Giuliano de' Medici

Giuliano de' Medici

MACHIAVELLI'S PRINCE IN LIFE AND ART

Josephine Jungić

Edited and revised
by Anne Leader

McGill-Queen's University Press
Montreal & Kingston | London | Chicago

ISBN 978-0-7735-5320-0 (cloth)
ISBN 978-0-7735-5368-2 (ePDF)
ISBN 978-0-7735-5369-9 (ePUB)

Legal deposit second quarter 2018
Bibliothèque nationale du Québec

Printed in Canada on acid-free paper

Funded by the Government of Canada | Financé par le gouvernement du Canada | Canada

Canada Council for the Arts | Conseil des arts du Canada

We acknowledge the support of the Canada Council for the Arts, which last year invested $153 million to bring the arts to Canadians throughout the country. Nous remercions le Conseil des arts du Canada de son soutien. L'an dernier, le Conseil a investi 153 millions de dollars pour mettre de l'art dans la vie des Canadiennes et des Canadiens de tout le pays.

Frontispiece: Michelangelo Buonarroti, *Head of Giuliano de' Medici, Duke of Nemours*, detail, from his tomb in the Medici Chapel (New Sacristy), San Lorenzo, Florence. Scala / Art Resource, NY

LIBRARY AND ARCHIVES CANADA CATALOGUING IN PUBLICATION

Jungić, Josephine, 1942–2013, author
Giuliano de' Medici : Machiavelli's Prince in life and art / Josephine Jungić ; edited and revised by Anne Leader.

Includes bibliographical references and index.
Issued in print and electronic formats.
ISBN 978-0-7735-5320-0 (hardcover).–ISBN 978-0-7735-5368-2 (ePDF).–ISBN 978-0-7735-5369-9 (ePUB)

1. Medici, Giuliano de', duca di Nemours, 1479–1516. 2. Medici, Giuliano de', duca di Nemours, 1479–1516 – Friends and associates. 3. Medici, House of. 4. Nobility – Italy – Florence – Biography. 5. Florence (Italy – History – 1421–1737. 6. Florence (Italy) – Politics and government – 1421–1737. I. Leader, Anne, editor II. Title.

DG738.14.M4J86 2018 945'.506092 C2017-907186-6
C2017-907187-4

Set in 11.5/14.5 Bembo Book MT Pro with TT Chocolates
Book design & typesetting by Garet Markvoort, zijn digital

Josephine Jungić was professor of art history at Capilano University for thirty-five years. She won numerous awards for teaching excellence and was recognized as professor emeritus upon her retirement in 2011. Her articles have appeared in *Art History*, *Gazette des Beaux-Arts*, *Journal of the Warburg and Courtauld Institutes*, and *Raccolta Vinciana*. She also contributed a chapter to *Prophetic Rome in the High Renaissance Period*, edited by Marjorie Reeves and published by Clarendon Press in 1992. Though Jungić had completed the writing and research of *Giuliano de' Medici* at the time of her death, she had only just begun the process of its publication, now brought to completion by her husband, Zoran Jungić, her son Orestes Pasparakis, and editor Anne Leader.

CONTENTS

ACKNOWLEDGMENTS

Toward the end of her teaching career, my mother, Josephine Jungić, embarked on what would be her final project. While she had published several well-received articles, and had introduced thousands of students to the art and architecture of Renaissance Italy, she was eager on her retirement to immerse herself more fully in the art and politics of sixteenth-century Rome and Florence. Other than the breaks she took to visit her grandson, she was happiest reading and writing in her study. She worked on the present book for five years, falling ill within days of completing its last chapter.

The scope of my mother's work was ambitious as she set out to provide the first major and sustained biography of Giuliano de' Medici (1479–1516), a significant member of the early sixteenth-century Medici family while they ruled Florence and Rome. The book starts with Giuliano de' Medici's tomb in the church of San Lorenzo and the words Michelangelo wrote on a sheet of sketches composed while designing Giuliano's resting place. This text had been largely dismissed as unimportant, primarily, as my mother shows so clearly throughout the book, because the fondness and respect shown for Giuliano by the artist so contradicted received opinion of the duke. It is with a re-examination of this text that the journey begins.

From there, the main argument, upon which several others depend, proceeds to show that Giuliano's negative reputation in most modern scholarship is the result of a deliberate campaign by his contemporaries within the Medici party to marginalize him and deny his legitimacy as a political actor. This animus arose primarily because Giuliano rejected their hard-line, autocratic politics. His affable, easy-going nature and advocacy for a restrained Medici presence – he favoured the retention of republican structures and traditions – made Giuliano quite popular in Florence, unlike the majority of his family members who were distrusted and disliked. Because of Giuliano's stubbornly independent and liberal politics, his kinfolk and those closest to them tended to write him out of the political scene, stressing instead the degree to which he was preoccupied with banquets and parties. Historians have largely followed suit. My mother argues to the contrary that Giuliano had considerable scruples and acted ethically and responsibly throughout his life, not only to help friends but also to find a harmonious resolution to the problem of Medici power in a city that was proud of its republican history. The narrative entwines the Medici family, Cesare Borgia, Machiavelli, Leonardo da Vinci, and Raphael; Florence, Venice, and Rome; it is an examination of art, politics, and history.

Although the chapters had been written and an extensive bibliography compiled, my mother had not yet approached any prospective publishers. With the generous help of her colleagues and friends, we set about finding an academic press. The list of those who have provided support through this difficult process is lengthy, and we are grateful to each of them, especially Alwynn Pinard, who helped us to navigate the heretofore unfamiliar world of academic publication, and Mark Jurdjevic, whose queries to colleagues eventually led us to Anne Leader. Anne readied the manuscript for submission to McGill-Queen's University Press and has addressed reader comments in way that was both thoughtful and consistent with my mother's argument and voice. Importantly, Anne was patient and always positive – making a challenging process less daunting. We are grateful to the three anonymous reviewers who provided such thorough evaluations, including important corrections and additional bibliography that my mother would have much appreciated. Without Anne's guidance through their commentary, we would not have succeeded in realizing my mother's wish to see her work published. We are also extremely grateful to Jonathan Crago and McGill-Queen's University Press for working with us through this process. It is a happy coincidence that Montreal was my mother's first home when she came to Canada as a teenager from London.

To celebrate finishing the last chapter, we were set to go as a family to Rome. My mother had already identified a number of ideas for her next book, which was to focus on Giuliano's brother Leo X, and she was giddy with excitement whenever she discussed her new project. She was also eager to show us the places where Giuliano had spent his days. Our plans changed quickly and unexpectedly. My stepfather, Zoran, and I are so pleased that my mother's work is now being published and again thank the many people that helped us bring it to fruition.

Orestes Pasparakis

Giuliano de' Medici

INTRODUCTION

Day and Night speak, and say: "We with our swift course have brought the Duke Giuliano to death. It is just that he, the Duke, takes revenge as he does for this, and the revenge is this, that as we [Day and Night] have killed him, he, dead, has taken the light from us, and with his closed eyes has locked ours shut, which no longer shine on earth. What then would he have done with us while alive?"

Michelangelo Buonarroti (1475–1564)[1]

Giuliano de' Medici, the youngest of seven children of Lorenzo the Magnificent (1449–1492) and Clarice Orsini (1452–1488), was born in Florence on 12 March 1479. In February 1515, just shy of his thirty-sixth birthday, he married Philiberte of Savoy (1498–1524), sister of Charles III (1486–1553), Duke of Savoy, and half-sister of Louise (1476–1531), mother of the king of France, Francis I (1494–1547). The following October, Francis I, crowned on 1 January 1515, conferred upon Giuliano the title of Duke of Nemours. Less than six months later, on 17 March 1516, Giuliano died from pulmonary tuberculosis, only five days after his thirty-seventh birthday. When Giuliano's nephew and rival Lorenzo de' Medici, Duke of Urbino, a title he received from his uncle Pope Leo X in 1516, died at the age of twenty-eight in 1519, Cardinal Giulio de' Medici (later Pope Clement VII) immediately commissioned Michelangelo to design and build a funerary chapel, the so-called New Sacristy, to house tombs for both Medici dukes in the family church of San Lorenzo in Florence[2] (Figs. 1–3). Around 1524 Michelangelo wrote the above lines of continuous prose on a sheet of architectural drawings of mouldings relating to Giuliano's wall tomb (Fig. 4). The first part of the text, a dialogue between Day and Night, causes no interpretive difficulty, signalling that the destructive force of time has brought Giuliano's early death, which in turn extinguishes the light of the world. The question in the last line, "What then would he have done with us while alive?" has puzzled observers, like Creighton Gilbert, who found "that the whole statement is incomprehensible, which has allowed its evidence to be put aside."[3] For Charles de Tolnay, the question posed by Day and Night was logically inconsistent with the rest of Michelangelo's dialogue, and he dismissed it as a "playful enigma."[4] Gilbert was inclined to see the entire note as a "statement of flattery" toward both Giuliano and Lorenzo, even though the latter was not named; Michelangelo, he believed, was offering an expression of "courtly adulation" for two dukes whose deaths have put out the "light of the world."[5]

However, Michelangelo's text clearly refers only to Giuliano. Gilbert's insistence that the artist refers to both Giuliano and his nephew exemplifies the common bias against Giuliano, wherein scholars cannot imagine that his death could possibly engender such dismay. Howard Hibbard also found the last line difficult, postulating that "it seems to mean that if the Duke could blind *Day* and *Night* after death, in life he could have done much more," a surely correct interpretation that Hibbard otherwise fails to elaborate. Acknowledging long-standing scholarly bias against Giuliano, Hibbard notes that "many writers have supposed that Michelangelo did not gladly participate in the task of honouring these two mediocre members of the increasingly degenerate Medici family,"[6] reflecting the view of historians like Ernst Steinmann, who in 1907 described Giuliano and Lorenzo as unimportant offshoots of a family that had fallen rapidly in stature.[7]

The central problem in interpreting Michelangelo's note is that many modern commentators find it impossible to imagine Giuliano as the inspiration for Michelangelo's words of hope and expectancy. Indeed, historians consistently portray Giuliano as a weak, ineffectual, and thoroughly dissolute figure. Though such criticisms date to his own lifetime, the most extreme views of Giuliano's character appeared in the nineteenth century, exemplified by historian Francesco Nitti (1851–1905), who accused Giuliano of pursuing a life solely dedicated to pleasure. While Giuliano's reputation for debauchery was not unwarranted, scholars like Nitti saw his passion for luxury and extraordinary excess as proof that he was also ineffective in public life and alienated from any worthwhile ambition. According to Nitti, Giuliano combined eroticism with mysticism and the practice of witchcraft; his supposedly melancholy and suicidal character left him without any quality whatsoever and unequal to the high purpose of his birth.[8] For Castiglione scholar Vittorio Cian (1862–1951), Giuliano was inherently lazy and uninterested in affairs of state, squandering both his time and his health by indulging in sumptuous banquets and orgies.[9] Papal historian Ludwig Pastor (1854–1928), following Nitti, concluded that Giuliano was "not fitted for high political aspirations" and "represented also the darker side of his family's characteristics, by his extravagant generosity, his boundless love of display, his desire for enjoyment, and his debauchery."[10] Giuliano's reputation did not improve in the twentieth century as historians continued to portray him as a man inclined to live a reckless and dissolute life, indulging in delights of the flesh and ruining his health in the process. Giuliano's constitution had always been weak because he had inherited a predisposition for tuberculosis from his mother, who died of the disease when Giuliano was only nine.[11] J.R. Hale (1923–99) best sums up the view of twentieth-century historians, assessing Giuliano in these terms: "Cultivated, somewhat moody, introspective, he had come to beguile his years of exile by devoting himself less to intrigue than to the pleasures of sex, luxury and the arts."[12]

In the twenty-first century, Giuliano's reputation has fared no better. In the *Dizionario Biografico degli Italiani*, Stefano Tabacchi summarizes his life with a focus on his sexual exploits and indolence. Of Giuliano's romance with Pacifica Brandano and the resulting birth of their son, Ippolito, Tabacchi notes: "This was one of the many fleeting love affairs that characterizes the biography of Giuliano, of which especially in the years of his exile [1494–1512], there appears to have been a balance between a refined laziness, at times tinged with mystical impulses, and an exasperating sensuality."[13] Tabacchi's source for Giuliano's alleged sexual proclivities is Giuseppe Fatini (1884–1963), who combined in his 1939 book an analysis of

Giuliano's early poetry with the first modern attempt at a scholarly biography.[14] While Fatini's book remains useful, he misrepresented Giuliano, as we shall see, because of a profound misunderstanding of the meaning and intent of much of Giuliano's youthful poetry.

Despite his acceptance of Giuliano's inherent laziness, Tabacchi warns that "we must not fall into the mistake of believing that Giuliano was an irrelevant figure";[15] in particular, he argues that he played a significant public and ceremonial role during the pontificate of Leo X (r. 1513–21), though citing only one example: Giuliano's organization of the great celebrations in Florence in June 1514 for the feast of St John the Baptist, patron saint of the city. Were this the only worthwhile activity Giuliano performed, then Michelangelo scholars could be forgiven for finding the last line of his note incomprehensible. But, of course, Giuliano did much more. Michelangelo, who knew him personally, placed the question in the mouths of Day and Night because he, like so many of Giuliano's friends, saw in him a potential for greatness, snuffed out by a premature death that brought a profound feeling of loss and even anger, expressed not only in Michelangelo's words but also perhaps in the image of a raging anthropomorphic head, fashioned from a pilaster base, on the same sheet as the artist's note (Fig. 4).

This new biography of Giuliano aims to understand why this particular Medici has so consistently been portrayed as irrelevant at best and as a degenerate at worst, exploring his politics as well as his alliances with key intellectuals, artists, and religious reformers. It seeks to construct a new narrative for Giuliano that shows how he was loved and admired by many contemporaries, including some of the most talented and famous men of his day, such as Michelangelo, Niccolò Machiavelli (1469–1527), Leonardo da Vinci (1452–1519), and Raphael (1483–1520). They have left in their various works of art, books, and letters testimony to how highly Giuliano was esteemed. A re-examination of Giuliano's relationships with these men shows him to have been, contrary to received opinion, a highly principled individual. Michelangelo, not only in the lines quoted above, but also in letters and, more potently, in his portrait of Giuliano for his tomb in the Medici Chapel at San Lorenzo, his greatest sculptural ensemble (Fig. 2), expresses eloquently the positive reception Giuliano enjoyed during his lifetime and upon his death. As Dale Kent has demonstrated in her study of the role of friendship in patronage networks,[16] personal fondness often developed among men of unequal status with positive benefits for the entire group. Indeed, as will be seen, Giuliano's relationships were themselves at the heart of some of the period's biggest cultural accomplishments. Moreover, his friendship with Machiavelli likely contributed to his persecution by Medici partisans who opposed Giuliano's ideology after the family's restoration to power in 1512.

Machiavelli's admiration for Giuliano can be found in letters and poems addressed to Giuliano, affection further conveyed through *The Prince*, written for him. Giuliano's relationship with Leonardo was much closer than was usual between patron and artist, since Giuliano revered Leonardo and treated the much older man as a brother. On Leonardo's part, his devotion to Giuliano was demonstrated in his notes, letters, and the various commissions he carried out for him in Rome and elsewhere. Giuliano came to know Raphael when both were at the Montefeltro court in Urbino. Later, their friendship was renewed in Rome when Raphael painted Giuliano's portrait (Fig. 38), which survives in several copies[17] (Fig. 5). Giuliano and Raphael formed part of a close-knit circle in Rome that included the Venetian cardinal Pietro Bembo (1470–1547), author of *Prose della Volgar Lingua*, and the Mantuan Baldassare Castiglione (1478–1529), who wrote the more widely known *Book of the Courtier*. In both works Giuliano was cast in an honoured role as one of the principal interlocutors. While a major concern of the present study has been to engage closely with the historical and political events that affected and helped give shape to Giuliano's life, much of its focus is given to examining these particular friendships. His close personal ties to Cesare Borgia (1475–1507), never fully explored before, are also investigated. These relationships offer overwhelming evidence that Giuliano deserves a more nuanced and balanced biography, which will allow historians to reconsider his role in early-sixteenth-century politics.

The maligning of Giuliano de' Medici began shortly after his return to Florence in September 1512, following an eighteen-year exile. Medici supporters did not like Giuliano because he was a relentless advocate of the popular government established after the collapse of the Medici regime in November 1494, as well as a supporter of the majority of Florentines who did not want a return of Medici-style, dynastic politics. In contrast, Giuliano's brother Giovanni, who became Pope Leo X in 1513, his first cousin Giulio, who took St Peter's keys as Clement VII in 1523, and his nephew Lorenzo, son of Giuliano's deceased eldest brother Piero (1472–1503) and Duke of Urbino after 1516, all wanted to restore a *governo stretto* under their control. This difference of opinion created a deep political divide between Giuliano and the rest of his family that has been dismissed as having had very little significance. Typically, when historians discuss the Medici family in this period, they do so as if it was a monolithic entity, with all members united in a single aim of strengthening the regime. Tabacchi's description of the Medici return to Florence after their long exile exemplifies this assumption: "[On] 1 September 1512, Giuliano entered the city in triumph with his brother."[18] Such statements disguise, if not ignore, the political differences that existed between the two brothers. Giuliano, in fact, entered Florence alone on that day and spent the next two weeks formulating a new constitution that would have allowed the republican institutions in the city to continue. It was only when Cardinal Giovanni de' Medici arrived two weeks later, on 14 September, accompanied by the Spanish army and Italian soldiers of the Holy League of Pope Julius II, that all vestiges of republican government were abolished and Medici control was imposed.

Many historians, when forming their opinions of Giuliano, appear to be unaware of the political tensions that existed between Giuliano and other members of his family, relying too heavily upon the accounts of politically biased contemporaries who were supporters of Cardinal Giovanni and the Medici regime. Indeed, divisions within the family were readily acknowledged by kinsmen, as seen, for example, in a letter written two years later by Alfonsina Orsini de' Medici (1472–1520), wife of Giuliano's brother Piero, to her son Lorenzo: "On one side is the Magnificent Giuliano de' Medici, Cardinal Bernardo Dovizi da Bibbiena, Contessina Ridolfi, and Mona Lucrezia Salviati; on the other side is Cardinal Giulio de' Medici, Lorenzo de' Medici, myself, Madonna Magdalena Cibo, Cardinal Cibo, Francesco Cibo, and all their adherents."[19]

Among the reasons why Giuliano's reputation was so tarnished could be the fact that the reign of Leo X coincided with widespread ecclesiastical abuses and corruption and with Martin Luther's attacks against the Roman Catholic Church and the onset of the Protestant Reformation in 1517. Some papal authorities, sensitive to Protestant attacks, may not have been inclined to write positively about the pope's younger brother for fear that Giuliano's integrity, recognized by many of his contemporaries, would only serve to highlight the shortcomings of Giovanni. Various dismissive comments about Giuliano stand in stark contrast to evidence that he led a purposeful, if short, life. During his exile, for example, he established very close, personal friendships with two Venetian aristocrats and scholars, Vincenzo Querini (1479–1514) and Tommaso Giustiniani (1476–1528), who subsequently became hermits at the reformed Benedictine hermitage of Camaldoli, relationships not mentioned in the biographies by Fatini or Tabacchi. As will be shown, Giuliano assisted his friends in their efforts to reform the Camaldolese order and was appointed its principal patron and benefactor. Furthermore, Giuliano seems to have inspired the hermits to see him as an important agent in their proposals for a sweeping reform of the church. In *Libellus ad Leonem X Pontificem Maximum* (1513), described as the most significant church reform document of the era, the hermits called for a crusade against the Turks and proposed an important role of military leadership for Giuliano. It is hard to imagine that they would have nominated Giuliano if he was simply the debauched layabout some commentators paint him to be.

Leo X's decision in 1515 to depose by force Francesco Maria della Rovere (1490–1538), in favour of the Duchy of Urbino passing to his nephew Lorenzo de' Medici, must have caused great friction between the two Medici brothers. Giuliano had formed very close attachments to both Francesco Maria, whom he regarded as a brother, and to the beloved dowager duchess Elisabetta Gonzaga (1471–1526), who had shown him the greatest affection and the utmost generosity and support during his exile. Mainstream historical literature has not made much of the fact that Giuliano fought as hard as he could to defend and protect Duke Francesco Maria against what was, as most realized at the time, the pope's blatant aggression toward Urbino and its people. Despite Giuliano's strong efforts to change his brother's mind (with pleas continuing even from his deathbed), the pope remained stubborn in his determination to proceed with his usurpation of Urbino in order to create a Medici dynastic state for his nephew.

The present biography also explores Giuliano's long friendship with Machiavelli, a relationship mostly overlooked in the vast literature on the politician. For example, Humfrey Butters's 2010 essay on Machiavelli and the Medici does not discuss any personal relationship between Machiavelli and Giuliano.[20] This omission is not at all surprising, however, for the consensus among Machiavelli scholars seems to be that there was very little, if any, direct contact between them. It is well known that, shortly after Machiavelli wrote *The Prince*, he penned a letter dated 10 December 1513 to his friend Francesco Vettori (1474–1539), Florentine ambassador to the papal court of Leo X. Machiavelli expressed his intention to dedicate *The Prince* to Giuliano. Most commentators firmly believe that Giuliano would not have been interested in Machiavelli's treatise, including James Atkinson and David Sices: "Although he had originally intended to dedicate it to Giuliano de' Medici, Machiavelli changed his mind, perhaps because Giuliano was never very interested in either Machiavelli or military theory, a topic fundamental to *The Prince* … [Machiavelli's] persistent belief in Giuliano de' Medici's … [engagement with his work] … [led him] to plan on dedicating *The Prince* to [Giuliano], but Machiavelli's intentions [were] frustrated by Giuliano's lack of interest in being a 'new prince' with military projects and by his early death."[21] Yet there is ample evidence showing that Giuliano was in fact genuinely immersed in politics. Furthermore, his interests extended to military matters, as seen in his 1513 invitation to Leonardo to join him in Rome. Giuliano was not in need of an artist (there is no evidence that Giuliano ever commissioned a painting from Leonardo) but rather required the services of a military architect and engineer. The specific tasks that Leonardo carried out for Giuliano during the last three years of Giuliano's life provide strong confirmation of his interest in both politics and the art of war, the subjects of Machiavelli's *Prince*.

Giuliano and Machiavelli first met in Imola in October 1502. Machiavelli, second chancellor to the Florentine republic, was sent to the court of Cesare Borgia (1475/6–1507) in Romagna, where he stayed for almost four months, at the same time that Giuliano was serving as a captain in Borgia's army. Their friendship resumed upon Giuliano's return to Florence in September 1512. In February 1513, when Machiavelli was incarcerated in the Bargello and tortured, accused of conspiring to kill Giuliano, he wrote two sonnets to him from his prison cell, imploring him to come to his aid. As we will see, Giuliano's special intervention during the general amnesty allowed Machiavelli, deemed an enemy of the government, to be released, thus avoiding certain execution or life imprisonment in the Stinche, Florence's notorious prison. In a letter to Francesco Vettori in Rome, Machiavelli wrote: "I can say that all that is left to me of my life I owe to the Magnificent Giuliano and your [brother] Paolo."[22] Butters raises doubts as to whether Machiavelli was right in thinking that Giuliano cared enough about him to save his life when he states that Machiavelli "believed, or affected to believe, that he owed his liberation to Giuliano."[23] Examining the evidence closely, however, makes certain that Giuliano did intervene on his behalf, despite the fact that others in his family remained deeply suspicious of the ex-chancellor. Machiavelli had been, of course, a loyal civil servant of the Florentine republic for fourteen years and thus was seen by many as a threat to the Medici. Medici suspicion of him became apparent in January 1515, a year before Giuliano's death, when rumours reached Rome that he was about to take Machiavelli into his service. On the orders of his cousin, Cardinal Giulio, a letter dated 14 February was quickly sent to Giuliano advising him not to have anything to do with Machiavelli.[24]

Nevertheless, Machiavelli seems to have written *The Prince* out of friendship because he was eager to offer Giuliano certain precepts that would serve to protect him and to ensure his success in establishing himself as a new prince in the dynastic state that Pope Leo was planning to establish in north-central Italy. The relationship between Giuliano and Machiavelli, as yet unexplored, possibly influenced the content of *The Prince*. New analysis of the context in which this well-known and much studied text was written reveals not only Machiavelli's motivations but also in what ways the book specifically addressed Giuliano's particular concerns as he embarked on a new stage in his life. It will be argued that the iconography of Raphael's official portrait of Giuliano, likely the damaged version now in New York's Metropolitan Museum of Art (Fig. 38),[25] portrays Giuliano as Machiavelli's new prince whose role was to bring good laws and institutions to his new state and to provide it with stability through the strength of arms. Commissioned in February 1515, several months after Giuliano had officially received possession of his state from his brother, Raphael's portrait, copied several times, established Giuliano's presence in Emilia and served as a proxy – reminding his subjects of his authority – during his absences.

In returning once more to Michelangelo's ducal tombs in the New Sacristy (Figs. 1–3), it is also hoped that this book will help lay to rest the lingering suspicion, first raised by Herman Grimm in the middle of the nineteenth century, that the identities of the two dukes or, as Michelangelo calls them, *Capitani* (Figs. 6 and 7), have been wrongly attributed.[26] The question arises because neither tomb carries an identifying inscription. Michelangelo carved representations of the deceased dukes as living figures sitting in centrally placed niches above their respective sarcophagi, Lorenzo on the left wall as the visitor enters the chapel (Fig. 3) and Giuliano opposite on the right (Fig. 2). For some observers, like Martin Weinbeger, "both statues express attributes of will and mind directly opposite to the characters of the men whom they now represent."[27] Seeing that the two *Capitani* were contrasted types, even Hibbard leaves a lingering doubt when he parenthetically notes that the figure of Giuliano, whose sarcophagus bears the personifications of Night and Day on its sloping lid, has a "characterisation [that] would seem more appropriate for Lorenzo, and there is even the faint possibility that they got confused, but according to Vasari Michelangelo set the two *Capitani* in their niches before leaving for Rome in 1534, and we surely have them right."[28] The issue resurfaced in two articles published by Richard Trexler, the first in 1981 and the second in 2000, who forcefully argued the case that a change in the identities of the *Capitani* occurred between the time of their conception about 1521 and the middle of the sixteenth century, so that what is generally regarded as the figure representing Giuliano (Fig. 6) is in fact his nephew Lorenzo, and conversely, the figure of Lorenzo (Fig. 7) should be given the designation of Giuliano.[29]

Both sculptures are clearly not portraits in the conventional sense, since neither bears any resemblance to the known facial features of the sitters. Michelangelo, nonetheless, has intentionally represented them as opposing types, interpreted by many as symbols of the active and contemplative life. Giuliano is youthful, powerfully built, and wears the form-fitting cuirass of a Roman general that reveals every detail of his Herculean musculature. He sits upright and alert in his niche, his head turned sharply to the left as he directs his gaze across the chapel to a seated figure of the Virgin and Child, placed atop the plain sarcophagus housing the remains of his father, Lorenzo the Magnificent, and his uncle and namesake, Giuliano. His relaxed hands rest lightly on the baton of the captain of the Church, an honour he received from his brother Pope Leo X on 29 June 1515,[30] that lies across his massive thighs. The pale, diffuse light that enters through the high windows of the chapel passes over the head of Lorenzo and falls directly onto Giuliano's face.[31]

Giuliano is invested with a psychic force that is entirely absent in the opposing sculpture of his nephew Lorenzo, who sits brooding in his niche on the opposite wall. His head rests in his left hand, and the burden of his thoughts is made visible by the weight of his large, lion-headed helmet. His supporting left arm is bent, the elbow resting on a moneybox placed on his knee,[32] and his right arm hangs down passively, his wrist touching the side of his thigh with the palm of his hand turned outward. Gazing in the direction of the Virgin, his face, less finished than Giuliano's, is partially hidden by a raised curling forefinger and is in perpetual shadow cast by the rim of his helmet. Since the eighteenth century this figure has been known as *il Pensieroso* (Thinker).

If we must begin, as seems logical, with the character of the dukes in order to determine their identities, then perhaps it is not surprising that some observers have misgivings about the artist's conception of each *Capitano*, since Giuliano, ten years older than his nephew, was reputed to have had a melancholy disposition. The young, bold Lorenzo, on the other hand, was by contrast known to have been impetuous and militaristic like his father, Piero, who was killed in action in 1503. Though Trexler's hypothesis, dismissed by a majority of art historians, has received little scholarly attention, it is hoped that by the time the reader reaches the conclusion of this book, the first major biography of Giuliano in English, all doubts, suspicions, and hesitations about the statues' assigned identities, as well as the nature of their personalities, will be finally put to rest. Instead, Giuliano will be recognized not as an inconsequential, womanizing, sybarite with little inclination, and even less ability, for politics, but rather as a popular Florentine leader who adhered to the republican principles that his countrymen held dear. Neither Michelangelo's "epitaph" nor his forceful portraits are misplaced. Giuliano, it will be shown, was a scrupulous, ethical, and responsible leader who sought harmonious solutions to the problem of Medici power in a fiercely republican city. His premature death and a campaign to malign his reputation have indeed "taken the light from us, and with his closed eyes / has locked ours shut, which no longer shine on earth." This biography seeks to answer Michelangelo's poignant question: "What then would he have done with us while alive?" His short life suggests that he would have been a tempering force to the monarchical aspirations of his kinsmen.

CHAPTER ONE

FLORENCE AND THE MEDICI

On 9 November 1494 the three sons of Lorenzo the Magnificent were expelled from Florence, bringing an end to sixty years of strong political influence by the Medici family (Fig. 8). Eighteen years later, in September 1512, they were given permission to re-enter the city on the understanding that they would remain private citizens. Barely two weeks after their return, however, the Medici orchestrated a coup d'état, which brought them into the centre of Florentine political life once more. While many modern studies are devoted to the end of the republic and the transition of Florence into a principate, very few pay much attention to the role of Giuliano de' Medici, Lorenzo's youngest son, who became the de facto head of the government.

Piero di Lorenzo, the eldest, had drowned in 1503 in the Garigliano River some sixty kilometres north of Naples. (He had joined French troops at war with Spain, who would gain total supremacy over the Kingdom of Naples.) The second son, Cardinal Giovanni di Lorenzo, was serving as legate to Pope Julius II in Bologna and in 1513 became Pope Leo X. What does not seem to be appreciated by modern scholars is that when Giuliano di Lorenzo returned to Florence on 1 September 1512, the first of his family to do so, he gave his support to the faction of leading families who had no wish to see the Medici returned to their former powerful position in the city. A close study of his actions reveals that he agreed with those patricians who wanted the popular government to continue. Some modern studies portray Giuliano as politically inexperienced and too compliant in nature, arguing that his weak personality enabled some of the Florentine patriciate to manipulate him easily. Yet a close focus on the first few weeks of the Medici restoration in September 1512 challenges the view that Giuliano was inexperienced or inept. On the contrary, he voted to retain the popular government that had been established following the collapse of Medici political power because he firmly believed that a republican system best suited the city. Although he intended to participate fully in Florence's political affairs, Giuliano was not seeking the power to rule, unlike his brother Cardinal Giovanni, his cousin Giulio di Giuliano (the future Clement VII), his nephew Lorenzo (1492–1519), son of the deceased Piero, and their close supporters.

Almost all modern studies describe how, on 16 September 1512, Giuliano played a major role in the coup d'état by leading an armed assault on the Palazzo della Signoria, which resulted in the abolition of the popular government. The fact that, upon his arrival in Florence, Giuliano appeared to support the republicans and their broadly based government, and then, two weeks later, switched his allegiance and spearheaded a coup against them, only confirmed to some historians that he was weak, could easily be led, and lacked all political conviction. A more critical study of the primary sources, however, reveals flaws in this narrative. Importantly, Giuliano took no part in the assault on the government on 16 September. The evidence shows quite the opposite. Not only did Giuliano stand up to Spanish soldiers and supporters of his brother's faction, but also he intervened to protect his republican friends gathered for a meeting in the council chambers from a certain bloodbath. One of the sources used extensively by historians of the early modern period is Bartolomeo Cerretani (1475–1524), but his reporting on Giuliano is untrustworthy in that the chronicler was politically biased. He was a staunch Medicean supporter and a severe critic of the broadly based popular government; consequently, when he described the events that took place during the Medici restoration in his *Dialogo della mutatione di Firenze*, his assessment of Giuliano was extremely negative. It is an assessment, unfortunately, that continues to dominate accounts of Giuliano's role in Florentine politics.

THE EXPULSION OF THE MEDICI FROM FLORENCE

For sixty years, from 1434 until 1494, the Medici had been the leading family in Florence. The first Medici regime was established by Cosimo di Giovanni "the Elder" (1389–1464) through his immense fortune derived from international banking, which he used to manipulate republican political life. His son Piero "the Gouty" succeeded him, but with his early death in 1469, Cosimo's grandson, Lorenzo the Magnificent, became the acknowledged, if unofficial lord, or *signore*, of Florence, at the young age of twenty. Inheriting much of his grandfather's political skill, Lorenzo was able to extend the period of strong Medici influence in the city for another twenty-three years. Following Lorenzo's death in 1492, his legacy, inherited by his then twenty-year-old son Piero, went unchallenged because many at the time, as Cerretani recorded, were hoping that the spirit of the father had descended into the body of the son.[1]

Better known in history as *lo sfortunato*, the Unfortunate, Piero di Lorenzo showed none of his father's moderation in domestic or foreign affairs. Francesco Guicciardini (1483–1540) wrote that by nature Piero was tyrannical and haughty and refused to trust even those Florentines who had been his father's closest acquaintances.[2] Instead of following Lorenzo's example of maintaining the semblance of a republican constitution, Piero's overweening ambition led him to aspire to absolute power as a prince. Soon after taking the control of the government, he embarked on a plan to transform Florence, with its centuries-old tradition of republicanism, into a principate.[3] It is doubtful whether Lorenzo the Magnificent, even after he extended control of the government following the Pazzi Conspiracy of 1478 that sought to assassinate him, would have ever entertained such an idea.[4] In fact, when Piero and several sons of Florentine ambassadors set out for Rome in November 1484 to congratulate Pope Innocent VIII on his election, Lorenzo wrote to Piero, reminding him that "although you are my son, you are no more than a citizen of Florence, like them."[5]

Influenced by his ambitious wife, Alfonsina Orsini, and her kin, Piero thought that his mother, Clarice, also an Orsini and, like his wife, a true aristocrat related to the Orsini barons of Rome, had given him Roman blood that distinguished him from all the other members of the patrician elite in Florence.[6] To ensure success for his new regime, Piero needed to align the Florentine state with powerful supporters and, without inviting the leading citizens to give their informed opinion on matters of state policy as expected of a leader of the republic, forged an alliance with King Ferrante of Naples (r. 1458–94) and his son Alfonso, Duke of Calabria (1448–1495). Piero promised them unlimited cooperation, completely ignoring the fact that Florence had always looked to France as its strongest ally and protector.[7] This alliance, Guicciardini says, was the beginning of the ruin of Piero di Lorenzo de' Medici.[8]

The political alignment of the Florentine republic with the ruling dynasty of Aragonese kings had immediate repercussions. It destroyed at once the delicate balance of power created by Lorenzo the Magnificent. Lorenzo was widely viewed as the master of Italian equilibrium, able to use his great diplomatic skills to deal with the two principal protagonists in the peninsula, the Milanese Sforza state in the north and the Aragonese kingdom of Naples in the south. Ludovico Sforza (1452–1508), believing that his state's security was directly threatened by the new Medici alliance, retaliated swiftly, inviting Charles VIII of France (1470–98) into Italy in order to pursue the dormant Angevin claim to Naples. In 1494 the French descended into Italy with one of the largest armies ever seen.

The invasion proved catastrophic for Piero, since it became the catalyst for the end of the first Medici regime and the family's political influence in Florence. Fearing that the French king would be hostile toward him because of his close ties to Spain, Piero tried to appease Charles VIII. In an audience at the French camp at Sarzana on 26 October, Piero surrendered, and as a sign of loyalty he pledged the Florentine fortresses of Pisa and Livorno, Florence's lifelines to the sea, as well as Pietrasanta and Sarzana on the northern Tuscan border, without first seeking approval from the Florentine Signoria. Florentines were especially proud of the fortress at Sarzana, which had been captured by the Genoese in the Pazzi War of 1478–80 but later retaken and rebuilt at tremendous cost.[9]

Piero was harshly criticized for his independent decisions, and his unlawful concessions of such valuable Florentine assets to Charles VIII outraged many in Florence. Even leading patrician families withdrew their support, despite past alliances with the Medici, who, therefore, quickly lost their political power. Acting swiftly, the Florentine government declared Piero and his younger brother Giuliano outlaws, stripping them of all their possessions. With supporters abandoning the Medici en masse, Piero fled the city on 9 November 1494, with the then fifteen-year-old Giuliano in tow.[10] In his diary, the Florentine apothecary Luca Landucci (1436–1516) recorded that "the poor young cardinal [Giovanni de' Medici] remained in his house, and I saw him at a window kneeling with joined hands, praying Heaven to have mercy. I was much touched when I saw him, considering him to be a good lad and of upright character. It was said that when he had seen Piero ride away, he disguised himself as a monk and took his departure also."[11]

THE MEDICI RETURN TO POWER

After nearly two decades of living in exile, the Medici were restored to Florence in September 1512, with the help of Pope Julius II (Fig. 9), whose obsessive desire was not only to rid the Italian peninsula of Louis XII of France (r. 1498–1515), who had occupied Milan since 1499, but also to overthrow the governments of Florence and Ferrara, still stubbornly tied to the French. This second Medici regime would be short-lived, lasting only fifteen years until the Sack of Rome in 1527, so poorly handled by the Medici Pope Clement VII.[12] In October 1511 Julius II established a Holy League composed of the papacy, the Republic of Venice, and the Kingdom of Spain. The League suffered a devastating defeat by the French during the battle of Ravenna on 11 April 1512,[13] but after the infantry of the Swiss Confederation, the most feared fighting force in Europe, joined the pope, the League won a decisive victory in June 1512. Louis XII was forced to abandon his hereditary claim to the Duchy of Milan, and his armies had to leave Italy entirely.

The pope's attention then shifted to the republican government of Florence and Piero di Tommaso Soderini (1452–1522), who had been elected to a life term as *gonfaloniere di giustizia* (Standardbearer of Justice), the highest republican office, in 1502. Julius saw Soderini as "that traitor" who was "to be sent to the devil" because he had refused to join the League against France.[14] Under pressure from Louis XII, Soderini had allowed a church council to be convened in November 1511 in Florentine territory at Pisa, an action seen as a direct assault on papal authority.[15] Soderini had reluctantly consented to the king's demands, fearing papal reprisal through interdict. His concerns were realized as Julius promptly punished Florence in exactly that way, with grave economic consequences to the Florentine state. The

Council of Pisa was attended by a small group of dissenting cardinals, whose chief aim was to challenge the pope's authority. They accused Julius of criminal negligence for failing to convoke a general council in order to address the issue of church reforms. They also declared him an enemy of peace and the promoter of warfare among Christians, because of his incessant warmongering. Pisan citizens and clergy opposed the council, which never did receive univocal support, because it was clear that Louis XII was not interested in church reform but rather used the council to act directly against Julius.[16] The council was short-lived and concluded within a few days.

Once the French left Italy, the Holy League met secretly on 21 August 1512 (Diet of Mantua) to discuss how the Italian states, especially Milan, would be reconstituted. The Florentine government was not officially represented, but Julius II made sure that both Giuliano and Cardinal Giovanni's secretary, Bernardo Dovizi da Bibbiena (1470–1520), were included in the papal delegation[17] (Fig. 10). As the secular head of his family, Giuliano spoke with great eloquence to the assembled representatives of the papal alliance, explaining why it was in their interests to return the Medici family to Florence. Isabella d'Este (1474–1539), Marchesa of Mantua (Fig. 34), who had befriended Giuliano during his long exile, gave him her support by holding a great banquet in Giuliano's honour. In Rome, the pope showed his own approval by praising Giuliano and sending him gifts.[18] The joint Spanish and papal armies, led by Ramón de Cardona (1467–1522), viceroy of Naples, were ordered to march to Florence, depose Piero Soderini, reinstate the Medici's political power, and recover their lost property. Cardinal Giovanni de' Medici was sent by the pope as a legate to Tuscany and to the army of the Holy League.[19] Julius, as we have seen, had good reason to bring Soderini down, but he may also have considered the advantages such an assault would accrue to him personally, especially since he was facing the prospect of having to pay the Spanish troops for their services to the League. The pope calculated that, by all accounts, if the soldiers attacked prosperous Florence and its surrounding territories, they would gain an opportunity to earn money by pillaging and thereby save him enormous sums, which would have to be otherwise spent on the army.[20] No one could foresee, however, the sheer brutal force that was unleashed against Prato (just twelve kilometres northwest of Florence) on 29 August. After hours of artillery bombardment, a breach was opened in the city wall, and soldiers poured through, killing, raping, looting, and burning. Some said that the Sack of Prato saw as many as five thousand men, women, and children massacred.[21]

As the news of the fall of Prato began to filter back to Florence, people panicked, fearing for their lives. Shops closed, houses were abandoned, and many tried to flee the city. A small band of young radical Medici supporters, determined to remove Piero Soderini by force and restore the Medici to power, took advantage of the chaos and broke into the Palazzo della Signoria in the early hours of 31 August. Led by Paolo Vettori, Antonfrancesco degli Albizzi, Baccio Valori, and Gino Capponi, they threatened to kill Soderini if he did not immediately resign his post as *gonfaloniere di giustizia*. After receiving assurances that his life would be spared, Soderini resigned, left the palace, and fled the city.[22] The Signoria, under force, formally sent the *gonfaloniere di giustizia* into exile, together with four of his closest male relatives who, not trusting the long arm of the Medici family, sought refuge in Castelnuovo on the Dalmatian coast, then under Turkish rule.[23] The next day, on 1 September, Giuliano de' Medici entered Florence. The Medici return consisted of two phases. During the first, from 1 until 16 September, Giuliano participated in political discussions that led to the adoption of a new constitution, one that preserved the popular government but at the same time gave a greater share of power to the Florentine patrician class. During the second phase, from 16 September, following the return of Giuliano's brother Cardinal Giovanni, the republican government and the new constitution were abolished, with a restricted government (*governo stretto*) imposed under tight control of the Medici. Writers have conflated the motives of Giuliano and Cardinal Giovanni, but, as we shall see, the brothers had different attitudes and ideals about the Medici return to Florence.

Historians often assume that, when Giuliano returned to the city on 1 September, he headed a faction that was dedicated to restoration of his family's influence.[24] While this may have been the ambition of his older brother Giovanni and other Medici, careful reading of contemporary sources makes clear that Giuliano was not seeking princely power but was content to see the institutions of the republic reinstated. Knowing that Florentine citizens were angry and resentful, his main concern was to convince the *populus* of his good intentions. They had already lost Soderini, despite his appointment as Standardbearer of Justice for life, and now they feared for their own liberty. Giuliano, therefore, did not enter the city at the head of a large contingent of Spanish soldiers, as his brother would two weeks later. Instead, he was escorted into Florence by only a small group of friends. Nor did he go directly to the Medici palace, where many Medici supporters had gathered to receive him. To their dismay, he went to stay with his young patrician friend Antonfrancesco di Luca degli Albizzi (1486–1537).[25]

Giuliano's choice of lodging demonstrated a certain independence from other members of his family. Dovizi da Bibbiena arrived in Florence only a few hours later but went directly to the Medici palace, unaware that Giuliano had gone to stay with the Albizzi.[26] Avoiding the Medici palace appears to have been deliberate on Giuliano's part, in order to signal to everyone that he was willing to abide by the laws of the republic. He had not yet received official permission to reside in the city, which was formally granted only on 5 September,[27] and his guest status at the Albizzi home indicated that he was abiding by the terms of his exile. The day after his arrival, Giuliano shaved his beard and, dressed in a rose-coloured sleeveless gown, or *lucco*, went walking in the streets with three of his friends.[28] To the people of Florence, the significance of these gestures was clear. Only aristocratic foreigners wore beards. Giuliano's act of shaving his beard was proof that he had put aside his aristocratic pretensions and wanted to conform to Florentine customs. Also, by wearing a *lucco*, the robe that had been worn by public officeholders since the thirteenth century, Giuliano was using another powerful symbol to demonstrate that he had returned to Florence not as a prince but as an ordinary citizen. In the fifteenth century, Giuliano's great-grandfather, Cosimo, and father, Lorenzo, always wore the *lucco* in public to show themselves as private citizens.[29]

In an attempt to allay the fear and distrust felt by many Florentines, the next day Giuliano went to visit Pierfrancesco the Younger (1487–1525), son of Lorenzo di Pierfrancesco de' Medici (1463–1503), cousins from the rival branch of the Medici family descended from Cosimo the Elder's brother Lorenzo (1395–1440).[30] Giuliano's aim was to show that he had returned in a spirit of reconciliation, prepared to make peace with all. His visit to the house of Pierfrancesco was meant to demonstrate, in an extraordinary way, that he wanted to right the wrongs done to Pierfrancesco's family by his father and brother. Pierfrancesco's father, Lorenzo, and uncle, Giovanni

(1467–1498), became wards of Lorenzo the Magnificent, their second cousin, after the death of their father Pierfrancesco the Elder in 1476. However, as guardian Lorenzo took advantage of these minors by using their very large inheritance, to the amount of 60,000 ducats according to Guicciardini,[31] for his own benefit, with threats that if the boys did not lend him the money, he would, as their guardian, simply confiscate it.

After Lorenzo's death in 1492, the brothers took their revenge by openly supporting the French king Charles VIII, becoming leaders of the opposition to their younger cousin Piero di Lorenzo.[32] In April 1494 the brothers were arrested and accused of treason and, according to Cerretani, Piero would have had them both beheaded but for the fact that his cousins were enormously popular and the magistrates might refuse to carry out his orders.[33] Instead, they were sentenced to permanent exile. After Piero was forced to flee the city himself, the cousins returned in triumph, and in December, because both brothers had always preferred a broadly based republican government, they renounced their family name and henceforth became known as Lorenzo and Giovanni, *i'Popolani'* (of the common people).[34] Giuliano's visit in September 1512 to the son of Lorenzo di Pierfrancesco "il Popolano" was therefore highly symbolic, meant to convey that he too was a devoted son of the republic and that he had returned to Florence with sincere reconciliation in mind, especially with his estranged Medici relatives.

Many citizens, as the Florentine chronicler Jacopo Pitti observed, could not believe that the Medici, with their history of political influence, could return after eighteen years in exile and consent to a diminution of power.[35] As we shall see, this was Giuliano's intent. The leading citizens of Florence were known as *ottimati*, from the Latin *optimates*, meaning "best ones," a term originally used to designate the senatorial aristocracy of the Roman republic. Several of these wealthy patricians, with great political influence in Florence, paid a visit to Giuliano in order to discuss the possible forms the new government could take. After days of intense negotiations, a new government was formed on 7 September. Giuliano surprised everyone assembled at the Palazzo della Signoria by voting to preserve the Great Council, clearly acting against the interests of his own family and of those radical Medicean supporters who wanted a more centralized form of rule.[36] But why was Giuliano so willing to support democratic republican institutions?

The Great Council had been established by law eighteen years earlier, on 22–23 December 1494, barely a month after the expulsion of the Medici, and became the cornerstone of the reinstated republican government. Modelled on the Venetian Consiglio Maggiore, the Florentine Great Council had received the enthusiastic endorsement of Girolamo Savonarola, a Dominican friar from Ferrara, who was prior of the Dominican convent of San Marco in Florence. Savonarola had risen to prominence not only because of his charismatic preaching at San Marco and the cathedral of Florence, where as many as fifteen thousand would attend his sermons, but also because of his remarkable prophetic gifts. Denouncing his fellow Italians for their vices, he had foretold the descent of Charles VIII with a huge army into Italy in 1494, and had warned his listeners that the French king was God's avenging instrument, a *flagellum Dei*, who had been sent by an angry God to punish the wicked for their sins.[37] Instead of sacking the city, Charles VIII entered Florence on 17 November in peace and agreed to hold negotiations with the Florentines. He stayed eleven days in the city, but at the urging of Savonarola and other citizens, the king resumed his march south to Naples, leaving Florence and its territories unharmed.[38]

After the departure of the French, Savonarola's prophetic message became much more optimistic. Florence, he preached, avoided destruction because God had chosen the city as the New Jerusalem. The city's unique destiny was to be the centre of a renewed Christianity that would spread throughout Italy and to all the peoples of the world. Florence would become rich and glorious. As the agent of this new, brighter vision, Savonarola's esteem in the city rose dramatically.[39] Many Florentines became his followers, convinced that he was divinely inspired. This was particularly evident among the cultural elite, which had formed part of Lorenzo the Magnificent's humanist circle. According to Lorenzo Polizzotto, elites "seemed to have joined *en bloc* the Savonarolan movement."[40] Devoted adherents were also found in the ranks of the patrician class, influential men such as Jacopo Salviati (1461–1533) and Giovanbattista Ridolfi (1448–1514), who had special political expertise and, in fact, helped ensure the initial success of the Savonarolan movement through their support.[41]

The initiative to create a Great Council in imitation of the Venetian Consiglio Maggiore came from a group of *ottimati* who appeared to have embraced the "myth of Venice." With its unique constitution, well-ordered and stable Venice was, for them, the realization of a perfect republic.[42] Venetian political wisdom, it was thought, had fashioned an exemplary constitution, one that reconciled justice, liberty, and security through its collegial decision making and state services. Patricians were subordinate to the republic, where personal ambition and self-interest were put aside for the common good.[43] One of the principal transmitters of this idea of the "myth of Venice" was the humanist Poggio Bracciolini (1380–1459), chancellor and historian of Florence. He wrote that, because of the virtue of their laws, institutions, customs, and constitution, the people of Venice had managed to keep their republic intact for seven hundred years. Furthermore, he wrote, in contrast to Florence and because of the excellence of its constitution, "there is no discord or dissent among the Venetians as to how to govern the republic, no feuding between citizens, no factions or quarrelling, no open enmities."[44]

Savonarola may have believed in the superiority of the Venetian constitution, but he preached in his sermons that the Florentine Great Council was created by God as part of His plan for the spiritual and moral regeneration of the city.[45] As early as 12 December 1494, in a sermon on Aggeus, Savonarola urged Florentines to base their new government on the Venetian model of the Consiglio Maggiore, seeing it as the best example of its kind. He believed it would encourage all those who qualified for government office to behave virtuously "for the sake of being so honoured."[46] Savonarola reiterated the benefit of the Venetian model for Florence at the end of his sermon, urging the Florentines to adopt this form of government, because it "is very good; let it seem no shame to you to learn from others, for the form they have was given them by God, and since they adopted it, there has never been civil dissension among them."[47]

A majority of citizens, eager to reclaim their ancient liberties and the institutions of the republic suppressed by the Medici, welcomed the Great Council, which soon became "the soul of the city."[48] The Venetian Consiglio Maggiore was based on a system of hereditary eligibility among the merchant elite, so the Florentines created their own quasi-hereditary model, granting the right to take part in the workings of the Great Council to those citizens of legitimate birth, over twenty-nine years of age, who were free of debt and whose direct male line over three generations of ancestors had occupied positions in government or were otherwise politically qualified. By reaching back three generations, the new government was not only establishing a connection with the previous Medici regime, ensuring that *ottimati* maintained influence, but also, and more importantly, it recognized the claims of those who had held office before 1434 and who had thus faced discrimination by the earlier Medici as led by Cosimo. Even though some 3,500 citizens were entitled to hold office, the original voting records show that no more than the required quorum of 1,000 would attend meetings. This number was reduced later to 600, because citizens either chose not to participate or were prevented from doing so by tax arrears. Furthermore, election to government offices was no longer manipulated and controlled as it had been under Medici control in the fifteenth century.

Members of the Great Council were given control of finances, taxes, and elections, and they were equally eligible for offices. Citizens who were elected to executive councils could once more exercise freely their traditional authority and independence.[49] In 1495 construction began on a huge hall in the Palazzo della Signoria known as the Sala Grande. This "great room" was to accommodate these newly re-enfranchised citizens, and, as if to reinforce their belief in the Venetian political model, it was built according to the exact measurements of the hall of the Venice Consiglio Maggiore.[50]

Even before returning to Florence in 1512, Giuliano had sympathized with members of the Savonarolan faction, possibly predisposing him to support later his brother-in-law Jacopo Salviati, a prominent figure among the friar's followers. In his youth prior to his exile in 1494, Giuliano could have listened to Savonarola's prophetic sermons himself, and was likely influenced by his father, who held deep respect for Savonarola. Indeed, when Lorenzo was on his deathbed in 1492, he summoned the Dominican preacher to the Medici villa in Careggi. Giuliano's tutor, Angelo Poliziano, described the friar's visit in a letter to a friend, saying that, just before Savonarola took his leave, Lorenzo asked for his blessings.[51] According to Roberto Ridolfi, this benediction proves that there were good relations between the Medici and Savonarola and that these relations remained excellent throughout Piero di Lorenzo's short involvement in Florentine politics.[52] The Florentine chronicler Jacopo Nardi (1476–1563) recounted how Giuliano was, by nature, much inclined toward religion.[53] His early personal encounters with the charismatic preacher seem to have left an indelible impression that could help explain why, when he returned to Florence from exile, he readily joined the faction of his brother-in-law Jacopo Salviati, giving his support to Savonarola's broadly based republican government.

Jacopo Salviati, married to Giuliano's eldest and favourite sister, Lucrezia, was an immensely rich banker who, like his close associates Lanfredino Lanfredini and Giovanbattista Ridolfi, was an experienced politician. All three men were held in the highest regard in Florence and were devoted to Savonarola. Even though it had been fourteen years since the friar had been executed in the city, after being spuriously charged with heresy, the preacher still exerted a tremendous influence and had many devout followers.[54] Referred to as *frateschi* (followers of the friar), they were in favour of preserving Savonarola's *governo popolare* because they subscribed to the Dominican's belief that, if a large portion of Florentine citizens were officeholders while in the Great Council, not only would it lead to greater stability but also many more citizens would be willing to support the popular government. Giuliano's actions upon returning to the city left no doubt that he shared these views. However, in the first weeks of political negotiations, he and his *frateschi* friends quickly realized that at least two urgent and significant constitutional reforms were needed. The first was to abolish the lifetime office of *gonfaloniere di giustizia* and the second was to establish a permanent patrician senate.

Before the year 1502, the republic's highest magistrate, the *gonfaloniere di giustizia*, and eight ruling priors, or *signori* (literally "lords"), were elected for a two-month term of office, with the *gonfaloniere di giustizia* presiding over the Signori. The short duration of service was intended to prevent anyone from usurping power and becoming a tyrant. However, as Guicciardini had pointed out, this political model created an untenable situation because "everyone tended to move cautiously, and no one felt personally responsible for public affairs."[55] As the year 1502 approached, the republic fell into a crisis. The government was paralyzed and split into rival factions. *Ottimati* wanted more control over finances, but representatives of the middle classes, also entitled to membership in the Great Council, resisted them, fearing the popular government would be overthrown. Thus, in 1502 the citizens once more turned to Venice as an exemplar and introduced a lifetime term for the *gonfaloniere di giustizia* in emulation of the Venetian doge. The Great Council approved this radical constitutional change, hoping it would bring continuity in government and usher in a new era of stability.[56] Many *ottimati* were in favour of the reform, particularly leading Savonarolans such as Giovanbattista Ridolfi and Jacopo Salviati, who could have been its main sponsors. There is evidence that Savonarola himself had advocated a *gonfaloniere di giustizia a vita*.[57]

From 236 candidates, the *frateschi* chose Piero Soderini, a politically neutral and highly respected diplomat, because he had promised that, if elected, he would continue constitutional reform and implement the proposal to create a Senate, thereby giving the *ottimati* wider representation. What appeared to work in Soderini's favour was the fact that, with no male siblings and very few living blood relatives, he was perceived to present no danger of founding a dynasty.[58] After Soderini was elected, however, he consistently refused to implement Senate proposals, afraid they would curtail his own powers.[59] Following Soderini's exile in September 1512, instead of appointing a new life-term *gonfaloniere di giustizia*, Giuliano, together with the rest of the *ottimati*, decided to reduce the term of office to just one year, arguing that it would give many more citizens the chance to be elected while maintaining some of the stability offered by a lifetime appointment. Their real aim, it seems, was to prevent any one person from having too much power in office.[60]

The second reform of the constitution was to give more leeway to the *ottimati*, and it appears that Giuliano was firmly in favour of the plan to transform the existing Consiglio degli Ottanta (Council of Eighty) to make it more closely resemble the Venetian Consiglio dei Pregadi (Senate). The Consiglio degli Ottanta, elected every six months by the Great Council, was an institution with limited powers. Many members of the new Senate were to be drawn from those *ottimati* who had held high offices in the previous republican government or those who became members through the elections held by the Great Council. Given the right to nominate fifty additional senators, the members of the Senate were granted greater authority, because the appointment was not for a year but for life, as in the Venetian Consiglio dei Pregadi. The Senate's function was to elect ambassadors, for whom patrician status was a prerequisite, to appoint administrators, and, most importantly, to handle government finances.[61]

Giuliano not only voted in favour of this constitutional reform but also was directly responsible for its adoption. According to Cerretani's account, Giuliano stayed in the Palazzo della Signoria until he was able to convince a majority of its members to pass the legislation, despite the fact that the new political body would effectively diminish the Great Council's powers.[62] Cerretani suggests that Jacopo Salviati and Lanfredino Lanfredini had compelled Giuliano to become involved.[63] However, given Giuliano's consistent political activity in Florence, it is more likely that he had formed his own political views long before returning to the city. During his exile he frequently found himself among members of the Venetian ruling class, from whom he would have gained first-hand experience of how well the Consiglio dei Pregadi served as a stable counterweight to the Venetian Consiglio Maggiore. The harmony of Venice's political institutions ensured the stability of the republic. Giuliano was eager to proceed with constitutional reforms because he understood the need for a Senate that consisted of members of Florence's elites, convinced that it would lessen dissension between *ottimati* and other members of the Great Council. Although the qualifying age in this new political body was forty, an exemption was made for Giuliano himself and a few others.[64] On 8 September, with Giuliano's endorsement, Giovanbattista Ridolfi, a widely respected patrician and acknowledged leader of the *frateschi*, whose nephew Piero had married Giuliano's sister Contessina, was elected *gonfaloniere di giustizia*. According to Cerretani, there was no one better in Florence to defend the Great Council.[65]

Giuliano had played a crucial role, therefore, in the creation of the new government on 7 September, and it was evident that he agreed with the political aims of his brother-in-law Jacopo Salviati and the *frateschi*. However, he alienated those most fervent supporters of the Medici, mostly men of the younger generation of *ottimati*, known as *palleschi*, derived from the balls (*palle*) of the Medici coat of arms. Guicciardini recounts that many of the sons of Florentine elites, driven by personal ambitions or pressing financial needs, saw definite material advantages in giving support to the Medici. Described as a "raucous" and "fast-living" bunch, these young *palleschi* lived according to whim and were often responsible for disturbing the civic order in the city.[66] Guicciardini specifically singles out Paolo Vettori, who figured prominently in the events surrounding restoration of the Medici, as one who was "deeply in debt because of his excessive expenditures."[67] Now that the Medici family had been restored in Florence, these young men expected their loyalty to Medici politics to be generously rewarded with dominant positions in a new Medici government.[68] During the first two weeks of September, the *palleschi* became increasingly agitated, because they saw how Giuliano had sided instead with the numerous and more powerful *frateschi*, advocating a popular government. The *palleschi* were also unhappy that Giuliano had managed to persuade them to agree to the constitutional changes, only to regret it bitterly afterwards.[69] Furthermore, there were still many former republicans occupying positions of power.

When the new *gonfaloniere di giustizia*, Giovanbattista Ridolfi, dismissed the Medici armed guard from the Palazzo della Signoria and removed the chains barring the entrance to the Great Council Hall, the *palleschi* decided to spring into action. Led by Giovanni di Bernardo Rucellai, son of the wealthy patrician, they rushed to nearby Campi in order to vent their anger directly to the head of the Medici family, Giuliano's older brother Cardinal Giovanni.[70] After the Sack of Prato, the cardinal had followed the army to Campi in order to be closer to Florence. His first cousin Giulio, son of Giuliano who had been murdered in the Pazzi Conspiracy of 1478, accompanied him. Cardinal Giovanni's nephew Lorenzo (Fig. 7), son of the deceased Piero, was also in the cardinal's company. The *palleschi* reported to Cardinal Giovanni that his younger brother had been badly advised in managing government affairs, thus undermining the security of the state. Moreover, they argued that Giuliano's good-natured approach in politics made him unsuited to the trials of governing. These *palleschi* informed the cardinal that Giuliano had allowed the enemy and their leader to get firmly established in the Palazzo della Signoria, and that this faction was only waiting for the Spanish soldiers to depart before taking further action to restore the republic.[71]

Cardinal Giovanni thus decided to move even closer to Florence, settling at the church of Sant'Antonio near the Faenza Gate, so that he could be seen to be soliciting the opinions of other Florentines. In his entourage were various mercenary captains, or *condottieri*, including the Marchese di Padula, Antonio Cardona (who was promised the position of captain-general of the Florentine forces), and the Bolognese captain Melchiorre Ramazzotto, in the service of the Medici with one thousand infantry. These soldiers were there, Cerretani observed "to frighten those who were thinking they had succeeded in their plot that nothing should be done."[72] No doubt Cerretani was referring to Jacopo Salviati, Lanfredino Lanfredini, and Piero Alamanni, who arrived at the church of Sant'Antonio certain that they could counter the arguments of the *palleschi* and persuade Cardinal Giovanni to accept the new government established with his younger brother's help on 7 September. Jacopo Pitti recounts how they told the cardinal that they did not want changes made to the Great Council because the people fully accepted it, and many citizens had been honoured by it during the previous eighteen years. They informed him that the Medici party was weak, since it had been deprived of men and resources, and that those who remained loyal were few in number and lacked caution. If the cardinal used Medici supporters to build the state and its security, they warned, he would become an agent of their greed and violence, but if he decided to stay with the present reformed government, everyone would embrace and honour the Medici. The citizens would rejoice, because the Great Council would be reconfirmed, and the *ottimati* would welcome the new reforms.[73]

Apparently, Cardinal Giovanni was unimpressed by these arguments. Filippo de' Nerli noticed that neither the cardinal nor his cousin Giulio believed their family could remain secure in Florence if the state stayed in the hands of the popular government. When the cardinal returned to his birthplace, he was firmly resolved to establish a *governo stretto* under Medici control.[74] The Florentine chronicler Giovanni Cambi described the cardinal's arrival this way: "On the fourteenth of September 1512, the day of Santa Croce, the Cardinal de' Medici entered Florence by the Faenza gate, and although he was papal legate to all of Tuscany, he did not want to enter by means of a procession, as was customary, and with a company of citizens, but in their place armed men and a great many foot soldiers from the Romagna and Bologna, and he went to dismount at his house."[75]

Jacopo Pitti provides more detailed description of the cardinal's armed escort, reporting that Giovanni was escorted by 400 lances, the *condottieri* Orsini, Vitello Vitelli, Rinieri della Sassetta, and Ramazzotto with his one thousand infantry, as well as other officers and soldiers of the Dominion.[76] It seems certain that the cardinal, in the midst of such a display of force, wanted to show that he was willing to crush any kind of resistance in the city, even if in contradiction to his younger brother's recent actions. Cardinal Giovanni's open display of force was intended also as a rebuke to those citizens who had humiliated his family by forcing them into long exile. Guicciardini claimed that from the very beginning, and despite his words to the contrary, the cardinal intended to restore his family's power, and he "would not have considered the restitution of his family as private citizens worthy reward for so much toil."[77]

Two days after the cardinal's arrival in Florence, a coup d'état, presumably on his orders, seized the Palazzo della Signoria. The contemporary chroniclers Landucci, Cerretani, and Pitti all record that Giuliano played a central role in the coup, describing how with soldiers and a band of armed *palleschi* he led an assault on the Palazzo while a meeting between *gonfaloniere di giustizia* Ridolfi and about sixty citizens was in progress.[78] Cerretani gave the fullest account of the rebellion in his *Dialogo della mutatione di Firenze*, through the words of Giovanni Rucellai, a participant in the seizure: "Giuliano armed with cold steel and in good company entered the meeting hall and met those citizens closest to him. Some of us wanted to take revenge on some of the magistrates but with great effort Giuliano stood between us so that no one got hurt, but the Palazzo and above all the munitions and some of the silverware fell into the hands of the soldiers."[79]

Modern historians appear to accept this standard narrative as fact.[80] But can these three chroniclers be believed? Unlike Landucci, Cerretani, and Pitti, the writers Guicciardini, Nardi, and Nerli make no mention of Giuliano storming the Palazzo with his armed men. Instead, they record that he was already in the Palazzo at the time of the attack, attending the council meeting with Ridolfi.[81] This version of events appears to be corroborated by an account written shortly after by one of the attackers, Prinzivalle della Stufa: "On 16 [September] Giuliano went in the morning into the Palace to consult on matters of the city, and all the friends gathered together, weapons in hand, and we found ourselves in the Palace, and we occupied it, and with loud voices confronted Giuliano[,] making him understand that this was the day on which he must order a state according to his way, and that we want him to make a popular assembly, and he must do this because this is the wish of all of us young friends of his."[82]

Niccolò Machiavelli gives further confirmation of Giuliano's lack of participation in the armed aggression. In a letter likely written to Isabella d'Este (Fig. 34), perhaps on Giuliano's behalf, at the end of September 1512,[83] Machiavelli observed: "On the sixteenth of this month the Signoria assembled many citizens at the Palazzo, and with them was the Magnificent Giuliano, and they were discussing governmental reform when there chanced to be an uproar heard in the Piazza, so that Ramazzotti with his soldiers and some other men seized the Palazzo shouting '*palle, palle.*'"[84]

Giuliano had taken a leadership role as conciliator and mediator, working closely with the *ottimati* to establish the reformed constitution on

7 September. There was no reason for him take up arms a few days later and instigate a violent assault against his fellow magistrates and citizens. The weight of evidence appears to support the view that Giuliano was already present in the council chambers that morning, attending the meeting with Ridolfi and about sixty citizens before the attack took place. But why was he there? Could it be that the members of his own family had not warned him beforehand that a coup d'état was being planned for later that day? The fact that Giuliano was in the *palazzo* at the time of the assault strongly suggests that he went there with the aim of protecting the *gonfaloniere di giustizia* and his *ottimati* friends. Cerretani admits as much, when, as we have seen, in his *Dialogo delle mutatione* Giovanni Rucellai claimed that "with great effort Giuliano stood between us so that no one got hurt." Jacopo Nardi writes how, following the seizure of the palace, members of the Signoria descended the stairs and walked out onto the *ringhiera*, the raised ceremonial platform erected in front of the town hall. They were led by none other than Giuliano, who held the hand of *Gonfaloniere di Giustizia* Ridolfi in full view of the large crowd summoned to the Piazza della Signoria by the ringing of its great bell. Nardi also adds that the men in the piazza were in large part not citizens but outsiders and soldiers.[85]

Calling the people to the piazza for a *parlamento,* or a popular assembly, was a political strategy used many times in the fifteenth century by the Medici in order to consolidate their power. Public meetings, held to ratify extraordinary laws related to constitutional reforms, had been prohibited since 1495. While appearing on the surface as an expression of the will of the whole community, these public meetings were able to bypass normal legislative channels. An injunction to this effect was engraved in the Great Council Hall: "He who wants to convene *parlamento* wants to take control of government away from *popolo*."[86]

Four hundred soldiers blocked all passages leading in and out of the piazza. The assembled crowd had little choice but to repeal the law banning *parlamenti* and to vote as they were instructed. Thereafter, with the presence of the Spanish soldiers in the city, the Medici slowly re-established the old system of government that suited them best. The Great Council, the Council of the Eighty, and the Florentine militia were all abolished by decrees, driving the last nail into the coffin of the republican government. In the past, the Sala Grande in the Palazzo della Signoria was the city's pride and joy. Savonarola often referred to the Sala Grande as "*sala di*

Cristo," believing that the Great Council was God's creation. Now it was desecrated by being turned into a barracks. In one corner was a tavern, in another gambling tables were set up, and a third corner was taken over by a brothel.[87]

The new government took the form of a *balìa*, meaning a body "having special power," composed of sixty-six citizens carefully appointed by Cardinal Giovanni for their loyalty. Its extraordinary powers gave the *balìa* unprecedented, unrestricted authority to introduce new institutional and legislative reforms, to distribute the offices of the magistracies, and to preside over matters of finance.[88] In spite of the fact that Jacopo Salviati, Lanfredino Lanfredini, and Giovanbattista Ridolfi had vehemently opposed the calling of a *parlamento*, Cardinal Giovanni appointed all three to the *balìa*, much to the disgust of the *palleschi*. The cardinal could have reasoned that it would be more prudent to include some of those patricians who had been prominent in the previous government, for their useful political experience, and their inclusion in the *balìa* would demonstrate to the disaffected that the new government was committed to broad political participation. A more pragmatic reason, however, could have been the cardinal's urgent need to pay the huge amounts of money demanded by the viceroy of Naples and his Spanish troops. These funds could only be raised by loans from the wealthiest of citizens. It would have been unwise for him to alienate those patricians who would potentially be the largest contributors. Indeed, both Jacopo Salviati and Lanfredino Lanfredini made sizeable contributions.[89]

According to Guicciardini, Giuliano presided over a regime that "governed much more imperiously and with much more absolute power than had their forefathers."[90] It was a government, moreover, that had been imposed on the people by military force rather than persuasion. Chapter 5 will examine more fully Giuliano's role in governing Florence from September 1512 until May 1513, at which point his brother, the newly elected Leo X, recalled him to Rome (Fig. 11). Giuliano's position as Florence's leading statesman was transferred in August 1513 to his nephew Lorenzo de' Medici. Contrary to the prevailing view that Giuliano "lacked sufficient interest in governing" and had "difficulty understanding Florentine politics,"[91] as will be seen further in chapter 5, evidence demonstrates his complete dedication to the affairs of the state and his efforts to reconcile the opposing factions. Despite the constraints placed upon him by his brother and the autocratic *palleschi,* he did his best to ensure that all citizens of Florence were treated fairly and equally.

The criticism that Giuliano mishandled affairs of state and that his good-natured approach in politics made him unsuited to the trials of governing can be traced to Bartolomeo Cerretani. In the fifteenth century, the Cerretani prospered because they had embraced Medicean politics and in return were rewarded with important government offices. For example, Bartolomeo's grandfather Niccolò served as *gonfaloniere di giustizia* in 1465, during the time of Piero di Cosimo the Gouty.[92] In 1480, two years after the Pazzi Conspiracy, his father, Paolo, was one of 210 citizens selected by Lorenzo the Magnificent to take part in administering special powers imposed at the time, showing recognition of Cerretani loyalty.[93] Bartolomeo continued the family tradition of Medici support, and, while it appeared that he might have had some sympathy with Savonarola's call for Church reform, he was greatly opposed to the preacher's political views.[94] Cerretani's disparaging remarks about Giuliano appeared first in his *Ricordi*, a diary kept from August 1500 until February 1524, a few months before his death in June.[95] Bartolomeo repeats these comments in his *Storia fiorentina*, composed between 1512 and 1514, and in his *Dialogo delle mutatione di Firenze*, completed in 1521.[96] This last text deals specifically with the change of government in 1512 and has become a treasure trove for historians.

Cerretani's *Dialogo* is a fictional account of conversations among four Florentines in the house of the historian Francesco Guicciardini, who was then serving as the governor of Modena and Reggio. Giovanni Rucellai, the radical *pallesco*, and the principal interlocutor in the dialogue, did in fact pass through Modena on his way to France in the early summer of 1520, having been appointed as Leo X's papal nuncio to Francis I.[97] Two of the four speakers were followers of Savonarola, who had been absent from Florence since June 1512, awaiting with interest to hear Rucellai's recollection of the *mutatione* of the government and his role in the events of 1512. Paolo Malanima believes that Cerretani used Rucellai as a fictional mouthpiece to espouse his own pro-Medicean views. For example, Rucellai states that the *ottimati* were divided between those who wanted nothing more than Piero Soderini's removal and the others, "of which I was one who wanted to make a new government with the Medici as head."[98] Because Cerretani was adamantly opposed to the popular government, he would have strongly disapproved of Giuliano's support of it, and it is hardly surprising that he would have nothing positive to say about Giuliano.

Bartolomeo Cerretani was highly regarded by the new Medici regime of Lorenzo de' Medici, who had replaced Giuliano as its head in August 1513 (Fig. 12). Indeed, Lorenzo himself apparently nominated Cerretani in 1514 to serve as one of the eight priors of the Signoria for March/April.[99] It appears, therefore, that Cerretani's partiality could be blamed for much of the criticism of Giuliano's character. Modern historians have, perhaps, relied too heavily on Cerretani as a credible source.[100] The modern writers who present Giuliano as inept and "politically inexperienced,"[101] as having a "pliable character,"[102] being easily manipulated[103] and lacking caution,[104] or being totally inexperienced politically, "more interested in letters than arms and having scarce inclination and aptitude for the questions of governing,"[105] certainly accepted Cerretani's bias against Giuliano.

Giuliano's support for the republican government brought him into conflict with his own brother, Cardinal Giovanni, who saw the *frateschi* as the greatest political enemy of the Medici. Not long after Giuliano's brother became Pope Leo X in 1513, and his power over Florentine affairs became increasingly absolute, repressive measures were taken in the state to suppress the followers of Savonarola. It would have been much easier from the outset if Giuliano had supported the "restricted government," but, as we have seen, he chose to endorse a model of popular governance. He was also responsible for the new constitution of 7 September, creating a Senate similar to that of Venice, granting a much greater share of power to *ottimati*. These events suggest that Giuliano's political outlook was fully formed before his return to Florence. In order to determine whether this was the case, it is necessary to examine the years of his exile and to discover who likely influenced his political and religious thinking, as well as what factors led him to side with Savonarola's reformists and republicans.

CHAPTER TWO

GIULIANO AND HIS VENETIAN FRIENDS

Upon the Medici expulsion from Florence in November 1494, the fifteen-year-old Giuliano left for Bologna with his older brother Piero. They were expecting to find refuge with and assistance from the Bentivoglio family, the rulers of the second-most-important city of the Papal States, who had benefitted greatly from the generosity of their father, Lorenzo the Magnificent. However, Piero and Giuliano were given a far from friendly reception. Piero was harshly rebuked for his cowardice, accused of fleeing Florence without putting up any resistance. Such defiance would have at least saved his dignity, instead of handing a complete victory to his enemies. Disillusioned and humiliated, the brothers continued on to Venice where, in great contrast to Bologna, not only were they received honourably, but also the Venetian Senate promised them help to return to Florence.[1]

Once before, in 1433, the Venetians had showed similar magnanimity toward the Medici when their great-grandfather Cosimo the Elder was forced to flee Florence. The Venetian republic welcomed Cosimo, not as the exile he was, but as a most honoured ambassador. He stayed for only one year, however, before being invited back to Florence by a new, pro-Medici Signoria, and with the tacit approval of Palla Strozzi (1372–1462), one of the most powerful patricians in the city, whom Cosimo would exile nonetheless. The Venetian Pope Eugenius IV (r. 1431–1447), who was in self-imposed exile in Florence for the better part of a decade, also voiced his strong support for Cosimo, wanting to preserve good relations with the Medici.[2] During the second Medici exile in Venice, fortunately for Piero and Giuliano, the Lippomano, patricians and prominent bankers, were happy and honoured to provide them with a house on the island of Murano in 1494. The Venetian government also granted an important concession when it allowed both brothers to carry arms and be escorted about the city by fifteen to twenty of their followers.[3]

Even though they had been given refuge in Venice, neither Piero nor Giuliano planned to stay long. Piero could think of nothing else but the need to raise troops in order to take back Florence by force, leaving the young Giuliano to make his own way in the city. Although Giuliano stayed for a while in Venice, in January 1496 he joined Ludovico Sforza's court in Milan, where he remained until April 1497, after which he returned to Venice.[4] Between 1498 and 1503 it seems he was constantly on the move, for the most part in northern Italy, although he did visit Rome twice in 1500 and make two journeys to France. These were the years in which the Medici had aligned themselves with Cesare Borgia, an alliance that will be discussed in the next chapter, hoping that he would be able to help them return to Florence. After Piero drowned in the Garigliano River in 1503, while attempting to retreat with French forces following a battle with a Spanish army, Giuliano became a frequent and much-favoured guest at the court of Guidobaldo da Montefeltro (1472–1508) and Elisabetta Gonzaga (1471–1526), Duke and Duchess of Urbino (Figs. 13 and 14). His close friendship with the ducal family continued after Guidobaldo's death, when Guidobaldo's nephew Francesco Maria della Rovere succeeded to the duchy. At certain intervals during his years of exile, however, Giuliano returned to Venice, drawn there by his strong ties of affection and friendship with a number of prominent Venetian patricians. These friendships had a formative influence on his thinking, particularly in relation to politics and religion, and would provide him with both an intellectual and a spiritual direction for the rest of his short life.

BERNARDO AND PIETRO BEMBO

Bernardo Bembo (1433–1519), Venetian ambassador to Florence in the 1470s, would certainly have been among the Venetian patricians who extended a warm welcome to Lorenzo the Magnificent's refugee sons in November 1494, particularly because he had shared an extraordinarily intimate friendship with their father. A member of one of the most illustrious families in Venice, Bernardo's more famous son, Pietro Bembo (1470–1547), poet, linguist, and later cardinal, became Giuliano's close friend (Fig. 15). Bernardo is known today for his patronage of the arts. Among the works that he seems to have commissioned was Leonardo da Vinci's famous 1474 portrait of the young Ginevra de' Benci, a work that revolutionized the tradition of female portraiture.[5] In Ravenna, Bernardo also commissioned a monumental marble tomb for the Florentine exile Dante Alighieri, who died in that city in 1321.[6]

Bernardo was a key player in the political affairs of the Venetian republic during the second half of the fifteenth century, twice serving as ambassador to Florence. It appears that he was primarily sent to encourage the Florentines to become more active against the Turks, a matter of vital interest to Venice. His first posting was from January 1475 to April 1476, and the second, much longer, from July 1478 to May 1480. While in Florence, Bernardo made a profound impression upon many Florentines because of his considerable intellectual interests, particularly among those humanists of the Laurentian circle, including Giuliano's tutor Poliziano, Cristoforo Landino (1424–1498), Giovanni Cavalcanti (1444–1509), and Marsilio Ficino (1433–1499).[7] He eagerly attended Ficino's Platonic academy, first conceived by Cosimo the Elder,[8] and after only one meeting, Ficino sang Bembo's praises and professed great affection for him. In a letter Ficino wrote: "You ask what the Academy does, my Bernardo? It loves Bembo. What else does it do? It reveres Bembo. Every man of letters among us agrees that Bembo above all is worthy of love and reverence, for his breast is the temple of the Graces, and his mind the fount of the Muses."[9] Bernardo also had a great love of vernacular poetry, especially the lyric verse of Petrarch (1304–1374), many of whose manuscripts he kept in his great library, which later became part of the Vatican Library in Rome.[10] One of his prized possessions was a manuscript of Petrarch's essay *De vita solitaria* (On the Solitary Life) written in the author's own hand.[11]

Bembo's admiration for Petrarch drew him to the attention of Lorenzo the Magnificent, and they soon developed a close rapport, as demonstrated by correspondence during Bembo's two-year absence from Florence between 1476 and 1478. Lorenzo sent generous gifts to Bernardo and his family as well as some of his own poems in order to solicit Bembo's approval, showing his respect for the Venetian. On his part, Bembo responded warmly to this demonstration of esteem and friendship, proclaiming many times in letters his devotion to the foremost citizen of Florence.[12] It appears that so great was Bembo's popularity among the ruling elite that efforts were made to prevent his recall from the city,[13] and it is certain that Lorenzo himself did not want to see his precious friend leave Florence. The high regard Bernardo garnered in Florence elicited suspicion in Venice, leading some, especially among the anti-Florentine faction in the Venetian Senate, to believe that Bernardo had so compromised himself that he could no longer serve the interests of Venice.[14] Indeed, it must not always have been easy for Bernardo to be impartial with someone who was so generous with his favours and who had "opened up such marvellous vistas of culture and poetry."[15]

Bembo eventually settled permanently in Venice, where he occupied some of the highest offices in the republic, and, because he was an expert on Florentine affairs, he was given the task of looking after Florentine ambassadors during their stays in the city.[16] Thus, Bernardo would have been among the first Venetian senators to welcome the two young Medici fugitives from Florence in 1494, and rescue them from their misery.[17] He would probably have shared his fond memories of Lorenzo and his family with young Giuliano. The Venetian diarist Marino Sanudo (1466–1536) recorded how in 1510 Giuliano stayed as a guest of the Bembo family in their palazzo on the Grand Canal near the Rialto Bridge, and mentions Giuliano's close friendship with Bernardo's son Pietro.[18] Given the close ties of friendship between Bembo and the Medici, it is very likely that Giuliano was given the same hospitality many times before as well as after that visit.[19]

In his travels during eighteen years of exile, Giuliano would have accumulated a wealth of knowledge about the different systems of governments in the various territorial states of Italy. He would have had much time to consider the reasons for his own exile, how in Florence *ottimati* had become openly hostile towards his family, finally withdrawing their support from his brother Piero in 1494 and forcing the Medici into exile. It would not have been difficult for him to realize that his older brother's blundering actions had led to these problems, above all the antagonistic feelings he had aroused among Florentines, because of his supreme arrogance in believing that he could turn the city, with two centuries of republican traditions, into a principate. Giuliano likely also recognized that, in the peninsula at the beginning of the sixteenth century, Venice and Florence had survived as powerful independent republics, along with Genoa, Lucca, and Siena. A comparison of his native city to Venice, however, would have shown him that the latter appeared stable and changeless, whereas Florence, after the fall of the Medici, was rife with factional strife and constant dissension, especially between many *ottimati* and members of the Great Council. The primary difference between the two constitutions was that Venice had a Senate, whereas in the Florentine republic, all power was vested in the Great Council.

Bembo surely knew that Giuliano loved his homeland deeply and harboured hopes of returning one day. Given Bernardo's love and respect for the memory of his father, Lorenzo the Magnificent, it is likely that Bembo played some part in Giuliano's political education and, as a senator of the Venetian republic, would have wanted to demonstrate why the Venetian constitution, admired by so many, including some Florentine *ottimati*, was superior to anything approaching a centralized form of rule. That Bernardo assumed the role of Giuliano's political mentor is, admittedly, speculative, but it is supported by Nella Giannetto's assessment of Bernardo's personality: when his affections and admiration were engaged, Bembo was generous with encouragement and support, especially to younger friends.[20] Evidence that Bernardo did care a great deal for Giuliano, who continued to be stateless, comes from his son Pietro who, returning on 13 November 1507 from Padua where he had gone to visit his ill father, wrote that it was one of Bernardo's more "intense desires" to see the house of the Medici returned to Florence.[21] Under Bernardo's guidance, Giuliano could have studied the subtleties of the Venetian constitution and seen first-hand how the Consiglio Maggiore worked in harmony with the Senate.

During the first weeks of September 1512 in Florence, not only did Giuliano vote to preserve a popular government with Soderini as *gonfaloniere di giustizia*, but also he used his considerable influence to persuade enough members of the Great Council to agree to legislation that would establish a Senate in imitation of the Venetian model. The fact that he was able to get such consent was a significant achievement that speaks to his gifts of oratory, tact, and leadership. His Venetian experience surely enabled him to advocate for this reform with so much conviction. That Venice was on his mind and in the thoughts of the other framers of this legislation is suggested by its prefatory statement of justification: "All ancient and modern republics which had a long life and ruled in peace and unity and did so because dignities and benefices were fairly distributed among its citizens." The preamble continues that good government requires "a republic [to] possess the institution of a Senate ... This had been considered and recommended by thoughtful citizens frequently in the past, but they were not believed till now when, with great losses for the city and danger to its freedom, experience proved them to be right."[22] Together with other *ottimati*, Giuliano was convinced that a Venetian-style Senate would be best model for Florence, restoring to the leading families their traditional right to a political voice while reducing friction between the patrician and middle classes. Moreover, Giuliano's leadership demonstrated clearly that he fully expected to assume an important role in governing Florence, but only as a permanent member of this new political body, not as an absolute ruler.

Unlike his father, Pietro Bembo chose to avoid the life of a Venetian diplomat and instead decided to devote his life to poetry and literary studies[23] (Fig. 15). He shared with his father a great love of Petrarch, and in 1501 and 1502 he worked with the Venetian printer-publisher Aldo Manuzio to prepare editions of Dante's *Commedia* and Petrarch's *Canzoniere* from manuscripts in his father's collection. Also in 1502, Pietro transcribed all the works of Dante and Petrarch to "imprint on his memory the phraseology and thoughts and lovely and noble conceits."[24] Both Bernardo and Pietro could have inspired the young Giuliano to write poetry in the Petrarchan lyric style, thus emulating his father, Lorenzo the Magnificent, who had been a prolific and accomplished poet. Giuliano's output, however, was limited to the first five years of his exile, from 1495 to 1500, during which time he seems to have composed more than seventy poems, mostly sonnets in the style of Petrarch.

Giuliano's friendship with Pietro Bembo was both close and long lasting. When his brother Giovanni was elected the first Medici pope in March 1513, one of his first papal acts, even before leaving the conclave, was to appoint Pietro and the Modenese neo-Latin poet Jacopo Sadoleto (1477–1547) as his apostolic secretaries, highly important and powerful posts charged with conducting correspondence with kings, emperors, and high-ranking clergy.[25] While Sadoleto was without doubt one of the greatest Latinists of his age, the nomination of Bembo, who only very recently had established himself as a foremost Latinist,[26] perhaps resulted from Giuliano's recommendation as well as being a gesture of gratitude by the newly elected Leo X toward Bernardo and Pietro Bembo for the generous support they had always given to his family.

Pietro Bembo publicly displayed his high opinion of Giuliano when he assigned an honoured role to him in his dialogue *Prose della volgar lingua* (Writings on the Vulgar Tongue),[27] a fictional conversation between four friends on how the literary language of fourteenth-century Tuscans, in the prose of Boccaccio and the poetry of Petrarch, should be elevated above all other vernacular models and become the universal literary language of Italy, in place of classical Latin. Pietro locates the dialogue in 1502 at the Venetian home of his younger brother Carlo while Pietro was away in Padua, the conversation reported to him upon his return. Even though the work was not published until 1525, it seems that Bembo had been thinking about the Tuscan language as early as 1497,[28] when he would have had his first contacts with Giuliano in Venice.[29] Because Giuliano is the only native speaker of Tuscan among the four interlocutors, who included the Venetian Carlo Bembo, the Genoese Federico Fregoso, and the Latin poet Ercole Strozzi from Ferrara, the young Medici was given a privileged position as an expert. Pietro, praising him for his "judiciousness,"[30] presents Giuliano in the best possible light. In the dialogue's third book, longer than the first two combined, the young Medici displays intelligence and competency as he gives a complete description of the Tuscan language and discusses the complexities of its grammar.[31]

VINCENZO QUERINI AND TOMMASO GIUSTINIANI

Pietro Bembo no doubt introduced the young Giuliano to his circle of Venetian friends, who were drawn together by a shared enthusiasm for literature, philosophy, and certain religious teachings. Among the group were Tommaso Giustiniani (1476–1528) and Vincenzo Querini (1478–1514), who were to form particularly strong bonds of friendship with Giuliano. Most of Bembo's friends had known each other at the University of Padua in the 1490s, but after returning to Venice they continued to meet informally on the lagoon island of Murano, where Giustiniani had a villa. Eugenio Massa speaks of a "Murano circle" of reform-minded humanists led by the charismatic and intensely intellectual Giustiniani. The friends gathered at his villa to participate in religious exercises and carry out studies of the Bible and writings of the Fathers of the Church. Most also displayed literary interests, and they often engaged in the writing of sonnets, composed in the style and tone of Petrarch, which they addressed to one another in celebration of their friendship.[32] Querini, a scion of one of the grandest Venetian families, had early on distinguished himself as a promising diplomat, but he was also an impressive humanist scholar, whose career culminated in his being nominated in 1505 to the post of lecturer in philosophy at the Rialto school.[33] Increasingly, however, in letters to friends written during the first decade of the sixteenth century, Querini complained about the demands of public service and expressed disgust for worldly ambition. He began to search for a more spiritual life, free from the distractions of the secular world, and adopted certain ascetic practices that better suited his temperament.[34]

This longing for a spiritual life is expressed in his Petrarchan sonnets written at the time, which were heavily influenced by Christian Neo-Platonic mysticism and Ficino's theology of divine love. A number of his poems are addressed to "an unknown *ma donna*," his divine beloved. They reject earthly love, expressing instead a desire for a spiritual love that has the power to penetrate and illuminate the soul.[35] Other friends in the group, particularly Pietro Bembo, whose father, we have seen, had known Ficino personally, shared Querini's interest in Ficinian Neo-Platonism. Neo-Platonic ideas permeate the imaginary of Pietro's dialogue *Gli Asolani* that he wrote in the vernacular and published in 1505. Dedicated to Lucrezia Borgia (1480–1519), Cesare's sister, who had married Alfonso d'Este, Duke of Ferrara in 1501, the treatise is a reflection on the nature of love in which Bembo weaves together the Petrarchan and Platonic traditions. In the third book, Pietro introduces a wise old hermit who treats love in its proper philosophical light, and the book ends with a discussion of the beauty of Plato's world of unchanging ideas and Ficino's concept of the contemplative ascent to God through love.[36]

It is not difficult to imagine that the younger Bembo, Querini, and Giustiniani would have warmly welcomed Giuliano, a kindred humanist and poetic spirit, into their circle of friends. The Florentine chronicler Jacopo Nardi described Giuliano's personality as "naturally inclined towards religion,"[37] and we can see an element of this spirituality expressed in his early poetry. It is evident that Giuseppe Fatini, the primary modern critic of Giuliano's poetry, did not think highly of Giuliano's work, especially those poems on the theme of love, which he finds devoid of genuine passion, repetitious, and characterized by a monotony that at times becomes "exasperating."[38] Fatini believes that these verses express Giuliano's love not for a single woman but for a number of different women met during his stays in Venice, Bologna, and Milan. He surmises that these women may have momentarily "distracted him from the painful uncertainties of his exile and the vain attempts made to return to Florence."[39] None of these women or loves, Fatini claims, give Giuliano's words the needed breath of humanity, sincere feeling, or thrill of joy, anger, or desire. Even though the aspiring poet almost always spoke of "unrequited love," "the expectation of disappointment," and "longed-for hope," none of his words, for Fatini, had the power to engender real passion. Furthermore, all these women appear to be equal in Giuliano's mind as he weaves his expressive longings together, using the usual images that many other courtly poets employed at the time: "fire that burns his heart," "tears that dissolve ice," "pain that joyously approaches close to death, since death is his only pleasure."[40]

These themes closely echo those that are found in Querini's sonnets, where his poems speak of a "sombre pleasure," a "false delight," a "doubtful hope and certain suffering," and where the approach of death is welcomed.[41] Not only is the thematic content similar but also almost a quarter of Giuliano's poems are likewise addressed to an unidentified "*ma donna*." Fatini does not seem to have considered the context in which Giuliano wrote many of these love sonnets, composed when he was either living in Venice or visiting the city during his first years of exile. Nor does he reflect on the fact that Giuliano at this time was absorbing the ideas of Florentine Neo-Platonism, so popular among his Venetian friends and their broader circle. Rather than being love poems in the conventional sense, perhaps Giuliano's Petrarch-inspired sonnets on love could be best understood and appreciated if they are seen as part of this expression of Christian mysticism rather than as proof of numerous affairs or an obsession with the pleasures of sex.[42] This is not to say that Giuliano was without paramours, for in 1511 in Urbino he fathered a son with the widow Pacifica Brandano. The child's name was changed from Pasqualino to Ippolito, and Pope Clement VII went on to appoint him cardinal in 1529 (Fig. 16).

Pietro Bembo and his Venetian humanist friends were in close contact with Paolo Orlandini, abbot of the Camaldolese monastery on the small island of San Michele, situated between Venice and Murano, who may have served as the inspiration for Bembo's old hermit in *Gli Asolani*. Before becoming abbot of San Michele, Orlandini had taken an active part in the intellectual life of Florence, where Lorenzo the Magnificent had assisted him in pursuing his humanistic studies, and Marsilio Ficino, whom Orlandini called his "'father and master' in everything that he knew,"[43] had been his professor of philosophy.[44] In 1488 Orlandini took his vows at Santa Maria degli Angeli in Florence, where, under the patronage of Lorenzo the Magnificent, the church became the locus of Ficino's informal Platonic academy beneath the rotunda of the first centrally planned church of the Renaissance, funded by Cosimo de' Medici and built by his favourite architect, Filippo Brunelleschi.[45] The spiritual and ascetic practices of the eleventh-century Camaldolese founder St Romuald had close affinities with the Platonists of the early Christian Church. In the fifteenth century the Camaldolese monks of Santa Maria degli Angeli forged close ties with the Platonists in Ficino's circle, who in turn saw in the mystical theology of the Camaldolese an embodiment of Platonic principles.[46]

Orlandini was prior of Santa Maria degli Angeli before moving to the Venetian monastery of San Michele, further tying the two Camaldolese houses together, and he, as argued persuasively by Dennis Lackner, served as the direct link between the Neo-Platonic circles in Florence and the humanists in Venice. Lackner also suggests that it was Orlandini's personal intervention together with the literary influence of Ficino that led Giustiniani and Querini to give up their lives of patrician privilege to become Camaldolese hermits,[47] a decision taken only after many years of thinking about the eremitical life. It seems that, early on, both Querini and Giustiniani had begun to prepare themselves for lives of poverty, solitude, and contemplation, making, for example, the commitment in 1501 to remain chaste[48] and then in May 1510 adopting the hair shirt.[49] Giustiniani joined the white-robed monks of the hermitage at Camaldoli, in the remote Apennine Mountains near Arezzo in July 1510, taking the name of Paolo. Querini, rechristened Pietro, followed him in October 1511.[50] Judging from the expression of mutual esteem in the letters passed between Giuliano and his two friends in the hermitage, and from the many times Giuliano was mentioned in the hermits' correspondence with their mutual friends in Venice, it appears that the friendship among Giuliano and the two Camaldolese monks, despite their seclusion at Camaldoli, continued to be very close.[51]

Not long after they adopted the eremitical life, Querini and Giustiniani began reforming their order's constitution to ensure a stricter observation of the rule. Their proposals brought them into conflict with the general of the order, Pietro Dolfin (1444–1525), who fiercely opposed their ideas and became an obstacle to their reform efforts.[52] Felix Gilbert argues that it was because of their particularly close friendship with Giuliano, whom they referred to in one of their letters as "amato da noi come il cuor nostro," that they were able to prevail in their struggle with Dolfin. Giuliano, using his influence, intervened on their behalf and obtained the support of his brother Giovanni, newly elevated as Leo X to the papal throne[53] (Fig. 11). Almost four months after taking office, on 4 July 1513, the pope issued a bull that permitted a radical reform of the Camaldolese order, one that brought all the religious houses – the hermitage at Camaldoli as well as the conventual and reformed observant monasteries – into one body under the jurisdiction of San Michele in Murano; moreover, the reform, together with the order's new constitution, resulted in the curtailing of Pietro Dolfin's power over individual houses.[54] It is doubtful that Giuliano would have personally become embroiled in this bitter religious dispute, or afterwards have consented to become the principal patron and benefactor of the order,[55] if he were unconcerned for the order's welfare or calls for religious reform. Indeed, he had known many priests and friars in his short lifetime and, as the brother of a cardinal who was now a pope, he had seen the abuses and excesses of the upper clergy, and was in a unique position to know how urgently the Church needed reform. Additional evidence for the shared desire of Giuliano and the hermits for Church reform can be found in Baldassare Castiglione's *Il Libro del Cortegiano* (*The Book of the Courtier*).

BALDASSARE CASTIGLIONE

A Mantuan of noble descent, Castiglione (1478–1529) first met Giuliano de' Medici in 1496 at the court of Ludovico Sforza in Milan, where Castiglione had been sent to complete his education (Fig. 40). Their friendship was renewed in Urbino in 1504, when Castiglione entered the service of Guidobaldo da Montefeltro (Fig. 13) in both military and diplomatic capacities, and where, as we have already seen, Giuliano was a frequent and much honoured guest. The Urbino court continued to flourish as it had during the times of Guidobaldo's father, Federico. Guidobaldo's connection to Pope Julius II (Fig. 9) through the papal nephew Giovanni della Rovere (1457–1501), married to his sister Giovanna, likely led to Guidobaldo's appointment as captain-general of the papal army as well as assurance of the pope's financial support. After Guidobaldo's death in 1508, Castiglione continued to serve his successor, Francesco Maria della Rovere (Fig. 17), nephew of both Guidobaldo and Julius II, who made even greater use of Castiglione's diplomatic and military skills on behalf of Urbino.[56]

Like Pietro Bembo, who had also been given a position at the ducal court in 1506, and where he remained until 1512, Castiglione held Giuliano in high esteem. This regard first becomes apparent in Castiglione's vernacular pastoral *Tirsi*, a dramatic eclogue composed for Carnival 1506, which has been described as a poetic prelude to the "idyllic" existence of the Urbino court later described in Castiglione's famous *Book of the Courtier*.[57] In the play, presented to Elisabetta, duchess of Urbino (Fig. 14), Giuliano is described as the one who comes across the mountains from Etruria, "a wise and learned shepherd, skilled in all the arts, whose praises are heard on every shore and by every fountain."[58] As we saw in Bembo's *Prose della volgar lingua*, in *Tirsi*, Giuliano inspired high praise for his personal qualities. He was stateless at the time, living upon the generosity of others, and so it is unlikely that either Bembo or Castiglione would have had anything to gain by praising Giuliano through hollow flattery or insincere statements.

Giuliano and Castiglione became close friends. Castiglione could have confided his worries about mounting debts, and perhaps it was Giuliano, in an attempt to help his friend, who first proposed marriage between Baldassare and his niece, Piero's daughter Clarice, in August 1507. She was the daughter of the widowed Alfonsina Orsini, then residing in Rome with her son and Giuliano's nephew Lorenzo. Clarice's dowry would certainly have solved Castiglione's financial problems. Although Alfonsina was at first vague in her response to Giuliano's suggestion, likely having more ambitious plans for her daughter, it appears that Giuliano was able to persuade his brother Giovanni to agree to the alliance. Cardinal Giovanni became anxious for the marriage to take place. In May 1508 Castiglione received word that the marriage had been agreed upon and that the dowry was 4,000 ducats, a rather small amount that would not even cover his existing debts.[59] He had high hopes, however, that he would eventually receive more, considering that Clarice's Medici uncle was a cardinal. No doubt he also looked forward to having family ties to Giuliano as well.

Castiglione waited patiently for all the arrangements to be concluded, but, as we learn from a letter he wrote to his mother in Mantua on 10 January 1509, it appeared that Cardinal Giovanni changed his mind, because quite suddenly, and without notifying Giuliano, he contracted a marriage for Clarice with the extremely wealthy Florentine Filippo Strozzi the Younger (1489–1538). This political move was intended to strengthen the Medici family in Florence.[60] Castiglione's disappointment was considerable, and in another letter to his mother he wrote: "We certainly had some cause of complaint, as on both sides troth had been plighted by word of mouth."[61] He assured her, however, that Giuliano had no share in breaking off the marriage. It was quite the opposite, he tells her, and "it had annoyed [Giuliano] excessively."[62]

One of the dialogues in Castiglione's *Courtier* points to Giuliano's views about the corrupt state of the Church. Julius II and his retinue were passing through Urbino on their way to Rome, after the pope's military success in 1506 over the Bentivoglio of Bologna, who fled rather than put up a fight. Because some of his courtiers were so captivated by the charm of the company at the ducal court, especially the gracious Duchess Elisabetta (Fig. 14), they decided to stay on after the pope's departure in March 1507.[63] As part of the four-day discussion regarding the ideal courtier, Duchess Elisabetta gave Giuliano the task of describing the qualities and virtues required of a lady at court, but he quite unexpectedly veers off in his defence of women to launch into a vitriolic diatribe against the abuses and corruption of friars, whom he describes as those:

> accursed hypocrites among men … who – forgetful, or rather scornful, of Christ's teaching … with their habits all torn, they deceive the simple. They do not refrain from forging wills, fomenting mortal enmities between man and wife, or from resorting sometimes to poison, from using sorceries, incantations, and every sort of villainy. And then out of their own head they cite a certain authority which says, *Si non caste, tamen caute* [if not chastely then discreetly]; and with this they think to cure every great evil, and to persuade with valid reasons those persons who are not very cautious that all sins, however grave, are readily pardoned by God, provided they remain hidden and a bad example is not set. Thus, under the veil of sanctity and in secret they frequently devote all their thoughts to corrupting the pure mind of some woman; sowing hatred between brothers; governing states; raising up one and putting down another; getting men beheaded, imprisoned, and proscribed; serving as instruments of crime and, as it were, repositories

> of the thefts that many princes commit. Others take shameless pleasure in appearing dainty and fresh, with well-shaven crown and fine dress, and, as they go along, lift their habit to show their neat hose – and bow to show their physique. Others use certain glances and gestures even while saying mass, and in so doing think they are graceful and that they cause others to pay attention to them. Evil and wicked men, utter strangers not only to religion but to all good conduct; and when they are reprehended for their dissolute life, they make a jest of it, laugh at all who speak to them about it, and almost pride themselves on their vices.[64]

Giuliano's polemic against degenerate clergy, so completely out of context for the evening's discussion, appears to upset one of his listeners, Signora Emilia Pia (Fig. 18), the faithful, constant companion of her sister-in-law Duchess Elisabetta. She reprimands him for straying from the topic and for speaking ill of friars, accusing him of doing a great wrong by whispering against them. Giuliano responds by pointing out that he was not whispering but "speaking quite openly and plainly," and by saying that he was only speaking ill of the bad and guilty friars, "about whom, moreover, I am not telling the thousandth part of what I know."[65]

Olga Pugliese traces the evolution of Castiglione's thought through a close study of the various drafts and redactions of the work from its earliest beginnings until the definitive text published in 1528, one year before Castiglione's death. What becomes apparent is the great care Castiglione took when selecting who would appear in the dialogue, all contemporaries of his with whom he had personal relations. Pugliese convincingly shows how the characters' identities were of utmost concern to Castiglione and that he often made changes, reassigning roles so that "the characters would have to illustrate in their words and actions, in mirror-like fashion, the type of art of courtly behaviour being advocated in the discussions."[66] So concerned was Castiglione with verisimilitude, he sent copies of the manuscript to those mentioned in the text in order to solicit their advice, writing, for example, to Pietro Bembo, another principal protagonist, (Fig. 15), that he was ready to make any changes "if what he has been made to utter in the text does not please him."[67]

In the final text, Giuliano replaced Camillo Paleotti (1482–1517) as the defender of the cause of women and critic of the Church.[68] Piero Floriani has suggested that the late substitution of Giuliano for Paleotti was because the latter had not achieved the greatness in life that had been expected of him by his friends. Paleotti was a rather obscure Bolognese professor who became an aide to Bernardo Dovizi da Bibbiena (Fig. 10), named cardinal in September 1513 and so exalted at the papal court that he was often referred to as the *alter papa*. By 1518, however, Paleotti was dead and Cardinal Bibbiena had fallen out of favour with Leo X. Floriani contends that Castiglione preferred Giuliano as an interlocutor because he was a more important personage.[69]

Pugliese suggests, however, that Castiglione's principal aim was for verisimilitude, and Giuliano's widespread reputation as a "lady's man" would therefore have made him much more credible in the role as defender of women.[70] While it is true that Giuliano was highly praised for his courtesy and civility, especially toward women, and that he had cultivated very close personal ties with the wives of the rulers at the courts of Italy, such as Duchess Elisabetta Gonzaga of Urbino, her sister-in-law Isabella d'Este in Mantua (Fig. 34), and Ginevra, the wife of Giovanni Bentivoglio II of Bologna, the fact that Giuliano was assigned a speech that attacks degenerate clergy suggests that the choice may carry greater significance than either Floriani or Pugliese has recognized.

Giuliano's outpouring of anger against the friars was clearly directed not only at clerics but also at the Church itself, for when he speaks about those who "govern states," "raising up one and putting down another, getting men beheaded, imprisoned and proscribed," he is hardly speaking only of friars. Vittorio Cian believes that Castiglione used Giuliano as his spokesperson, and that in this instance the author was expressing Castiglione's own feelings of anger towards the Medici papacy.[71] This ire comes because, as Cian explains, in 1516 Leo X deposed Castiglione's employer, Francesco della Rovere, from his duchy in Urbino (Fig. 17) in favour of his own nephew Lorenzo (Fig. 12). The move follows the pope's diplomatic failure to create a hereditary principality for Giuliano in north-central Italy. Leo wished to acquire a dynastic state for Lorenzo that would guarantee a line of descent independent of Florence, which might not always remain secure and stable for the Medici.[72] Cian argues that this blatant act of nepotism explains why, in the *Courtier*, the tenaciously loyal Castiglione gave Giuliano a central and most sympathetic role in the cast of characters, while his brother Giovanni was nowhere explicitly mentioned.[73] Moreover, Cian believes that Castiglione wrote the *Courtier* as a form of gratitude to his former employer, Duke Guidobaldo, but, at the same time, as an indirect protest and spiritual retaliation against the cruelty and evil of those men who brought dispossession to his successor, Francesco Maria, as well as war and persecution to the state.[74]

Giuliano was vehemently opposed to his brother's designs on Urbino via his nephew Lorenzo, and in May 1515 he gave reassurances to Francesco Maria, whom he regarded as a brother, that he would never consent to such a crime, however much it was desired by the pope.[75] In his protestations to his brother, Giuliano reminded Leo of how their family, Giuliano especially, had found refuge and generous hospitality at the Urbino court. Giuliano warned that, if the pope proceeded with this violent usurpation, it would forever be a black stain of ingratitude on the Medici house. Giuliano had been Francesco Maria's most powerful ally, but by the summer of 1515 he was unable to continue his support because he had fallen seriously ill in Florence with the tuberculosis from which he would not recover. Giuliano's failing health did not prevent him from pleading Francesco Maria's cause, even from his deathbed.[76] On 1 March 1516 Leo issued an ultimatum to the duke, advising him that if he did not present himself in Rome within eighteen days, he would be declared a rebel and his duchy would be in default and thereby confiscated.[77] Giuliano died in Florence seventeen days later. Francesco Maria della Rovere ignored the pope's summons and lost his estate to Lorenzo de' Medici, who was formally invested with the title of Duke of Urbino in August 1516[78] (Figs. 12 and 19).

Even if Cian is correct in his assessment that Giuliano's stinging attack on the Church reflected Castiglione's own feelings, Giuliano still may have shared these views. Given what we now know about Castiglione's concern for verisimilitude, it seems inconceivable that Castiglione would give Giuliano this harsh speech if he had not been known to hold these opinions. It appears, however, that Castiglione waited until after the death of Leo X in 1521 to change the designation of the speaker from Paleotti to Giuliano in the final redaction of his text.

LIBELLUS AD LEONEM X PONTIFICEM MAXIMUM

Giuliano, as we have seen, forged a close friendship with the Camaldolese monks Querini and Giustiniani, and it could be argued that their friendship endured in part because of shared concerns for Church reforms. We know that Giuliano attended the Fifth Lateran Council, held in Rome on 17 June 1513; the council had originally been convoked by Julius II to challenge the schismatic 1511 Council of Pisa but was reconvened by Leo X to address mounting calls for reform.[79] Giuliano, in all likelihood, supported the reform proposals that Giustiniani and Querini set out in their 1513 *Libellus ad Leonem X Pontificem Maximum*, which has been described as the most impressive and boldest Catholic reform document of the era.[80] The *Libellus* called for sweeping changes and addressed such encompassing issues as papal power, ecclesiastical reform, the extension of Latin Christendom, and the crusade against the Turks. By addressing the tract directly to Leo X, the hermits hoped that it would provide a guide for the Fifth Lateran Council. Section three of the document concerns the conversion or defeat of the Muslims, who were seen as a serious threat to Christendom because of their encroachment on Europe's eastern flank. The Venetian hermits consequently called for a crusade against the Turks that would either see them converted to Christianity or utterly defeated. They envisaged an important role of military leadership for Giuliano, writing: "The faithful would have the Supreme Pontiff Leo residing in the Holy See, and the infidels would feel another Leo, Giuliano the brother of the Supreme Pontiff, leading an army into battle against them."[81]

Querini and Giustiniani certainly would not have nominated Giuliano for this critical undertaking if he had been known to be weak or inept, or to be living a dissipated life. Instead, the two Camaldolese hermits designated Giuliano as leader of their proposed crusade, convinced that he possessed the requisite leadership qualities to ensure military success. Indeed, it is not unreasonable to think that they had discussed their ideas with him prior to writing the *Libellus*. The fact that they could imagine Giuliano in such an exalted role certainly stands in sharp contrast to his many detractors, such as the prejudiced Florentine chronicler, Bartolomeo Cerretani, who insisted that Giuliano did not have the necessary qualities to govern Florence.

In early May 1513 the two hermits wrote directly to Giuliano, once again expressing their hope that he would lead a crusade. However, it appears that Leo failed to initiate a crusade against the Turks, because, as Stephen Bowd suggests, his court was less concerned with military action than with arts and letters.[82] Another reason for Leo's failure to heed the monks' call for crusade could be that his attention in the summer of 1513 was less focused on the wider interests of Christendom and more on expanding

Medici dynastic interests. The pope had other plans for his brother, namely the establishment of a hereditary Medici state in north-central Italy, and sending him off on a military expedition would interfere with that goal.

There can be little doubt that the Camaldolese hermits, Giuliano's good friends, helped to shape his spiritual direction. When he returned to Florence in 1512, he was well disposed to support the faction of his brother-in-law Jacopo Salviati given the fact that Savonarola, the greatest religious reformer of his day, had previously established a popular government in a spirit of religious renewal. Moreover, Giuliano would have known about the strong ties of friendship between the hermits and the Savonarolans at San Marco in Florence, located a short distance from the Camaldolese Santa Maria degli Angeli.[83] Giuliano's close attachment to both Bernardo and Pietro Bembo, as well as to Querini and Giustiniani, likely played a significant part in forming his political and religious outlook. However, we will see in the following two chapters how Giuliano's relationship with two other prominent contemporaries, Cesare Borgia and Niccolò Machiavelli, also contributed considerably to the moulding of his political thinking.

CHAPTER THREE

GIULIANO AND CESARE BORGIA

Cesare Borgia (1475–1507) is judged most severely in the historical records and he is, without doubt, among the most reviled figures in early modern history. A dashing portrait of a gentleman by Altobello Melone may represent the brooding Duke of Valentino (Fig. 20). His nineteenth-century descendants certainly thought so, and the picture has played a significant role in modern characterizations of the papal bastard.[1] An exploration of Cesare's career free of such bias reveals him to have been an important role model for Giuliano. Despite Borgia's later poor reputation, his deeds in fact correspond to Machiavelli's prescription for good leadership as outlined in *The Prince*.[2] Duke Valentino, as Cesare became known during his lifetime, was nevertheless detested in Italy by a great many of his contemporaries, especially those lords whose lands in the Romagna and the Marches he successfully recovered for the Church. Cesare was the illegitimate son of the Spanish Pope Alexander VI (r. 1492–1503) and was consequently loathed by his father's many political and religious enemies,[3] who despised Alexander because "foreign birth, to their eyes, made his emotions all the more uncontrollable, his nepotism all the more pernicious, and his political manoeuvrings all the more suspect."[4]

Following the pope's death, condemnation of all things Borgia began in earnest when Julius II (Fig. 9), his successor and harshest critic, did all that he could to ruin the reputations of both his predecessor and his bastard son.[5] Cesare's infamy has not diminished, and popular literature still characterizes him as an "inhuman monster" and a man "terrifying in his evil."[6] But in his day, Valentino did have his admirers. One was Niccolò Machiavelli, an astute observer of people. Another was Giuliano de' Medici. From their very first meeting in 1502, Machiavelli was greatly impressed with Cesare, writing in his dispatches to the Florentine government: "This lord is truly splendid and magnificent."[7] Machiavelli's positive view remained unchanged over the years, so that, when he came to write *The Prince* in 1513, he described Borgia's actions as "prudent and virtuous" and those of a man who possessed "great courage and high goals."[8] Indeed, Cesare was his ideal prince: "I would not know of any better precepts to give to a new prince than the example of his deeds."[9] Cesare, the just ruler concerned with the good governance of his newly acquired territories, also served as an important model for Giuliano's own political formation.

Giuliano knew Cesare Borgia personally and shared Machiavelli's high regard for the man to whom he looked as an exemplar. Like Borgia, Giuliano would marry into the French royal family and be named a French duke. He also was captain-general of the papal army, and, being the close relation of a reigning pope, he had the full backing of the papacy in his quest to carve out a Medici hereditary state on Church lands. In his biographical sketch of Giuliano, Fatini glosses over the years in which Giuliano had contact with Borgia; his interpretation of Giuliano's character makes it impossible for him to conceive the existence of a significant relationship between the two. However, Giuliano did have close personal interactions with Cesare over a two-year period, as seen through various notices in Sanudo's Venetian diaries, which collected diplomatic correspondence from 1496 through 1533.[10] Taken together, they show how Giuliano trusted Borgia, who in turn did all that he could to restore Giuliano to Florence. Moreover, Giuliano's admiration for Cesare was no doubt considerably enhanced after the duke, against all expectations and despite the wishes of the pope, made great gestures of magnanimity towards Giuliano's close friends, the Bentivoglio of Bologna.

Following his expulsion, Piero de' Medici made three attempts between 1496 and 1498 to reclaim Florence by force, each ending in dismal failure.

During the third campaign, Giuliano was given command of his own contingent of three hundred cavalrymen. On this occasion Piero seemed destined for success, since he had the full support of the Venetian republic and of Giovanni II Bentivoglio of Bologna. Riding with Annibale Bentivoglio into the Val di Lamone at the foot of the Apennines in September 1498, Giuliano arrived before the town of Marradi and ordered the people to surrender the fortress. When the inhabitants saw the nineteen-year-old captain, they immediately opened the gates, shouting "Marco, marco, palle, palle" (the former referred to the Venetians and the latter to the Florentines who constituted Giuliano's fighting force).[11] The short-lived military victory was soon followed by a humiliating defeat. Giuliano pressed forward with his troops, reaching the hill town of Bibbiena in the Tuscan territory of the Casentino in the middle of November 1498, when heavy snow in the rugged mountain terrain prevented further advances. The Florentines responded by sending the renowned *condottiere* Paolo Vitelli (1461–1499) to lay siege to Bibbiena.

Trapped in Bibbiena, life became increasingly difficult for Giuliano, who was reported to be ill with quartan fever and distressed by the infighting among the various military captains. When it became obvious that Venice had lost confidence in the campaign, preferring to initiate negotiations with Vitelli rather than send the desperately needed money and supplies to Bibbiena, Giuliano's soldiers began to desert. On 27 March 1499 four hundred infantry managed to leave, with Vitelli unable or uninterested in capturing them. With great courage, Giuliano repeatedly refused the promise of safe conduct offered by Vitelli, even though he faced continued hardship and the prospect of famine. Where once a ransom had been offered only for his older brother Piero, the Florentines now put a price of 5,000 ducats on Giuliano's head for his live capture, 4,000 if returned dead. In an attempt to bring this senseless war to an end, Venice and Florence agreed to the arbitration of Ercole d'Este (1431–1505), Duke of Ferrara. Florence initially consented to safe conduct for the Venetians but rejected the same for Giuliano, who in their eyes was an outlaw and a rebel. However, after further negotiations he too was allowed to leave and return to Venice.[12]

Piero and Cardinal Giovanni were undeterred by this defeat. Within six months of Giuliano's ordeal in Bibbiena, they sent him to the French court to press their case before Louis XII. The Medici had received word that the king was planning a new Italian expedition that had the support of Pope Alexander VI and the Venetians. Experience had shown the Medici that a French descent into Italy would bring in its wake an inevitable political shake-up, as had happened in 1494 with Charles VIII. The elder Medici brothers were convinced that, if the new king were approached with the promise of a large sum of money and their pledge of allegiance, he could be persuaded to restore them to Florence. Hence, Giuliano was dispatched to the French court.[13] While it appears nothing concrete was achieved by his visit, other than establishing good relations with the king, it did give Giuliano an opportunity to meet Cesare Borgia, who had been in France for almost a year to negotiate a new French-papal alliance on his father's behalf. As part of this diplomacy, King Louis named Cesare Duke of Valentinois and Diois (hence the sobriquet Il Valentino) and gave him an estate near Avignon plus a very generous yearly pension and a company of one hundred French lances.[14]

Giuliano arrived in Lyons for his own audience with Louis XII a few months thereafter, sometime in late August or early September 1499, where he surely met Cesare as the court was making final preparations for the king's descent into Italy. Giuliano could not fail to notice that Borgia was highly regarded by the king. Among the many marks of favour Louis XII had bestowed upon Cesare, perhaps the greatest honour was the collar of the Order of St Michael, usually reserved for hereditary princes.[15] Borgia had also been appointed lieutenant of the king of France for the invasion of Italy. Ludovico Sforza fled to the court of the Holy Roman Empire in advance of the arrival of the French army in Lombardy. On 17 September the citadel of Milan surrendered, preparing the way for the triumphant entry of King Louis XII into the city on 6 October 1499. Castiglione described the procession and noted how gallant the pope's son appeared, riding in a splendid cavalcade accompanied by Gonzaga and Ercole d'Este, Duke of Ferrara.[16] In early November, Louis XII returned to France and Cesare, with all his obligations to the king met, immediately set out to retake lands of the Romagna from unruly vicars on behalf of the Holy See.[17] Borgia first took Imola and Forlì, ruled by the tyrannical Riarii,[18] who were so detested that when Valentino's army arrived each town's citizens opened their gates without a shot being fired, welcoming Valentino as the pope's lieutenant and as their liberator.[19] The speed of these conquests certainly made a profound impression on Giuliano and others.

Valentino was ready to advance on his former brother-in-law Giovanni Sforza (1466–1510), lord of Pesaro, but his French forces were recalled to defend the Duchy of Milan from Ludovico il Moro, who had suddenly reappeared in Lombardy with Swiss mercenaries; il Moro's force successfully recovered Sforza's dominion on 5 February.[20] Forced to halt his campaign to recover the Romagna for his father, Borgia decided to return to Rome, where the city was host to many thousands of pilgrims in the midst of celebrating the Jubilee of 1500. The pope's son arrived on 26 February to a tumultuous and joyful welcome. All along the route from the Piazza del Popolo to the Vatican, jubilant crowds cheered, hailing Cesare as a conquering hero. Dressed in his usual coat of black velvet that reached to his knees, and wearing the gold collar of the Order of St Michael, Cesare was escorted by all the cardinals and followed by a long line of ambassadors, dignitaries, and officials. The cavalcade slowly made its way through the city, over the Ponte Sant'Angelo, past the elaborately decorated Castel Sant'Angelo. It then passed through the Borgo along the new Via Alessandrina, the first straight street since Roman times, named in honour of Cesare's father, who had built it in order to commemorate the Jubilee. The street led directly to the Piazza of St Peter's, where, from his private loggia above the entrance to the Vatican, the pope watched his son's great victory procession. In an elaborate ceremony held on 29 March, Alexander conferred the offices of *gonfaloniere* and captain-general of the Church upon his son and granted Valentino the title to the vicariate of Imola and Forlì.[21]

Giuliano arrived in Rome from Bologna soon thereafter with twelve of his friends.[22] Since his brother Cardinal Giovanni and cousin Giulio were not in Rome and not expected to return until May,[23] it could be, in light of Cesare Borgia's victories in the Romagna, that Giuliano had taken the initiative to travel to Rome to renew his acquaintance with the duke and approach him directly to discuss his family's case. He might also have been attracted to the circle of poets and scholars seeking Valentino's patronage in Rome. Cesare's military reputation has perhaps overshadowed his interests in learning and the arts. He was widely known to have had an extraordinary intellectual brilliance, first seen when he obtained a degree in canon and civil law at Pisa in 1492.[24] Though Stephen Kolsky has suggested that Borgia "*needed* a court which would help him appear less a 'cut-throat bandit' and more like a 'Renaissance prince'; it might even lend a sense of legitimacy to a most illegitimate regime,"[25] Borgia could very well have created his household out of a genuine interest in promoting literature and the arts.

In the summer of 1500, many artists, scholars, and poets sought Cesare's favour, and he received them graciously. Leading the literary circle of Valentino's Roman household was his secretary, the humanist scholar Agapito Geraldini (d. 1515), an experienced diplomat, administrator, and a disciple of Giulio Pomponio Leto (1428–1498), the founder of an informal Roman academy of antiquarians dedicated to classical studies and the mastery of good Latin. Poets from all over central Italy had followed Cesare to Rome, including Battista Orfino of Foligno, Francesco Sperulo from Camerino (1463–1531), and Pier Francesco Giustolo of Spoleto (d. 1511).[26] They would gather for meetings, together with other Roman literati, in the house of Tuscan humanist Paolo Cortese (1465–1510).[27] When Giuliano's close friend Vincenzo Querini travelled from Venice to Rome in the summer of 1502 to present his *Conclusiones* to Alexander, he praised the pope's son in the book's dedication for his great skill in military matters. Querini also expressed the opinion that there had hardly been a greater friend to literary studies than Cesare.[28]

It is not too difficult to imagine that Borgia would have extended this same cordiality to Giuliano, son of the illustrious Lorenzo the Magnificent. Giuliano was already well acquainted with the star of Cesare's Roman household, the charismatic *strambottista* Serafino Aquilano (1466–1500), who was the most celebrated Petrarchan poet in Italy at the time. Giuliano had befriended Serafino in 1496, when both men were in Milan at the court of Beatrice d'Este Sforza (1475–1497). Aquilano was famous for composing vernacular verses (*strambotti*) sung to the accompaniment of a *lira da braccio*. He suddenly died from an attack of quartan fever on 10 August 1500 at the age of thirty-four, shocking many, including Cesare, who ordered his secretary to arrange a great public funeral and burial in Santa Maria del Popolo, site of the Borgia family chapel.[29] Giuliano was unable to attend the funeral because he had already left Rome for Bologna that July to escape the deadly summer heat. However, when he received news of Serafino's death, he immediately composed his own sonnet of lament, *Pro morte Seraphini*, which begins: "Why did Serafino have to die, did he offend so many?"[30] Giuliano's poem was subsequently published in an anthology of tributes to the dead poet in Bologna in 1504.[31]

On 2 October 1500 Valentino marched his army out of Rome north along the Via Flaminia to undertake his second campaign to conquer the Romagna, this time with a formidable force of ten thousand professional mercenaries of diverse nationalities.[32] Valentino also took with him a full household, including many Roman nobles who had accompanied him before to France, as well as advisers, secretaries, physicians, and three bishops designated to be the future administrators of the conquered Papal States. Just as the leading *condottieri* wanted to share in Cesare's good fortune, so did the poets and scholars who followed him to Romagna. These included his loyal secretary Geraldini; the poets Giustolo, Sperulo, and Vincenzo Calmeta (d. 1508); the Florentine sculptor-turned-soldier Pietro Torrigiani (1472–1528); and many other members of Valentino's Roman household.[33]

By early November 1500, the duke had repeated his earlier successes by quickly repossessing the Adriatic cities of Pesaro and Rimini from Giovanni Sforza and Pandolfo Malatesta respectively.[34] Next, Valentino marched northwards along the Via Emilia, toward the heavily fortified town of Faenza, which would prove more difficult to conquer. The lord of Faenza was the fifteen-year-old Astorre III Manfredi, whose subjects were fiercely loyal to him. He was the grandson of Giovanni Bentivoglio II of Bologna, who had sent armaments and money, fearing that after Faenza Valentino would strike against Bologna.[35] Valentino's army arrived on 19 November and began to bombard Faenza's fortifications with heavy artillery, but the citizens refused to surrender and mounted a vigorous and courageous resistance, managing to repulse their enemy and inflict the first serious casualties for Valentino. The taking of Faenza proved to be so arduous that Valentino decided to lift the siege and, while leaving town under blockade, billet his soldiers in winter quarters spread along the Via Emilia from Forlì to Rimini. He chose to spend the winter months in Cesena, intending to return to Faenza in the spring.[36]

After Valentino's departure from Rome, the Medici had been very active, now more than ever convinced that the Borgia duke presented the best prospects for their restoration to Florence. In Bologna, where Giuliano surely received news of Cesare's latest conquests, his thoughts had often turned to Florence, and in July Giuliano wrote to a trusted family friend in Venice, Piero Dovizi (c. 1456–1514), the brother of Cardinal Giovanni's secretary, Bernardo da Bibbiena (Fig. 10). Giuliano told Dovizi that "now was the time to take action against Florence."[37] Upon returning to Rome in May, Cardinal Giovanni had set about to improve his standing with the pope, knowing that Alexander's support was essential if any move was to be made against the government in Florence. William Roscoe contends that Alexander was hostile toward the Medici cardinal because he thought that Giovanni's behaviour lacked moderation and respectability.

However, during the summer of 1500, Alexander's attitude toward Cardinal Giovanni had noticeably changed, as seen in correspondence wherein the pope wrote with the respect and attention due to Giovanni's rank.[38] By October, Giovanni was able to announce in a letter to Piero Dovizi that the "Medici are now in the good graces of the pope."[39] Giuliano was recalled from Bologna to Rome during the same month,[40] but he did not remain there, for he was immediately dispatched back to Romagna on a secret mission,[41] in all likelihood with a concrete proposal for the Borgia duke. Cardinal Giovanni's choice of Giuliano to approach Valentino, rather than their older brother Piero, supports the likelihood that Giuliano had already established a good rapport with Cesare, who seemed to have been responsive to whatever the Medici offered. In November, while the siege of Faenza was still underway, Valentino called Piero de' Medici, who was in Pisa at the time, to join him in his camp, probably to discuss Florence.[42] Biagio Buonaccorsi (1472–1522), a minor civil servant in the Florentine government, and among those Florentines nervously tracking Giuliano's movements, noted in his diary that Giuliano had left Rome and had gone to Bologna "on account of this expedition."[43]

This contact between Cesare Borgia and the Medici was enough to frighten the Florentines into believing that the Medici would soon be returning to Florence. In January 1501 rumours began to circulate in the city that a Medici return would happen with Borgia's help; it was also reported that the Strozzi and Nerli, supporters of the Medici, were already stockpiling weapons in their houses in Florence.[44] The Florentines had cause to worry because their long war with Pisa had left them without a fighting force or any money to pay soldiers. Furthermore, they suspected that Valentino's military commanders, Vitellozzo Vitelli and the Orsini brothers, were urging the duke to overthrow their republican regime. Vitelli wished to avenge the beheading of his brother Paolo by the Florentine government in October 1499 on the grounds of treason, and the Orsini, because they were related by marriage to the Medici, could see their own power and prestige increase if the Medici were returned as the city's most influential family. A move against Florence, however, could not be contemplated before Astorre Manfredi was dispossessed and Faenza returned to the Papal States.

Valentino tried diplomacy once more in order to convince the people of Faenza to surrender voluntarily, but his offer was rejected outright, the

Faventines resolving to defend the dominion of the Manfredi to the end.[45] The French ambassador, Louis de Villeneuve, Baron de Trans, arrived in Bologna on 7 January 1501, carrying specific instructions from Louis XII for Giovanni Bentivoglio. As Giovanni himself informed Piero Dovizi in his letter, the king warned him not to lend assistance to his grandson Astorre but to leave Valentino free to take possession of Faenza.[46] By this time, the duke's patience with the Faventines must have been wearing thin, but another letter from Giovanni Bentivoglio to Dovizi suggests that Cesare had not entirely given up on diplomacy because he had agreed to allow the French ambassador, together with Giuliano, to go to Faenza and try to negotiate a surrender.[47] It was in Borgia's best interest to resolve this situation peacefully, and the fact that he was willing to send the young Medici to Faenza further suggests that Giuliano had gained the respect and trust of the duke.

Giuliano, who had close relations with the ruling family in Bologna, may also have agreed to this mission on behalf of Borgia because of the particular concerns of Giovanni Bentivoglio and his wife, Ginevra, who were no doubt anxious about the welfare of their grandson. When Giuliano stayed in Bologna, which he did very often, he was a guest of their daughter Bianca and her husband, Conte Niccolò Rangoni of Spilamberto, captain-general of the Bolognese forces, a man universally respected and liked, who lived close to the Bentivoglio palace.[48] We know that Ginevra had the highest esteem for Giuliano's father because, in conversations with the Ferrarese ambassador to Bologna, Pandolfo Collenucci, she made it known that she would like to see Lorenzo's conduct and policy followed in Bologna.[49] Perhaps Ginevra saw in the young Giuliano something of his father's acclaimed skills of mediation. Neither the French ambassador nor Giuliano, however, was successful in convincing Astorre Manfredi to surrender. The Faventines remained adamant in their refusal to make an accord with Valentino. As Bentivoglio wrote in his letter to Dovizi, "Trans and Giuliano returned to Bologna with heavy hearts."[50]

In late February 1501 reports stated that a courier had turned up in Faenza, bringing money to the besieged town but refusing to say who sent it. It was widely thought that a worried Florentine government had made this gesture of support because they had heard that Giuliano was still in Valentino's camp.[51] Sanudo noted in early March that Giuliano was in France again, and that Cardinal Giovanni had said he was sent there in accordance with Cesare Borgia's wishes.[52] Sanudo is likely more accurate than Biagio Buonaccorsi, who recorded in his diary that Giuliano was dispatched on the orders of the pope and ambassador Trans.[53] It is quite doubtful that the pope was involved here, because, as we shall see later on, Alexander VI had his own reasons for not wanting Florence attacked and the Medici restored to power.

Giuliano's visit to France suggests that Cesare himself had agreed to reinstate the Medici and was prepared to go against the wishes of his father. Guicciardini recorded that Giuliano was well received at the French court, that he was even "coddled and given long audiences," while the two Florentine ambassadors, sent to France with offers of money to buy the king's protection against the Borgia duke, "wasted eight months there in vain, without ever receiving a kind word … always repulsed very barbarously by the king, by Rouen, and by the whole court."[54] Returning to Italy after such a warm reception in France, Giuliano would perhaps have been justified in believing that he had received the blessing of the king and that the way was now clear for Cesare to restore the Medici to Florence. But if he did entertain such hopes, they were sadly misplaced. Louis XII may have shown that he was ill disposed toward the Florentines because they had failed, after so many years, to win the war against their former subject Pisa,[55] and had not made payments to him at the requisite times stipulated in the articles of their treaty. However, as Guicciardini makes clear, though the king "knew that in case of need he could make use of the Medici far more readily than he could of [the Florentine] government … he was too ashamed to restore them by his own arms, because our behaviour and our loyalty deprived him of any just reason."[56]

On 16 April 1501 Cesare resumed the bombardment of Faenza with the full force of his artillery. After days of heavy shelling and fierce fighting, and with deplorable losses suffered on both sides, the exhausted Faventines, with their ammunition depleted and no possibility of further resistance, finally agreed to surrender. The terms of capitulation, signed by Cesare on 25 April, appear honourable and generous, and included safe conduct for Astorre, members of his family, and his close supporters, as well as the promise of life, liberty, and property for all subjects. Paying the fullest respect to the civic dignity of the Faventines, Borgia did not make a ceremonial entry into the city as its conqueror, nor did he allow his troops to quarter within its walls.[57]

With the victory of Faenza behind him, Cesare turned his attention to Bologna. He was angered by the fact that Giovanni Bentivoglio had repeatedly refused to hand over the fortress of Castel Bolognese, situated strategically between Imola and Faenza on the Via Emilia, for the use of the duke's troops during the winter, even though Bentivoglio had been ordered to do so by both Louis XII and Alexander VI.[58] Cesare knew that he had his father's full support for an assault against Bologna. The pope was determined to incorporate Bologna, the largest city in Emilia, into the Papal States and overturn the special rights of civic autonomy that had been granted by Pope Nicholas V in 1447.[59] Even though Bentivoglio thought he had protection from France, bought at the immense cost of 40,000 ducats, he knew that Cesare posed an immediate threat and on 28 April sent ambassadors to Borgia with an offer of peace. On 30 April an accord was reached whereby Bentivoglio agreed to consign the Castel Bolognese to the duke's jurisdiction and give him military assistance for a period of three years. On Borgia's part, he promised to restore the fortresses of San Pietro, Guelfo, and Medecina currently occupied by his troops, free all prisoners, and reconfirm with the pope the ancient privileges of the Bolognese commune and the Bentivoglio.[60] Giuliano attempted to bring a lasting peace to the two sides by negotiating the terms of a marriage contract through his agent, the Bolognese merchant Girolamo da Casio, whereby Giacoma, the daughter of Borgia's captain Giulio Orsini, would be betrothed, without a dowry, to Ermes Bentivoglio, one of Giovanni's four sons.[61] This was the second time Giuliano had assumed the role of a peacemaker, and here his efforts seemed to have paid off. The marriage took place in autumn of 1504.[62]

VALENTINO AND THE FLORENTINE REPUBLIC

As soon as Cesare had ratified the peace accord with Giovanni Bentivoglio, Alexander VI ordered his son's immediate return to Rome, warning him to take the eastern road and the Umbrian plain in order to skirt Tuscan territory. Even though the pope knew Florence was under the protection of Louis XII, he was nonetheless worried that Vitellozzo and the two Orsini captains would exert pressure on Cesare and compel him to attack Florence. He understood that this would play into the hands of the Orsini because a return of the Medici to Florence would only serve to aggrandize the Roman Orsini barons, who, while allied with the Borgia today, could very well become their enemies tomorrow.[63] Cesare chose to ignore his father's commands, and at the end of the first week of May he turned his army south and marched into Tuscan territory. William Woodward has assessed Valentino's refusal to obey his father's orders as "wholly in keeping with the adventurous spirit of Cesare Borgia,"[64] who wished to appease his captains, Vitellozzo Vitelli and the Orsini. However, it is unlikely that he would have acted against the pope just to satisfy the demands of his *condottieri*. A more convincing explanation is that he wished to carry out his promise to reinstate the Medici. Galeazzo Bentivoglio, Giovanni's son, joined Cesare with three hundred cavalrymen and two thousand infantrymen. Giuliano de' Medici also arrived from Bologna with the intention of remaining in the duke's camp, but when the army reached Lojano, a village in Bolognese territory at the foothills of the Apennines, he was ordered by Borgia to remain in the rear.[65] A few days later, Giuliano's brother Piero, wanting to join this alliance against Florence, arrived on the Sienese border but was refused an audience with Cesare. According to Edoardo Alvisi, the reason for holding back the Medici brothers was that Borgia did not want to give the appearance of contradicting what he had earlier assured the Florentine ambassador Galeotto Pazzi in Bologna, namely, that the Florentines had nothing to fear and that all he wanted was free passage through Tuscany.[66] However, the duke's subsequent actions show otherwise.

On 12 March Cesare arrived with his forces at Barberino in the Mugello, where he met with three ambassadors sent from Florence: Piero Soderini, Alamanno Salviati, and Jacopo Nerli. Fatini claims that Cesare never had any intention of keeping the promise he had made to Giuliano to bring him back to Florence, for the simple reason that Valentino sought only to serve his own interests.[67] He bases his conclusion on the belief that, during Cesare's consultations with the Florentine ambassadors, nothing was discussed about the Medici.[68] While it is true that, in their official dispatches to Florence, the ambassadors did not mention the Medici per se, contemporary Florentine sources record that Cesare was insisting that the Medici be readmitted to the city.[69] According to contemporary chronicler Jacopo Nardi, the duke made four demands. First, he was to be appointed captain of the Florentine forces in order to maintain peace between his state in Romagna and Florence. Second, the Florentines were not to render any assistance when he expelled the lord of Piombino, Jacopo IV of Appiano (whose family had held this small state situated on the coast, south of Pisa, since 1348). Third, the city would hand over six citizens to be nominated by Vitellozzo (to include Paolo Vitelli's imprisoned chancellor Cerbone). The final demand, in the words of Nardi, was that "Piero de' Medici would be readmitted to Florence, where he would form a state that would be so secure it would solve everything, and know that the promise made was firmly complied with."[70]

Was this a reference to the promise that Borgia had made to the Medici that he would return them to Florence? If it was, he was unable to do anything other than to intimidate, threaten, and bluff the Florentines into accepting a change of government because he was severely constrained by both the pope and Louis XII. Already on 1 May, the Borgia duke had received a papal bull ordering him to avoid Tuscany altogether and now a second bull arrived commanding him not to touch Florence. Cesare was well aware that any move he made against Florence would bring swift and decisive retaliation from Louis XII.[71] Nonetheless, he moved his army on 14 May to Campi, a few kilometres from Florence. This highly provocative move was certainly intended to terrorize the population and force the government into submission. Landucci reported that Valentino's troops were doing great damage in the countryside, burning, robbing, and cutting corn and that the duke had issued Florence an ultimatum that, if his demands were not met, he would sack the city.[72] In Romagna, Cesare imposed strict discipline on his army, but in Tuscany he appeared to sanction pillaging and plundering by his soldiers, surely as another tactic to exert maximum pressure on the Florentine government. The Signoria, anxious for Cesare's army to leave their territory, responded hastily and accepted all his demands except to reinstate Piero de' Medici, which they adamantly refused to consider. On 15 May, Cesare signed the terms of an agreement that did not include Medici restoration,[73] the same day on which Pope Alexander issued a bull conferring upon his son the title of Duke of Romagna. Cesare could now consolidate all the lands of the Papal States into one entity in order to form a hereditary Borgia state that would survive long after the pope's demise, a pleasing thought for both Alexander VI and his son.[74]

Despite the Borgia duke's best efforts, he was unable to force the Florentines into accepting the return of the Medici. Once again, the Medici had failed in their attempt to win back their city, and Giuliano could now only watch from the sidelines as Cesare resumed his military conquests elsewhere. In June 1501 Giuliano was in Milan,[75] and then in Genoa with his sister Maddalena (1473–1519),[76] who was married to Franceschetto Cybo, the illegitimate son of Pope Innocent VIII. Perhaps, after so much disappointment, he wanted to remove himself from all the political turmoil.[77]

In June 1502, at the instigation of Vitellozzo Vitelli and Piero de' Medici, the citizens of Arezzo and Valdichiana rose up and rebelled against the Florentine republic, proclaiming their allegiance to the Medici. Nardi reports that at this time Giuliano was back at the court of Louis XII, trying to convince the king that he would be much better served by a Medici government in Florence.[78] In the same month, Borgia surprised everyone when, instead of marching his army to the vicariate of Camerino in the Marches so he could depose the papal vicar Giulio Cesare Varano, he suddenly advanced upon Urbino, forcing Duke Guidobaldo to flee. Cesare occupied the city on 21 June unopposed. Borgia justified his action on tactical grounds because he knew that Guidobaldo had sympathy with the Varano family and thus might combine his forces with theirs and threaten his lines of communication to the coast.[79]

Cesare was now seeking an alliance with Florence, but he also wanted the Florentines to know of his dissatisfaction with them because they had not lived up to the terms of the accord signed a year earlier. The Florentine republic sent their ambassador, Francesco Soderini, to Urbino, accompanied by Machiavelli, but the first meeting between the parties on 24 June ended on an ominous note, when Borgia was reported to have said: "This government of yours does not please me, and I cannot trust it; you must change it and give me a pledge that you will observe everything you promised; otherwise you will soon realize that I have no intention of going on like this, and if you do not want me as a friend, you will find me your enemy."[80] Cesare, clearly annoyed by the republican government, may still have hoped that by insisting upon a change of government, he could achieve Giuliano's return. The duke's words were faithfully recorded in Machiavelli's dispatch dated 26 June to the Signoria but, astonishingly, the letter also included a glowing assessment of Borgia's qualities: "This prince is very splendid and magnificent, and in war he is so bold that there is no great enterprise that does not seem small to him, and to gain glory and territory he never rests or knows danger or weariness: he arrives at a place before anyone has heard that he has left the place he was in before:

he wins the love of his soldiers, and has got hold of the best men in Italy. These things make him victorious and formidable, and are attended with invariable good fortune."[81]

If Machiavelli, not known to exaggerate or be easily impressed, could write such effusive praise about the Florentine republic's greatest enemy, it is not surprising that Giuliano was also captivated by the duke's personal appeal. In August 1502 Borgia had paid a visit to Louis XII, who was visiting Milan, wishing to renew his personal friendship with the French king and counter the mounting opposition among some Italian princes and his own captains who were alarmed at his growing power and who feared for the safety of their own states. He was also seeking a military accord for his next conquests in Italy. Giuliano, according to Nardi, was with the king in June, and he could have accompanied the king to Milan, since there is no evidence of him being anywhere else at the time. Cesare might have invited him to join his camp in Imola, which could account for Sanudo's notice that places him there in November 1502.[82]

IMOLA

Since early September 1502, Valentino had established a makeshift court in Imola, a town of about five thousand inhabitants in the Romagna region. At this stage, however, the duke's position was threatened by his Italian captains Vitelli, the Baglioni of Perugia, the Orsini, Oliverotto of Fermo, and Pandolfo Petrucci of Siena, who had all witnessed Cesare's brazen usurpation of Urbino the previous June. Most likely, they had also heard about the duke's secret mutual understanding with Louis XII, when the two met in August in Milan, that, while the king would continue to protect Florence, he was now willing to sacrifice Bologna in order to please Alexander VI, because he was planning his march on Naples and indeed needed the pope's support. If the Bentivoglio were forced out of Bologna, Cesare's captains thought that their own fiefdoms would be next, particularly those such as Perugia and Città di Castello, belonging by rights to the Church, as did part of the Orsini estates. At the beginning of October 1502, the captains revolted and, gathered in the fortress of Magione near Perugia, conspired together for their leader's downfall by forming an opposition league. As if to show Borgia their resolve, they attacked the lightly defended city of Urbino and restored it to Duke Guidobaldo.[83]

Cesare demanded Florence send an ambassador to Imola to negotiate an alliance. According to Guicciardini, the Florentine Signoria, fully realizing that Borgia's position was now considerably weakened, responded by dispatching "their chancellor Niccolò Machiavelli to Imola as a token of our goodwill, to keep the duke's favour."[84] But, by sending the second chancellor, a civil servant without the power to commit the republic, the Signoria demonstrated that it was not interested in an alliance. Machiavelli's purpose was only to buy time, observe Borgia closely, and report on his intentions toward the republic, and especially on his handling of the conspirators at Magione. The Florentine secretary arrived in Imola on 7 October, bringing assurances to the duke that, although the Florentines had been invited to participate in the discussions at Magione, they had refused to do so, wanting to continue their friendship with France and the duke.[85] But, if his rebellious captains were threatening his security, Cesare at the time seemed unperturbed and instead focused his attention on raising troops that would be loyal only to him and no one else, and taking care of the civil administration of Romagna. To this end, in September he summoned Antonio Ciocchi del Monte, granting him the office of *presidente di Romagna*, which added to the post he already held as the chief justice of the Supreme Court of the duchy.[86] In Machiavelli's opinion, Del Monte was "a most learned man of the highest repute,"[87] a view shared by many, including Pope Julius II, who ordained him cardinal in 1511.[88] Borgia's choice of Del Monte as his first civil official in the new state was significant and confirms his intention to bring good government to Romagna. Guicciardini can be believed, therefore, when he writes that the people of the Romagna loved Borgia "dearly on account of the great justice and integrity with which his administrators governed."[89] As Machiavelli later wrote in *The Prince*: "After the Duke had taken the Romagna and had found it governed by powerless rulers – more anxious to plunder their subjects than to correct them, and who had given them reason for disunity rather than unity, so that the entire territory was full of thefts, quarrels, and every other kind of insolence – he decided that if he wanted to make the region peaceful and obedient to his regal power, it would be necessary to give it good government."[90]

Besides the fact that Cesare was still the only man in Italy who had the power to return him to Florence, there may have been other reasons for

Giuliano to be close to him. Guicciardini, an otherwise bitter critic of the Borgia, wrote that "Valentino came to be highly respected – especially since he had a good army, was a capable ruler, and was beloved by his soldiers, toward whom he was very liberal."[91] Another factor might have been Cesare's personal magnetism, which enabled him to attract some of the most capable men to his service, including, as we have seen, the distinguished jurist and administrator Ciocchi del Monte. Cesare was also able to attract the Florentine artist Leonardo da Vinci to serve him in the capacity of military architect and engineer. Giuliano had formed a close bond of friendship with Leonardo at the Sforza court during his stay in Milan between 1496 and 1497, and he was able to renew this friendship in Imola where Leonardo stayed for three months. Giuliano could have also greatly admired how Cesare, who had made so many enemies in Italy, was able to maintain the personal admiration of Louis XII. He could have witnessed this admiration first-hand during Cesare's visit to Louis XII in Milan in the summer of 1502. Niccolò da Correggio wrote to Isabella d'Este in Mantua on 8 August, giving her an account of their meeting: "His most Christian Majesty welcomed and embraced him with great joy and led him to the castle, where he had him lodge in the chamber nearest his own, and he himself ordered the supper[,] choosing diverse dishes, and that evening three or four times he went to his room dressed in shirt sleeves, when it was time to go to bed. And he ordered yesterday that he should dress in his own shirts, tunic and robes, for Duke Valentino brought no baggage wagons with him, only horses. In short, he could not have done more for a son or a brother."[92]

While in Imola in late 1502, Giuliano would have been preoccupied with the negotiations that would eventually decide the fate of the ruling family of Bologna. Anxious to have Pope Alexander's support for his forthcoming campaign against Naples, the French king agreed during his meeting with Cesare in Milan to withdraw his protection from Giovanni Bentivoglio and return Bologna to the jurisdiction of the Church, thus annulling the special privileges that had allowed the city to enjoy suzerain authority as well as all the rights of self-government.[93] The pope moved quickly, and on 2 September he summoned Giovanni Bentivoglio and two of his sons to appear in Rome within fifteen days on the pretext that Giovanni had misgoverned the vicariate and had given support to rebels who were enemies of the Church.[94] The driving force behind the plan to depose the Bentivoglio was clearly the pope, rather than Cesare, since the evidence shows the duke felt no ill will toward the Bentivoglio and had always planned to make Cesena his capital, not the more populous city of Bologna.[95] Louis XII sent his ambassador Savoyard Claude de Seyssel to Bologna, to confirm verbally his desire that Bologna should be ceded to Cesare.[96] Giovanni Bentivoglio disregarded the pope's summons and, as he had done previously, when Bologna was under threat, began peace negotiations directly with his son.

Given Giuliano's close attachment to the Bentivoglio, there can be no doubt that he would have involved himself in the negotiations that took place during October and November between Cesare and Giovanni. One of Giovanni's sons was regularly at Imola,[97] and Giuliano, having the confidence of both Cesare and Giovanni, would have escorted the younger Bentivoglio and vouched for his security. On 2 December 1502 the peace accord was finally ratified in Imola, after having been signed, albeit with great reluctance, by the pope in Rome. The peace was guaranteed by Louis XII, the Signoria of Florence, and Ercole d'Este, Duke of Ferrara, whose son Alfonso had married Cesare's sister Lucrezia a year before. It is noteworthy that Cesare issued a separate edict, announcing to all the people of Romagna that his differences with the Bentivoglio had been resolved amicably, and that his friendship with Giovanni had been fully restored in perpetuity.[98]

Modern scholars remain perplexed by Cesare's apparent refusal to mount an attack on Bologna "when it lay within his grasp." Cecilia Ady, for example, finds it "one of the puzzles of his career."[99] Borgia could have taken advantage of the discontent among the citizens of Bologna; some prominent Bolognese families had already approached him, urging that he act to deliver them from the Bentivoglio. The fact that he preferred friendship is surprising and, as Ady notes, "his refusal to take a risk for a great prize is not easy to reconcile with the reputation which Cesare Borgia enjoys as the ablest and most intrepid of Italian adventurers."[100] Giuliano would have been overjoyed by this renewal of friendship between Cesare and the Bentivoglio and also much relieved by this good outcome. The great magnanimity that Cesare so clearly displayed toward Giuliano's Bolognese friends could only have served to increase his admiration for the duke.

Cesare's dramatic ascendancy in Italy ended suddenly in August 1503 when Pope Alexander VI, at the age of seventy-two, died from malarial fever, particularly virulent in Rome that hot summer. Cesare was seriously stricken by the same illness, but his youth and strength enabled him to recover gradually, though he remained weak.[101] On 1 November, the day that Cardinal Giuliano della Rovere was elected pope Julius II (following the death of Pius III, who reigned from 22 September until 18 October), Cesare admitted to Machiavelli, who was on a diplomatic mission to Rome, that "he had thought about what might happen on his father's death, and had found a remedy for everything, except that he had never dreamed that at the time of his father's death he, too, would be at death's door."[102] Machiavelli, in a dispatch to Florence dated 14 November 1503, reported that the bishop of Elna, an old confidant of the duke, had told him how Borgia "has lost his head and does not know himself or what he wants to do. He is fretful and irresolute."[103] It seems certain that, if Cesare had been in good health, he would not have made the decision to accept the election of Giuliano della Rovere, his father's bitter enemy, as pope or would have been deluded enough to believe his assurances of his full support. On 18 November, Julius ordered Borgia's arrest at Ostia, where he was about to sail with his troops to Livorno, intending to march from there across to Romagna, where his support was still strong. Cesare was brought back to Rome but allowed to leave the city after all his fortresses in the Romagna had agreed to surrender. Expecting his Spanish allies to assist him, he went to Naples, but he was arrested again and put on a ship bound for Spain, where he was imprisoned on the orders of King Ferdinand V, who wanted to improve his standing with Julius and take advantage of the fact that the new pope despised his French rivals. Cesare escaped from prison in 1506, but a year later, at the age of thirty-two, he was killed in a skirmish at Viana in northern Spain, fighting with his brother-in-law, the king of Navarre.

CHAPTER FOUR

GIULIANO AND MACHIAVELLI

On 10 December 1513 Niccolò Machiavelli wrote to his friend Francesco Vettori (1474–1539), Florentine ambassador to the papal court of Leo X, and announced that he had "composed a short study, *De principatibus*" (*On Principalities*) and that he was "dedicating it to His Magnificence Giuliano"[1] (Fig. 21). Most Machiavelli scholars hold the view that Machiavelli's choice did not necessarily mean there was any personal contact between him and Giuliano, looking especially to the years from 1498 to 1512, when Machiavelli held the important posts of second chancellor of the republic and secretary to the foreign policy committee known as the Ten (Dieci di Balìa), when, as Butters notes, Machiavelli hardly referenced the Medici at all in either his diplomatic or his personal correspondence.[2] Contrary to this view, it will be shown here that a close relationship did exist, that it was first established in Imola in 1502, and that it was sustained until Giuliano's untimely death in 1516.

When Giuliano returned to Florence in 1512, his initial aim was to keep the republican institutions intact but at the same time establish a Venetian-style Senate that would strengthen the influential power of the Florentine elite. Following the coup d'état, Giuliano might have thought that, together with his brother-in-law Jacopo Salviati and the new *gonfaloniere di giustizia*, Giovanbattista Ridolfi, all appointed to the balìa by Cardinal Giovanni de' Medici, he would still be able to bring good government to the citizens of Florence. Furthermore, given Machiavelli's long experience as appointee to the second chancery of the republic and as secretary to the Ten, Giuliano would be able to avail himself of Machiavelli's astute political judgment when navigating the fraught, factional world of Florentine politics. But all this was wishful thinking because, early in November, Cardinal Giovanni, before leaving the city to resume his duties as papal legate to Bologna, bowed to the demands of the radical *palleschi* and removed both Salviati and Ridolfi from his brother's side in order to ensure that they were no longer in a position to influence him. In addition, Cardinal Giovanni not only ordered the dismissal of Machiavelli from all his governmental posts but also saw that he was banished from entering Florence for one year.

Most writers on Machiavelli believe that he was fired from the chancery during the first week of November 1512 because of his close association with the former *gonfaloniere di giustizia*, Piero Soderini, which proved to be politically compromising. Yet, while Machiavelli's loyalty toward the new regime was suspect in some quarters, his removal seems to have been specifically linked to his friendship with Giuliano, for certain *palleschi* had convinced Cardinal Giovanni that his younger brother's friendship with Machiavelli represented a danger to the interests of Medicean power. As will be discussed shortly, Machiavelli's first overtly partisan political tract, commonly known as the *Ricordo ai Palleschi*, which he wrote in early November 1512, was not, as is generally thought, an attack on the *ottimati* but instead was written as a warning to Giuliano not to take counsel from those same *palleschi* who had effected Machiavelli's dismissal from office. The history of this friendship provides important context for the vicissitudes of 1512.

In October 1502 the Florentine government sent Machiavelli on a diplomatic mission to the court of Cesare Borgia at Imola, where he remained until the middle of January 1503 and surely met Giuliano, who was serving as a captain in Borgia's army. Another close friend of both Florentines, the artist Leonardo da Vinci, had been appointed as Borgia's military architect and engineer and was in residence at Imola during this entire period. It seems highly likely that the three Florentines spent time in each other's company. Machiavelli did not mention Giuliano in his dispatches to the

Florentine government, nor did he refer to Leonardo, but this is not surprising, since Borgia was considered a threat to Florence, and it would have been unwise for Machiavelli to mention a member of the Medici family, given the fact that they were condemned to exile, or to write about Leonardo, who was in the employ of the enemy. Two poems composed by Machiavelli, whose chronology and meaning have been disputed, suggest that he befriended Giuliano in Imola. Mario Martelli first proposed that these poems were addressed to Giuliano, written before the Medici expulsion of 1494, when Giuliano was between the ages of thirteen and fifteen. Martelli later revised his opinion to suggest that the longer of the two poems was composed between 1514 and 1518 for Giuliano's nephew Lorenzo di Piero, later Duke of Urbino (Fig. 12). Martelli's original supposition that both poems were dedicated to Giuliano seems to be correct, but, as we shall see, were written not in Florence between 1492 and 1494 but rather in Imola in 1502.

On 7 October of that year, Machiavelli arrived in Imola on his second diplomatic mission to Borgia, in response to the duke's demands for a representative from the Florentine republic. Machiavelli stayed in the city until early December, moving with Borgia's entourage from Imola to Cesena. Giuliano, as a captain in Borgia's army, frequently visited Imola while involved in the peace negotiations between his friends Giovanni Bentivoglio and Borgia. As John Najemy has noted, Machiavelli's "early poetry suggests some degree of youthful friendship with Giuliano."[3] Though undated, two poems in particular were likely written in the period when both men were at Imola. The poems form part of a collection of fourteen copied out in the hand of Biagio Buonaccorsi, Machiavelli's close friend and colleague in the Florentine chancery. In this *Libro di ricordi*, compiled between 15 April 1495 and 24 January 1525,[4] Buonaccorsi included one poem each by Lorenzo di Pierfrancesco de' Medici (1463–1503) and Agnolo Poliziano (1454–1494), interspersed with the two by Machiavelli, and followed by ten written by Giuliano's father, Lorenzo the Magnificent, which led Mario Martelli to posit that the poems all date to the late fifteenth century, prior to the 1494 Medici exile.[5]

Machiavelli's first poem, "Se avessi l'arco e le ale, / giovanetto giulío" (If you had wings and a bow / young Giulio), 24 lines in length, is clearly addressed to Giuliano.[6] The second poem, "Poscia che a l'ombra, sotto questo alloro" (Now that in the shade under this laurel),[7] 124 lines long, was in the style of Virgilian allegorical bucolic verse, where Machiavelli, in the guise of a shepherd, sings the praises of a youth called Giacinto (Hyacinth). Martelli initially proposed that both poems were addressed to Giuliano, based on the fact that when Machiavelli was accused of conspiring to assassinate Giuliano and was imprisoned and tortured in 1513, he addressed two other poems, subsequently known as the "prison sonnets," to Giuliano, imploring him to come to his aid. Martelli reasoned that there must have been some prior contact between Machiavelli and Giuliano before he penned the prison sonnets. He further speculated that Machiavelli could have sought Giuliano's protection and patronage before the Medici expulsion from Florence, as exemplified by the two earlier poems.[8] Carlo Dionisotti agreed with Martelli's suggestion that Machiavelli, ten years older than Giuliano and an aspiring poet in Medicean Florence, could have become a member of a circle of friends and clients that Giuliano formed following the death of his father in 1492. Giuliano, who would have been between the ages of thirteen and fifteen, might have formed such a group as a gesture of independence from the tutelage of his older brother Piero, helping to explain why many years later, in Machiavelli's hour of greatest need, he addressed his poems to Giuliano with so much confidence and faith.[9]

Martelli later revised his hypothesis about the longer poem because three verses celebrate Hyacinth's military virtues – "Fierce Mars, that you might shine the more"[10] – and he saw this statement as more applicable to Giuliano's nephew Lorenzo between 1514 and 1518 than to Giuliano in 1492, who would have been rather young to be compared to the god of war.[11] The younger Lorenzo di Piero (1492–1519), aged twenty-one when he was appointed to lead the Medici in August 1513 by his uncle Pope Leo X, took after his father and appeared to be more interested in military affairs than civil administration. This affinity was especially apparent in 1515 when, manipulating the Signoria, the younger Lorenzo became captain-general of the Florentine forces, thus violating the provision in the city's constitution that prohibited a citizen of Florence from occupying that post. Giuliano was stridently opposed to this move, which was also widely condemned in Florence.[12] Martelli suggested that another suitable occasion for dedicating the longer poem to the younger Lorenzo might have presented itself when Machiavelli changed the dedication of *The Prince* to him, possibly following Giuliano's death in March 1516. To support this hypothesis, Martelli drew attention to the laurel tree mentioned in the opening line, a familiar topos for Lorenzo the Magnificent easily extended to his namesake. Martelli argued that, by evoking the laurel (*lauro*), Machiavelli was referring to both grandfather and grandson.[13]

The first poem, "Se avessi l'arco e le ale," has been widely accepted as "obviously addressed to Giuliano."[14] Did Machiavelli write one poem for Giuliano between 1492 and 1494 and then, much later, write another for Giuliano's nephew Lorenzo di Piero? Why would Buonaccorsi have copied these two poems, without any others, if they were not seen as a pair? When the two poems are considered together, as they evidently were when Buonaccorsi copied them, the similarity in their content strongly suggests that they were composed at the same time and for the same person. Both are encomia that sing the praises of a youth. Though several Machiavelli scholars have accepted Martelli's revision that "Se avessi l'arco e le ale" was an early poem for Giuliano while "Poscia che a l'ombra" was written later for his nephew Lorenzo,[15] his initial hypothesis that they were both for Giuliano can be substantiated,[16] though with a new dating that resolves other conflicts in Martelli's analyses. Rather than written when Giuliano was a young teenager in Florence, it seems that both poems were composed for him during his diplomatic mission to Imola in 1502, when Machiavelli was still posted at the chancery and working with his assistant Buonaccorsi prior to their dismissal after the Medici return in 1512. In the shorter poem, "Se avessi l'arco e le ale," Machiavelli, himself a master orator, praises the power of his dedicatee's rhetorical skills:

> The mouth and the words
> Are the bow and the arrows that you have:
> There is not a man under the sun
> That you cannot wound when you draw.[17]

In the longer poem, "Poscia che a l'ombra, sotto questo alloro," the dedicatee, called Iacinto, is again celebrated for his eloquence:

> Then from the splendour that reigns in that face, and from
> every part examined for itself, we learn how great is the force of nature.
> See then the rest in harmony with her; hear, then, the sound of
> his pleasing words, such as to make a marble-stone, a rock show life.
> So that earth smiles where you set foot, and the air grows

happy wherever the welcome sounds of your voice are heard.
When you depart, the little plant that was flowering withers
and is left in misery, and the air deprived of you shows grief.[18]

Letters written to the Signoria suggest that Machiavelli was very well informed about the ongoing negotiations for the peace accord between Borgia and the Bentivoglio, and in the longer poem Machiavelli appears to allude to Giuliano's central involvement in these discussions in lines 55 to 63:

All the shepherds who live in this forest, without regarding
your youth, have submitted to you their quarrels.
You with your accomplished and lordly genius, with varied
ways and diverse inventions make them return to their fold in happiness.
Full of pity you are; if you see a shepherd wretched through
adverse fortune or through love, with your pleasing speech you
gladden him.[19]

Lines 91 to 93, which celebrate the military *virtù* of Hyacinthus, "Fierce Mars that you might shine the more," prompted Martelli to conclude, with good reason, that they were entirely inappropriate for Giuliano, only a youth in the early 1490s. However, these words are even more applicable to Giuliano when he was in Imola in 1502, twenty-three years old and in his prime, having served as a soldier for four years and now one of Borgia's captains. Moreover, Imola seems to be the context for writing the poem because Machiavelli makes direct reference to Borgia: "Fierce Mars, that you might shine the more, within your noble / breast enclosed a heart like that of Cesare, duke of all the dukes."[20]

Given Machiavelli's use of the present tense, a dating of this poem prior to Borgia's death in 1507 seems appropriate, again pointing to Giuliano as its dedicatee in 1502 rather than his cousin Lorenzo after 1514. Both Joseph Tusiani and Allan Gilbert have translated the poem as referring to Julius Caesar, rather than to Cesare Borgia,[21] quite clearly unable to conceive that Machiavelli could describe the latter as having a heart enclosed in a noble breast. However, it is doubtful that with the phrase "Cesar, duca alli altri duci"[22] Machiavelli was alluding to the Roman, who was not a duke, because in his *Discourses on Livy* (1.10.3) he was unsparing in his criticism:

"Caesar is so much more detestable as he who had done an evil is more to blame than he who had wished to do one."[23] Further, Julius Caesar had placed a yoke of slavery on Roman necks (1.17.1), and as a staunch republican Machiavelli condemns Caesar for being the "first tyrant in Rome, such that never again was the city free" (1.37.2).[24]

On the other hand, when Machiavelli first met Borgia, he praised him effusively as one who "is truly splendid and magnificent" and who wins the love of his soldiers. Machiavelli's admiration for the duke was both genuine and long-lasting because in *The Prince*, which he wrote in 1513, Borgia is held up as the exemplar of the ideal prince, a man who was both "prudent" and "virtuous," who "laid sturdy foundations for his future power," and whose example a new prince should imitate.[25] It is important to bear in mind that, if Machiavelli could write so glowingly about Cesare Borgia, there is every reason to believe that Giuliano shared this same exalted view, especially because, as we have already seen, when Giuliano served as a captain in his army, Borgia showed by his actions in Romagna that he both favoured and trusted Giuliano and that he had tried to do all that he could to restore him to Florence.

The last lines of the longer poem also reveal Machiavelli's feelings for his dedicatee, when he wrote:

> I shall keep concealed the love I cherish, and home I shall go
> with my herd, hoping one day to return more famous
> to sing your praises, and more happy.[26]

These lines do not make sense when applied to Giuliano's nephew Lorenzo, since there would have been no reason for Machiavelli to "conceal" his love for the younger Medici after the family's return to Florence (Fig. 12). Machiavelli would, however, have had every reason to hide his affections for Giuliano during the Medici exile, where even the fact of meeting him, a declared outlaw perceived to be acting against the republic, had to be kept secret. When Machiavelli writes "and home I shall go," he seems to allude to his return to Florence from Romagna.

When Giuliano later returned to Florence, Machiavelli was at the chancery, still serving as second chancellor to the Florentine republic. Although he must have deeply regretted the demise of the republic and the return of the Medici to power, at the same time he could draw some solace from knowing that he would now be serving his friend Giuliano. In a curious twist of fate, Machiavelli fulfilled the desire that he first expressed in the longer 1502 poem:

> O gift of so many gods, condescend to accept me among
> your faithful subjects, if to have such a servant you do not scorn.
> And if I see that my song will delight you, these valleys and
> these little hills will echo in your praise verses splendid and measureless;
> for my thoughts are so strained to please you that my desire is
> only that I shall think of obeying, you commanding.[27]

That Machiavelli hoped to retain his post in the chancery and continue working under the new administration is demonstrated by a letter written to a noblewoman, likely Isabella d'Este (Fig. 34), that was discovered among his papers by his nephew Giuliano de' Ricci.[28] He describes the Medici as his "new masters," and while it has been suggested that he is being "moderately obsequious" in using this phrase,[29] in light of Machiavelli's encomiastic poems, attributed here to have been for Giuliano, there is good reason to believe that he was being sincere.

The letter, in Machiavelli's hand, perhaps a copy of one sent or simply a draft, is addressed to a woman, although no name is indicated. Not surprisingly, this "letter to an unknown woman," as it has been called, has generated much speculation. Machiavelli's nephew thought it might be addressed to a Medici, perhaps Alfonsina, the widow of Piero and the mother of Giuliano's nephew Lorenzo. Other historians have proposed that the mysterious woman could be Giuliano's niece, Alfonsina's daughter Clarice, or one of his sisters, either Contessina or Lucrezia (Fig. 8). In 1978 Roberto Ridolfi argued convincingly that neither Alfonsina nor any other member of the Medici family would require a description of Prato or, indeed, would need to be told that Prato was ten miles from Florence. Moreover, Ridolfi explained, the letter's designation of "V.ra S.ria illustrissima" clearly denotes that the intended addressee was a noblewoman, not any of the Medici women.[30]

In 1982 Brian Richardson presented a compelling case to support his identification of the noblewoman as Isabella d'Este, Marchioness of Mantua, a proposal also put forward by Franco Gaeta.[31] Richardson suggested that Machiavelli wrote the letter between 17 and 30 September 1512 on the instructions of Giuliano de' Medici, who was responding to Isabella's request for information about recent changes that had taken place in Tuscany, to which Machiavelli refers at the beginning of the letter. Giuliano's close rapport with Isabella was apparent when she arranged a great banquet in his honour during the Diet of Mantua. Ten days afterwards, on 31 August, Giuliano wrote from Prato, informing her of his imminent return to Florence. Isabella replied on 3 September, expressing her great happiness at the news of his return home with the consent of the citizens of the republic and without the spilling of blood.[32] Machiavelli's letter could, therefore, be seen as part of this correspondence that flowed between Giuliano and the Marchioness of Mantua in the late summer of 1512. As Richardson points out, Isabella would have had good reason, apart from her natural curiosity, to be preoccupied with the consequences of the Diet of Mantua because she had ceased to be a disinterested spectator. Now that Piero Soderini had been deposed in Florence, Julius II had turned his sights on her brother Alfonso, Duke of Ferrara, as his greatest enemy because of d'Este's pro-French ties and his adamant refusal to switch his allegiance to the Holy League. To make matters worse, Isabella's eldest son, the twelve-year-old Federico, was being held hostage in Rome at the papal court.[33]

Machiavelli would have been a natural choice to write such a letter because the second chancellor was surely well acquainted with the marchioness from his diplomatic missions to Mantua in 1505 and 1509. A good part of the letter concerns military matters so that, in his capacity as the administrator of the Florentine militia, he would also have been in a position to provide Isabella with valuable information. Machiavelli recounts what decisions and kinds of preparations were undertaken to protect the strongholds in Tuscany and repel an attack against Florence itself. Giuliano also knew that Machiavelli would be sensitive in his reporting of the Sack of Prato, and, indeed, Machiavelli does refrain from describing gory details of the massacre of Prato's population: "In order to spare Your Ladyship cause for worry in your spirit." He did, however, inform her that more than four thousand had perished and that even the virgins "cloistered in holy sites" were not spared, falling victim to "rape and pillage."[34] Because Isabella had known the Soderini family personally, having been invited on several occasions during her private visit to Florence in 1506 to the Palazzo della Signoria as a guest of Soderini's wife Argentina,[35] Machiavelli also took care, when describing the last days of Piero Soderini, to assure her that he had left the city safely for Siena "with the Signoria's consent and with a large escort."[36] At the end of the letter, Machiavelli could even be expressing Giuliano's own sentiments when he writes optimistically: "The city is now quite peaceful and hopes, with the help of these Medici, to live no less honoured than it did in times past, when their father, Lorenzo the Magnificent, of the most happy memory, governed."[37]

Despite Richardson's persuasive argument, accepted tentatively by Gaeta, and without hesitation by Giorgio Inglese and the present author,[38] Francesco Bausi did not accept the identification of Isabella d'Este as the noblewoman in question. He counters that, although Machiavelli was still formally in his post at the chancery, he was not given any official duties to perform or official letters to write, and his past collaboration with Piero Soderini made it "certain that the Medici would not have regarded him well."[39] Instead, Bausi proposed that the letter could have been fictive, a sort of "open letter" with no particular recipient in mind, and that in writing it, Machiavelli perhaps wanted to gain the sympathy of the Medici in order to compensate for the fact that he was living under a cloud of suspicion.[40]

While Bausi is correct in assuming that Cardinal Giovanni and other members of the Medici family would not have "regarded him well," Giuliano was not among them. If, as seems likely, the letter was intended for Isabella, then it demonstrates how Giuliano saw Machiavelli as a trusted servant of the state who could write correspondence on his behalf. Indeed, Machiavelli was more than willing to put his experience and skills of diplomacy in the service of Giuliano. Bausi, along with a majority of Machiavelli scholars, believes that Machiavelli was severely compromised by his association with the former Soderini government, reason enough for his dismissal in early November 1512.[41] However, it is argued here that Machiavelli's downfall was not so much because of a close connection with Soderini, whose trusted confidant he certainly had been, but because of the fears he aroused among the radical *palleschi*, who felt directly threatened by his friendship with Giuliano.

PAOLO VETTORI

The *palleschi* lost no time in going to Campi after the Sack of Prato to voice their complaints directly to Cardinal Giovanni de' Medici about Giuliano's perceived inadequacies when it came to the task of governing Florence. Paolo Vettori (1477–1526), one of the *palleschi* who had entered the Palazzo della Signoria and had forced Piero Soderini to resign as *gonfaloniere di giustizia* on 31 August 1512, once more raised the issue of Giuliano's leadership with the cardinal, then making preparations to return to Bologna and planning to leave Florence in the hands of his younger brother. Vettori remains a somewhat elusive figure, even though he seems to have been one of the key players in the overthrow of Soderini. His older brother Francesco (1474–1539), however, is much better known because of his various written works, such as his *Sommario della Storia d'Italia dal 1511 al 1527* and his *Vita di Lorenzo de' Medici*, Giuliano's nephew who died in 1519.[42] Francesco has also achieved renown because of his two-year correspondence with Machiavelli while serving as the Florentine ambassador to Rome. Their letter exchange began in March 1513, almost immediately after Machiavelli's release from prison, and continued until the end of January 1515.[43]

Filippo de' Nerli (1485–1556) identified Francesco's brother Paolo as one of the *giovani* who had begun, as early as 1505, to speak out against Piero Soderini. He was very cunning, Nerli says, because although he opposed the *gonfaloniere di giustizia* and criticized his actions, Francesco always stayed close and affected respect for Soderini.[44] Guicciardini recorded that, many months before the restoration of the Medici, Paolo Vettori conspired with several others to restore the Medici family in Florence and secretly met with Giuliano's cousin, the exiled Giulio de' Medici (later Cardinal and then Pope Clement VII), at the Vettori villa at Paneretta, within Florentine territory near Siena, in order to plan how to return the Medici to power.[45] Lorenzo Strozzi, whose brother Filippo had married Giuliano's niece Clarice in 1508, confirmed this account by saying that only Paolo Vettori met secretly with Giulio at his villa, so that they could decide how the city was to be governed and who among the citizens could be trusted. Strozzi also described how Vettori and Antonfrancesco degli Albizzi (1486–1537) had falsely presented themselves as intimate friends of Piero Soderini so that they could more easily carry out their designs in favour of the Medici. Vettori and Albizzi proved to be so convincing in their deception that Piero Soderini trusted them more than all his other friends and relatives.[46] It is significant to note, however, that Paolo Vettori's motive for opposing Piero Soderini, to whom he was related and from whom he had benefited privately,[47] may have been for selfish reasons rather than for any particular feelings of loyalty to the Medici. Guicciardini maintained that Paolo had massive debts. Apparently these were incurred by the failure of an iron foundry, a business venture with Soderini, which had ruined Paolo financially.[48] He may therefore have thought that, by conspiring against Soderini to bring back the Medici, he would have his revenge on his former business partner. Perhaps Vettori had also calculated what he could gain by a change of regime, and that if he took personal risks to restore the Medici, he could then look forward to being generously rewarded for his actions. Indeed, it appears that Paolo was appointed the commissary of the five hundred foreign infantry retained in the city by the Medici for their personal protection. Not long after, he was apparently forced to relinquish his command to Giulio de' Medici.[49]

Paolo Vettori was deeply unhappy with Giuliano's leadership and with the new *gonfaloniere di giustizia* Ridolfi, as well as with the composition of the Dieci di Balìa because the *frateschi* Jacopo Salviati, Lanfredino Lanfredini, Piero Alamanni, and Piero Guicciardini had been appointed as members while he and other *palleschi* had been kept out.[50] Vettori also feared that, once Giovanni de' Medici returned to Bologna to resume his duties as papal legate, the cardinal's absence from the city would make him vulnerable to discontent from the many citizens who had loved their popular government and had respected Soderini. These fears may have led Paolo to express his concerns directly to Cardinal Giovanni in his "Memorandum to Cardinal de' Medici about the Affairs of Florence."[51] Most likely, Paolo wrote the memorandum sometime in late September, after he had lost command of his infantry troops to Giulio de' Medici.

The document, written in Paolo Vettori's own hand, is remarkably revealing and warrants close scrutiny because it provides valuable insights into the thinking of this radical Medici partisan. Vettori was clearly anxious for protection against the *frateschi*, whom he saw as his enemies. In the memorandum, Vettori asked Cardinal Giovanni to make changes to the institutional structure of the government before his anticipated departure for Bologna. Changes would not only strengthen the Medici hold on the government but also would provide Vettori with some protection against his opponents. His three demands can be summarized as follows: the security of the state must be enhanced, Giuliano must at all times be closely supervised, and reorganization of the Florentine chancery must take place. With regard to security, Vettori writes: "Your ancestors, from Cosimo to Piero, maintained power [*questo Stato*] more by skilful management [*industria*] than by force [*forza*]. But you need to use force more than skilful

FIGURE 1 | Michelangelo Buonarroti, Medici Chapel (New Sacristy), view toward tomb of Giuliano de'Medici, San Lorenzo, Florence. Scala / Art Resource, NY

FIGURE 2 | Michelangelo Buonarroti, tomb of Giuliano de' Medici, Duc de Nemours, c. 1519–34. Marble. Medici Chapel (New Sacristy), San Lorenzo, Florence. Scala / Art Resource, NY

FIGURE 3 | Michelangelo Buonarroti, tomb of Lorenzo de' Medici, Duke of Urbino, c. 1519–34. Marble. Medici Chapel (New Sacristy), San Lorenzo, Florence. Scala / Art Resource, NY

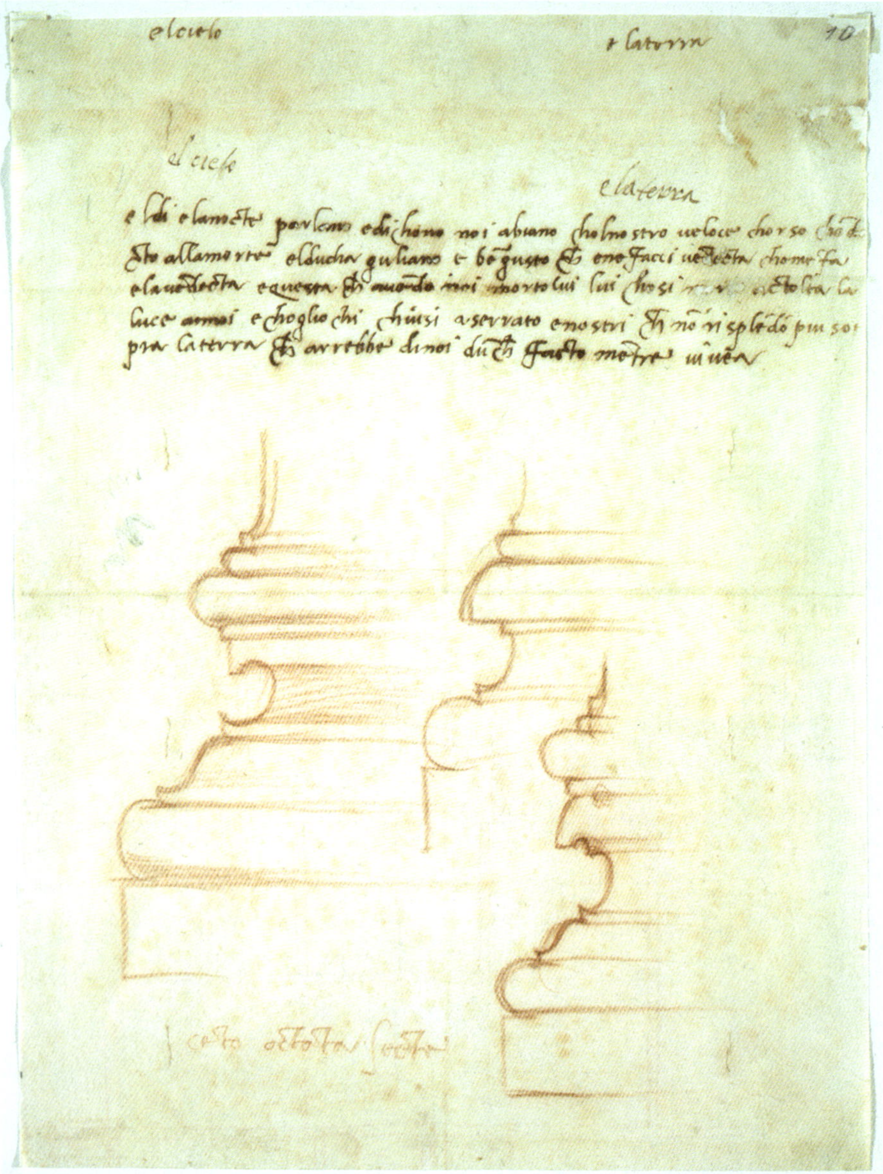

FIGURE 4 | Michelangelo Buonarroti, drawing for the profile of pilasters in the Medici Chapel (New Sacristy), c. 1524. Red chalk, pen, and brown ink, 28.3 × 28.1 cm. Casa Buonarroti, Florence, inv 10a. Scala / Art Resource, NY

FIGURE 5 | Alessandro Allori, *Portrait of Giuliano de' Medici Duke of Nemours, after Raphael.* Palazzo Pitti, Galleria Palatina e Appartamenti Reali, Florence, inv 1890, n. 775.

FIGURE 6 | Michelangelo Buonarroti, tomb of Giuliano de' Medici, detail of Giuliano installed in niche. Marble. Medici Chapel (New Sacristy), San Lorenzo, Florence. Scala / Art Resource, NY

FIGURE 7 | Michelangelo Buonarroti, tomb of Lorenzo de' Medici, detail of Lorenzo installed in niche. Marble. Medici Chapel (New Sacristy), San Lorenzo, Florence. Scala / Art Resource, NY

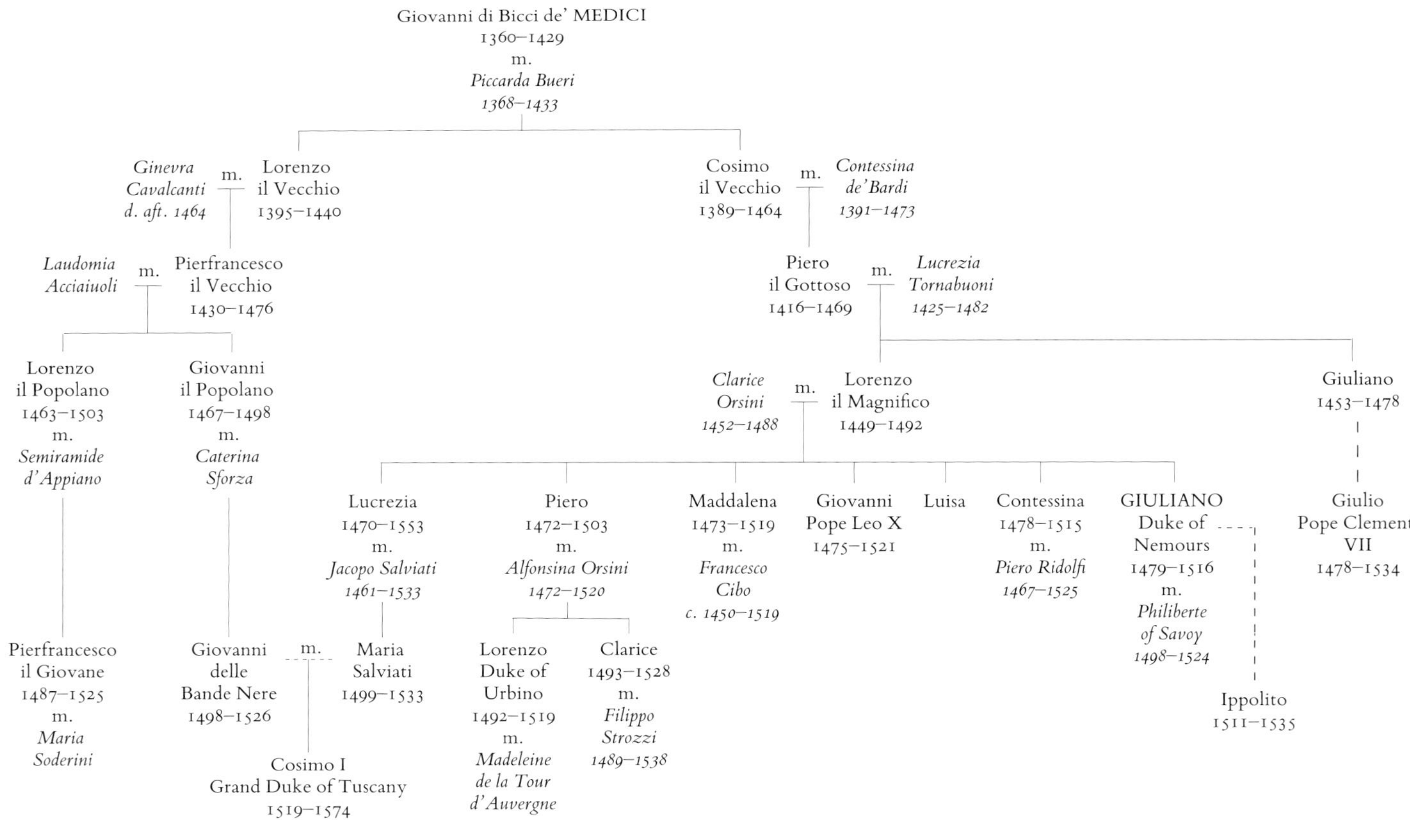

FIGURE 8 | Medici family tree showing relations discussed in this book. Adapted from Simonetta, *Volpi e Leoni*.

FIGURE 9 | Raphael, *Portrait of Pope Julius II Rovere*, mid-1511. Oil on poplar, 108.7 × 81 cm. National Gallery, London, ng27 © National Gallery, London / Art Resource, NY

FIGURE 10 | Raphael, *Portrait of Cardinal Bibbiena*, c. 1516. Oil on canvas, 85 × 66 cm. Galleria Palatina, Palazzo Pitti, Florence. Scala / Art Resource, NY

FIGURE 11 | Raphael, *Portrait of Pope Leo X (Giovanni di Lorenzo de' Medici) with Cardinals Giulio de' Medici (left) and Luigi de' Rossi (right)*, c. 1517. Oil on wood. 155.5 × 119.5 cm. Uffizi, Florence. Scala/Ministero per i Beni e le Attività culturali / Art Resource, NY

FIGURE 12 | Raphael, *Portrait of Lorenzo II de Medici, Duke of Urbino*, c. 1518. Musée Fabre, Montpellier. Josse/Scala/ Art Resource, NY

FIGURE 13 |
Raphael, *Portrait of Guidobaldo da Montefeltro*. Uffizi, Florence. Alinari / Art Resource, NY

FIGURE 14 |
Raphael, *Portrait of Elisabetta Gonzaga*, 1504. Wood. 52.5 × 37.3 cm. Uffizi, Florence, inv 1441. Erich Lessing / Art Resource, NY

FIGURE 15 | Raphael, *Portrait of Pietro Bembo*. Oil on panel. 54 × 39 cm. Museum of Fine Arts (Szepmuveszeti Muzeum), Budapest. © Museum of Fine Arts Budapest/Scala / Art Resource, NY

FIGURE 16 | Titian, *Portrait of Cardinal Ippolito I de' Medici*, 1533. Oil on canvas, 138 × 106 cm. Galleria Palatina, Palazzo Pitti, Florence. Scala / Ministero per i Beni e le Attività culturali / Art Resource, NY

FIGURE 17 | Raphael, *Portrait of Francesco Maria della Rovere*. Oil on wood. 48 × 35.5 cm Uffizi, Florence, inv 1890: 8760. Scala / Ministero per i Beni e le Attività culturali / Art Resource, NY

FIGURE 18 | Raphael, *Emilia Pia da Montefeltro*, c. 1502–04. Oil and possibly tempera on wood panel. 42.5 × 28.6 cm. Baltimore Museum of Art: Jacob Epstein Collection, bma 1951.114. Photography by Mitro Hood.

management, because you have more enemies here and not very much ability to satisfy them; therefore, since you cannot win them over again, you will need to become so strong and secure that they will be afraid to attack you."[52]

Vettori advocated for the government to keep an army of well-paid soldiers, but he also argued that these troops would not be enough for a city as large as Florence, where too many citizens were discontented. That is why, he thought, it would be necessary to establish extra security. He doubted that the allegiance of citizens could be won because the last ten years had brought them prosperity, and now, with a regime change, most would be resentful and hostile. The inhabitants of the *contado*, the subject territory closest to the city, however, had been badly governed, and therefore, the cardinal must arm the *contado* and protect it from oppressive provincial administrators and public officers in Florence.

By doing so, Vettori says, "within six months you will be safer than if you have an army of Spaniards in Prato ready to help you."[53] Vettori was, in fact, advising the cardinal to re-establish the Florentine militia that had been dissolved on 19 September. Florence's first citizen army had been created on the initiative of Machiavelli, who came to hate mercenaries when he realized that the traditional practice of employing the services of *condottieri* was not only excessively expensive because of their greed but also was no guarantee against incompetence or treachery.[54] Machiavelli would later argue in his *Art of War*, written between 1519 and 1520 and published in Florence in 1521, that, paradoxically, "only a part-time soldier can be trusted to possess a full-time commitment to the war and its purposes."[55] A citizen soldier would be content in a time of peace to return home and resume his occupation, whereas the mercenary, with no home but a camp, would make no attempt at resolution because he is only happy if the war drags on indefinitely, and he continues to be paid.[56] In 1506 Machiavelli began to supervise the recruitment of peasants in the surrounding countryside and to organize them into a citizen army. On 6 December of that year he was given a third office as chancellor of the newly created Nine of the Militia Ordinance, responsible for overseeing the levying and training of troops.[57] There was, however, one crucial difference between Machiavelli's militia and the one Paolo Vettori proposed to Cardinal Giovanni. Whereas Machiavelli's infantry was intended to defend the liberty and independence of Florence, Vettori's militia was its antithesis, owing its loyalty only to the Medici, so that in times of political strife it could be turned against the citizens themselves.[58] Vettori advised the cardinal to appoint someone who was loyal to the Medici to serve as commissary of this new militia, and here it is certain that he was angling for a position for himself.

After calling for enhanced security, Vettori's memo turned to concerns about Giuliano, urging the cardinal to decide before leaving Florence "how Giuliano should act and from whom he should seek advice about both internal and foreign policy." Vettori warned the cardinal that, "if the matter is not dealt with properly, confusion and harm could result." He recognized that it was the authority of the cardinal that kept the citizens "united in obedience," and he expressed the fear that, once the cardinal had gone from the city, those ambitious and self-seeking citizens "will create discords that Giuliano will be unable to overcome by himself because he does not yet understand our affairs, and very serious troubles could result from this."[59] Vettori knew that the cardinal shared his opinion that Giuliano could pose a danger to the state because he had seen how swiftly the cardinal had taken charge in Florence after he had arrived in the city on 14 September. When Vettori repeated that Giuliano would not realize when he was given biased advice because "he is not yet well versed in the affairs of the city," he was really saying that Giuliano and whomever he chose to advise him could not be trusted with running the affairs of Florence. Therefore, Vettori asked the cardinal to choose ten or twelve citizens who would advise Giuliano on every matter of governance; also, he advised that, since it was possible for disagreements to occur, no more than two of these men should be singled out as principal advisers.[60] Again, Vettori might have been hoping that the cardinal would appoint him as one of the two. In selecting counsellors for Giuliano, Vettori warned, the cardinal must be careful to "choose among those who want to share in the fortunes of your family."[61]

Mikael Hörnqvist has interpreted the memorandum as proof of the "problem of finding trustworthy advisers among the Florentines … who out of exaggerated deference or excessive ambition" could not be expected either to be loyal or to give good advice.[62] Vettori may be alluding to the cardinal's own brother-in-law Jacopo Salviati and *gonfaloniere di giustizia* Ridolfi as men unsuitable for the task and potentially dangerous if allowed to advise the Medici. Giuliano had aligned himself with Salviati and the *frateschi*, upholders of the Savonarolan popular government, rendering both Giuliano and the friar's supporters suspect in the eyes of the *palleschi*.[63]

Vettori was clearly afraid that, with Cardinal Giovanni out of the city, the followers of Savonarola, who had Giuliano's ear, would do everything in their power to undermine the stability of Medicean governance. Giovanni Rucellai, one of the ringleaders of the *palleschi*, and the principal spokesman in Cerretani's *Dialogo della mutatione di Firenze*, expressed the same fears when he noted that Salviati did his utmost to subvert the Medici in the early days of their restoration: "Their brother-in-law played an insignificant part in their return and then afterwards he did all in his power to reintroduce and keep alive Savonarola's party, since he was such a devoted follower of the friar. And he was successful in this thanks to the bad way in which the *balìa* had been set up, something which was very frequently discussed by us and brought us to the verge of despair because we could see how efficiently that party was being revitalized."[64]

The view that Jacopo Salviati could not be trusted was widely held among the *palleschi*. For example, in a letter dated 5 August 1513, Francesco Vettori gave his brother Paolo some advice that demonstrates his lack of trust in Salviati while nevertheless suggesting that Paolo should adopt dissimulation when it served him. It appears that Paolo still feared that the actions he had taken against Piero Soderini had made him despised in some quarters in Florence. Francesco tells Paolo that he should learn from the example of Jacopo Salviati, who, when he found himself among Medici *amici*, would declare that all his actions since 1494 had been directed toward securing the return of the Medici, but when he was with those whom he knew were Medici enemies, and who had supported the former Great Council, would declare that he always wanted to stand firm with this government and that he had never had another intention.[65]

Almost immediately, Paolo's memorandum seems to have had its desired effect. On 3 October Jacopo Salviati was appointed as Florentine ambassador to Pope Julius II, likely at the suggestion of Cardinal Giovanni,[66] thereby removing him physically from Florence and denying him the possibility of influencing Giuliano. Some observers at the time seem to confirm that this appointment was made to satisfy the demands of the *palleschi*. Nerli claimed that Salviati was sent to Rome because the *palleschi*, desiring a restricted form of government, had convinced the Medici that Salviati was their adversary and that it was necessary to remove him and the Savonarolans from Florence, since they favoured and honoured Salviati as a supporter of the popular, broadly based government.[67] Pierre

Hurtubise believes that Salviati's appointment as ambassador to Rome was inspired less by a consideration of his merits, which were indisputable, than by the exigencies formulated by his own supporters, who could not forgive this close relative of the Medici for being Savonarola's faithful disciple and counsellor.[68]

Salviati left for Rome on 4 November,[69] two days before the cardinal's own departure for Bologna.[70] Salviati's mission was expected to end when Francesco Vettori, the new ambassador elected on 30 December 1512, would arrive in Rome. The Dieci di Balìa, together with Giuliano, expected Salviati to return on 12 February. It appears, however, that the wishes of the cardinal overrode the Florentine government, and Salviati was forced to remain at the papal court. Following the death of Pope Julius II on 22 February, Salviati once again fully expected to be recalled to Florence, but this was not to be. After making repeated requests, which were all ignored, he was allowed to return only in August 1513, that is, after Giuliano had moved permanently to Rome.[71] On 16 October 1512 the Dieci di Balìa ordered the resignation of Giovanbattista Ridolfi from his position as *gonfaloniere di giustizia* on the grounds that "although he was most wise and experienced in affairs of state, he lacked good enough health for the office."[72]

The third and final matter upon which Vettori's memorandum had urged the cardinal to act concerned a reorganization of the Florentine chancery, which consisted mainly of civil servants whose functions were to administer the internal affairs of the state, conduct foreign policy, and carry out policies determined by the various magistracies and councils. These career civil servants followed the tradition of maintaining bureaucratic neutrality in order to be assured of their permanent salaried posts. Most of the officials who were first elected in 1498, therefore, were able to remain in office after the Medici were restored.[73] In his *Ricordi*, Vettori asked Cardinal Giovanni to decide where he would like the affairs of the state to be handled. "Dealing with all of them privately [in the Medici palace] would be too troublesome." In the Palazzo della Signoria, the Dieci di Balìa "must deal with them, because the Signoria has always been the instrument and not the decision-making body of the government."[74] Since, as we shall see, the only civil servants to lose their offices in this recommended reorganization of the Florentine chancery were Machiavelli and his good friend and junior colleague Biagio Buonaccorsi, by drawing the cardinal's attention to the critical importance of the Dieci di Balìa where Machiavelli was still secretary, Vettori may have laid the grounds for Machiavelli's removal.

Vettori lists the names of the chancery personnel and gives a brief description of each position's functions, wishing the cardinal to be better acquainted with the body's workings. He began with the first chancellor, Marcello Virgilio Adriani, appointed to his post in 1498, who continued in office under the new Medici regime until his death in 1521. Adriani handled correspondence dealing with other rulers, and Machiavelli, nominated second chancellor on 19 June 1498 and on 14 July of the same year appointed secretary to the Dieci di Balìa, attended to internal affairs. He then provided the names of minor officials who occupied less important posts. Machiavelli's name comes up again, when Vettori writes: "At present, the duties of the Chancery of the Ten and the Chancery of the Signoria are not entirely distinct, because messer Marcello deals with letters to and from the Ten, and Machiavelli dealt with letters about internal affairs, before he went to the [Nine of the Militia Ordinance]."[75] At the time of writing, Vettori would have been aware that Machiavelli had lost his post as administrator of the Nine because it had been disbanded by government decree on 19 September but that Machiavelli was still secretary to the Dieci di Balìa. Finally, Vettori named Buonaccorsi (Machiavelli's good friend who had copied the two poems written by Machiavelli for Giuliano while at Imola), describing him as the assistant to Adriani. Buonaccorsi had replaced Machiavelli when he took up his post at the Nine.[76]

Vettori's memo then asked the cardinal to think about how the staff of these chanceries could be reduced, and if he wishes, "the affairs of state to be controlled by the Ten, Giuliano will need to meet with the Ten at least once a day and have with him some of those citizens chosen to advise him; and the replies to be given to ambassadors should be decided there." The chancellor "attached to the Ten [should have] much experience of internal and foreign affairs, and this man should also write on Giuliano's behalf to the ambassadors about those things that concern your own rule, not deviating in any way from what has been decided."[77] Vettori concludes this section: "Moreover, if you found someone experienced or trusted to serve this purpose, this would be an excellent thing in these early days of your government, because it is necessary as anything else you institute."[78]

Only Machiavelli and Biagio Buonaccorsi were dismissed from their posts in November 1512;[79] Machiaveli's experience and, in the eyes of

Giuliano, his trustworthiness could not save him. Apparently, these dismissals occurred on 6 November, the very day Cardinal Giovanni set out with his entourage from Florence for Bologna (although most commentators give the date of his dismissal as 7 November, when the official decree was passed unanimously).[80] Were these two events, the departure of the cardinal and the dismissal of Machiavelli, merely a coincidence, or was Machiavelli's removal from office intended to be a very public display of the "excellent beginning" of the cardinal's rule? Hörnqvist has posed the question of whether Machiavelli collaborated with Vettori on his *Ricordi*, writing those parts that are "general and theoretical" and leaving Vettori "to work out the details of the concrete proposals,"[81] a division of labour that may have cost Machiavelli his job.

Many historians who address the question of why Machiavelli was relieved of his posts in the chancery explain his dismissal as the inevitable outcome of the restoration of the Medici; he was fired, in this telling, because he had been the political confidant and close collaborator of Piero Soderini. If true, and he was seen as so contaminated by his service to Soderini, why was he allowed to remain in office until early November? Robert Black and John Najemy have both given thought to this question. Black, focusing his attention on Machiavelli's fourteen and a half years as a public official in the Florentine chancery, compares Machiavelli's career as a public servant with the chancery service of other public officials and found no evidence to support the idea that Machiavelli was ever involved in partisan politics. Moreover, he says that there was nothing to justify a dismissal because there simply is no evidence that Machiavelli behaved any differently than any other chancery official, and that he conformed to the expectations of political neutrality throughout his years of service.[82] Black concludes that the dismissal resulted from the hatred felt among the Florentine conservative patricians, who resented Machiavelli's intellectual arrogance and self-assertiveness and despised his success in climbing the Florentine social ladder. This loathing was as much to blame for Machiavelli's dismissal as was his connection to Soderini.[83] Najemy explains that Machiavelli's humiliating ejection from office was because he had managed to alienate many who disliked his exacting judgment of their policies. Beneath the mask of neutrality, Najemy writes, Machiavelli "harboured a multitude of negative and often scathing judgments about the political leaders, institutions and policies served," and it was an awareness of this attitude that caused him to be removed from office.[84]

In the *Ricordi*, as already seen, Vettori described the Dieci di Balìa as the place where the important government decisions were made. Machiavelli was, as secretary to the Ten, dismissed on 6 November. That step was certainly essential to curbing Machiavelli's influence on Giuliano, as it had been with Jacopo Salviati and Giovanbattista Ridolfi. The decision to remove "an experienced and trusted man" was the cardinal's, and it was made on the very day of his departure from Florence. But if this were so, what could be the reason for Buonaccorsi's dismissal at the same time? Black emphasizes that Buonaccorsi was a minor civil servant of almost complete political detachment whose writings were "largely devoid of political comment or prejudice."[85] If Machiavelli's removal stemmed from a desire to isolate Giuliano from any possible contact with Machiavelli, Buonaccorsi, as Machiavelli's good friend, may have been perceived as a possible conduit between them, and therefore had to go as well.

On 10 November the Signoria banished Machiavelli from Florence for one year, effective immediately, but required him to stay within the Florentine state. Furthermore, he was obliged to find a surety of 1,000 gold florins, a considerable sum, which his friend Francesco Vettori together with Filippo and Giovanni Machiavelli guaranteed.[86] Ten days later, on 17 November, another decree was issued, forbidding him to cross the threshold of the Palazzo della Signoria for twelve months, a prohibition that was also extended to Buonaccorsi.[87] It was at the point of being removed from office that Machiavelli wrote his first partisan political tract, commonly referred to as *Ai Palleschi*, perhaps in retaliation for the removal of himself, Salviati, and Ridolfi as potential aides and advisers to Giuliano.

MACHIAVELLI'S *AI PALLESCHI*

In his discussion of Machiavelli's service in Florentine government chancery, Black draws attention to Machiavelli's *Ai Palleschi*, pointing out that it is profoundly different from all Machiavelli's previous political writing because it specifically addressed the partisan struggles in Florence after the fall of the Soderini government and consequently was the first to focus on internal politics, rather than on foreign or military affairs.[88] An autograph copy of this short political statement survives but does not in fact carry a title. At the top of the first page are the words "notate bene questo scripto" (note well this writing). When the text was first published in 1868, Cesare Guasti presented it as the *Ricordo di Niccolò Machiavelli ai Palleschi del 1512* (Memorandum of Niccolò Machiavelli to the Medici Faction).[89] Bausi suggested that a more accurate title would be *A un pallesco* because Machiavelli adopts the *voi* throughout, "*Io vi voglio advertire*" (I wish to warn you) "*e che voi guardiate*" (and that you look), and that this formal address was perhaps used specifically for a member of the Medici family.[90] Since the text is generally thought to date from early November 1512, we could surmise that it was intended for Giuliano in his capacity as head of state.

If Giuliano is the "*voi*" in question, which seems highly possible, then we should consider the document as though it was meant for Giuliano alone, and not addressed to the *palleschi* faction as a whole, as is commonly thought. And, if we assume that Giuliano was the intended recipient, we can propose that Machiavelli wrote to alert him to the danger of taking counsel from those who argued that the Medici, in Machiavelli's words, "would benefit by exposing Piero Soderini's shortcomings in order to blacken his name among the populace."[91] Throughout the text Machiavelli seems compelled to caution his reader about the dangers of listening to the advice from "enemies of Soderini" who "persistently countered him in Florentine politics," and who now say that Soderini must be "exposed" in order to "destroy his reputation." Machiavelli warns his reader that Soderini's enemies want Giuliano to believe that, if the Medici lay bare Soderini's defects, their newly restored government would be empowered. To the contrary, Machiavelli insisted, discrediting Soderini would not give power to the Medici but rather would only benefit his enemies, for "their faction will have drawn the hatred of the populace upon themselves unless they can now prove that he was evil and deserved their enmity." Machiavelli writes: "The current opinion of the people is that the faction in question wished Soderini ill, so it could seize the government for itself. If, however, Soderini could be defamed to the Florentine people, they would say: 'The enemies of Soderini were telling the truth! They are, after all, upright citizens who are blackening Soderini because he merits it! If things have turned as they have it is not because they planned it that way.' These enemies would then have more influence with the populace. This is in no way to the advantage of the Medici government … The reason they want to free themselves of the populace's hatred is so that they can promote their own interests, not those of the Medici."[92]

Machiavelli saw these "enemies of Soderini" as the real nemesis of the Medici, urging his reader to "look those individuals carefully in the eye and see what is motivating them … not to benefit the new Medici government, but to strengthen their own faction."[93] Indeed, it is surely Giuliano who must "find a way for this faction to be despised, not prized, by the people." Machiavelli repeats: "Airing Soderini's defects does not raise the standing of the Medici government but that of Soderini's enemies, while the Medici government would only weaken itself by attacking a man who is in exile and cannot harm it."[94] For Machiavelli, only Soderini's foes would benefit from his denigration, "so that they can cast off the burden they bear with the people for having been its enemy. But they are doing this for themselves, not for the Medici, nor for those who wish to stand by the Medici in good and bad fortune."[95]

But to whom was Machiavelli referring? Who were these "enemies of Soderini"? Most agree that Machiavelli was attacking the *ottimati*. Jean-Jacques Marchand has provided the deepest analysis of the text, identifying the target of Machiavelli's attack as those *ottimati* who, when the Medici returned, "feigned loyalty" to the new government. He has suggested that Machiavelli wrote *Ai Palleschi* in response to the political discontent that confronted the Medici on their return to power and the new Dieci di Balìa, and that this displeasure had strengthened "the party of the friar" led by former *gonfaloniere* Ridolfi, fuelled by fears of a resurgence of *ottimati* power. As proof, Marchand cites the passage in Cerretani's *Dialogo delle mutatione* concerning Jacopo Salviati, where the *pallesco* Giovanni Rucellai laments Jacopo's untrustworthiness and despairs that the party of the friar was being revitalized.[96] For Marchand, therefore, Machiavelli's "enemies" were the *frateschi*.

Robert Black claims that Machiavelli was displaying his hatred for "aristocrats" and that the emergence of these views in *Ai Palleschi* shows that all along, when outwardly he conformed to the code of bureaucratic neutrality, Machiavelli had "been restraining his true political opinions."[97] Najemy, too, believes that Machiavelli was expressing "strong anti-*ottimati* sentiments,"[98] and he emphasizes the contempt that Machiavelli felt for these elites, suggesting that he was excoriating the same *ottimati* whose "cooperation and benevolence" the Medici were trying to seek in order to construct their new regime.[99] Martelli is of the opinion that *Ai Palleschi* perfectly frames the situation in Florence because the real opposition was not between the Medici and the previous Soderini government but between the *ottimati* and the Medici. Since Machiavelli had been Soderini's man, he too had become an enemy of the elite.[100] Bausi agrees, arguing that the danger came no longer from Soderini but from *ottimati* who, "in their habitual, ambiguous behaviour," hoped to restore the "'old order' of the former elitist government."[101] Dotti suggests that Machiavelli's text aimed to urge the *palleschi* to unite with the supporters of the old Soderini regime and to face together a "dictatorship of the *ottimati*, hostile to both parties."[102] Similarly, Butters argues, "Machiavelli was clearly referring to the Salviati group, rather than to the *ottimati* as a whole," advising in his memorandum that "in order to secure their undivided loyalty, the Medici had to ensure that Salviati and his friends were loathed by the people."[103]

The assertion that Machiavelli identified the "enemies of Soderini" with Ridolfi, Salviati, and the followers of Savonarola appears, however, problematic. The *frateschi* were devoted to the friar's popular government, and this fact alone makes it hard to imagine that they would have incurred the hatred of the people. Although the *frateschi* preferred the republic to continue, their leaders, having been elected to the balìa, were expecting to effect change from within the government and, therefore, it is doubtful that they would pose a danger to the Medici such as would prompt Machiavelli to write these words of warning. Moreover, the citizens of Florence did not despise either Ridolfi or Salviati. In fact, the opposite was true. Lorenzo Strozzi wrote glowingly of Ridolfi, saying that he was a person of great prudence and reputation, who possessed every civil quality and that he was unequalled.[104] Guicciardini was also very positive in his assessment of Ridolfi, declaring that he was a noble citizen, "reputed to be very wise," whom the people respected because of his great virtue, which gave him authority in the city, especially among the elite.[105]

At the time that Machiavelli wrote *Ai Palleschi*, and there is no reason to doubt Marchand's proposed dating of early November 1512,[106] Jacopo Salviati was leaving the city to take up his position as an ambassador to the papal court and therefore could not have posed much if any threat. But was Salviati in fact an enemy of Piero Soderini? Could he be considered one of Machiavelli's "enemies of Soderini"? Salviati had wholeheartedly endorsed Soderini's candidacy for the office of permanent *gonfaloniere di giustizia* in 1502.[107] It is true that afterwards Salviati grew disillusioned because of Soderini's increasing independence and his failure to continue the reform of the Florentine constitution that would have allowed *ottimati* more control of the affairs of the state, but it is doubtful that he harboured hatred for him personally. Even though Salviati is described as Soderini's political opponent, Butters believes that both Guicciardini and Nerli "tend to exaggerate the divide that separated Soderini from some of his opponents such as Salviati or Giovanbattista Ridolfi, and to see in it a rigidity of outline it did not possess."[108] Salviati, together with other *frateschi*, continued to hold high office during the Soderini regime, and twice Salviati was sent on important diplomatic missions, first to Cesare Borgia in 1503 and then to the king of Naples in 1506.[109] It must also be remembered that both men shared the common purpose of advancing the cause of the popular government.

Further proof that there was no enmity between Salviati and Soderini can be seen shortly after Cardinal Giovanni de' Medici was elevated to the papacy in March 1513 as Leo X. The new Medici pope, wanting to fulfill his obligation to Piero's brother Cardinal Francesco Soderini, who had helped to elect him, proposed a pardon for Piero and other members of the Soderini clan who had been exiled from Florence. Salviati was vigorous in his support for this plan, whereas his fellow Florentine, Bernardo Rucellai, a leading representative of the Florentine elite, who was described by Guicciardini as the "arch enemy" of Soderini,[110] was outraged by the mere suggestion and sent two emissaries from Florence to protest.[111] Moreover, not long after Soderini's arrival in Rome, where he had elected to take up permanent residence, he paid a visit to Jacopo Salviati's house.[112] While perhaps simply a courtesy visit, this encounter raises questions about the conclusions of Marchand and Butters that the enemies alluded to by Machiavelli in *Ai Palleschi* belonged to the *frateschi* faction. Most importantly, however, Machiavelli would of course have known of the close-knit friendships that existed between Ridolfi, Salviati, and Giuliano. If *Ai Palleschi* was indeed intended for Giuliano, there would be no reason for Machiavelli to warn him about his friends. Giuliano held no grudge against Piero Soderini either; immediately after his brother became pope, Giuliano, who was still in Florence at the time, wrote to Soderini's sister to express his gratitude and formally recognize all that Cardinal Soderini had done to help Giovanni become pope, advising her that his brother had given permission to Piero Soderini and all members of his family to return from exile.[113]

To complicate matters further, Machiavelli referred to the "ordine vechio" as the Medici's enemies in *Ai Palleschi*: "It is not Piero Soderini who is the enemy of this government, but the old order."[114] For most scholars, the "old order" appears once again to signify the *ottimati*. However, because Florence was such a fractious society, torn apart by political factions, it does seem important to be more specific about what he meant when he used the terms "enemies of Soderini" and the "old order" in his first partisan political tract.

That Machiavelli was taking aim at the "party of the friar" is doubtful. However, could Machiavelli's "enemies of Soderini" and the "old order" refer specifically to that patrician faction that had set itself apart from other *ottimati* and, in particular, apart from the *frateschi*, whom they disliked, in the struggle against Piero Soderini? These were the radical *palleschi* who had gravitated to the orbit of Bernardo Rucellai, whose deep-seated animosity towards Piero Soderini, stemming, according to Guicciardini, from personal, rather than political reasons, was well known. In addition to Piero Soderini, Bernardo Rucellai also detested the popular government.[115] Before Rucellai went into voluntary exile between 1506 and 1511, "because he could not tolerate the Gonfaloniere and his ways,"[116] a number of young patricians met in Rucellai's gardens, where they freely criticized the *gonfaloniere di giustizia* and his policies. There were rumours that Rucellai's son Giovanni, who had inherited his father's "mind and manners," was sent several times to Rome secretly to plot with the Medici because, as Guicciardini writes, "Rucellai's hatred for the Gonfaloniere was greater than his ancient enmity towards [the Medici]."[117] These radical *palleschi*, who Nerli says were well trained in the "school of the Rucellai gardens,"[118] had conspired with the exiled Medici against Piero Soderini, forcing him to resign on 31 August, and then complained bitterly to the cardinal at Campi regarding Giuliano's leadership. They also joined in with the Spanish troops on 16 September to seize the Palazzo della Signoria.

Of all the *palleschi*, perhaps Paolo Vettori, who according to Nerli, regularly attended the meetings in Rucellai's gardens, did the most to facilitate the return of the Medici, which would have brought upon himself the loathing of the people since they would have held him responsible for the loss of the popular government. In fact, Francesco Vettori's letter to his brother of 5 August 1513 refers specifically to the people's hatred of Paolo because of his participation in *parlamento*, stating that even Paolo's own relatives were ill disposed towards him, out of respect for Piero Soderini.[119] In the same letter, Francesco tells his brother that he had asked Giulio de' Medici (appointed archbishop of Florence in May 1513 by his cousin Leo X), who was about to return to Florence, to protect his brother because, of the three men who had forced Soderini's resignation, Paolo had the most reason to fear when members of the Soderini clan returned from exile to Florence. Unlike the other two *palleschi*, Baccio Valori and Antonfrancesco degli Albizzi, he had by far the fewest relatives to protect him and, as Francesco had already pointed out to his brother, because of their displeasure with his actions, Paolo would not be able to count on any of them for support.[120]

It is possible that, when Machiavelli wrote *Ai Palleschi*, he was thinking of the danger Paolo Vettori posed for Giuliano. Was Paolo the one who had been agitating for the Medici to attack the reputation of the exiled *gonfaloniere di giustizia* in November 1512? Did he wish to make Soderini appear evil to bring the people on his side and lessen their hostility toward him? Did Machiavelli have Paolo Vettori in mind when he wrote: "Some individuals who play the whore between the people and the Medici are very hostile to Soderini and would welcome the opportunity to denigrate him so that they can cast off the burden they bear with the people for having been its enemy"?[121] Was he in fact warning Giuliano about Paolo Vettori?

For Machiavelli, his dismissal from office and banishment from Florence signalled a bitter end to the public service that had been his vocation and livelihood, but this was not the worst of what was to come. Just a few months later, inconceivably, he would be imprisoned and tortured, being accused of conspiring with others to assassinate Giuliano de' Medici. The circumstances of this tragic event and the alleged conspiracy will be fully explored shortly. First, we will examine Giuliano's brief participation in the Florentine government that lasted until May 1513 when his brother Leo X compelled him to stay in Rome. Despite the constraints put upon him by his brother and the opposition from the *palleschi* faction, and measured by his wide popularity, Giuliano did succeed in bringing good government to the city with his politics of peace and reconciliation. Perhaps we will be able, at last, to see clearly that the negative connotations attached to Giuliano for so long are nothing but a part of a joint effort by his political opponents to ruin his reputation.

CHAPTER FIVE

GIULIANO, *CAPO* OF FLORENCE

Cardinal Giovanni de' Medici was without question the real authority behind the government of Florence after the return of his family to power, but following his election as Pope Leo X on 11 March 1513, his control over Florentine affairs became even stronger (Fig. 11). Shortly after the new pope's younger brother Giuliano arrived in Rome in May 1513 at the head of an official Florentine delegation sent to congratulate the recently elected pontiff, he relinquished his position of influence in Florence, perhaps by force, in favour of his young nephew Lorenzo (Fig. 12). Giuliano's removal from Florence points toward fundamental political differences between him and other members of his family. Alfonsina Orsini de' Medici, mother of Lorenzo and sister-in-law of Giuliano, confirmed as much in a letter dated 9 February 1514 and sent from Rome to her son in Florence, in which she described how the family was divided into two factions. On one side, she wrote, were Giuliano and his two sisters, Lucrezia, wife of Jacopo Salviati, and Contessina, married to Piero, a nephew of Giovanbattista Ridolfi (Fig. 8). On the other side were Giuliano's cousin Giulio di Giuliano (later Pope Clement VII), herself, her son Lorenzo, and Giuliano's third sister, Maddalena, and her husband, Franceschetto

Cybo (d. 1519), the illegitimate son of Pope Innocent VIII (d. 1492). Each faction, she informed her son, had its followers, "except that there are more of us and we are wiser."[1] This divide, caused by conflicting political ideologies, set Giuliano and his supporters, who wanted the republic with its broadly based government to continue, on one side, with other family members, who insisted on a more absolute rule, on the other. Alfonsina did not include Pope Leo X in either bloc, but there can be little doubt that he stood with her.

This political division within the Medici family has been overlooked, and many historians have consequently treated the Medici as a monolithic entity, with Giuliano seen as weak and lacking "aptitude for dealing with Florentine affairs."[2] Yet, in spite of all the constraints placed upon him by Cardinal Giovanni and the *palleschi* in Florence, Giuliano was nevertheless able to bring good government to this fractious city during his short involvement in its management from September 1512 until May 1513. He displayed moderation while exercising his power, and though his politics of reconciliation surely antagonized his opposition, it brought him widespread praise from the people of Florence.

A set of *Instructions* he seems to have written in Rome in the summer of 1513 for his nephew Lorenzo, who was about to return to Florence to take up his position of power, strongly suggests that Giuliano was neither apolitical and uninterested in governing Florence nor "a licentious dilettante [who] soon wearied of the responsibilities associated with governing, and [thus] moved to Rome."[3] These *Instructions* have either been neglected or not properly attributed to Giuliano. Tommaso Gar first published the text in full in 1844, attributing its authorship to Giuliano, whom he believed wrote the instructions at the command of the pope for their nephew, sent to take Giuliano's place at Florence.[4] Gar dated the text to between May and August 1513 and noted that Lorenzo the Magnificent had written a similar document, in the form of a letter, for his son Cardinal Giovanni when he left for Rome.[5] Some historians, however, discuss the instructions as though Leo X himself, or another of his advisers, was their author.[6] A close analysis of the text, however, indicates that Giuliano was, as Gar first suggested, responsible for the document, since several of its views on good governance are in line with Giuliano's thinking and not necessarily those of his brother. Moreover, the *Instructions* suggest that Giuliano had gained valuable insights about the governance of Florence, had understood the complex workings of government, and, most importantly, took his role as head of the government very seriously.

In the preamble we read that the author "will record for Lorenzo, *figliolo carissimo*, what is in his opinion, from the little time he has lived in Florence, all that to him was useful and necessary to know about governing the city," and that he is giving Lorenzo "a way to use your power more lightly so that you will be better able to think of the health and preservation of our country."[7] At the end of a fairly long discourse that gives full particulars on the care Lorenzo must take in leading Florence, the author says that he is writing these instructions to "satisfy the command of the pope," thus suggesting that the document was not penned by Leo X directly.[8] Given the familiarity of the instructions' language, and various references to Medici relations, the most likely candidate for the text's authorship is, as Gar first suggested, Giuliano himself. Were the document written by another papal adviser, one would expect either a more formal tone or reference to the Medici only in the third person. Similarly, if the voice were to be Leo's, there would be no need to indicate that the document was written on the pope's behalf. Even though Giuliano states clearly that he writes on behalf of his brother, it becomes evident that his primary concern was to curb Lorenzo's autocratic inclinations, in the hope that his young nephew would not cause harm to the prestige of Florence's great patrician families or offend their dignity.

Lorenzo di Piero il Giovane was only two years old when the Medici were expelled from Florence in 1494, and he grew up mostly in Rome among his Orsini relatives in an environment of aristocratic privilege and rituals that were in every sense alien to the republican customs and mercantile mentality of the Florentines.[9] His politically ambitious mother, Alfonsina, had, moreover, long encouraged her son's seigniorial tendencies. She had never been satisfied with his social standing and was always seeking ways to advance his political and financial fortunes.[10] Giuliano had good reason to fear, therefore, that Lorenzo would repeat his father Piero's mistakes and entertain the idea of turning Florence into a principate (which indeed transpired a few years later).

In writing this guide for Lorenzo, the author recounts his own experiences, and the text is clearly personal, describing situations that had "often happened" to him. For example, when there was discord among the magistrates, a frequent occurrence, he would swiftly intervene to remedy the situation by putting in some "good words."[11] To acquaint Lorenzo with the workings of the republic, the author gives a detailed analysis of its three principal magistracies, which had been allowed to continue to function, presumably in order to preserve the outward appearance of the republic, although power was invested in the Dieci di Balìa, whose members had been hand-picked by Cardinal Giovanni, now the pope. The *Instructions* list the Signoria (eight elected priors) and the office of *gonfaloniere di giustizia*, the Dieci di Balìa, and the Otto di Guardia. Albertini found it rather strange that the *Instructions* do not discuss the balìa in depth and suggested that Leo X may have reserved for himself and his cousin Giulio control of this council.[12] On the other hand, this omission is likely additional proof of Giuliano's authorship, since it reflects his own thinking that the *balìa* should not have so much power and his hope that it would be short-lived. The absence of the *balìa* from the text supports the notion that its main purpose was to educate Lorenzo about the traditional republican institutions of Florence, which, Giuliano surely hoped, would earn his nephew's respect.

In describing his experiences in dealing with the magistrates of these various councils, Giuliano emphasized how important it was for his nephew to win Medici friends in all the key magistracies, and how it would be necessary to employ spies and informants to keep him apprised of the developments taking place in each one. To assist him, the author recommends that Lorenzo use the services of Niccolò Michelozzi (1444–1526), Machiavelli's replacement as a secretary in the chancery. Michelozzi was loyal and highly experienced, having served in the same capacity in the previous period of Medicean dominance, when he acted as Lorenzo the Magnificent's confidential secretary. The *Instructions* urge Lorenzo to pay special attention when choosing a *gonfaloniere di giustizia*, because this officer must be selected from among the most respected citizens and have the highest social standing in the city, given that he would have authority over all the other magistrates.[13] Whatever Lorenzo does, Giuliano warns, he must be careful not to offend the dignity of the great patrician families who are "used to having the state" by giving offices to those who have less social standing.[14] Giuliano's own choice of *gonfaloniere* had been his in-law Giovanbattista Ridolfi, one of the former republic's most respected and influential citizens, whose reputation, both within and outside of Florence, was, according to Guicciardini, unequalled.[15]

Although he no longer took part in running the government of Florence, Giuliano demonstrates through the *Instructions* that he still cared a great deal about the city and the welfare of its citizens and wanted to instill in his nephew a respect both for the constitutional forms of the republic and for the traditional claims to authority of the great houses in the city. The text refers to how things were "in the government of my father [Lorenzo the Magnificent] and then of yours [my brother Piero]."[16] Yet Giuliano's advice to his nephew goes far beyond the practices of his father, whose position in the Florentine republic, as the grandson of the most powerful of all the patricians Cosimo il Vecchio, had always been an awkward one, since Lorenzo the Magnificent held neither official nor constitutional office and his family's pre-eminence depended largely upon the tacit approval of the city's leading families.

Following the turbulent events of the Pazzi Conspiracy in 1478, however, when Lorenzo and his younger brother Giuliano were attacked during Sunday Mass in the cathedral – Lorenzo survived with a wound to his neck but Giuliano succumbed to seventeen stabbings – Lorenzo became much more autocratic. Instead of seeking *ottimati* opinions as he had done in the past, he increasingly took unilateral decisions that in turn alienated the *ottimati*. He tightened his grip on all aspects of the government by establishing in 1480 the Council of Seventy, whose members, sworn to secrecy, were responsible for making important decisions. By concentrating power in fewer hands, he did as much as he could to keep the *ottimati* down.[17] Lorenzo felt that he could no longer trust them and was in constant fear that the patricians who had the greatest wealth and power and extensive family connections would challenge him and deprive him of his position. It was this suspicion and mistrust of *ottimati*, Guicciardini writes, that was the elder Lorenzo's greatest fault, leading him to promote reliable but mediocre men with little power or status in their own right who would not pose any threat to him. Such was the case of Bartolomeo Scala, Lorenzo's chancellor, whom he made *gonfaloniere di giustizia* in 1486, "much to the outrage and contempt of all the leading citizens" since Scala was the son of a provincial miller.[18] Giuliano's political strategy, as outlined in the *Instructions*, especially in relation to choosing a *gonfaloniere di giustizia*, shows that he did not wish to follow his father's practice of putting pressure on men wholly beholden to him but tried instead to move Florence closer to an elitist form of government, where *ottimati* could return to their traditional role of participating in a meaningful way.

The magistrates of the Dieci di Balìa, in charge of foreign policy, should also be men of great reputation and experience, the *Instructions* explain.

Again, in sharp contrast to the practices of Lorenzo the Magnificent, the document notes that it is not always necessary to choose Medici loyalists because in the magistracy it is much more important to have people of genuine merit and ability.[19] "For me," Giuliano counselled, "there is none better than Jacopo Salviati [my brother-in-law through Lucrezia] and Lanfredino [di Jacopo Lanfredini]."[20] It is clear that Giuliano was hoping that his nephew would heed advice from these two pre-eminent men of the political class. The recommendation of Salviati points again toward Giuliano's authorship since it seems unlikely that a member of the opposing Medici/Orsini faction would recommend him. Indeed, as made clear in the aforementioned letter from his mother, Alfonsina, relations between Lorenzo the Younger and Salviati were far from cordial.[21] Jacopo Salviati was forced to leave Florence and take up the post of Florentine ambassador to Rome, but in August 1513 Leo X gave him permission to return to Florence, after Giuliano was permanently domiciled in Rome.

Barely two months after the return of Lorenzo and Salviati to the city, dissension arose between them. Lorenzo wrote in confidence to his uncle Giulio in Rome, who in September became a cardinal, complaining bitterly about how Jacopo was objecting strongly to a marriage he was arranging between the Salviati and Alamanni families, a matter about which Cardinal Giulio was apparently fully aware. Having been elevated to an influential political role in Florence, Lorenzo was following in the footsteps of his grandfather, who in his day was the prime marriage broker in the city, arranging marriages between Florentine patricians as a way of building political alliances.[22] Lorenzo related to Giulio how Salviati had threatened him, saying that if Lorenzo forced the issue Salviati would appeal directly to the pope and to Giuliano for help, knowing they would always take his side against their nephew.[23] However, and not surprisingly to anyone save perhaps Salviati, the pope decided in favour of his nephew, and the contested marriage was concluded in December.[24]

In February 1514 Alfonsina reported to her son that his aunt Lucrezia de' Medici Salviati was deeply upset about how he was treating her husband and had pleaded with her brother the pope to recall Jacopo to Rome, for not only was Lorenzo forcing marriages on the free citizens of Florence, he was at the same time insulting her husband. Alfonsina appears to have had little respect for her sister-in-law, saying to Lorenzo: "In truth, Lucrezia has not been taken seriously by the pope [and] the Cardinal [Giulio] …

or by anyone else here, even by the foreigners, and no one has any regard for her."[25] Replying a few days later, Lorenzo protested that he had never been disrespectful toward his uncle Jacopo, although he added that, as far as he was concerned, he would not be disappointed if Salviati were recalled to Rome.[26]

Another major magistracy that Lorenzo had to consider carefully was the Otto di Guardia, responsible for criminal justice. Again, the *Instructions* emphasize how essential it was to know exactly what transpired during every deliberation. Giuliano gives the example of his use of the chancellor of the Otto, Ser Zanobi del Pace, who had been, like Michelozzi, a trusted servant of Lorenzo the Magnificent. Ser Zanobi, who would later be elected on 28 June 1525 as notary to the republic,[27] served as Giuliano's personal informant, reporting back to him on every new event.[28] He intervened on Giuliano's behalf when there was discord among the magistrates and passed on instructions from Giuliano to the Otto. This relationship lends further credence to the theory that it was Giuliano, through the *Instructions*, who recommended that Lorenzo was not to pervert the course of justice either for favours or for money, that he was to ensure that any punishment was just, and that, when the Otto di Guardia was judging crimes against the state, its verdicts had to be vetted.[29] The *Instructions* declare that the ban on carrying weapons must be rigidly enforced and that Lorenzo must disarm his guards in order not to provoke the resentment of those citizens who had been deprived of their right to bear arms.[30] Lorenzo the Magnificent had also prohibited the carrying of weapons in the city after the Pazzi Conspiracy, but he made exceptions for himself, his supporters, and his bodyguards. In this context, it is interesting to note that one of the first laws to be passed by the popular government after the fall of the Medici in 1494 was one that restored the ancient right of all citizens to bear arms, so that they could fight and defend themselves against the enemies of their liberty.[31] The *Instructions*' provocative call for the indiscriminate prohibition of arms was the source of great anger among radical Mediceans, a fact that offers further support for Giuliano's authorship of the document. Indeed, Cerretani would criticize Giuliano for mismanaging the state governance with such a weapons ban in his *Dialogo della mutatione di Firenze*.[32]

The *Instructions* reminded Lorenzo of his duties toward all the people living in the state of Florence, not only in the city proper. He must never make himself scarce when it came to conducting audiences, and he must give them to any who wanted them, whether citizens, women, peasants, or even the poor. Giuliano warned that the people will pester him with infinite requests and, although he tells Lorenzo that he must be open in hearing them all, he warns him not to make too many promises and only to grant favours to those who merit them. Above all, he must never offend nor oppress the poor or the peasantry.[33] The *Instructions* emphasized to Lorenzo that he must be prepared to give the people the opportunity to solicit favours, especially since they had been deprived of government participation. Lorenzo rejected this advice, for not long after he took the helm, complaints arrived in Rome concerning his mismanagement, especially when it came to granting audiences. Letters, including one from Cardinal Giulio, were sent from Rome in February and March 1514 to Lorenzo, urging him to set aside an hour every morning and evening for audiences.[34]

As this analysis of the *Instructions* to Lorenzo makes apparent, Giuliano was its likely author, who based his advice on his own experience in the day-to-day running of the government. Claims that he lacked either understanding of or interest in the politics of Florence are indeed unjustified. His direct involvement in governing the city can be found in various actions during the few months when he was guiding the affairs of government, prior to his recall to Rome. Though often minor, Giuliano's acts of governance show him to be engaged, above all in the promotion of political reconciliation.

In the fifteenth century, the Medici were known to use small committees to introduce arbitrary tax assessments,[35] and this practice was reintroduced early on in their restoration when tax concessions were used to reward clients and loyal supporters.[36] Unfair taxation could also be used as a weapon against those citizens who were perceived to be unsympathetic to the Medici. It appears that this may have been the case with Ludovico Buonarroti, the father of Michelangelo. In October 1512 Ludovico wrote to Michelangelo, who was in Rome finishing the frescoes of the Sistine Chapel ceiling for Pope Julius II, complaining that he was being assessed a new tax of sixty ducats, an amount he was unable to pay. Ludovico may have been singled out because, as Michelangelo revealed in a letter he wrote to his father the same month, there were rumours circulating in Florence that the artist had uttered disparaging remarks about the Medici. Michelangelo wrote: "As to the matter of the Medici, I have never said a single thing against them except in the way that every man did generally, as over the affair of Prato, which the stones would have talked of too, if they had known how to talk."[37] Upon hearing back from his father, Michelangelo replied, saying that he thought the sixty-ducat fee was a "dishonest" charge and that he had "suffered very much over it."[38] With his letter, the artist enclosed a separate two-line note addressed to Giuliano, advising his father, "Read them, and if you would like to take them to him, take them to him, and you will see if they help at all" to have the fine forgiven.[39]

Michelangelo, four years older than Giuliano, would have known him well from the time when the young sculptor lived in the Medici palace from 1490 until 1492, one of a number of Florentine artists who were members of Lorenzo the Magnificent's household. Michelangelo's service continued under Piero di Lorenzo until October 1494, when the artist left for Venice, one month before the Medici were exiled.[40] Michelangelo feared that his father and brothers would be treated badly, and he worried about them living under the new government. He hoped that his short note to Giuliano would relieve his father of the sixty-ducat fee. If Giuliano does not help, Michelangelo wrote, Ludovico should think about which of their possessions "might be sold, and we can go and live elsewhere."[41]

Fortunately, it was not necessary for them to take this drastic step because it appears that Giuliano did intervene on behalf of Ludovico, who was able to inform his son that he had been absolved from paying the tax.[42] Ludovico wrote to Giuliano directly, a few months later, asking to be reinstated as comptroller of customs, a position given to him by Lorenzo the Magnificent but lost following the Medici expulsion.[43] While it is difficult to ascertain whether Giuliano was able to accommodate Ludovico's request, the mere fact that Ludovico felt free to write to him personally does indicate that Giuliano was fulfilling expectations of leadership, participating in the patronage network of the city, and involving himself in the dispensing and brokering of favours and largesse. Cerretani would take specific aim at Giuliano on this subject in his *Dialogo della mutatione*, using Giovanni Rucellai to declare that Giuliano's mild nature made him inclined to grant all manner of requests such that disorder would soon set in. Cerretani unfavourably compared Giuliano to his cousin Giulio, whose patience, caution, and sense of justice counterbalanced what he saw as Giuliano's inadequacies.[44]

There were other instances, besides the one involving Ludovico Buonarroti, when Giuliano intervened to protect the welfare of citizens. Such was the case of Giovacchino Guasconi, *gonfaloniere di giustizia* when *condottiere* Paolo Vitelli was executed for treason. Vitelli had been appointed captain-general of the Florentine forces in 1498, specifically to wage war against the rebellious maritime city of Pisa. Vitelli was accused, however, of collaborating with foreign powers to lose the war and of colluding with the Medici. While blockading Bibbiena, he was suspected of conducting negotiations with the exiled rebels Piero and Giuliano de' Medici.[45] Although the Florentine government possessed no hard evidence that treason had been committed, and many at the time thought Vitelli innocent of all charges,[46] he was brought back to Florence, tortured for twenty-four hours, and, having confessed to nothing, beheaded in the early evening of 1 October 1499.[47] The Vitelli, lords of Città di Castello, held ancient family ties to the Medici and were much in their favour, always supporting the Medici cause. Vitello Vitelli, nephew of the executed Paolo, was one of the leading mercenary captains who rode into Florence with Cardinal de' Medici on 14 September 1512. He took part in the seizure of the palace on 16 September and continued to serve Cardinal Giovanni after he became Leo X.[48]

After the execution of Paolo Vitelli, members of his family had been agitating for revenge, and it would have been easy for Giuliano to give in to their demands. Instead, he gave Guasconi, who was now living in fear for his life, full protection.[49] Having been in Bibbiena, where the alleged treason took place, Giuliano would have known whether Vitelli colluded with his brother Piero, but this clearly was not an issue in 1512. As an influential figure in the state, Giuliano's principal concern was to stop private vendettas and family feuds that would cause disorder in Florence. Giuliano's protection of Guasconi was consistent with his earlier attempts to prevent acts of vendetta, such as when he protected citizens on 16 September during the seizure of the palace. Nardi records that Giuliano tried to reassure Guasconi "and with great gentleness, promised on his own faith that no harm would come to him and that his order would be respected."[50]

As we study Giuliano's actions, it becomes clear that his aim was to pursue the same policy of rapprochement followed by his brother and their cousin Giulio. A majority of citizens had been content with their Great Council and were proud of their two centuries of republican government. Consequently, they remained largely antagonistic towards the Medici. Having already made peaceful overtures to the rival, cadet branch of the Medici, Giuliano now wished to extend the same offer of reconciliation to all those in the city who were traditionally opposed to his family in order to show that he harboured no resentment, even toward his most intractable enemies. This is why he made a very public visit to the house of the austere republican soldier, Antonio Giacomini (1456–1518), who had fought against him in the Casentino during the failed Medici campaign of 1498–99. Everyone knew that Giacomini and his family had suffered long periods of exile at the hands of the Medici in the fifteenth century and that Giacomini was unremitting in his hatred toward them. Giacomini had a most distinguished career as general commissioner of the army during the second republic, and in their admiring biographies both Jacopo Nardi and Jacopo Pitti recorded Giuliano's surprising visit to Giacomini, which must have caused a great stir in Florence.[51] Pitti says that Giuliano went to Giacomini's house because he was full of admiration for the old soldier's valour and integrity, and that he listened patiently as Giacomini, now very old, blind, and suffering from old wounds, lamented the changes that had taken place in the republic, whose liberty, regrettably, he could no longer defend. In an effort to console him, Giuliano spoke many words of affection and said that he too had high hopes for Florence. He would not have sought to return, he declared, if it was not within his power to demonstrate how much he was a devoted son of the city. Considering Giacomini's age and the fame that surrounded him, Giuliano then made an important concession to the old warrior, proclaiming that, as long as he was in charge of the state, Giacomini would be permitted to keep in his house the arms that he had won in war, a privilege that was not extended to others in the city, especially those whose loyalty to the Medici was under suspicion.[52]

Giuliano's conciliatory gesture towards the old warrior appears to have been part of his wider political strategy to bring his enemies around, but he may have wished to pay special tribute to this gallant soldier after having had conversations with Machiavelli, who was, in the early months of the Medici restoration, still serving as second chancellor. For Machiavelli, Giacomini represented the ideal of bravery and self-sacrifice.[53] Apart from Giacomini's steadfast dedication to the cause of Florentine liberty, Machiavelli also revered him because he had been one of the earliest and most vocal supporters of the secretary's militia project.[54] In 1514, when Machiavelli wrote his Second Decennale, recounting Florentine history from 1504 to 1509,[55] he eulogized Giacomini in the following lines:

> And Giacomino, through his virtue, through his fate, attained
> glory and renown as much as ever did private citizen.
> For his native city this man bore much, and long he sustained
> with great justice your army's dignity.
> Covetous of honour, generous with money, and capable of such
> virtue he is, that he merits honour much higher than I give him.
> Now neglected and scorned he lies in his house, poor, old and
> blind. So greatly displeasing to Fortune is he who does well.[56]

Any lingering sentiment in government for this old warrior disappeared entirely after Giuliano's departure from Florence in May 1513, for under the new Medici governance the city indeed became a hostile place for such republican heroes as Giacomini, who died in abject misery in 1518.

In mid-November 1512, in an attempt to win over the citizens, Giuliano decided to form a company of his peers who would be responsible for staging public spectacles that had been so much a part of the Laurentian age, especially during the last years of Lorenzo the Magnificent's life.[57] Giuliano's intention was not only to gain the support of citizens by fostering a general sense of optimism and well-being; he also, perhaps more importantly for him, wanted to channel the destructive energies of the young nobles, who as a group had traditionally participated in the production of these elaborate spectacles, so that they would not, as Machiavelli warned in his *Ai Palleschi*, be so ready to "bite" him.[58] Guicciardini must be exaggerating when he says that when Lorenzo the Magnificent was alive, "every day, the people were treated to shows, feasts, and novelties."[59] Machiavelli, emphasizing the political significance of these public spectacles during the time of Lorenzo, also writes in his *Florentine Histories* that "he kept his fatherland always in festivities: there frequent jousts and representations of old deeds and triumphs were to be seen; and his aim was to keep the city in abundance, the people united, and the nobility honoured."[60]

The idea for public festivals that included floats drawn by animals through the streets of Florence was inspired by the example of classical models of imperial Rome. Although Lorenzo the Magnificent's engagement in these public spectacles had been sporadic, in the last years of his life, he seems to have shown a renewed interest in triumphal pageantry.[61] He financed the Seven Triumphal Pageants of the Seven Planets, as described by Ptolemy, during Carnival in 1490, for which he wrote *canzoni*, as well as during the *festa* of 1491 celebrating St John the Baptist's day on 24 June. For this last festival, Lorenzo's Compagnia della Stella, now operating as the Confraternity of the Magi, organized a magnificent civic spectacle on a theme that was invented by Lorenzo himself. It was the first non-Christian subject ever to be performed on the feast day of San Giovanni. It consisted of a procession of fifteen floats pulled by forty or fifty pairs of oxen, recounting how Paulus Æmilus returned to Rome in triumph after conquering the East and bringing so much treasure that Romans did not pay any taxes for the subsequent fifty years.[62] This dazzling and costly spectacle must have impressed the citizens, who would have identified Lorenzo with the glory and magnificence of Paulus Æmilus and thus seen him as the source of the city's wealth – a point, no doubt, he clearly wanted to make.

Giuliano surely did not forget these spectacles of his youth and the very positive effect they had had on the morale of the populace. Cerretani described how Giuliano invited thirty-six young nobles to dine with him one evening at the Medici palace, almost all of them being the sons of those who had former dealings with Lorenzo the Magnificent's company. Addressing his guests, Giuliano reminded them of how his father and their families had previously "happily entertained the city," ordering a festival to be prepared for the coming Carnival. To honour the memory of his father, Giuliano gave the name *Diamante* to his company, after Lorenzo's personal emblem of a diamond ring. Giuliano's young nephew Lorenzo attended the dinner, but he chose not to join his uncle's company, preferring instead to organize a competing company of his own, made up of young men of his own generation and social rank, among whom, according to Cerretani, there was no lack of those who persuaded Lorenzo to believe that, as Piero's son, the eldest of Lorenzo the Magnificent's three male children, the city rightfully belonged to him.[63] Lorenzo called his company the Broncone, a reference to the device of a truncated branch of laurel sprouting new leaves. Lorenzo the Magnificent had made the laurel (*l'alloro*) his personal emblem, since the eternal evergreen (appropriated from Petrarch's Laura) was a play on his name Laurentius – Laurus – Lauro.[64] The younger Lorenzo's father, Piero, had a *broncone* embroidered on his vest to signify a resurgence of the Medici, and the same device appeared again on the floats decorated by Lorenzo di Piero's Compagnia del Broncone.[65]

The Broncone parade took place on 6 February 1513, followed two days later by that of Giuliano's Diamante. The chronicler Jacopo Nardi, given the task of inventing a theme for Lorenzo's company, chose the Triumph of the Golden Age. Nardi knew that association would be made to the age of his grandfather Lorenzo the Magnificent, since the poets in his humanist circle had frequently invoked the ancient myth of bounty and liberality in order to flatter him. An example would be Aurelio Lippi Brandolini, who wrote:

> The golden age owes less to Saturn, and Augustus's
> glorious age less to him, than ours, made golden by
> your bounty, acknowledges to you, to you, Lorenzo.[66]

Clearly, the theme was carefully chosen for its propaganda value. By reviving the idea of a coming age of gold, Lorenzo the grandson, conflating his name with that of his grandfather, thereby appropriated the elder's magnificence and publicly proclaimed that he, and not Giuliano, was the legitimate inheritor of Lorenzo the Magnificent's state.

Giorgio Vasari, the sixteenth-century biographer of numerous Italian artists, gives the fullest account of the Carnival of 1513 in his life of Jacopo Pontormo, describing how no cost was spared to excite and delight the people.[67] Using Roman models, Nardi created an elaborate allegory that highlighted the new Medici government in the form of seven extravagantly decorated triumphal wagons, designed and painted by some of the most notable artists in the city, including Pontormo and Andrea del Sarto.[68] The carts were drawn through the streets by an assortment of horses, oxen, buffaloes, and heifers, some disguised as winged griffins or elephants while others were lavishly draped with the skins of lions, tigers, and wolves, their claws gleaming with gold paint. The first float showed the figures of Saturn and Janus, rulers of the original Golden Age with Fury tamed under their feet, followed by five Roman triumphs: Numa Pompilius, second king of the Romans and founder of religion and laws; Titus Manlius Torquatus, Roman consul after the end of the first Carthaginian War, when Rome was at the height of her prosperity and virtue; Julius Caesar Octavianus, triumphing on his victory over Cleopatra; Augustus, accompanied on horseback by six pairs of poets who had bestowed upon him eternal fame; and Trajan, the Roman emperor who embodied the idea of the just ruler. The seventh wagon, didactically proclaiming the Return of the Golden Age, showed a huge globe on top of which a man, lying face down as if dead and wearing rusted armour, represented the Age of Iron. From his back a gilded naked boy emerged to symbolize the new Age of Gold that would bring the promise of future happiness for all the people.[69] Scores of noble youths, splendidly attired in sumptuous costumes appropriate for each subject, accompanied the glittering wagons that were in turn illuminated by hundreds of torchbearers. Lorenzo's Broncone had mounted a splendid spectacle, so much so that Cerretani, writing many years after the event, could remark that everyone thought that they were once more living in the time of Lorenzo the Magnificent,[70] a result that was intended to bolster the younger Lorenzo's standing in the city and the claim of his faction that he, and not his uncle Giuliano, was the rightful heir.

The humanist Andrea Dazzi, who since 1502 had lectured in Greek and Latin studies at the University of Florence, was given the responsibility of designing the parade of Giuliano's Diamante company held two days later. He selected a more modest theme of Time and Change, as symbolized by the Three Ages of Man. Even though five hundred torches accompanied the three pageant wagons, representing Boyhood, Manhood, and Old Age, the smaller parade, compared to Lorenzo's seven carts, must have struck many onlookers as anti-climatic, even melancholic, dwelling as it did on the transitory nature of youth and the inevitability of death. Antonio Alamanni composed a poem for the occasion that began, "Round and round go the years, the months, and the hours," and concluded with "everything at last then dies."[71] How much Giuliano was involved in selecting this theme is not known, and he might have simply trusted Dazzi to choose one that was appropriate, but in this case he does not seem to have been well served by the professor.[72] Lorenzo had exerted tremendous effort and far greater cost than his uncle's Diamante, showing his increasing jealousy of Giuliano's position in Florence and his determination to set himself up as his rival.

The Carnival of February 1513 offered the perfect occasion for Giuliano to continue a tradition of his father and great-grandfather Cosimo through the commission of a portrait medal that would not only commemorate his return to Florence but also assert his own claims to power. Honouring contemporary rulers and family members with portrait medals was concentrated primarily in the Renaissance princely courts of Milan, Naples, Mantua, Rimini, and the Este court at Ferrara, reflecting the growing interest in the culture of imperial Rome, especially as a precedent for their own claims to absolute power.[73] Together with painted profile portraits, medals appeared as part of the new and rapidly expanding cult of fame, in particular imitating Roman imperial coins.[74]

A comparison of medals struck for Cosimo and Lorenzo the Magnificent, together with one created for Giuliano during the Carnival of 1513, is both instructive and illuminating and provides further important insight into Giuliano's political aspirations in Florence. After Cosimo's death on 1 August 1464, a communal decision conferred upon him the honorific title *pater patriae* (Father of the Country), a title derived from republican Rome. It reflected Cosimo's unique position in a republic where he held no constitutional title to power. The edict issued in March 1465 represents Cosimo as one who had possessed "the greatest virtue, benevolence and piety" and who had "conferred upon the Florentine republic innumerable benefits in times of both war and peace, and always with absolute piety preserved his *patria*."[75] The creator of Cosimo's bronze medal, which exists in two slightly different versions, is unknown. First cast between 1465 and 1469, the medals show Cosimo in profile on one side and an allegory of Florence on the other. The obverse bears a portrait likeness of his aged profile head facing left, wearing a flat cap that is broad at the top (Fig. 22). The inscription around Cosimo's head reads: MAGNVS COSMVS MEDICES P[RIMUS] P[ATER] P[ATRIAE] (Cosimo de' Medici the Great, First Father of the Country).[76] The reverse shows a woman facing left, wearing a tunic, mantle, and veil in the classical style (Fig. 23). She sits on an antique Roman folding chair, which rests on the Medici yoke, a symbol of reconciliation. She holds an orb, which could also be seen as a Medici *palla*, in her outstretched right hand and in her left a sceptre in the form of a triple olive branch. Her elbow is bent and rests on the back of the chair. At the bottom she is identified with the inscription FLORENTIA. The inscription around her reads: PAX LIBERTAS QVE PVBLICA (Public Peace and Liberty). This inscription acknowledges Cosimo's part in creating stability in the city and peace in Florence's relations with the other Italian states.[77]

Lorenzo the Magnificent's medal, attributed to Niccolò Fiorentino, was created in 1490, two years before his death.[78] The obverse shows Lorenzo looking left (Fig. 24). Compared to the fine carving of Cosimo's features, his are more crudely modelled, and Fiorentino's blunt realism accurately depicts the rather coarse features of Lorenzo's face and his flattened nose. He is shown without a hat, and his long, striated hair reaches down to the collar of his gown. There seems to be a concern to show more of his upper torso than in Cosimo's medal, undoubtedly to emphasize that he is wearing the Florentine *lucco*, with its plain collar and soft folds, identifying him, not as a prince but as a citizen of Florence. The inscription around reads: MAGNVS LAVRENTIVS MEDICES (Lorenzo de' Medici, the Great). The reverse shows a woman, identified as FLORENTIA by the inscription across the lower field (Fig. 25). She sits upright on a rock, facing to the right, her back supported by the trunk of a laurel tree, which was Lorenzo's personal symbol. On closer inspection, however, the trunk seems to be growing out of her drapery, in order to emphasize the idea that Lorenzo has total authority and that Florence and the Medici are one. The trunk rises up and its branches extend over Florentia's head to become a flourishing canopy of laurel leaves, symbolizing Lorenzo's protective reach over the entire city. She has long, striated hair, wears a tunic and mantle, and holds in her outstretched right hand a stalk of three Florentine lilies, while her left hand clasps the edge of her mantle to reveal the flowers gathered in her lap. The inscription around reads: TVTELA PATRI[A]E (Protector of the Homeland).[79] In Lorenzo's medal, the theme has changed from one proclaiming the ideal of Public Peace and Liberty to one of Protection, reflecting his determination, in the face of insecurities caused by the Pazzi Conspiracy, to hold on to power. The iconographic source for Florentia sitting under a laurel tree is Poliziano's *Stanze Cominciate per la Giostra del Magnifico Giuliano de' Medici* (Giuliano's uncle and namesake, assassinated in the Pazzi Conspiracy of 1478). Poliziano composed his poem between 1475 and 1478, where he addresses the honouree's brother Lorenzo:

> And you, well-born Laurel, under whose shelter happy Florence rests in peace, fearing neither winds nor threats of heaven, nor irate Jove in his angriest countenance: receive my humble voice, trembling and fearful, under the shade of your sacred trunk; o cause, o goal of all my desires, which draw life only from the fragrance of your leaves.[80]

The maker of Giuliano's medal is not known. Like the medals of his father and great-grandfather before him, the obverse shows Giuliano's profile head and shoulders facing left (Fig. 26). As in the case of his father's medal, Giuliano wears a soft pleated garment with a simple collar, recognizable as the traditional civic *lucco* that distinguishes him as a citizen of the Florentine republic. Also like Lorenzo, Giuliano is clean-shaven according to Florentine custom, and he wears a flat cap with the back turned up. His head is held high, and his jaw is thrust forward, giving him an air of confidence. His benign expression contrasts sharply with that of Lorenzo, who, looking straight ahead, has a severe expression consistent with his role as the city's protector.

Most assume that Giuliano's medal was struck in Rome to commemorate his receipt of Roman citizenship, an elaborate ceremony performed by his brother Leo X on 13 September 1513 on the Campidoglio, Rome's civic centre. This conjecture originated with George Hill, who transcribed the inscription on the obverse as: IVLIANVS MEDICES. L[AURENTI] F[ILIUS] P[ATRICIUS] R[OMANUS] (Giuliano de' Medici, son of Lorenzo, Roman Patrician), a reading that has been widely accepted.[81] However, given Giuliano's Florentine costume on the obverse, and the presentation of Florentia on the reverse (Fig. 27), it seems that the transcription instead should read, as Giuliano's biographer Guiseppe Fatini first proposed, *Laurentii Filius Pater Reipublicae* (Son of Lorenzo, Father of the Republic).[82] Indeed, the inclusion of Florentia and his local costume make little sense if Giuliano were now permanently domiciled in Rome and the medal honoured his new home. Indeed, in this medal Giuliano is not the Roman patrician but is commemorated as Lorenzo's son and his heir as father of the Florentine republic, giving him legitimacy to rule Florence, represented allegorically on the medal's reverse.

Furthermore, several small medals show a bust portrait of Giuliano looking much like a Roman emperor with personifications of Rome on the reverse side (Figs. 28 and 29). Given their small size, a little over three centimetres, these medals were likely struck in 1513 for distribution among the crowds celebrating Giuliano's admission to the Roman citizenry and patriciate.[83] More like large coins in size and weight, these much smaller medals should be associated with Giuliano the Roman Patrician, not the larger, Florence-themed one. Some scholars have suggested that the larger medal's reverse showing Florentia reclining on a Medici coat of arms refers to Giuliano's return to Florence in September 1512,[84] a dating more consistent with the allegory, inscription, and costume. Shown as a son of the

Florentine republic, the medal was likely struck sometime between his September return and his departure for Rome in May 1513, after which the smaller, Roman-themed medals were created.

In contrast to Lorenzo's personification of Florentia, who is seated in profile view (Fig. 25), the reverse of Giuliano's medal shows her reclining, supporting her head with her bent right arm resting on top of a Medici shield emblazoned with six *palle* (Fig. 27). Her relaxed body is turned toward the front as she calmly contemplates the viewer. Although she is not explicitly identified by name, this allegorical figure is surely Florentia. A laurel tree, an allusion to Lorenzo, grows out of the Medici shield. Placed at the extreme left of the composition, the tree is much less noticeable and prominent than that shown in Lorenzo's medal. Even more significantly, its branches no longer offer protection to Florentia. The smaller tree, placed in the background, conveys the idea that the time of Lorenzo has passed to his legitimate successor Giuliano, who brings peace to Florence, but only because Florentia, resting on the family shield, relies upon the protective might of the Medici.

The inscription around her reads: RECONCILIATIS CIVIBVS MAGNIFICENTIA E[T] PIETA[T]E (Citizens having been reconciled [because of] generosity and respect). Unlike the protection afforded by a stern Lorenzo the Magnificent, under Giuliano, Florentia is now at perfect peace, signified by her relaxed pose and announcement of generous and respectful reconciliation. The medal emphasizes the qualities that Giuliano exhibited during his short tenure as head of the Florentine republic, which strongly suggests his involvement in devising its iconography. The most appropriate, and perhaps only, occasion for Giuliano to commission such a commemorative medal would have been during the Carnival of 1513, when he was still guiding the affairs of the state. Viewed in this context, the medal takes on great historical value because it shows Giuliano as a strong Florentine leader, experience that enabled him to write his *Instructions* shortly thereafter in August 1513. We have already seen how he strove to bring fair and balanced government to the city, and there is no doubt that he would have achieved this goal – as well as peace and reconciliation among the citizenry – but for the actions of other members of his family. Only days after the Carnival celebrations were concluded, as we shall see in the next chapter, Giuliano's life changed dramatically, when he was removed from his position as head of the government, in favour of Lorenzo di Piero, his autocratic nephew.

CHAPTER SIX

GIULIANO AND THE BOSCOLI-CAPPONI CONSPIRACY

Immediately following the Carnival celebrations of 1513, two events occurred that not only put an end to Giuliano's attempt to create concord and consensus among the citizens of Florence, but also led to his permanent removal to Rome. The first was the execution, on the orders of Cardinal Giovanni de' Medici, of two Florentine noblemen who were accused of conspiring to assassinate Giuliano. Even more momentous was the election of his brother as pope on 11 March (Fig. 11). The Boscoli-Capponi Conspiracy, as it has come to be called, refers to the alleged plot to kill Giuliano and, some sources say, other members of the Medici family. The conspiracy has always been accepted as fact, even though the various contemporary accounts reporting on the events are full of inconsistencies. Roberto Ridolfi, in his biography of Machiavelli, took a cautionary approach when he simply declared that it was one of those conspiracies that was "more literary than bloodthirsty,"[1] although he offered no further elucidation. However, in the most recent discussions, it seems to be a given that Pietro Paolo Boscoli and Agostino Capponi conspired to kill members of the Medici family.[2]

One of the principal aims of this book is to examine the nature of the relationship between Giuliano and Machiavelli, and since Giuliano was the intended victim of the conspiracy, and Machiavelli was one of the accused, a fresh look at the evidence is necessary. A review of the facts leads to the conclusion that there is no concrete evidence of the conspiracy's existence. Moreover, a strong argument can be made that Cardinal Giovanni de' Medici fabricated the plot to kill Giuliano out of political expediency. Also problematic is the view held by a majority of writers on Machiavelli, especially in more recent years, that Machiavelli was freed from prison during the general amnesty proclaimed the day after the election of the Medici pope. It is much more likely that Giuliano ordered Machiavelli's release from prison some days prior to Cardinal Giovanni's elevation to the papacy, believing deeply in Machiavelli's innocence and finding it unthinkable that Machiavelli could ever be a party to such a plot, especially in light of the admiration and affection he had expressed for Giuliano in his early poems. In May 1513, less than two months after the alleged conspiracy, and much against his will, Giuliano lost his position as head of the government in Florence and was compelled by the new pope to move permanently to Rome.

Jacopo Nardi's account of the events leading up to the arrest of twelve Florentine citizens on the evening of Friday, 18 February 1513 describes how a short time before news of the illness of Pope Julius II reached Florence, a certain Bernardino Coccio of Siena, who was a guest at the house of the Lenzi, relatives of the deposed Piero Soderini, found a piece of paper which had inadvertently fallen from the pocket of Pietro Paolo Boscoli. The paper listed the names of about eighteen or twenty *giovani*. Thinking that the note looked suspicious, Coccio took it to the magistrates of the Otto di Guardia.[3] Filippo de' Nerli's account differs from Nardi's, saying that these events took place slightly later, during the illness of the pope. Nerli claims that Agostino Capponi and Pietro Paolo Boscoli were the ringleaders of a conspiracy to kill both Giuliano and his nephew Lorenzo in Florence when Cardinal Giovanni was on his way to Rome to attend the conclave to elect a new pope. Nerli also mentions the list, but says it fell from Capponi's pocket instead of Boscoli's. Moreover, he believed that the names on the list were of those who were expected to be sympathetic to a plan to assassinate members of the Medici family, but not of those actually involved in plotting the undertaking. He identifies Coccio as the faithful secretary of Pandolfo Petrucci, *signore* of Siena, and implies that Coccio was thinking of personal gain when he took the list directly to the Medici.[4]

Francesco Vettori, in Rome at the time serving as Florentine ambassador, wrote in his *Sommario* that Capponi and Boscoli conspired to kill Giuliano.[5] According to Vettori, the list of names was taken to Cardinal Giovanni de' Medici (who had returned to Florence from Bologna on 19 January),[6] and that he, and not the Otto, ordered the arrest of Boscoli and Capponi as well as others whose names were on the list. Vettori's account is then rather vague, reporting that those arrested were interrogated but only Boscoli and Capponi were found guilty and condemned to death.[7] Nardi is more forthcoming when he writes that, during their interrogations under torture, neither Boscoli nor Capponi confessed to plotting against the state, although they did admit that they had longed for the liberty of their country and that they may have spoken to each other using words that could have been misconstrued by others.[8]

Without doubt, Giuliano was aware of the arrest and interrogation, having a special informant in the Otto di Guardia, its secretary Ser Zanobi del Pace. Ser Zanobi reported directly to Giuliano everything that was said during the questioning of prisoners, as indicated in Giuliano's *Instructions* to Lorenzo.[9] The letters that Giuliano wrote to his friends at the time are also revealing, allowing us to examine his thoughts about the alleged conspiracy and related events. One day after the arrests, on 19 February, Giuliano sent a letter to his friends in Mantua, the Marchese Francesco Gonzaga and his wife, Isabella d'Este, calmly informing them of what was known of the plot thus far. He wrote that some malicious citizens were planning to do violence to his person after the death of the pope (Pope Julius II died during the night of 21/22 February) when his brother Cardinal Giovanni would be absent from Florence to attend the conclave in Rome. Giuliano noted that the ringleaders and all other suspects, ten in number, "have been arrested and from yesterday until today nothing has been drawn from them but the discovery of a bad intention, or some meetings against us, and although the arrested men are noble, they are weak in character, are of little account and have no followers; therefore, they present no danger to the state."[10] He reassured his friends in Mantua by saying that everything is progressing calmly, "without change or any alteration: and in this case all will result for our benefit."[11]

On the same day, he wrote to Piero Dovizi in Venice, repeating much of what he shared with the Gonzaga, namely, that nothing had been extracted from the prisoners except their bad intentions. They were without an organization, substance, or following, which meant that they did not pose any danger to the state.[12] He also reassured Dovizi by adding that the people have come together and are united, and especially the close relatives of the "delinquents": "e *maxime* de' primi parenti de' delinquenti."[13] To describe the conspirators as "delinquents" rather than traitors is significant, because it suggests that Giuliano was satisfied regarding the investigation and that a true conspiracy did not exist, nor had there been a threat to his own security or the security of the state. At the end of the letter, Giuliano listed the names of the twelve men who had been arrested, many of whom Dovizi would have known personally. Machiavelli's name appeared in the seventh place on the list.[14]

Four days later, in the early hours of 23 February, in an act of swift retribution that allowed for no appeal of the sentence, Boscoli and Capponi were beheaded. Nardi reports that Cardinal Giovanni had left Florence for the conclave in Rome the day before, after being assured of the final sentence.[15] Fatini believes that Giuliano would probably have ended this incident with a magnanimous gesture of benevolence, but instead Lorenzo, Giulio, and perhaps even Cardinal Giovanni did not consent to a pardon because they believed the execution was an opportunity for them to show severity as an example and warning to all.[16] In his edition of Vettori's *Sommario*, Enrico Niccolini has correctly raised doubts as to whether there ever was a list of conspirators and, if it did exist, whether Boscoli would have been so reckless as to lose it. Niccolini argues that claims of a list could have been a convenient excuse for the Medici to cover up the fact that they had used an informant to collect the names of Soderini's friends and supporters, particularly those who gathered regularly at the Lenzi household. To make it appear as though a conspiracy against the Medici was being fomented, it was announced that a bogus list had been discovered.[17] Niccolini's assertions suggest the very real possibility that the conspiracy was spurious, and that it was part of the ongoing rivalry between the Medici and Soderini families. Could it have been that, when news reached Florence of Pope Julius's grave illness from which he was not expected to recover, the cardinal invented a conspiracy because he was afraid that the security of the current regime would be put at risk while he was attending the conclave in Rome? Was he, by ordering the round-up of Soderini supporters who might be emboldened to act in his absence from Florence, trying to pre-empt the possibility of an assault against the state?

Little is known about the two principal presumed conspirators, Pietro Paolo di Giachinotto Boscoli (b. 1481) and Agostino di Bernardo Capponi (b. 1471), since neither of them had achieved distinction other than as friends of the Lenzi, who from time to time hosted them as guests in their house. Some valuable insights into their personalities can be gleaned, however, from Luca Della Robbia's *Recitazione*, a moving and, at times, harrowing narrative of the last hours of the two condemned prisoners as they prepared for their execution.[18] Della Robbia (1484–1519), a humanist scholar of some note and a devout follower of Savonarola and his evangelical preaching, was a close friend of Pietro Paolo Boscoli. In the preface to his *Recitazione*, he described how he arrived at 8 o'clock on the evening of 22 February at the Palazzo del Podestà, where all the accused men had been taken, "drawn by great compassion to console (as much as I could) Pietro Paolo, to whom I was very close."[19] He was present the whole night until 4 o'clock the next morning when the beheadings took place, performing the role of a loving comforter, guiding Boscoli toward salvation. Della Robbia prayed with Boscoli and read passages to him from Scripture, as well as from the sermons of Savonarola, in order to encourage his friend to accept his fate without resistance and to approach death peacefully, with his thoughts focused only on Christ. While Della Robbia's narrative has great value as one of the foundational documents in the tradition of a "comforting text,"[20] at the same time it serves as an important historical source. Della Robbia, a devout Christian, assures his readers that he offers an accurate version of events in the preface to his *Recitazione*, where he wrote: "Let everyone who will read this present recollection know that he can trust it as a thing told truly and without passion, for it would disturb my conscience more than a little to write lies, especially on such a subject which, if I am not mistaken, pertains strongly to the Christian faith."[21]

According to Della Robbia's *Recitazione*, only Boscoli, who was described as "a man of singular intellect and well educated and that he spoke with great vigour,"[22] harboured treasonable thoughts against the Medici. He was a staunch republican and, steeped in the reading of Roman history, had begun to see himself, after the restoration of the Medici, as a second Brutus whose love of liberty over tyranny had inflamed his desire to assassinate Giuliano.[23] In conversations with Della Robbia during his last hours, Boscoli at one point pleaded with him, saying: "Ah, Luca, pull Brutus from my head, so that I can make this passage entirely as a Christian."[24] Della Robbia may have been motivated to record what was said that night to show how he had tried to comfort his friend.

If Boscoli comes across as a young, headstrong, republican idealist, what can be said of Agostino Capponi? Capponi, a decade older than Boscoli, seems initially to have been much more courageous in facing his imminent death, even encouraging his younger friend by saying that he should not be afraid and that they should both go to their deaths "willingly." Della Robbia had the opportunity to speak with Capponi while Boscoli was confessing to the Savonarolan Fra Cipriano da Pontassieve and must have been quite perturbed when he heard Capponi, who clearly was convinced of his own innocence, declare to him: "I die willingly although innocent."[25] Capponi had not, therefore, accepted the supremacy of the judgment against him that all comforters desired from condemned men, so that they would die quietly and acquiescent, forgiving their enemies, judges, and executioner. Indeed, far from being peaceful, Capponi became increasingly restless and mentally agitated as the night wore on.[26] Boscoli himself, in his earlier conversations with Della Robbia, confirmed that Capponi was innocent. Boscoli had admitted to Della Robbia that, while he was being tortured, he had implicated Capponi in the drawing up of the conspiracy.[27] Now, lamenting what he had done, he asked Della Robbia whether he should ask for Capponi's forgiveness. Della Robbia replied that Boscoli should first confess to God, and only then seek Capponi's forgiveness.[28] As dawn approached, Boscoli pleaded with Capponi: "I beg your pardon for anything I have done to offend against you in this life, and especially that I offended against you in the interrogation."[29] While the *Recitazione* indicates that Boscoli was guilty of having thoughts of assassinating Giuliano, it suggests that Capponi was not a participant in any plot against him. The decision to execute both men seems to have been made in order to legitimize the greater charge of conspiracy.[30]

Boscoli was also distressed about what he had said under torture about another of the accused, Niccolò Valori (1464–1528), whose name appeared in third place on Giuliano's list of suspects. Boscoli feared that what he had said during his interrogation would lead to Valori's execution. He begged Della Robbia to go to Ser Zanobi del Pace to tell him that he should remove certain words from his testimony, "and so it was done" according to Della Robbia.[31] Valori escaped the executioner's axe in all likelihood because the incriminating remarks were removed from Boscoli's statement.[32] Instead, he was sentenced to two years' imprisonment in the dungeons of the fortress of Volterra and thereafter exiled for life to Città di Castello. Fortunately for him, he was released in the general amnesty and was allowed to return to live in Florence. Valori wrote his own account of the events surrounding his arrest in his *Ricordanze*. He described how Boscoli came to see him, and, after some preliminary chatter, asked, most inconsiderately in his estimation, what they should do now that the pope was dying. Boscoli opined that Giuliano could be cut down because when he goes about the city late at night, he had few friends to protect him.[33] Valori wrote that he was horrified that Pietro Paolo would come to him and speak in this way because he should have known that he bore all the responsibility for supporting the Valori family with its many children. Moreover, Niccolò felt that he held sufficient honours and offices, and, as Boscoli should have realized, was both content and inclined toward peace.[34] Recognizing the significance of Boscoli's words, Valori asked Boscoli if he did not know the city abhorred the shedding of blood, that he himself had never liked violence, and that they were not suited for such acts? Valori further told Boscoli that the death of Giuliano would have no effect whatsoever because Cardinal Giovanni, Lorenzo, and Giulio de' Medici would remain alive and in their positions of power.[35] Though Boscoli left Valori quietly, that same night he was arrested and, under torture, he confessed to having conspired with Valori. Soldiers came for Valori in the middle of the night and took him straight to the Otto.[36] Valori's *Ricordanze* suggests that Boscoli's intention was to kill only Giuliano, and not Lorenzo or Giulio, as Della Robbia asserted in the preface to his *Recitazione*.

Even though Boscoli had implicated Niccolò Valori, the Medici may have already looked upon him with great suspicion because he had been an ardent supporter and close friend of Piero Soderini, and he had held prominent offices during the republic. Valori was also a very close friend of Machiavelli, standing godfather to his youngest son Bernardo.[37] It is more difficult to explain why Giovanni Folchi was put on the list of plotters because he had never held public office and was not in any way involved in politics.[38] In Folchi's confession, made during his interrogation on 1 March 1513, he admitted that on several occasions he had read Aristotle's *Politics* with Boscoli, especially those parts dealing with how cities are governed, and that one time Pietro Paolo had asked him whether he thought Giuliano was secure when he went about the city. Folchi said that he thought he was, first because the Medici were good and treated everyone well, and second, that the citizens were not armed as they were in Bologna and Perugia. Perhaps it was Folchi's long and close friendship with Machiavelli that had brought him to the attention of the Medici,[39] for his interrogators appeared to be interested in their relationship. In Folchi's confession there is a summary of his conversations with Machiavelli. They had spoken about the deeds of Piero Soderini, but more about the war than the city. Machiavelli also had once said that it seemed to him "that this state could not be governed without difficulty because it lacked someone to stand at the tiller, as Lorenzo de' Medici had properly done so."[40] It was also noted in the confession that, according to others, Folchi was always with Machiavelli.[41] He was condemned to two years in the dungeons of the fortress of Volterra, and thereafter to permanent exile. However, he served only a little of his sentence because, like Valori, he was set free in the general amnesty.

Machiavelli was also arrested and brought to the prison, where he was tortured. The form of torture used on prisoners was the *strappado* (meaning to rip or tear), referring to a rope that hung from a pulley attached to the ceiling (Fig. 30). One end of the rope was tied to the victim's wrists held behind the back and several men pulled the other end of the rope down so that the victim's body was hoisted high into the air. The rope was then suddenly released and the body plunged to the ground, but, at the very last moment, it was pulled again to stop the fall. These actions resulted in extreme pain either from broken shoulders or from arms being wrenched from their sockets. On average, *strappado* was administered four times during interrogations.[42] From Della Robbia's *Recitazione*, we learn that Boscoli was given eight drops from the rope,[43] whereas Capponi was subjected to two.[44] During the first days of Machiavelli's imprisonment, his interrogators administered six drops. Given the seriousness of the charge and the fact that his interrogators seemed intent on extracting a confession, Machiavelli turned to Giuliano, pleading for help. He would hardly have done so if Giuliano had treated him with the same suspicion and disdain that other members of the Medici had displayed toward him in the early months of their restoration. He was given permission to write to Giuliano, which he did in the form of a sonnet, addressing him as a friend and fellow poet:

> I have, Giuliano, a pair of shackles on my legs,
> with six hoists of the rope upon my shoulders;
> my other miseries I do not want to talk about,
> as this is the way poets are treated.
> These walls exude lice,
> sick with the heaves no less, that [are as big as] butterflies,
> nor was there ever such a stench in [the massacre of] Roncesvalles,
> or among those groves in Sardinia,
> as there is in my so dainty inn.
> With a noise that sounds just as if at the earth
> Jove was striking lightning, and all Mount Etna,
> One man is being chained, and the other shackled;
> with a clatter of keyholes, keys, and latches;
> another shouts: "Too high off the ground!"
> What disturbed me most
> was that close to dawn while sleeping,
> I heard chanting: "We are praying for you."
> Now they can go their own way,
> if only your mercy may turn toward me
> good father and these criminal bonds be untied.[45]

His tormentors were not able to break him and, as he wrote afterwards, he was rather proud and perhaps a little surprised by the way in which he had endured all the hardships during his imprisonment: "I have borne [these troubles of mine] so straightforwardly that I am proud of myself for it and consider myself more of a man than I believed I was."[46]

The chanting he complained about in the sonnet, being loud enough to wake him, involved the singing of psalms by the Compagnia de' Neri, a group appointed to comfort the souls of Boscoli and Capponi before their imminent death. The fact that he could hear them meant that he was being held in a cell close to theirs, which may have increased his fears that he too would soon be executed. Under these circumstances, it is understandable that he could write the line, "Now they can go their own way," and not feel compassion for Boscoli and Capponi. He believed that these two had dragged him into a conspiracy against Giuliano. In the last line, he addressed Giuliano, ten years his junior, as his "good father." Though De Grazia suggests this appellation resulted from his confused sense of identity while pleading desperately for help, more likely it resulted from the fact that Giuliano, in his position of head of the Florentine government, inherited the honorific title of Cosimo the Elder, *Pater Patriae* (Figs. 22 and 27), and with it the capacity to offer clemency.[47]

Machiavelli wrote a second sonnet, this time using humour that he knew would appeal to Giuliano. He begs the Muses to console him by going to visit Giuliano so that they can make his excuses for him, but when one enters his cell and he tells her his name, she viciously hits him in the face and shuts his mouth, saying that he cannot be Machiavelli but, instead, he is Dazzo (a reference to Andrea Dazzi who, as we have seen in chapter 5, was responsible for devising the theme of Giuliano's Carnival floats). The Muse does not recognize him because his legs and heels are bound together, and he is chained up like a lunatic. He entreats Giuliano to bear her witness and tell the Muse that "I am not Dazzo but I am who I am,"[48] suggesting perhaps that Andrea Dazzi had been the butt of a long-standing joke between them.

On 7 March, after the executions of Boscoli and Capponi had been carried out and all the other sentences had been handed down, Giuliano wrote a second letter to Piero Dovizi in Venice, informing him that the city had shown the greatest affection for the Medici, for which he felt an "eternal obligation." The ringleaders, Agostino Capponi and Pietro Paolo Boscoli, were "young and from good families but they had no followers. They meant to dispossess us and had drawn up a list of young men whom they believed were discontented with us. They had spoken with Niccolò Valori and Giovanni Folchi and secured their attention and for this reason the two principals, Agostino and Pietro Paolo have been executed."[49] His matter-of-fact tone conceals his true feelings about the harshness of the judgment meted out, because he knew full well from Ser Zanobi del Pace that only Boscoli had admitted to having had treasonable thoughts and that neither Boscoli nor Capponi had confessed to a conspiracy. His letter continues: "Niccolò [Valori] and Giovanni [Folchi] have been confined to the dungeons of the tower of the fortress of Volterra for two years … and some others, such as Francesco Serragli, Pandolfo Biliotti, Duccio Adimari,

Ubertino Bonciani, have been imprisoned for some years in *contado* at various locations. The others who were found to be innocent of treason have been released."[50] Since Giuliano makes no mention of Machiavelli, it seems that he was among the others who were set at liberty as innocent men, on the payment of a fine. In his *Ricordi*, Cerretani writes that, after Machiavelli had been tortured, he was confined for life in the Stinche,[51] a prison situated close to the Church of Santa Croce. When the news reached Florence that Giovanni de' Medici had become the new pope, (Fig. 11), the Otto, in a spirit of magnanimity (presumably on the orders of Giuliano), opened all the prisons on Saturday, 12 March, and everyone was freed, including all those who had been sentenced for the conspiracy.[52]

Villari, contradicting Cerretani on this point, writes that the judges found Machiavelli innocent and he was freed,[53] and Ridolfi, citing Giuliano's letter of 7 March, also believes that Machiavelli was released on or before that time.[54] More recent commentators on Machiavelli, however, tend to follow Cerretani and write that Machiavelli was set free during the general amnesty on Saturday, 12 March.[55] Machiavelli's letter to Francesco Vettori, Florentine ambassador to the papal court, dated Sunday, 13 March 1513 in Florence, may confirm this assessment, for he says that he "got out of prison, amid the city's universal rejoicing."[56] Perhaps, however, Machiavelli did not mean it literally but for its literary effect. Certainly, as he was writing his letter on that Sunday, all around him he could see and hear the sheer madness that had overtaken the city and that had continued unabated since the moment the news had reached Florence that Cardinal Giovanni de' Medici was the new pope, the first Florentine to be so honoured. Throngs of people had descended into the streets to celebrate in high spirits, shouting *Palle! Palle! Papa Lione!* Church bells were rung day and night and cannons big and small were continually fired. Great bonfires blazed in every street, and all over the city people rushed around gathering up baskets, barrels, and furniture – even ripping down entire wooden roofs – to feed the flames. The noise and smoke prompted one observer to exclaim that it looked as if the whole city had turned itself upside down and "anyone who had seen it from overhead would have said: 'Florence is burning down the whole city.'" Landucci reported that "on Monday [it was] worse than ever."[57] In writing that he had been released from prison "amid this city's universal rejoicing," Machiavelli was perhaps simply describing what was taking place all around him on that Sunday, after having a few days of freedom that allowed him sufficient time to recover from his terrible ordeal.

Had Machiavelli been held in prison until the amnesty was proclaimed, it would mean that in the eyes of the authorities he was not one of those who were found innocent but was under the suspicion of having taken part in the conspiracy and thus a man not to be trusted. Would it have made sense for Machiavelli, considered guilty by the Medici, to write to Francesco Vettori the day after his release and ask him to recommend his younger brother Totto for the new pope's household in Rome? Or, even more bizarrely, to end his letter with the plea to Vettori: "If it is possible, remind Our Lordship about me in order that, if it should be possible, either he or his family might start engaging my services in some way or other, because I believe I shall do honour to you and do something useful for me."[58] Only if Machiavelli had been fully exonerated by the judges in Florence would he then write such a letter. Despite being a convinced republican, his participation in such a wicked plot, let alone bringing it to closure, seems highly unlikely, especially owing to his shared deep bond of friendship with Giuliano. He proclaimed his innocence some months later, in a letter to his nephew Giovanni Vernacci: "it is a miracle that I am alive, because my post was taken from me and I was about to lose my life, which God and my innocence have preserved for me."[59] Along with all the others who had been rounded up and put to torture, Machiavelli was innocent, for the evidence shows that no crime had taken place. It seems that only Pietro Paolo Boscoli, in his thoughts, sought to harm the Medici, but his thinking was not shared, and we can conclude that no conspiracy existed.[60] On 4 April 1513 the balìa, certainly on the orders of Giuliano, granted full pardon to those suspected of complicity in the plot.[61]

FRANCESCO VETTORI

Machiavelli's letter to Francesco Vettori was the first in a series that passed between the two men during a two-year period. Their friendship dated back to 1508, when Machiavelli, as second chancellor and secretary to the Dieci di Balìa, spent six months with Francesco, the republic's appointed envoy to Emperor Maximilian. Vettori, a successful diplomat, belonged to one of the great families of Florence, part of the city's closely knit and intermarried elite, socially removed from Machiavelli, the salaried bureaucrat from the more modest upbringing that he claimed taught him "how to scrimp rather than to thrive."[62] These differences may help to explain the awkward tension that sometimes surfaces in their letters.[63] Despite having been informed of Machiavelli's imprisonment by Totto, who had dispatched a courier to Rome the moment Machiavelli was arrested, Vettori could do nothing to assist him. On 15 March, responding to a letter written by Machiavelli two days earlier, Vettori expressed his dismay over his lack of power to remedy Machiavelli's predicament. He insisted that he had tried: "I did so when the pope was elected [four days ago] and I asked him for no other favour than your liberation, which, I am happy, had already taken place."[64]

It could very well be that Machiavelli initially wrote to Vettori following his release from prison because he hoped that his friend might be inclined to compensate him for not having helped him earlier, and that he would now recommend his brother and himself to the new pope. Vettori, it appears, was unable or unwilling to help Machiavelli, probably because he was aware that such a request would have annoyed Pope Leo X, who was ill disposed toward Machiavelli.[65] The very fact that his name had been put on the list of Soderini's sympathizers and was arrested strongly suggests that Cardinal Giovanni de' Medici had been suspicious of Machiavelli. Perhaps Giuliano's friendship with the ex-secretary further aggravated the new pope's animosity. Vettori was clearly anxious not to be seen to be too closely associated with Machiavelli, fearing that this would jeopardize his own standing with the new pope, especially since he hoped to be able to obtain favours for his brother Paolo. In November 1513, in recognition of his services, Leo X did indeed appoint Paolo Vettori as treasurer of the *decima*, a tax levied on the Florentine clergy, although, according to Melissa Bullard, the debt-ridden Paolo apparently used the treasury funds to pay his own creditors.[66]

On 18 March 1513 Machiavelli wrote again to Francesco: "I can say that all that is left to me of life I owe to the Magnificent Giuliano and your Paolo."[67] The good-natured Giuliano had often intervened, as we saw in the previous chapter, to help citizens who were being harassed by the new Medici regime, and it is difficult to imagine that he did not come to Machiavelli's aid, ensuring that he was released as one of the innocents, thereby saving him from possible execution or life imprisonment. Ridolfi may be right when he says that Paolo could have "commended the sonnets and the poet to Giuliano and thus spared him a worse imprisonment."[68] In the absence of Cardinal Giovanni and his cousin Giulio, perhaps Vettori had acquired some authority again with the soldiers of the Otto that allowed him access to the prison cells at the Palazzo del Podestà. Delivering Machiavelli's poems would have given Paolo the opportunity to ingratiate himself with Giuliano and affect respect for him, just as he had done with the deposed *gonfaloniere di giustizia* Piero Soderini.[69] It is difficult to agree with Ridolfi, however, when he writes that Giuliano had great affection for Vettori and trusted him.[70] As a radical *pallesco*, Paolo had taken an active part in bringing down Soderini and the republican regime and, moreover, was the author of the *Ricordi* addressed to Cardinal Giovanni, in which, as we saw in chapter 4, he expressed his fears that Giuliano and his supporters could not be trusted with the handling of the regime. It would be unrealistic to assume that Giuliano could have had overly warm feelings for him. Because he knew that his brother admired Paolo, specifically recommending him to their cousin Giulio,[71] Giuliano would have maintained an outward show of guarded civility, although inwardly he was likely suspicious of Vettori's motives.

On 16 April 1513 Machiavelli informed Francesco Vettori that Giuliano would soon be coming to Rome, as a member of a Florentine delegation sent to congratulate the new pope, adding: "You will find him naturally disposed to please me."[72] This suggests that there had been some friendly contacts between Machiavelli and Giuliano after his release from prison. We have to ask why Giuliano, unlike his nephew Lorenzo, did not rush to Rome immediately following his brother's election either to take pleasure in his great fortune or to attend Leo X's coronation on 11 April, one of the most extravagant and costly ever held in Rome. On 22 March, Giuliano was elected as one of the ambassadors who would go on behalf of the Florentine government to pay tribute to Pope Leo X, but in this case he seems to have delegated someone else take his place.[73] Fatini says that Giuliano deferred his visit to Rome, first to April and then to the beginning of May, because he was still bound by his responsibilities in the government,[74] but there could be more to it than that (Fig. 26). Did he fear, now that the new pope had total authority over Florence, that he would be replaced by his more autocratically inclined nephew Lorenzo, as indeed happened? We have already seen that there was an ideological rift between certain members of the Medici family, and perhaps Giuliano knew that his brother and cousin Giulio were far from satisfied with his conciliatory politics, especially towards his *frateschi* friends, who were perceived by the Medici to be enemies of the state. Moreover, Lorenzo and his mother, Alfonsina, were resentful of Giuliano's overwhelming popularity and princely ambitions, as seen clearly in letters exchanged between mother and son.[75]

Evidence of Giuliano's widespread public approval was seen in May 1513, before his departure for Rome, when, according to Cerretani, the authorities granted him far wider powers than was the usual diplomatic practice, appointing him syndic and procurator of the commune, with a mandate lasting until September, to conduct affairs of the state, to hire anyone he chose as captain of the Florentine army, and to negotiate war or peace. In fact, his powers were so broad that he could literally "do anything." Cerretani also reported that many members of the balìa were unhappy with the powers given to Giuliano and they voted against his appointment.[76] These opponents must certainly have been the pro-Medici supporters, who continued to be upset with the way Giuliano was handling the government. Some have suggested that these extraordinary powers granted to him were a reflection of the better position that the Medici enjoyed after they returned to Florence in 1512,[77] whereas others are of the opinion that the increase in Giuliano's powers was mandated by Leo X.[78] However, it is more plausible to think that it was those citizens not closely allied with the Medici who voted in favour of this measure, because in Giuliano they recognized a committed leader who was devoted to bringing them good government and, above all, would always protect their interests.

Giuliano finally arrived in Rome on 4 May, and it was not long afterwards that discussions were held regarding who would be the new ruler of Florence. The two principal sources of these deliberations are Cerretani's *Dialogo delle mutazione* and Francesco Vettori's *Sommario*, but, alas, they give contradictory accounts. Cerretani recorded that there was a heated debate over who was to govern Florence and that the substitution of Lorenzo for Giuliano only came after a protracted dispute, including the pope and leading members of the Medici family. He also reports that Giuliano was "annoyed and dismayed" at having to give up his office to his nephew.[79] The contemporary chronicler Piero Parenti also wrote about a "long dispute" between Giuliano and Lorenzo, and how Lorenzo, after he had emerged victorious, was determined not to relinquish his position to his uncle.[80] Francesco Vettori, on the other hand, comments that neither Medici wanted to remain in Florence. Giuliano, he wrote, thought of "excessive grandeur" and, not being satisfied with Florence, fantasized about having a much larger state, such as the kingdom of Naples.[81] After realizing what an important position a pope's nephew could enjoy in Rome, Lorenzo also opted to stay put, because in Florence "he would have to behave with a thousand cautions while in Rome he needed not one."[82] Vettori also writes that the pope preferred that Giuliano return to Florence because he was now older and would be more acceptable to the Florentines. However, Giuliano refused to leave Rome, and since the pope did not want to remove Giulio from the Church (in May he had been appointed archbishop of Florence), he had no alternative but to send Lorenzo to govern Florence.[83]

Did Rome's attractions for Giuliano really outshine those of Florence, as some modern historians suggest?[84] Even Fatini appears to believe that it would have been easy for the pope to persuade Giuliano to pass up Florence for Rome, because, he says, in Giuliano's own heart, he desired nothing more than to delight in a life of luxury and enjoy worldly amusements and, with the benefits that would come through his association with the papacy, he would be able to carry out his innate vocation, which was to become a princely patron.[85] Yet the portrayal of Giuliano as being either overly ambitious or willing to exchange Florence for the life of a Roman Maecenas is difficult to reconcile with the fact that, after he was deprived of his Florentine state in May, the Dieci in Florence still referred to him as "our colleague," sending their dispatches directly to him, sometimes bypassing the ambassadors altogether. In one letter to Giuliano of 29 July 1513, the Dieci wrote: "We speak with you about everything freely and without reserve, as we do among ourselves, and, as you will find, to our ambassadors we have kept silent on many points."[86] It appears that Giuliano, according to Nerli, always regretted giving up his position to Lorenzo[87] and was closely in touch with his former secretary Michelozzi. He wanted Michelozzi to keep him informed of all important government matters while he was in Rome. Michelozzi was to give the Florentine ambassadors certain information, "so it appears that they are valued," but he should avoid revealing any state secrets.[88]

Francesco Vettori's version of events is difficult to trust, because he was personally antagonistic towards Giuliano and he knew that he was being excluded from conversations about Florentine affairs. This is especially apparent in the letters he wrote to his brother Paolo, expressing his frustration, shortly after Giuliano arrived in Rome.[89] To Francesco it seemed that Jacopo Salviati, appointed ambassador to the papal court in order to prevent him from giving counsel to Giuliano in Florence, resented his presence when public business was being conducted, because Salviati suspected that Vettori took his brother Paolo too much into his confidence. Apparently, Jacopo Salviati had received a letter, probably from Matteo Strozzi, the third ambassador in Rome, who had just returned to Florence, informing him that Paolo Vettori was talking as if he was aware of many state secrets. Francesco warned Paolo not to show his letters to anyone in Florence and to be careful with whom he conversed.[90] Perhaps it is not surprising, therefore, that Francesco complained to Paolo how he found it very difficult to have a word with Giuliano, and that it was much easier to approach the pope.[91] In his letters to Machiavelli, there is further evidence that Giuliano was keeping the ambassador at bay, since, in a letter dated 23 November 1513, Francesco wrote that, as a rule, he spoke twenty words with the pope, ten with Giulio, and only six with Giuliano, and if he could not talk directly to him, he spoke instead with Giuliano's secretary Piero Ardinghelli. Francesco also informed Machiavelli that he often dined with Cardinal Giulio de' Medici,[92] raised to the office in September (Fig. 11). This all suggests that Vettori's relationships with both Leo X and Cardinal Giulio were very close, but with Giuliano not so much.

Francesco Vettori was also bitter about the fact that, through lack of money, he was forced to live an ordinary life, neither wearing the long customary ambassadorial vestments nor entertaining, and keeping no more than a minimum number of horses. He was powerless to further the interests of his friends in Florence, because everyone turned to Jacopo Salviati for help, and not to him.[93] In another letter to Paolo, he revealed how resentful he was toward Giuliano, saying that Giuliano's expenditure was such that his papal provision of 6,000 ducats *carlini* a year would not suffice even for the upkeep of his stables.[94] On 14 August he again complained bitterly about how much money Giuliano was spending.[95] Giuliano and Jacopo Salviati most likely kept their distance from Vettori, because it was clear to them that, since Francesco was on intimate terms with Leo X and Cardinal Giulio, he could not be trusted.

The correspondence between Machiavelli and Vettori came to an end in January 1515 at the same time that Leo's hostility toward Machiavelli became public knowledge. On 14 February 1515 the papal secretary Piero Ardinghelli wrote to Giuliano the following: "Cardinal de' Medici asked me yesterday, in very strict confidence, if I knew whether your Excellency had taken Machiavelli into your service, and when I replied to him that I had no news of it, nor did I believe it, his most reverend lordship spoke to me the following formal words: I don't believe it either; however, because there is news of this from Florence, I remind him that this suits neither him nor us … Write to him on my behalf that I advise him to have nothing to do with Machiavelli; and I say this not so as to teach him what he needs to do, but moved by love, etc."[96]

When Francesco Vettori returned permanently to Florence in the summer of 1515, having been relieved of his ambassadorial duties, he became closely associated with the autocratic Lorenzo di Piero de' Medici and, together with Filippo Strozzi, acted as his closest adviser,[97] before Lorenzo's early death from syphilis in 1519.[98] Benedetto Buondelmonti, a Florentine and a Medici supporter, seems to sum up Francesco Vettori's flawed character in his letter to Filippo Strozzi, written soon after Francesco's departure from Rome, in which he severely criticized Francesco for his servile and submissive attitude toward the Medici, and stated that such behaviour was unbecoming for a man in his position. The honour of Florence warranted much more from its ambassador. He compared his conduct "unfavourably with Jacopo Salviati's behaviour, concluding that one should know how to gain esteem rather than humble oneself."[99] In the meantime, Giuliano had established himself in Rome, but he still maintained close ties to Florence and stayed for long periods of time in his beloved city, even though his nephew was now the nominal head of government.

CHAPTER SEVEN

GIULIANO AND LEONARDO DA VINCI

In May 1513, following Cardinal Giovanni de' Medici's elevation to the papacy on 11 March, Giuliano was relieved of his government position in Florence and settled permanently in Rome (Figs. 11, 28, and 29). He took up residence in the Palazzo Monte Giordano belonging to his Orsini relatives, located in the heart of old Rome.[1] In June it was rumoured that Leo X wanted to nominate Giuliano as a cardinal,[2] but soon it was revealed that the pope had other plans for his younger brother, namely, to establish a Medici dynastic state in north-central Italy that would be completely independent of Florence. At some point during the summer of 1513, Giuliano must have sent a messenger to Milan with an invitation for the Florentine artist Leonardo da Vinci (1452–1519) to come to Rome. Leonardo's own records state that he left Milan with his small entourage, heading for Rome on 24 September. Why did Giuliano issue this invitation? Carlo Vecce has suggested that, as a lover of arts and poetry, Giuliano offered his protection to Leonardo because although he had collected around him an impressive circle of humanists and learned men, he still felt the need to have an artist who combined both excellence in art and excellence in knowledge.[3]

Leo's predecessor, Julius II, had already attracted some of the finest artistic talent of the day to Rome, eager to exploit their new classicizing language for the display of papal power. Architect Donato Bramante was commissioned to demolish the thousand-year-old Constantinian basilica of St Peter's in order to construct a massive, Roman-inspired, centrally planned church intended to house the pope's tomb, an undertaking of imperial scale equal to the pope's grandiose vision. First commissioned to build Julius's tomb, the Florentine sculptor Michelangelo was diverted in 1508 to paint the ceiling of the Sistine Chapel, built by Julius's uncle, Sixtus IV. After the pope's death in February 1513, Michelangelo resumed work on the tomb, having signed a new contract with the heirs of Julius for a scaled-down version to be placed in San Pietro in Vincoli. Raphael also received a major commission in 1508 to fresco the pope's new apartment in the Vatican Palace, apparently because Julius could no longer stand to live in the six-room Borgia suite, decorated with family portraits and the heraldic bull of his bitter enemy, Alexander VI.[4] The work of decorating the so-called Stanze remained unfinished at Julius's death but was continued under the patronage of Leo X. Now that a Medici pope, known for his liberality, had ascended the papal throne, artists everywhere must have seen Rome as an exciting and attractive place to be, offering the very real prospect of more lucrative papal commissions. But did Giuliano invite Leonardo to Rome, as Vecce seems to imply, so that the artist could become the prized ornament of his Roman household, or did he have a more urgent reason for requiring Leonardo's presence?

Leonardo spent less than three years on and off in Rome. Some months after Giuliano's death in March 1516, the artist entered the service of King Francis I of France, where he died three years later. Despite exhaustive scholarly investigation of Leonardo's life and work, the years he spent in Giuliano's employ have garnered relatively little attention or serious examination of the projects he carried out for Giuliano.[5] This oversight stems in large part from Giorgio Vasari's dismissal of Leonardo's Roman activity as limited to "an infinite number of follies."[6] For Vasari, though Leonardo "went to Rome with Duke Giuliano de' Medici," his focus on scientific exploration did not satisfy Vasari's criteria for artistic success because he did not produce much in the way of painting, especially in comparison to his earlier career.[7] Vasari claimed the pope shared his disappointment, reportedly saying, "Alas! this man will never do anything, for he begins by thinking of the end of the work, before the beginning."[8] Though this sentiment is surely that of Vasari projected onto Leo X, it points to the long-standing bias against Leonardo's Roman period. Indeed, we will see that Leonardo was invited to Rome, and given a salary and an apartment at the Villa Belvedere, not because of his artistic reputation but because he was regarded as one of the most experienced and talented military engineers of his day.

Leonardo worked on three separate engineering projects for Giuliano. The first, in accordance with the wishes of Leo X, involved surveying the lands that would constitute Giuliano's future state in northern Italy. The second was a project to drain and reclaim for agricultural use the malarial-infested swamplands of the Pontine Marshes, a huge tract of uninhabitable land situated southeast of Rome. His final task was to facilitate research on building a new, supreme instrument of war – a burning mirror to protect Rome and its environs from incursions of the Turkish fleet in the Tyrrhenian Sea. He also kept himself busy reworking paintings like the *Mona Lisa* and preparing notes for a never-realized treatise on geometry, both seemingly with Giuliano's blessing and support. Furthermore, he is thought to have painted several works now lost, both for Giuliano and other notable patrons, including Baldassare Turini, datary to the pope, and Leo X himself.[9]

Between 13 and 18 September 1513, a spectacular festival was held in Rome's civic centre on the Capitoline Hill to celebrate the rebirth of the city under the new pope, simultaneously symbolizing the unity of Florence and Rome. Honorary titles of Patrician and Citizen of Rome were conferred upon Giuliano and Lorenzo di Piero (who was absent in Florence), as well as on the whole house of the Medici[10] (Figs. 28 and 29). The Roman humanist Marcantonio Altieri, one of the eight planners of the celebration, wrote the following: "Then with magnificence and honourable company, they gave [Giuliano] a sumptuous and splendid meal, with a welcome demonstration of public happiness, applying such solemnities to the birthday of Rome and calling it the *Palilie*, since in a manner of speaking, Rome was reborn, *that is freed by His Holiness from the troubles and woes and given the beginning and the means for a happier life together with the hope of a better condition*."[11] With the privilege of Roman citizenship came also the obligation to protect the city and defend the citizens of Rome. Giuliano was responsible for guiding Leonardo's project to drain the Pontine Marshes in order to rid the city of the pestilential air that wreaked havoc with the health of Rome's citizens and his plan to design weapons of war intended to repel any coastal attack from the Turkish fleet. This oversight clearly conveys that Giuliano took his new obligations of Roman citizenship very seriously. The last three years of his life, however, have not escaped criticism, such as, for example, Connell's charge: "In Rome he became famous for a dissipated lifestyle and for consorting with artists, poets and astrologers, while neglecting papal and family business."[12] As we shall see, this critique is not borne out by the facts of Giuliano's time in Rome.

A NEW STATE FOR GIULIANO – PARMA, PIACENZA, MODENA, AND REGGIO

Following the total defeat of the French invaders by the armies of the Holy League and the retreat of the French from Milan and Italy in the summer of 1512, League members, with the backing of Emperor Maximilian, agreed to restore the Duchy of Milan, an imperial fief, to Massimiliano, the nineteen-year-old son of Ludovico Sforza, who had been raised at the court of his namesake.[13] Nevertheless, Julius II took advantage of Milan's weakened position and seized the cities of Parma and Piacenza and their territories from the duchy. He justified his actions, as reported to Francesco Gonzaga by his agent Folenghino in August 1512, by asserting: "The Church's legal claims were 'so old that it was shameful even to discuss them.'"[14] Julius was, no doubt, referring to the legacy left to the papacy by Countess Matilda of Canossa in the eleventh century.[15] At the same time, the pope recovered the former Matildine cities of Modena and Reggio, also located in the lower Po valley, from Alfonso d'Este, Duke of Ferrara who, like the Duke of Milan, had held them as Imperial fiefs.[16] Because the pope was able to restore these cities to the Papal States and increase the temporal power of the papacy, he gained high praise for his actions; not only was he seen as a liberator because he had freed Italy from the tyranny of the French, but also, by using military might, he had "made great kings fear the arms of the Church."[17]

When Julius died in February 1513, Parma and Piacenza were quickly recovered for Milan,[18] but, as we learn from Francesco Vettori's letter to Machiavelli, the loss of these Papal States caused great consternation for the new pope: "This judgment, that [Leo X] wants to maintain the Church in its states and its pre-eminence, I make on the basis of the words I have heard him speak and also on the actions he has taken; because, since Julius occupied Parma and Piacenza without any just title and the duke of Milan took them back when the pontificate was vacant, the pope thought at first of nothing else than getting them back."[19] Within two months of Leo's election in March, the territories were returned to the Papal States, despite the pleadings of the young Massimiliano who, desperately in need of their revenues, begged the new pope to have compassion for the disastrous financial situation in which he found himself.[20] Vettori, in the same letter, also informed Machiavelli that the new pope was thinking of giving states to Giuliano and Lorenzo, though he did not speculate where, because, he wrote, "the past popes, Calixtus, Pius, Sixtus, Innocent, Alexander, and Julius, have done so; if any did not do so it was because they were not able to."[21]

A decade earlier, as mentioned in chapter 3, Cesare Borgia had attempted to carve out a principality in the Papal States of Romagna, and his example surely was on the pope's mind, as well as on those of his immediate circle, including Giuliano. Valentino had ultimately failed, but his lack of success was widely perceived as being the culmination of what Machiavelli called "an extraordinary and extreme instance of contrary Fortune,"[22] with the sudden death of Alexander VI and the election of Cardinal Giuliano della Rovere as Pope Julius II, an enemy of the Borgia.[23] Instead of dissuading Leo X from his plan to form a state for Giuliano, Valentino's example appears to have served as an inspiration, because in 1513 there was good reason to believe that Giuliano's fortune would be greater than the duke's. Cardinal Giovanni de' Medici had been elected pope at the unprecedented age of thirty-seven and could have been expected to live for many more years (even though his poor health, exhibited during the conclave, induced some to believe that his pontificate would not be of long duration).[24] With the power of the papacy and the papal treasury behind him, Giuliano would be given all the support he would need to establish a state peacefully or, if necessary, with arms.

The idea of forming a state from the northern central cities of Parma, Piacenza, Modena, and Reggio was first discussed by the Medici pope in early July 1513 in conversation with the Mantuan ambassador, Alessandro Gabbioneta, on behalf of Francesco Gonzaga. The plan found particular favour with Gonzaga, who was hoping to acquire both the sympathy of Leo X and the advantage of having a friendly state near to his own, even though he knew that the interests of the dukes of Milan and Ferrara would be badly served.[25] Rumours that the pope was planning to create a state for Giuliano spread quickly throughout Italy, as attested by the notice in Sanudo's diary of July 1513, which reports: "Giuliano wants to become the lord of Modena, Reggio, Parma and Piacenza; so that this pope is worse than Pope Julius."[26]

The evidence appears to confirm that in July 1513, in order to further his dynastic ambitions, the pope intended to create a Medici hereditary state, carved out of lands in north-central Italy. Giuliano seems to have been in favour of his brother's idea,[27] perhaps recognizing that it was just compensation for his departure from Florence. In making preparations for the possession of his new state, like any other prince at the time, Giuliano would have required the services of a military architect and engineer, and as we have seen, one of the first actions he took in the summer of 1513 was to invite Leonardo to Rome. He had first met Leonardo at the Milanese court and then again at Imola in the autumn of 1502, being well aware that Leonardo had occupied the role of military architect and engineer for both Ludovico Sforza and Cesare Borgia. Moreover, he could also count on having the pleasure of Leonardo's company in Rome. According to Benedetto Varchi, Giuliano treated Leonardo more like a brother than a friend.[28]

LEONARDO AS MILITARY ARCHITECT AND ENGINEER TO LUDOVICO SFORZA AND CESARE BORGIA

In order to understand fully why Giuliano moved so quickly to secure the services of Leonardo in the summer of 1513, and then, when the artist had arrived in Rome, provided so generously for him and his entourage, it is important to understand Leonardo's work as a military engineer, which is often overshadowed by his fame as a painter. It was his pre-eminence in this field that brought Leonardo to Rome in 1513, and there is no direct evidence that Giuliano ever commissioned a painting from Leonardo. However, in October 1517, Antonio De Beatis reported that he had seen three pictures in Amboise, *The Mona Lisa*, the *Virgin and Child with Saint Anne*, also now in the Louvre, and a portrait of "a certain Florentine lady, made from life at the instigation of the late Giuliano de' Medici,"[29] raising the possibility that Leonardo did paint for Giuliano. Some have identified several copies of a half-length female nude, known as the *Nude Mona Lisa* or *Monna Vanna*, as evidence of the lost portrait[30] (Fig. 31). But De Beatis may simply have been referring to Leonardo's unfinished *Mona Lisa*, rather than a separate portrait, which Giuliano could have urged Leonardo to complete when he saw it unfinished in Rome.[31]

Giuliano first met Leonardo in 1496 during his extended stay at the Sforza court, where the artist had been residing for many years, having arrived in Milan sometime between September 1481 and April 1483. At the time of Leonardo's arrival, Ludovico Sforza was acting as regent for his young nephew Giangaleazzo Sforza, who had inherited the title of duke in 1476. In 1491 Ludovico married Beatrice d'Este (1475–1497), sister of Isabella d'Este. After the sudden death of Giangaleazzo in 1494, he received the title of duke from the Emperor Maximilian. Ludovico's court, modelled on the courts of northern Europe, was aristocratic and military in character, and rivalled them in grandeur and opulence.[32]

Leonardo, during the almost two decades spent at the Milanese court, produced surprisingly little in the way of art. In addition to his role as designer and organizer of the lavish theatrical productions and festivities that were a feature of the Sforza court, especially during the time of Beatrice d'Este, his actual commissioned works for Ludovico, not counting of course those that may not have survived, are very few: the ill-fated clay model of the horse for the proposed gigantic bronze equestrian monument to honour Ludovico's father Francesco Sforza, which was destroyed in 1499 by French soldiers who used it for target practice; the mural of *The Last Supper* in the Refectory of the Dominican friary of Santa Maria delle Grazie, 1495–97; the ceiling decoration in the seigniorial apartment in the Castello Sforzesco, referred to as the *Sala delle Asse*, during the period 1496–97; and a portrait of Ludovico's mistress Cecilia Gallerani in 1489–90.[33]

During his eighteen years at the Milanese court, Leonardo primarily worked as a military engineer, as indicated in a letter, probably dating from 1482–83, in which Leonardo offers Ludovico his services as an inventor of war machines, only mentioning at the very end his proficiency in architecture, sculpture, and painting. His preamble reads: "I shall endeavour, without prejudice to anyone else, to explain myself to your Excellency showing your Lordship my secrets, and then offering them to your best pleasure and approbation to work with effect at opportune moments as well as all those things which, in part, shall be briefly noted below."[34] Leonardo informs Ludovico that he can build an endless variety of light and strong bridges that are indestructible by fire and easy to carry when pursuing or fleeing the enemy, but that he also has methods for burning and destroying the bridges of the enemy. During a siege, he knows how to drain trenches and dig tunnels without making any noise, even under rivers; he can make covered ways and scaling ladders; and he has methods for destroying rock or any fortress built on rock. He can supply big guns, mortars, and light ordinance, and when bombardment is impractical, he can produce war machines of marvellous efficiency, not in common use, such as covered chariots that are immune from attack, catapults, mangonels (machines that fire small stones, having the effect of a violent hailstorm), which will cause "great terror to the enemy,"[35] and *caltrops* (iron balls with sharp prongs) to impede cavalry. In the event of war at sea, he has many machines, "most efficient for offence and defence; and vessels which will resist the attack of the largest guns and powder and fumes."[36] Whether any of the above-listed machines of war were simply "technological dreams," as Paolo Galluzzi believes,[37] the product of Leonardo's highly fertile imagination and beyond the engineering capabilities of his time, is an open question. However, a significant number might have been possible, and Leonardo could thus confidently write at the end of his letter: "And if any one of the above-named things seem to anyone to be impossible or not feasible, I am most ready to make the experiment in your park, or in whatever place may please your Excellency – to whom I commend myself with the utmost humility, &c."[38]

Leonardo must have impressed Ludovico, whose patronage extended to two other renowned military architects and engineers, Donato Bramante, who left for Rome after 1499, and Francesco di Giorgio Martini of Siena (1439–1501). Although we have no knowledge of the actual conditions under which Leonardo was employed at the Sforza court during his eighteen-year stay, if we consider the approximately six thousand extant pages of notes and drawings, well over half of them deal with technical and scientific studies.[39] This corpus strongly suggests that most of his energy was devoted to his engineering and technical work, and that this was his main source of income.[40] The notes and drawings are divided between those intended to become formal treatises on various subjects, such as, painting, mechanics, hydraulics, and anatomy, and the notebooks that he always carried with him in which he recorded personal notes and observations. Even though as much as 75 per cent of Leonardo's notes may have been lost, what survives offers a fairly balanced representation of his extraordinarily far-ranging interests.[41]

Between 1483 and 1490, Leonardo made finished drawings of most of the machines proposed in his letter of introduction to Ludovico, and although there is no evidence that any were ever built, his designs and the feasibility of their realization might have served as a point of discussion with the duke and his military advisers. An example of his early ideas for new weapons is the single sheet, now part of the so-called Codex Atlanticus, where he attempts to solve the ubiquitous problem of the slow rate of cannon fire with three alternative ideas for a multi-barrelled machine gun, each comprising twelve cannons mounted on an easily movable gun carriage (Fig. 32).[42] Another sheet shows an ingenious device to prevent the enemy scaling the battlements, where a series of wooden beams are concealed in the castellated walls and activated by an interior winch, extending outward and knocking the assault ladders down to the ground (Fig. 33).[43] Beginning in 1485, Leonardo turned his attention to military architecture and strategic engineering for Ludovico, and, judging from the large body of drawings and notes that has survived, his study of fortified architecture became one of the most important aspects of his work until about 1517 or 1518.[44] The most urgent problem of the day was how to minimize the impact of cannon fire on fortresses, and Leonardo's notes and sketches show the evolution of his thinking about the issue; he made many studies of triangular bastions with sloping sides, as well as square, polygonal, and round bastions, together with watchtowers, escarpments, moats, and trenches. He also produced designs to improve the fortifications of Milan's Castello Sforzesco.[45] It is not surprising, therefore, to find Leonardo described as *Leonardus de Florentia ingeniar, et pinctor* (engineer and painter), in a document, dated 1490, from the Sforza archives.[46]

When Ludovico Sforza was forced from Milan by the French conquest under Louis XII late in 1499, Leonardo returned to Florence. He stopped first in Mantua as an honoured guest of Isabella d'Este, who, having admired his portrait of Cecilia Gallerani in Milan, desired to obtain her own portrait painted by him. Leonardo, however, was far more interested in pursuing his engineering projects than in painting, although he did manage to produce a sketch of Isabella's profile in black and red chalk (Fig. 34) before moving on to Venice, where he presented his credentials as an expert in military fortifications.[47] The Venetian republic at once sent him to examine the Isonzo River in the Friuli region, because it was there that the Venetians feared an imminent overland attack by the Turks. An incomplete draft of a report survives in his notes, probably intended for the Venetian Senate, in which he recommends the construction of a water barrier, although it seems that soon afterwards he left Venice and it is not known whether he submitted a final report.[48]

By the end of March 1500, Leonardo was back in Florence. He stayed there for the next two years but was still reluctant to re-establish himself as painter, as made clear in letters sent to Isabella d'Este by Fra Pietro da Novellara, vice-general of the Carmelites, who was acting as her artistic agent in Florence. Isabella was anxious to acquire a painting by Leonardo.[49] Fra Pietro responded that Leonardo was working hard at geometry, with "absolutely no patience to spare for painting."[50] Two weeks later, he wrote again to say that he had seen Leonardo in person and that "his mathematical experiments have so distracted him from painting that he cannot bear the sight of a paintbrush."[51] Just before leaving Milan in December 1499, the artist had transferred a rather large sum of 600 florins to his bank account in the Hospital of Santa Maria Nuova in Florence,[52] allowing him to refuse commissions, even from such an illustrious a patron as Isabella d'Este.

In May 1502 Leonardo, now aged fifty, accepted a position to serve Cesare Borgia as architect and engineer (Fig. 20). Leonardo almost certainly had first met the duke in early October 1499, when Valentino had accompanied Louis XII into Milan. His willingness to enter Borgia's service suggests that he was pleased at the prospect of resuming his career as a military architect and engineer, although, as Kemp suggests, it might also have been because he found it difficult to resist Cesare's great personal magnetism.[53] His second meeting with Valentino occurred in July 1502 in the Duchy of Urbino, which, in a surprising move, as we saw in chapter 3, Valentino had captured from Duke Guidobaldo (Fig. 13). According to Vecce, Leonardo would have been especially eager to superintend the military installations of the duke's new lands, giving him the opportunity to study up close the web of castles and strongholds executed for Guidobaldo's father, Federico da Montefeltro, by Francesco di Giorgio Martini, widely acknowledged to be the leading master of fortification.[54] While in Sforza's service Leonardo had served as architectural consultant to Francesco di Giorgio in Pavia in 1490 and owned one of his treatises on architecture and machines.[55]

Vecce also draws attention to Leonardo's red-chalk portrait of a bearded man in the Biblioteca Reale, Turin (Fig. 35), which might represent Cesare

Borgia and date from this time in Urbino.[56] On a sheet measuring 111 × 284 millimetres Leonardo has drawn a man with a bushy, curly beard and long, wavy hair from three different vantage points. On the left, he is drawn in profile, in the middle, in a three-quarter view, and on the right, from the front. The head at the centre of the sheet is shown wearing a round cap with an encircling headband reaching down almost to the eyebrows, whereas the figure on the right is bareheaded. If these heads really do represent Duke Valentino, as many believe,[57] they are quite remarkable. Leonardo's *Notebooks* contain many independent male head studies, but these are either preparatory studies for paintings or, more often, heads in profile that form part of his systematic investigation into ideal types or grotesques.[58] The Turin drawing, showing different views of the same subject, is unique in Leonardo's surviving work. The profile head depicts an energetic, virile man, with his head held high looking to the right, whereas the two other heads express a more reflective, pensive mood. These three-quarter and frontal heads show Cesare as if sitting in a relaxed pose across from the artist, his head lowered and his eyes cast down as though absorbed in deep thought. If Leonardo was able to share such an unguarded, intimate proximity to the duke, then both men must have felt at ease being in each other's company. Such an introspective Borgia is clearly at odds with the public perception of the pope's bastard son, summed up for example, in Machiavelli's first dispatch to the Florentine *Signoria*, where he wrote that Valentino "never rests or knows danger or weariness."[59] In the summer of 1502, Borgia was twenty-seven, which would be consistent with this youthful, "partly idealized" portrait.[60] The iconic frontal view of the head at the right edge of the sheet is also exceptional, and for some commentators it suggests the tradition of the depiction of Christ as *Salvator Mundi*.[61]

After their meeting in Urbino, Cesare's high esteem for Leonardo was revealed a few weeks later when, on 18 August in Pavia, he issued a *patent*, a kind of passport, allowing Leonardo to travel through his territories unharmed. Written in elegant humanist script and addressed to all his lieutenants, castellans, captains, *condottieri*, officers, soldiers, and subjects, the duke hails Leonardo as his "Most Excellent and Most Beloved Familiar Architect and General Engineer," notifying them that Leonardo and his company have been given the commission to survey the strongholds and fortresses of all his states. They are to be given free passage and a friendly reception and are to be exempt from all tolls. Leonardo can order as many men as he needs on his requisition, and all engineers are compelled to consult with him and conform to his opinion. Cesare ends with an admonition: "And to this may none presume to act in opposition if it be his pleasure not to incur our indignation."[62] Leonardo obviously felt flattered by the sweeping authority he was given, and, although he remained in the duke's employ for less than a year, he must have treasured this *patent,* because it was found carefully preserved among his personal effects after his death in 1519.[63]

Giorgio Vasari made no mention of Leonardo's contacts with Borgia in his biography written in the mid-sixteenth century and perhaps, as we saw with Giuliano's twentieth-century biographer, Giuseppe Fatini, his motive may have been to protect the reputation of the artist. Nonetheless, there are numerous entries in Leonardo's so-called Manuscript L, now in Paris,[64] consisting of notes and studies made in the summer of 1502 during his journeys through Borgia's conquered domains in central Italy – Piombino, Urbino, Pesaro, Rimini, Porto Cesenatico, and Cesena. In Cesena, selected as the capital of Cesare's new state,[65] Leonardo stayed for more than a month before making his way in early September to Imola, where he received new instructions from Cesare. The notes demonstrate that he was primarily concerned with military architecture, inspecting and strengthening defence systems and supervising repairs and the rebuilding of fortresses.[66] He has also left numerous notes on the port of Cesenatico and plans for digging a canal to link Cesena to the sea.[67] But there were also imaginative schemes to improve the region. The evidence shows that when Leonardo arrived in Imola in September he received new orders for harbour works in Cesena, as well as for the construction of new university buildings and a Palace of Justice to accommodate the High Court.[68] Having accurate maps of all his domains was a major concern for Borgia, and during the time Leonardo worked for him, the artist made maps of Tuscany, Umbria, the Val di Chiana, and Castiglion Fiorentino, on which the exact measurements of distances are marked out between the various towns and fortresses.[69] The result was to give the duke great strategic advantage, enabling him to take the shortest route, so that when Machiavelli wrote in his dispatches to the Florentine Signoria that Valentino "arrives at a place before anyone has heard that he has left the place he was in before,"[70] he was not exaggerating.

Leonardo remained in the small fortress town of Imola for three months, giving him the opportunity to spend time with fellow Florentines Machiavelli and Giuliano, then a captain in Borgia's army. Giuliano visited frequently from Bologna during the negotiations between Borgia and Giovanni II Bentivoglio. During this time, Leonardo made a beautiful bird's-eye-view map of Imola (Fig. 36), measuring 44 × 60.2 centimetres and drawn in pen and ink and watercolour.[71] Inscribed in a circle, Imola is divided into eight main segments radiating from the centre, showing fortified walls, the great fortress in the southwest corner, and every street, square, house, and garden carefully delineated and delicately colour-coded, with public squares painted deep yellow, streets white, houses shaded in pink, and the winding river at the bottom of the circle a delicate blue. The distances between each feature were paced out on the ground to give exact measurements, resulting in a map that was remarkably precise, surely pleasing to Cesare. Indeed, the aesthetic aspect of the map convinces some that it must have been made as a presentation drawing for Valentino.[72]

It is not difficult to imagine how Leonardo would have impressed many at the ducal court with his knowledge of surveying and his skill at map making. Years later, writing in chapter 14 of *The Prince*, Machiavelli stressed how important it was for the prince to have knowledge of geography: "The hills, valleys, plains, rivers, and swamps of Tuscany, for example, have certain similarities to those of other territories, so that by knowing the lie of the land in one territory, one can easily come to know it in others. A prince who lacks this expertise lacks the most important quality in a commander, because it teaches you to find the enemy, choose a campsite, lead troops, organize them for battles, and besiege towns to your own advantage."[73] Giuliano surely remembered the vital services, cartography included, that Leonardo provided for Cesare Borgia, and it is certain that he would have wanted to avail himself of this same expertise when planning for his own new state eleven years later.

NICCOLÒ MACHIAVELLI

Evidence that Leonardo's friendship with Machiavelli had flourished in Imola can be found in the fact that, when the artist left Borgia's service and returned to Florence in March 1503, Machiavelli, a close adviser to *gonfaloniere di giustizia* Soderini, obtained two prestigious government contracts for his friend. The first drew on Leonardo's long experience as a hydraulic engineer in Lombardy, where he had consulted on the building of shipping and irrigation canals, as well as his more recent projects for canal digging in Cesena. In their interminable war with Pisa, the Florentines had concocted a scheme to divert the Arno River toward Livorno by means of a canal, thus depriving the Pisans of fresh water. A second, equally ambitious scheme, one that had been suggested at least as early as 1347, was to dig canals wide enough to render the Arno navigable between Florence and the sea, in order to bring increased trade and prosperity to the city. Even though a start was made on the first project, it was quickly abandoned on account of insurmountable difficulties and the enormous costs involved. All that remains of the second scheme are Leonardo's series of maps that show proposals for converting the Arno into a navigable canal.[74] The other government commission called for a huge fresco on the wall of the Great Council chamber in the Palazzo della Signoria, but that project was also soon abandoned.[75] The subject chosen for the fresco was the victory of the Florentines over the Milanese forces in 1440 at Anghiari.[76] Even though Leonardo made a start on the mural's central section, depicting the fight for the standard, the painting was never completed. In May 1506 the artist went to Milan and, although he returned to Florence in September 1507, he was back north again April 1508, working for Charles d'Amboise, the French governor of the city, on designs for a suburban villa.[77] Charles was, in all probability, a more generous and congenial patron than the republican government officials in Florence.

From Leonardo's own notes, as we have already seen, we know that he left Milan and headed for Rome on 24 September 1513, travelling with a small entourage and transporting his entire studio, with many books, pictures (including the unfinished *Mona Lisa*), and voluminous notes, as well as all sorts of specialized equipment.[78] Perhaps he thought that, now that he had reached the age of sixty and had secured Giuliano's protection, he would be able to settle permanently in Rome and never have to embark on another long and arduous journey again. On his way, Leonardo would have passed along the Via Emilia through Giuliano's projected state of Piacenza, Parma, Modena, and Reggio before making his descent south at Bologna through the Apennines, where he would have made a brief stop in Florence.[79] It is also highly likely that, on resuming his journey, he stopped in San Casciano, a few kilometres from Florence, on the main road south to Rome, to visit Machiavelli.[80] Following his release from prison, Machiavelli was exiled from Florence and confined to his farm at Sant'Andrea in Percussina, living an isolated, solitary life, far from the political excitement of the city that had once been his intellectual lifeline. A visit from

Leonardo would have certainly lifted his spirits, as would the news that Leo X intended to create a state for Giuliano from the northern cities of Parma, Piacenza, Modena, and Reggio. The fact that Leonardo had been appointed to the post of architect and military engineer may have given Machiavelli reason to hope that Giuliano would employ him too, and thus save him from a life of inactivity and obscurity.

In a letter to Francesco Vettori dated 10 December 1513, Machiavelli informed the ambassador that he had "composed a short study *On Principalities* (*De principatibus*) that was more or less finished; he intended to dedicate it to Giuliano.[81] Could news of Giuliano's new state have inspired Machiavelli to write *The Prince*? Did he begin to write his little treatise after a visit from Leonardo, who was on his way to enter Giuliano's service in Rome? One of the most contentious issues among Machiavelli scholars today is the question of whether *The Prince* was written, as some believe, as a piece of disinterested political writing, or whether Machiavelli's intention was more focused and practical, writing his book as a guide for Giuliano, about to take over a new state. This question will form the subject of the next chapter.

LEONARDO IN ROME

By late November, Leonardo and his household were, no doubt, installed in rooms in the Villa Belvedere of the Vatican, where many artists working for the pope resided, including Raphael, who, two years later, would paint a portrait of Giuliano in his studio in the Belvedere, as discussed in chapter 9 (Figs. 5, 38, and 39). Built as a summer retreat by Pope Innocent VIII (r. 1484–92), the Villa Belvedere rests on the top of a steep escarpment and, as its name implies, affords magnificent views of the city and surrounding countryside. It was connected to the Vatican Palace by Bramante's great court, constructed at the request of Julius II to house the papal collection of ancient statues.[82] An itemized list survives, dated 1 December 1513, showing that extensive renovations were planned for Leonardo's quarters, including repairs to the ceilings and floors, the enlargement of a window, and construction of wooden room dividers to create several bedrooms, a kitchen, and a studio, as well as provision for furniture, such as wardrobes, benches, a chest, stools, and tables, one of which was designated for the mixing of colours.[83] Leonardo confirms Giuliano's generosity and patronage in a notation regarding the solution to a mathematical problem: "Finished on the seventh day of July, at the twenty-third hour, in the Belvedere, in the study given to me by the Magnifico, 1514."[84]

Leonardo received thirty-three gold ducats as a monthly allocation, a considerable sum,[85] and Giuliano appears not to have imposed any restrictions on the artist, thus allowing him to continue anatomical research. He paid special attention to embryology and the activity of the heart, perhaps with the view to publishing a treatise on anatomy. Scholars have long thought that Leonardo conducted dissections at the nearby hospital of Santo Spirito, but research by Domenico Laurenza suggests instead that the hospital of Santa Maria della Consolazione, located on the slopes of the Campidoglio, unlike other Roman hospitals, had a long tradition of the study of anatomy.[86] Although little else is known of Leonardo's own interests and activities during these Roman years, we do know that he undertook projects on behalf of Giuliano, including the aforementioned territorial survey, a drainage plan for the water-logged Pontine Marshes,[87] and, what certainly was Leonardo's most important commission for Giuliano, research into the development of a huge parabolic burning mirror.

Shortly after his notes of July 1514, Leonardo embarked north for Emilia, a journey possibly timed to escape Rome's oppressive August heat and unhealthy air while providing him an opportunity to carry out inspections and surveys for Giuliano. Leonardo recorded his presence in Parma on 25 September 1514 and on the banks of the Po River at Sant'Angelo two days later. Though Giuliano was shortly to become governor of Parma and Piacenza,[88] his engineer must have been travelling on his own. Sanudo records that Giuliano had been in Florence since June, having attended the festivities of St John the Baptist in the company of four cardinals and likely happy to have left behind a stiflingly hot Rome.[89] Giuliano remained in Florence until sometime in October, when Leo X sent him to Bolsena, so that he could escort Isabella d'Este to Rome together with Cardinal Bernardo Dovizi (Figs. 10 and 34). Isabella, having heard rumours that the pope was intent on acquiring states for his relatives, was anxious to win his friendship and ward off any further designs on the Duchy of Ferrara, a direct threat to her brother Alfonso d'Este,[90] or the Duchy of Urbino, which would likewise deprive her beloved sister-in-law Elisabetta Gonzaga of her husband's patrimony. (Although the pope made no move against Ferrara, he did usurp Urbino in 1516 for his nephew Lorenzo, an action harshly condemned by both Giuliano and Isabella, as well as many others.) On 18 October 1514 Isabella made her entrance into Rome, where she remained until March 1515.[91]

On 14 December 1514 Giuliano petitioned the pope, requesting title to a huge tract of land situated southeast of Rome, known as the Pontine Marshes. This land, hemmed in by a chain of mountains and the Tyrrhenian Sea, encompassed low-lying marshland that was susceptible to constant flooding because the coastal dune system prevented the many watercourses that flowed down from the surrounding mountains from properly draining into the sea. Even in Roman times, this land was notorious as a place where the stagnant swamps were "putrid, and emit vapours of a heavy and pestilent nature."[92] Plans to drain the marshes had been considered by Julius Caesar but nothing was achieved, so that in Giuliano's day the Pontine Marshes were populated only by brigands and malaria-infested mosquitoes that during the summer affected the health and well-being of the Roman population. Giuliano proposed to undertake all the expenses and risk to drain the marshes in return for hereditary title to the reclaimed lands. His plan, shown on a topographical relief map, drawn by Leonardo, and now housed in the Royal Library at Windsor (Fig. 37), involved two separate interventions. The first was to widen the existing Rio Martini, shown on the left side of the map, that flows into the sea, and the second, to construct a new drainage canal to carry water from the swamps at the place marked Badino, located half-way up the coast, on the right side of the map.[93]

Given Leonardo's extensive experience and his great interest in hydraulics, this detailed map suggests that he may have worked out a plan to drain the marshes before approaching Giuliano with the idea. It is likely that this map was used to accompany Giuliano's petition to the pope on 14 December to propose the scheme. The fact that Leonardo's assistant Francesco Melzi marked the place names legibly on the map strongly indicates that his intention was to present the map to others.[94] The pope readily consented to his brother's request, but since Leonardo was engaged on another important project for Giuliano in Rome, the work was entrusted to Fra Giovanni Scotti, whom Leonardo could have known from his days in Milan.[95] News of the death of Giuliano in March 1516 suspended all activity; the plan to drain the marshes was completely abandoned following the death of Leo X in 1521.[96]

Soon after his arrival in Rome, Leonardo began work on another, more ambitious undertaking for Giuliano: the construction of an enormous parabolic burning mirror. Leonardo's interest in the burning properties of concave mirrors dates back to his years in Florence where, as early as 1480, he was drawing devices for grinding parabolic mirrors.[97] Throughout the workshops of Florence at the time, burning mirrors were used to solder metal alloys, and it is interesting to note that in Rome in 1515, at the very time he was working on his parabolic mirror for Giuliano, Leonardo wrote: "Keep in mind how the ball of Santa Maria del Fiore was soldered together in sections."[98] Leonardo was remembering the time he served as an apprentice in Andrea del Verrocchio's workshop, when Verrocchio, the leading sculptor in Florence, was given a commission in 1468 to make the gilt copper ball, or *palla*, for the top of the lantern of the Florence cathedral. The ball, made from eight separate pieces of copper, was soldered together using a burning mirror.[99]

Leonardo scholars appear divided, however, in their views about how Giuliano was to utilize Leonardo's burning mirror. Pedretti believes, citing Leonardo's own note, which he dates c. 1513–14, that Leonardo's intention was to use these parabolic mirrors for industrial purposes and to utilize solar energy to heat large boilers in dyeing factories. Leonardo wrote in his notebook now known as the Codex Atlanticus: "One wonders whether the 'pyramid' can be condensed to bring so much power to one single point, and whether it acquires more density than the air that sustains it. With this one can supply heat for any boiler in a dyeing factory. And with this a pool can be warmed up, because there will always be boiling water."[100] Pedretti suggests that the Medici, after one of their family members had been elected to the Holy See, may have been very keen to develop a textile industry in Rome, like the one in Florence, assuring the economic prosperity of the Florentines.[101] Martin Kemp, on the other hand, while not discounting the possibility of using such mirrors to boil water in dyeing works, also suggests that the parabolic mirror "may well have been a burning mirror for military use."[102] Vecce also speculates about a military use for the parabolic mirror: "Any eventual military use of the burning mirror could not help but bring to Leonardo's mind the image of Archimedes and the siege of Syracuse."[103] Vecce is, of course, alluding to the legend of how Archimedes, the Greek mathematician, set fire to the Roman fleet using a giant burning mirror, during the siege of Syracuse from 215 to 212 BCE, in the Second Punic War. By reviewing the evidence, one could easily come to the conclusion that Leonardo's project to construct a burning mirror was for military use, but before going any further, it is important to establish how much Leonardo actually knew about Archimedes and his legendary weapon.

Some years before Leonardo embarked on a serious study of the geometry and mathematics of Archimedes, he had shown a keen interest in Archimedes' machines of war. He had invented a version of Archimedes' *Architronito* in Milan, as seen in notations from about 1487–90 that accompany three drawings of his machine: "'The *Architronito* is a machine of fine copper, an invention of Archimedes, and it throws iron balls with great noise and violence.'"[104] Leonardo's source for this weapon was the drawings of cannons in *De Re Militari* by Roberto Valturius (1405–1475), who stated that Archimedes invented the cannon. Leonardo owned a copy of Valturius' book, but his drawings show that he had reinvented Archimedes' weapon using the power of steam instead of the already well-established gunpowder.[105] Both Pedretti and Kemp emphasize how much Leonardo admired and respected Archimedes.[106] Perhaps Leonardo hoped that he too would be honoured as a "second Archimedes" in the same way that the noted Florentine architect Filippo Brunelleschi (1377–1446) had been in the previous generation.[107] Laird has shown that, in the early Renaissance, Archimedes was famous for being a practical designer and builder of ingenious instruments and machines, and that it was this aspect, rather than his reputation for mathematics and geometry, that the early humanists had promoted. Petrarch, for example, hailed him as the greatest mechanic and designer of machines. Only in the first part of the sixteenth century was Archimedes rediscovered for being a mathematician of sublime and formidable ability.[108] Luca Pacioli (1445/50–1517), Leonardo's close companion at the Sforza court and later in Florence,[109] was one of those early mathematicians who had discovered Archimedes' mathematics and geometry, and although he had little direct knowledge of Archimedes' works, he did play an important role as the disseminator of Archimedean mathematics.[110] Significantly for Leonardo, Pacioli was the first Renaissance writer to refer to Archimedes' use of burning mirrors at Syracuse.[111] In his *De viribus quantitatis* Pacioli wrote: "Archimedes was accustomed to say that if he had enough material he would be able to make a mirror which would burn up the whole world just as at Syracuse he set fire to one transport and another ship."[112]

Leonardo must have discussed with Pacioli the feasibility of building such a weapon, especially when Leonardo was working for Cesare Borgia in 1502, when he began in earnest to search for manuscripts by Archimedes, noting: "Borgia will get me the Archimedes of the Bishop of Padua and Vitellozzo the one at Borgo di San Sepolcro,"[113] perhaps hearing of the existence of this last manuscript from Pacioli himself. Many years later in Rome, Leonardo was still anxiously searching for manuscripts. In 1515 he noted: "There is a complete Archimedes in the possession of the brother of Monsignor of Santa Giusta in Rome. The latter said that he had given it to his brother who lives in Sardinia. It was formerly in the Library of the Duke of Urbino and was carried off from there in the time of Duke Valentino."[114] On the same folio as this notation Leonardo drew a diagram relating to the study of reflections of a burning mirror.[115] Perhaps he had come across the tantalizing passage in the second-century *Apologia* of Lucius Apuleius, author of the famous *Golden Ass*, in which he refers to a monumental volume by Archimedes that included a section on burning mirrors.[116]

We know that, even before Leonardo's arrival in Rome, Giuliano had established a workshop in the Belvedere for the making of mirrors and had hired the services of an expert German mirror-maker, the most technologically advanced at the time,[117] who was known in Italy as Giovanni degli Specchi. In April 1514, a few months after Leonardo's arrival, Giuliano sent Isabella d'Este a gift of a golden mirror,[118] and Leonardo himself confirmed, in a draft of a letter he wrote in the summer of 1515 to Giuliano, then in Florence, that there were "a number of workmen making numerous mirrors to send to the fairs" and that this Giovanni had filled the whole Belvedere with workshops for making mirrors.[119] Giovanni degli Specchi worked independently of Leonardo, but, as Leonardo complained in his letter to Giuliano, the German was always hovering about in the workshop, wanting to discover Leonardo's secrets, and was highly critical of anything that he did not understand. What was worse, he wrote, this same Giovanni degli Specchi had denounced Leonardo before the pope and the hospital (most likely Santa Maria della Consolazione), accusing him of engaging in sacrilegious practices: "This other hindered me in anatomy, blaming me before the Pope; and likewise at the hospital."[120] Leonardo believed the German had acted out of jealousy, since Leonardo's presence at the Belvedere, as he informed Giuliano, "had deprived [master Giovanni the mirror-maker] of the countenance and favour of your Lordship."[121] It remains a mystery why Leo X, who was renowned for his great liberality, took the accusations against Leonardo seriously, but he did, prohibiting Leonardo from carrying out his anatomical research and also forbidding the artist from entering the hospital.[122] This same Giovanni also had a malign influence over another German mirror-maker, Giorgio, who had been assigned to work directly with Leonardo, but who, as we learn from Leonardo's letter, was insolent and caused the artist nothing but grief. He refused either to work with Leonardo or to learn Italian, and preferred to spend his days shooting birds with the Swiss Guards.[123]

Leonardo's burning mirror was to be of "enormous size"[124] and made from a great quantity of reflecting pieces held together by a structure known as a *sagoma* that ensured the perfect curvature of the mirror.[125] The most urgent technical problem was to find the angle of reflection, or locus of the point of combustion of rays, that would create the maximum concentration of heat. Pacioli, summoned to Rome in 1514,[126] was in all likelihood appointed to work with his old friend Leonardo on the geometry of the parabolic mirror. If Leonardo's burning mirror was designed not for industrial purposes but as a weapon of war, it must be considered within the context of the rising fears in Rome about the great threat posed to Christendom by the Turks, of which both Giuliano and Leonardo were only too aware. Giuliano had many discussions regarding this matter with the Venetian hermits Querini and Giustiniani; and Leonardo had been called a decade earlier by the Venetians to be consulted on the land defences in the Friuli region. Giuliano attended the seventh session of the Fifth Lateran Council, which opened on 17 June 1513;[127] there, he would have heard Balthassar del Rio make an urgent, impassioned appeal to the pope to mount a crusade, warning "that the Lateran Basilica itself was in danger of being put to the torch by the Turks."[128] Fears of a Turkish attack were greatly intensified in December 1513, following the opening of the eighth session of the Lateran Council on 19 December 1513, when a Knight of St John of Jerusalem, Giovanni Battista de Gargha of Siena, implored the pope and "Christian princes to awaken from their perilous slumber, take up arms on behalf of the Church."[129] He warned that the Turks were preparing for war, having assembled a huge fleet, soldiers, and cannons, and he spoke about the sightings of Turkish navy in the Tyrrhenian Sea, declaring: "Was it not shameful that they could even raid the shores of the Roman campagna?"[130] Giuliano did not attend this session of the Lateran Council because, as Sanudo reports, both he and Cardinal Bernardo Dovizi were unwell and remained in Giuliano's palace,[131] but they certainly would have been informed about the subject of the address.

In February 1514 Giuliano spent several weeks on the coast at Civitavecchia,[132] and it is quite possible that a worried Leo X sent him there to inspect the fortifications of the harbour. Leonardo accompanied Giuliano on this occasion and made drawings of the plan of the port, the docks, fortress, and quay.[133] Perhaps it was while conducting surveys of Civitavecchia that the idea was first broached about the feasibility of building a giant burning mirror to defend the coast from an attack by the Turkish fleet, just as Archimedes had done in Syracuse. Belief that burning mirrors could be made powerful enough to burn ships was widespread in the Renaissance, and it was not until the end of the seventeenth century that this certainty turned to skepticism.[134] When Leo X recalled his brother to Rome,[135] Leonardo must have continued his inspection of the coastline, travelling south, until he reached the Pontine Marshes. After conducting a survey of the whole area, perhaps it was at this time that Leonardo came up with his plan for the two drainage canals. Leonardo probably presented his topographical map later on, after both he and Giuliano had returned to Rome, in the autumn of 1514.

Giuliano's death in March 1516, at the age of thirty-eight, brought to an abrupt end Leonardo's work on the burning mirrors. The loss of his friend and patron meant that Leonardo was now without any protection. Leo X did not share his brother's great esteem for Leonardo's talents or even take him seriously as a painter, as indicated in Vasari's *Life* of the artist.[136] The pope preferred instead to support Michelangelo and Raphael, awarding a commission to Michelangelo to design a new façade for the Medici family church of San Lorenzo in Florence and, most surprisingly of all, given his youth and inexperience, appointing Raphael to take over as principal architect of the new St Peter's following Bramante's death in 1514.[137] Leonardo was still in Rome in August 1516, but, without any hope of securing a patron in either Rome or Florence, he had no alternative but to leave Italy altogether. Old and in poor health, he once again loaded up all his possessions and embarked on the long, and what must have been difficult, journey crossing over the Alps. He found his final refuge at Amboise, France, where King Francis I graciously received him as an honoured guest.

CHAPTER EIGHT

GIULIANO AS MACHIAVELLI'S *IL PRINCIPE*

The friendship between Giuliano de' Medici and Niccolò Machiavelli, built upon a profound love of their native city of Florence and a shared passion for vernacular poetry, has already been discussed in previous chapters. Two eulogistic poems, argued in chapter 4 to have been composed in Imola in 1502, make apparent that the youngest son of Lorenzo the Magnificent made a profound impression on Machiavelli. In September 1512, as noted in chapter 1, it seems that Giuliano entrusted Machiavelli to write his "Letter to a Noblewoman" to Isabella d'Este in Mantua on his behalf. Indeed, there is every indication that Giuliano wanted Machiavelli to remain in his secretarial post in the chancery. As has been proposed in chapter 4, Machiavelli wrote his *Ai Palleschi* just before he was dismissed from government service in November 1512, as a warning to Giuliano not to listen to the advice given by radical *palleschi*. Soon thereafter, as one poet to another, Machiavelli sent two sonnets to Giuliano from prison in his hour of greatest need. Giuliano responded to Machiavelli's pleas, so that, later, Machiavelli could write that he owed his life to the "Magnificent Giuliano." Found innocent of conspiracy, he was set free despite those who still saw him as a dangerous enemy who had plotted against the Medici during his tenure as second chancellor of the Florentine republic.

In the last months of 1513, when he had to endure a forced idleness at his farm in Sant'Andrea in Percussina, Machiavelli wrote his famous, or infamous, as it came to be seen later in the sixteenth century, book *The Prince.*[1] The work has generated a vast literature and an array of divergent and conflicting interpretations, not only regarding the book itself but also about Machiavelli's political views. Two central questions have puzzled readers. First, what did Machiavelli intend to achieve by writing *The Prince*, and second, who was the presumed audience? Was it meant as a handbook to teach a new prince the rules of political power, including that evil deeds may have to be committed in order to acquire and maintain his new territories? Or was it a piece of disinterested political theory to prove to everyone, as Viroli contends, that even though he had been removed from office, his knowledge of the art of statecraft was unparalleled, and that he was a better political thinker than all the men of antiquity, particularly Cicero and his modern followers?[2] Another great puzzle is that, in his *Discourses on the First Ten Books of Titus Livy*, composed at more or less the same time, Machiavelli spoke with the voice of a resolute republican, as he had in other writings, and adhered to a completely different political outlook and value system than that set out in *The Prince*. Described by Mansfield and Tarcov as a "decent and useful book," the *Discourses* "advises citizens, leaders, reformers, and founders of republics on how to order them to preserve their liberty and avoid corruption."[3] How could the political philosophy of *The Prince*, transgressing conventional morality, seemingly written by one who had no use for moral principles, be reconciled with that of the *Discourses*? As has been demonstrated, Giuliano and Machiavelli knew each other personally, a relationship that sheds new light on questions concerning Machiavelli's intentions in writing *The Prince*. By rejecting Ciceronian and Christian moral precepts, he chose to instruct the new prince in the ways of an evil deed.

Machiavelli's famous letter, dated 10 December 1513 and addressed to Francesco Vettori, Florentine ambassador to the papal court, announced that he had just composed a little study, *De principatibus* (Of Principalities), "in which I delve as deeply as I can into the ideas concerning this topic, discussing the definition of a princedom, the categories of princedoms, how they are acquired, how they are retained, and why they are lost. And if ever any whimsy of mine has given you pleasure, this one should not displease you. It ought to be welcomed by a prince, and especially by a new prince; therefore I am dedicating it to His Magnificence Giuliano."[4] This passage strongly suggests that Machiavelli wrote the book with Giuliano's special circumstances in mind.[5] As postulated in the previous chapter, Machiavelli may have learned of Pope Leo's plans to create a new principate from Leonardo, newly appointed as Giuliano's military architect and engineer. Given that the artist likely stopped off on his way to Rome to pay a visit to his old friend in Sant'Andrea in Percussina, the news that Giuliano was poised to take possession of a principate surely would have come up. If the two did meet in early October 1513, the idea to write *The Prince* may have been inspired by Leonardo's visit. What better way for Machiavelli to remind Giuliano of his existence than to write him a small book of advice for his new state?[6] He had already written a short political tract for Giuliano, his *Ai Palleschi*, headed "Note well this writing," as if to warn Giuliano of the dangers he faced from the radical *palleschi* in Florence. Could the impetus to write *The Prince* have been similar? Did he write his book to alert Giuliano to the new political realities that would confront him outside Florence? Was it his intention to make Giuliano think less like a good republican, as he knew Giuliano to be, and more like an absolute prince, whose opposing precepts, set out clearly in *The Prince,* he must now adopt if he was to survive in the treacherous waters of Italian politics? Machiavelli seems to have written his "little study" at a feverish pace, since the manuscript was essentially finished by early December, not long after Leonardo's presumed visit. He informs Vettori in his letter that all that was required to complete the text was some "fattening" and "currying."[7] Did he fervently hope that his book of advice on principalities would lead to his being hired by Giuliano?

Brian Richardson observes that "one of the striking features" of the work "is its lack of the polish which one would expect in artistic prose."[8] This unadorned language and almost complete absence of fine, ornamental words or rhetorical flourishes was part of Machiavelli's strategy, Richardson believes, to "shock [readers] into awareness that fine words were not enough" so that when they read his book they would "stop dreaming about imaginary states" and focus on the "actual truth of the matter."[9] Machiavelli was the voice of practical experience, and his aim was to instruct the new prince on how to hold on to power by using any means necessary. In his later prose works, such as the *Discourses*, the *Art of War*, and the *Florentine Histories*, Machiavelli abandoned this blunt, matter-of-fact style, because he was now writing for a much larger audience, being conscious of his responsibility to demonstrate the superiority of the Tuscan language over other dialects on the Italian peninsula. Could this isolated use of straightforward language, then, indicate, as Richardson seems to imply, that *The Prince* was meant as "a practical advice document," with an intention to be circulated among a small, select circle of readers?[10]

Machiavelli wrote *The Prince* in the vernacular and gave each of the twenty-six chapters a heading in Latin. The book is divided into four sections: chapters 1 through 11 discuss principalities (hereditary, mixed, new, civil, and ecclesiastical) and how they are acquired (with Fortune and the arms of others, or by one's own troops and virtue); chapters 12 to 14 deal with military matters and various sorts of troops, be they mercenary, auxiliary, mixed, or citizen-soldiers; chapters 15 to 19 concentrate on the moral character of the prince, how princes are praised or held responsible, whether they should be benevolent or close-fisted, cruel or merciful, and how a prince should keep his word and avoid being loathed; chapters 20 to 25 cover a variety of questions, such as the usefulness of fortresses, the selection of ministers, the necessity of acquiring esteem and avoiding flatterers, and the role of Fortune in human affairs. The book concludes with a chapter entitled "An Exhortation to Seize Italy and to Free Her from the Barbarians." Most chapters are quite short in length, on average between five and seven paragraphs; three of them are, however, much longer, indicating their relative importance: chapter 3, consisting of fourteen paragraphs, deals with mixed principalities; chapter 7, with its thirteen paragraphs, describes the exemplary role of Cesare Borgia; and chapter 19, having sixteen paragraphs, gives advice on how the prince must avoid being disliked.

In a letter to Francesco Vettori of 31 January 1515, Machiavelli relayed that his brother Paolo had told him about Giuliano's promise to appoint him a governor "of one of those cities over which he is currently taking control." Significantly, however, Machiavelli made it clear that Paolo had not divulged which cities were to comprise Giuliano's state, since he wrote: "And having understood – not from Paolo but from a rumour – that His Magnificence is to become lord of Parma, Piacenza, Modena, and Reggio, I think this is a rule that would be considerable and would be strong."[11] Machiavelli wrote also about the need to unify these cities into one state body, which could explain what he had in mind in chapter 3 when he talked of "mixed states." The letter continued with advice on how this could be achieved, and, as many have observed, the advice given is essentially a gloss on *The Prince*.[12] All this would indicate that, at the time of writing in 1513, he knew, possibly from Leonardo, where the state was to be located, but that he purposely chose not to reveal the identity of the four Emilian cities because it was still a secret. This also would explain why chapter 3, seemingly concerned with Giuliano's particular circumstances, received so much prominence.[13]

Machiavelli's reason for writing *The Prince* was to give Giuliano helpful advice on how to acquire and maintain his new state. We know that Giuliano already had his own political opinions and convictions by the time he took over the reins of the Florentine government in 1512. He exercised his power moderately, showing magnanimity toward his enemies and promoting tolerance and reconciliation among the citizenry. The *Instructions* that he wrote for Lorenzo di Piero de' Medici in the summer of 1513 also revealed his political thinking; there, as explained in chapter 5, he attempted to instill in his nephew a respect for the republican institutions of Florence, as well as for the great families of the city, urging him, among other things, to be mindful of the right social precedence when distributing favours and patronage. Giuliano's portrait medal (Figs. 26 and 27), struck to commemorate the Florentine Carnival of 1513, also expressed his political aspirations for the people of Florence, whom he wanted to reconcile with *magnificenta e pietà*. Niccolò Guicciardini,[14] nephew of one of Machiavelli's friends, the historian Francesco Guicciardini, confirms his many virtues, writing in 1519, three years after Giuliano's death:

> And it is true that all the people were profoundly distressed by his death because in him there was a singular humanity and kindness, for he had a good nature and a great love for all the citizens [of Florence] that it was almost impossible to imagine, and toward all citizens he was so easy and graceful in audience and love, that it is impossible to estimate, and because this humanity in similar great men is the most rare and most gracious virtue that is possible to imagine. It was obvious to everyone how deeply he regretted

> how things had gone in Florence, because he was most ready to make people love him rather than fear him and he desired always to help them and to gain his enemies favour rather than oppress them through revenge.[15]

If we accept the proposition that *The Prince* was conceived for the benefit of Giuliano, and that Machiavelli, as his friend, was deeply concerned for his future as the prince of a new state, could this explain why he laid so much stress on teaching Giuliano how "not to be good"? Was he trying to protect him because he feared that Giuliano's innate goodness would cause him to fail in his new enterprise? In many ways Machiavelli's *Prince* was typical of a class of books intended to guide the practice of princes, and according to Clough, there already existed at least fifty or sixty books of the same genre.[16] The great originality of *The Prince*, however, lies in the fact that Machiavelli had dared to put into writing advice that rejects the convention whereby princes were taught by their educators to be just, noble, and virtuous. Instead, his book teaches an amoral pragmatism whereby, if the new prince wished to perpetuate his state, he must be willing "to learn how not to be good": "Many writers have imagined republics and principalities that have never been seen nor known to exist in reality. For there is such a distance between how one lives and how one ought to live, that anyone who abandons what is done for what ought to be done achieves his downfall rather than his preservation. A man who wishes to profess goodness at all times will come to ruin among so many who are not good. Therefore, it is necessary for a prince who wishes to maintain himself to learn how not to be good, and to use this knowledge or not to use it according to necessity."[17]

All that mattered to Machiavelli was "to search after the effectual truth of the matter rather than its imagined one."[18] He had no illusions about human nature and a bleak view of his fellow man, which must have become much darker after experiencing torture first-hand, as expressed in Book 1, chapter 3 of the *Discourses*, where he writes that those who desire to found a state and give it laws must begin with the assumption that "all men are bad, and that they always have to use the malignity of their spirit whenever they have a free opportunity for it. When any malignity remains hidden for a time, this proceeds from a hidden cause, which is not recognized because no contrary experience has been seen. But time, which they say is the father of every truth, exposes it later."[19]

Addressing princely conduct in chapter 16, Machiavelli wrote that the prince should avoid liberality, because he would never get recognition for it and could only attain grief. To sustain a reputation for generosity, he must always be lavish in his gifts and ostentatious in displays, but this would soon exhaust his resources, leading to impoverishment and forcing him to impose extortionate taxation on his people, who would then certainly detest him for it.[20] In chapter 18, Machiavelli used the famous simile of the ferocious lion and the cunning fox, derived from Cicero's *De Officiis*, where the author condemns using fraud or force because they imitate the nature of beasts and are wholly unworthy of men.[21] Machiavelli rejects the Ciceronian precept that, if a prince wanted to attain glory and preservation of his state, he must be virtuous,[22] arguing that his survival depended on him making good use of both the nature of man and the nature of the beast, but since the first act is often ineffective, "a prince must know how to make use of the nature of the beast, [and] he should choose from among the beasts the fox and the lion; for the lion cannot defend itself from traps, while the fox cannot protect itself from the wolves. It is therefore necessary to be a fox, in order to recognize the traps, and a lion, in order to frighten the wolves."[23] Furthermore, a prince who wished to retain his state must "not depart from the good if it is possible to do so, but he should know how to enter into evil when forced by necessity."[24]

It is very disconcerting for some readers, given Cesare Borgia's reputation for cruelty and treachery, to find that Machiavelli presented him as the ideal prince.[25] He writes: "I would not know of any better precepts to give a new prince than the example of his deeds." For Machiavelli, the duke possessed "great courage and high goals" and "did everything and used every method that a prudent and virtuous man ought to employ," proposing that all those "who have risen to power through Fortune and with the troops of others" should imitate him.[26] There is no doubt about Machiavelli's sincerity because his high regard for Cesare had not diminished since the first effusive praise he penned in his dispatches to the Florentine government in 1502. As mentioned in chapter 4, Machiavelli's adulatory 1502 poem to Giuliano described Cesare as the "duke of all the dukes," whose breast encloses "a noble heart." By presenting Cesare as his hero and model, Machiavelli knew that his words would give immense pleasure to Giuliano, because he, too, shared this high esteem for the duke. Not only had Giuliano's own rise to power been possible with the aid of "Fortune and the troops of others," but also he was now on the verge of creating his own hereditary state and could have been pondering Cesare's example in the Romagna.

In chapter 17, Machiavelli spoke of cruelty and mercy, writing, "Cesare Borgia was considered cruel; nonetheless, this cruelty of his brought order to the Romagna, united it, and restored it to peace and loyalty."[27] He states that Cesare was "more merciful than the Florentine people, who allowed the destruction of Pistoia in order to avoid being considered cruel."[28] Machiavelli was referring, of course, to the eruptions of violence that took place in 1499 and 1500 in Pistoia, a provincial town located thirty-five kilometres from Florence and a part of the Florentine state, between supporters of the two most powerful local families, the Panciatichi and the Cancellieri.[29] Since medieval times, the quarrels of these two factions, in Guicciardini's words, "had infected and stained the whole city and countryside."[30] In 1499 intense fighting broke out once more, aided by soldiers brought from Bologna, and for two months bloody street battles raged and many men were murdered, palaces destroyed, shops ransacked and burned, and the entire community made to suffer.[31] Giuliano would have understood why Machiavelli had used the example of Pistoia because, like many others, he had been horrified by the news of the killings and destruction in the city, so much so that he composed a sonnet (probably sometime in 1499 or 1500), in which he condemned those who were responsible for the savagery and carnage. Without choosing sides, Giuliano expressed revulsion for all those Pistoiese who were filled with so much hatred and abominations, and in anger he enumerated all their vices. His poem culminated in a cry of lament for Italy and a call for action: "Poor Italy, no better than sheep, that the inhabitants of / Tuscany chose to emulate the barbarians! / Return Italy, once more to your accustomed courage!"[32] Machiavelli's discourse on cruelty further asked whether "it is better to be loved than to be feared or the contrary," then answering his own question by saying that it is safer to be feared if either emotion is missing among the people. Men, he writes, are ungrateful and disloyal, liars and deceivers, quick to avoid danger but nonetheless greedy for profit. Hence, they more readily inflict injuries on those who are loved, because "love is held together by a chain of obligation that, since men are a wretched lot, is broken on every occasion for their own self-interest; but fear is sustained by a dread of punishment that will never abandon you."[33] Could Machiavelli be speaking for himself in this last line? Was he still haunted by the thought of his own harrowing experience of torture?

A vivid example of how the prince must be willing to use cruelty to win the support of the populace is given in chapter 7, and it concerns the nobleman Don Ramiro de Lorqua (Remirro de Orco), one of Borgia's Spanish captains, whom he had appointed governor of Romagna. Ramiro did bring peace and unity to the state, but he used excessive force and cruelty against the population, incurring the people's wrath. Borgia tried to show that the harshness was not his idea but that it originated in Ramiro's violent nature and, in an effort to win the people over, he ordered Ramiro's execution by beheading on Christmas morning 1502. His headless body was cut in two pieces and placed on a mat in the main square of Cesena, beside a block of wood and a bloody sword, where it lay until the following evening, for all to see. The ferocity of the act and the public staging of the body "left that population satisfied and stupefied at the same time."[34] While some readers of *The Prince* may conclude from this horrid episode that Borgia's reputation for evil-doing was fully justified, and even feel some pity for his "betrayed underling who was following his master's orders,"[35] in Machiavelli's eyes (he was present in Cesena when the execution took place) Borgia's use of cruelty was very effective, and it benefited his subjects. He was able to win the support of the people by dispensing cruel justice in this particular instance.

Did Ramiro deserve Cesare's act of brutality? Borgia had appointed Ramiro de Lorqua as *governatore e luogotenente* of Romagna in 1501, but on 14 August 1502, for unknown reasons, he relieved Ramiro of his governorship and confined him to his military role. A day after his imprisonment on 22 December in the fortress of Cesena, a proclamation was sent to all the cities of Romagna announcing Ramiro's arrest, ascribing it to the charges laid against him for a series of crimes, including oppression, extortion, and fraud.[36] The most egregious offence, it read, and contrary to strict prohibitions, was that he was trafficking in great quantities of grain for his own profit and at the expense of Borgia's army and the people of his state. This necessitated the importation of grain, at enormous cost, from outside the region. For these reasons, Ramiro had been arrested and charged, and his sentence would be just and would serve as an example to all present and future officials.[37] Alvisi wrote that the people of Cesena and Faenza, who had been subjected to the brutality of the governor, were generally pleased that the duke had been able to accommodate them by sacrificing such an important minister, "who by his imperious manner had hidden the most sordid rapacity."[38] Sacerdote makes the point that Borgia's method of wielding justice was not extraordinary for the times, and he believes that in his proclamation's carefully chosen words, Borgia showed that he really was a just ruler, and for this his people admired him.[39]

Machiavelli juxtaposed the names of Ramiro and Paolo Vettori in a letter he wrote to Paolo's brother Francesco dated 31 January 1515:

> Since Duke Valentino, whose deeds I should imitate on all occasions were I a new prince, was aware of this necessity [to create a firm foundation in his state], he appointed Messer Ramiro president in Romagna; this decision united those peoples and made them afraid of his authority, fond of his power, and trusting in it; all the love they felt for him, which was considerable, considering his unfamiliarity to them, resulted from this decision. I believe that this point, because it is true [that the duke was loved], could easily be proved; should this situation happen in your Paolo's case, it would be a step toward making him known not merely to His Magnificence but also to all of Italy; along with profiting and honouring His Lordship, he would provide prestige for himself, for you, and for your family. I spoke to him about this idea; he liked it and will consider how to avail himself of it.[40]

Given what we know from *The Prince* about Ramiro's grisly end, it is certainly strange that Machiavelli would seem to assign Paolo to the same role. Vettori, who had lost his position as *depositario* only a year before when Lorenzo replaced him with his young cousin Galeotto de' Medici, was seeking a position within the new Medicean state, eventually earning the role of Giuliano's *maggiordomo*.[41] Is Sebastian de Grazia correct when he proposes that "our political thinker" was so carried away by the idea of a "central Italian lordship ... beautiful and strong ruled over by a Florentine lieutenant [Paolo]" that he ignored Ramiro's horrific end when comparing Vettori to De Lorqua?[42] Or is Najemy nearer the mark for suggesting that Machiavelli was "piling irony upon irony" when he wrote the above passage, acknowledging that "love, fear, and political power are all bound up with each other in ways that *The Prince* sought to deny"?[43] Najemy argues that Machiavelli could have been warning Paolo not to get too "carried away with his hopes for glory in the service of a Medici prince as to lose sight of the dangers of being too successful."[44] Was he hinting that, if he was not careful, Paolo might very well end up by sharing Ramiro's fate? In drawing this parallel, it could well be that Machiavelli was reminding Francesco of how far Paolo had fallen from the good graces of Lorenzo. In November 1513, in a gesture of gratitude to Paolo for his efforts to return the Medici to Florence, Leo X named him *depositario* of the ecclesiastical *decima* in Florence. As we have seen previously, however, the cash-strapped Paolo had amassed enormous debts, and the temptation to use the funds for his own needs was too great. Lorenzo needed *decima* funds for his own expenses and for those of the regime and complained to his uncle, Cardinal Giulio, openly accusing Paolo of misappropriating the commune's funds.[45] Machiavelli was no doubt aware of Francesco's difficult position when it came to defending his troublesome brother before Lorenzo, who replaced Paolo with Galeotto de' Medici as *depositario*, one of several administrative roles given to him by his cousin.[46]

Before *The Prince* was finished, as he told Francesco in his letter of 10 December 1513, Machiavelli had shown the manuscript to his friend Filippo Casavecchia, possibly knowing that Casavecchia was shortly going to see Vettori in Rome. Machiavelli was certain that Vettori would be interested in his treatise and find pleasure in reading it. After months of forced idleness in the country and seeing his finances dwindle, Machiavelli was expecting that his book would redeem him in the eyes of the Medici, and, as he wrote in his letter, he hoped it would finally open the way for them to begin to engage his services. He asks whether it would be a good idea for him to come to Rome to present his book to Giuliano himself, or whether he should send it to Vettori: "Against presenting it would be my suspicion that he might not even read it and that that person Ardinghelli [the papal secretary] might take the credit for this most recent of my endeavours."[47] His reluctance to go to Rome himself was made very clear in the letter; he noted that he would feel obliged to visit the ex-*gonfaloniere a vita* Piero Soderini (who after being recalled from exile, chose to live in Rome) and talk with him, but, because the regime in Florence was still suspicious of him, he was afraid that upon his return he might "not count on dismounting at home but rather I should dismount at the Bargello." He begs Vettori "to make this fear evaporate, and then, come what may," he writes, "I shall come and see you in any case at the time mentioned."[48] Machiavelli was fearful of the reception he might receive in Medicean Rome, especially since he had no official position or protection, and that he might not be allowed access to Giuliano. It is also apparent that he was hoping Vettori would offer to present his book to Giuliano, and thus relieve him of these anxieties.

Impatient for Vettori's response, he sent another letter to Rome on 19 December, writing: "I wrote you eight or ten days ago and told you what made me uncertain about my going there. I am waiting for your opinion and then I shall do whatever you advise."[49] Vettori's reply of 24 December was filled with gossip about how Casavecchia and Giuliano Brancacci, their mutual friends from Florence, were adapting to Vettori's living arrangements in Rome, where they were his guests, and only toward the end of his letter did he refer to Machiavelli's book: "You write me, and Filippo has also told me, that you have written a certain work about states. I shall be grateful if you send it to me; and although I am not an authority, I judge it proper that I should judge your thing; so far as knowledge and judgment are lacking, affection and trust will make up for them. When I have seen it, I shall tell you my opinion about presenting it or not to the Magnificent Giuliano, as it may seem to me."[50]

As for him coming to Rome, he reassured Machiavelli by saying that since the Soderini had not appointed him to his post in the chancery, nor had given him any special favours or rewards, he should not feel obligated to them in any way. One courtesy visit to Cardinal Soderini was perhaps all that was required and, in his opinion, this would not get Machiavelli into any trouble. However, if he chose not to visit, nobody would think he was ungrateful. As for the ex-*gonfaloniere* Piero, he writes, "I do not think he would be happy to be visited, and especially by you." He noted Machiavelli's previous comments about his difficult financial situation and that he was not able to earn money in Florence, but was somewhat blunt in responding: "We have studied the question, and here in Rome we do not find anything suitable for you."[51]

Apparently, Machiavelli did send Francesco some chapters of *The Prince*, but in Vettori's reply of 18 January 1514, instead of giving his opinion of the book, which he clearly knew was what Machiavelli most wanted, the ambassador chose to write a lively and entertaining description of a dinner party he had staged for his guests Brancacci and Casavecchia, who had cajoled him into inviting his neighbour, a Roman widow from a prominent family. She arrived accompanied by her "virtuous" fourteen-year-old son, over whom Casavecchia hovered in predatory glee, and her "supremely beautiful" twenty-year-old daughter, Costanza, soon monopolized by Brancacci. Vettori tells Machiavelli that by the end of the evening he himself had succumbed to the charms of the daughter, writing: "Out of a wish to please my friends I have become a prisoner of this Costanza." Obviously taking great pleasure in recounting in detail how they had passed the time, "telling stories, jokes and silly talk," he then made a brief and somewhat, as Atkinson and Sices call it, "offhand" comment about the book, as though it was an unimportant afterthought: "I have seen the chapters of your work, and I like them immeasurably. But since I do not have the entire work, I do not want to make a definitive judgment."[52] Until he had seen the rest of the work, he was not prepared to say whether or not he should show it to Giuliano. This is the last Vettori reference we know of regarding *The Prince*. Machiavelli evidently did not comply with his request to send the entire manuscript, and the work was never mentioned again in their correspondence.

What more Vettori thought of the chapters he had already received is unknown, but it is quite certain that he was not interested in discussing the book nor did he wish to play the role of intermediary between Machiavelli and Giuliano. He knew this would not have pleased either the pope or Cardinal Giulio, and his loyalty was to them, after all. He had tried to indicate to Machiavelli in his letter of 23 November 1513, as noted in chapter 6, that he had closer relations with the pope and Cardinal Giulio than with Giuliano, to whom he had some difficulty speaking, describing what happens when he would go to the palace every two or three days: "There, on occasion, I speak twenty words with the pope, ten with Cardinal [Giulio] de' Medici, six with Giuliano the Magnificent; and if I cannot speak with him I speak with Piero Ardinghelli, then with whatever ambassadors happen to be in those chambers; and I hear a thing or two, though little of any moment. Having done that, I go back home; except that sometimes I dine with Cardinal de' Medici."[53] Vettori was obviously aware of the political differences between members of the Medici family, and was evidently unwilling to jeopardize his own standing with Pope Leo X and Cardinal Giulio for the sake of Machiavelli.

But was Francesco Vettori the only line of access that Machiavelli had for reaching Giuliano? Perhaps this was the case in Rome where, without the Florentine ambassador's protection, the disgraced ex-secretary would have had no other means of reaching Giuliano. However, as we learn from

Sanudo, Giuliano left Rome for Florence on 17 June 1514, accompanied by a group of cardinals who were invited to participate in the festival of St John the Baptist, the city's patron saint, on 24 June. The celebrations were to last from 21 to 28 June.[54] Giuliano stayed on in Florence until the middle of October when, as we saw in the previous chapter, Leo X sent him to Bolsena so that he could escort Isabella d'Este to Rome. Machiavelli's period of exile from Florence had expired, and he was now free to return to the city, where there would have been many occasions for Machiavelli and Giuliano to meet and for a personal presentation of *The Prince*.

Almost all surviving copies of the work that were circulating in Florence before *The Prince* was finally printed in 1532 include a dedication letter addressed to Giuliano's nephew, Lorenzo; apparently no version of *The Prince* with a dedication to Giuliano has ever been found, leading some to conclude that the text was never formally presented to Giuliano.[55] According to Connell, most scholars now believe that the presentation to Lorenzo took place in 1515, possibly at the same time when he was created captain-general of the Florentine forces,[56] which has raised questions about whether, in changing his dedication, Machiavelli would have also revised his text.[57]

Although no formal dedication letter exists for Giuliano, Hugo Jaeckel has convincingly argued that Machiavelli's third undated sonnet addressed to Giuliano, written at some point following his release from prison, might have served the purpose of a dedication for *The Prince*.[58] The sonnet read:

> I send you, Giuliano, some thrushes, not because this gift is good or fine, but that for a bit Your Magnificence may recollect your poor Machiavelli.
> And if you have near you somebody who bites, you can hit him in the teeth with it, so that, while he eats this bird, to rend others he may forget.
> But you say: "Perhaps they will not have the effect you speak of, because they are not good and are not fat; backbiters will not eat them."
> I will answer such words that I am thin, even I, as my enemies are aware, and yet they get off me some good mouthfuls.
> Won't Your Magnificence give up your opinions, and feel and touch, and judge by the hands and not by the eyes?[59]

Jaeckel believes that a literal reading of the sonnet is absurd because, if these were real thrushes, Giuliano would completely lose his appetite: as Machiavelli admits, the thrushes are neither good nor fat. Their role was metaphorical, because the sonnet is in miniature a work of deliberate rhetoric, intended to persuade Giuliano to welcome his gift of *The Prince*, and to read it, but not to eat it.

Verse was often adopted in dedications, but in this case the sonnet has a particular significance because, during his imprisonment, Machiavelli had already used poetry as a mode of discourse to appeal to Giuliano. The principal message of the sonnet is found in the second stanza, where Machiavelli advises: "And if you have near you somebody who bites, you can hit him in the teeth with it so that while he eats this bird, to rend others he may forget."[60] This is also the principal theme, Jaeckel contends, of *The Prince*, where the men who surround the "affable" Giuliano are only too ready to offend him. If he is careful, however, and observes the rules set out in the book, he will remain safe and secure in his new state. Security, therefore, Jaeckel argues, seems to be the dominating idea of both *The Prince* and the sonnet.[61] Interestingly, this imagery in the sonnet of "men who bite" also appears in the last line of *Ai Palleschi*, where Machiavelli warned Giuliano about the "many mouths that will surely and most readily bite."[62]

Riccardo Fubini fully endorses Jaeckel's argument and finds additional support in the last stanza of the sonnet: "Won't Your Magnificence give up your opinions, and feel and touch, and judge by the hands and not by the eyes?"[63] The source for this saying, Fubini writes, is the *Facetiae* (ribald tales) of the Florentine humanist Poggio Bracciolini.[64] The proverb tells the story of a thrush that sees a man killing other thrushes in the cage, and as he grabs each bird he utters a moan with tears in his eyes. The thrush then says to the others in the cage, "Be of good cheer because I see him weeping, and now he will have compassion for us." But the oldest bird replies: "My son, do not look at his eyes but at his hands." Poggio comments that this example shows how we should not heed the words of others but rather their actions.[65] Machiavelli echoes this precept in chapter 18 of *The Prince:* "Men in general judge more by their eyes than their hands: everyone can see, but few can feel."[66] Jaeckel suggests that the expression in the sonnet to "judge by the hands" could be taken in its literal sense, now that *The Prince* has been placed in Giuliano's own hands.[67] Although there is no direct evidence that Giuliano ever received or read the book, given their history and the fact that Giuliano was vitally interested in politics and was making plans for his new state, it would have been extraordinary if he did not read it.

Another matter arising from Machiavelli studies that concerns *The Prince* is the issue of whether the final chapter, titled "An Exhortation to Seize Italy and Free Her from the Barbarians," was conceived as a part of the work from the beginning or whether it was added at a later date. As the title of the epilogue indicates, there is a new fervency and an emotional tone that contrasts sharply with the cold pragmatic language of the other chapters. Machiavelli began the chapter by writing: " [I am] wondering to myself whether at present in Italy the times are suitable to honour a new prince, and if there is the material that might give a prudent and virtuous prince the opportunity to introduce a form that would do him honour and bring benefit to the people of Italy, it seems to me that so many circumstances are favourable to such a new prince that I know of no other time appropriate to this."[68]

According to Connell, a majority of scholars now believe that the first twenty-five chapters were indeed probably written for Giuliano in 1513–14 but that chapter 26 was added later, composed at the same time that the new dedication was written for Lorenzo, sometime in 1515.[69] In contrast, Hans Baron excluded the possibility that chapter 26 could have been composed for Lorenzo. Baron argued that no member of the Medici family is mentioned by name in the epilogue, which only references "Your Illustrious House," phrasing that would have been offensive to Lorenzo since he was a proud and imperious young man and would have expected Machiavelli to address him by name. Rather, Baron suggests that chapter 26 was written for Giuliano, but that it was only added in the first quarter of 1515, when Machiavelli's "suitable time" presented itself following Giuliano's appointment as captain-general of the papal troops and when he was about to take possession of his new state in north-central Italy.[70]

On the other hand, Bausi and Martelli, like Connell, agree with most scholars that chapter 26 was intended for Lorenzo and that it was an addition, but they propose a much later date of 1518, because in their view it was only then that the times were propitious enough for Machiavelli to write that "this opportunity, therefore, must not be allowed to pass by, so that Italy may behold her redeemer after so long a time."[71] They believe that the young and bold Lorenzo, who for some years had held the

FIGURE 19 | Michelangelo, *Lorenzo de' Medici, Duke of Urbino*, detail from his tomb, c. 1519–34. Marble. Medici Chapel (New Sacristy), San Lorenzo, Florence. Scala / Art Resource, NY

FIGURE 20 | Altobello Melone, *Portrait of a Nobleman, Perhaps Cesare Borgia*, c. 1520. Oil on wood, 56 × 47 cm. Accademia Carrara, Bergamo. Erich Lessing / Art Resource, NY

FIGURE 21 | Rosso Fiorentino, *Portrait of Niccolò Machiavelli*. Casa del Machiavelli, Sant'Andrea in Percussina. Scala / Art Resource, NY

FIGURES 22 (above, left) and 23 (above, right) | Unknown, *Cosimo de' Medici* (obverse) and *Florentia* (reverse), c. 1480–1500. Bronze, 7.7 cm. Victoria and Albert Museum, Salting Bequest, A.284–1910. © Victoria and Albert Museum, London

FIGURES 24 (below, left) and 25 (below, right) | Niccolò Fiorentino, *Lorenzo de' Medici* (obverse) and *Florentia* (reverse), c. 1490. Copper alloy, 8.8 cm. National Gallery of Art, Samuel H. Kress Collection 1987.34.2.a and 1987.34.2.b. Courtesy National Gallery of Art, Washington

FIGURES 26 (above, left) and 27 (above, right) | Unknown, *Giuliano II de' Medici, Duc de Nemours* (obverse) and *Florence Leaning on the Medici Shield* (reverse), c. 1513. Copper alloy, 8.77 cm. National Gallery of Art, Samuel H. Kress Collection 1957.14.834.a and 1957.14.834.b. Courtesy National Gallery of Art, Washington

FIGURES 28 (below, left) and 29 (below, right) | Unknown, *Giuliano II de' Medici* (obverse) and *Rome Holding a Figure of Victory* (reverse), 1513. Copper alloy, 3.41 cm. National Gallery of Art, Samuel H. Kress Collection 1957.14.835.a and 1957.14.835.b. Courtesy National Gallery of Art, Washington

FIGURE 30 | Domenico Beccafumi, *Torture by Strappado*. Pen and brown ink, brown wash, black chalk on beige paper, 24 × 20.6 cm. Musée du Louvre, Paris, inv 256. Photo: Thierry Le Mage. © RMN-Grand Palais / Art Resource, NY

FIGURE 31 | After Leonardo da Vinci, *Portrait of a Female Nude*, c. 1527. Black chalk on brown paper, 72.4 × 54 cm. Musée Condé, Chantilly, France, inv de32. Photo: Gérard Blot © RMN-Grand Palais / Art Resource, NY

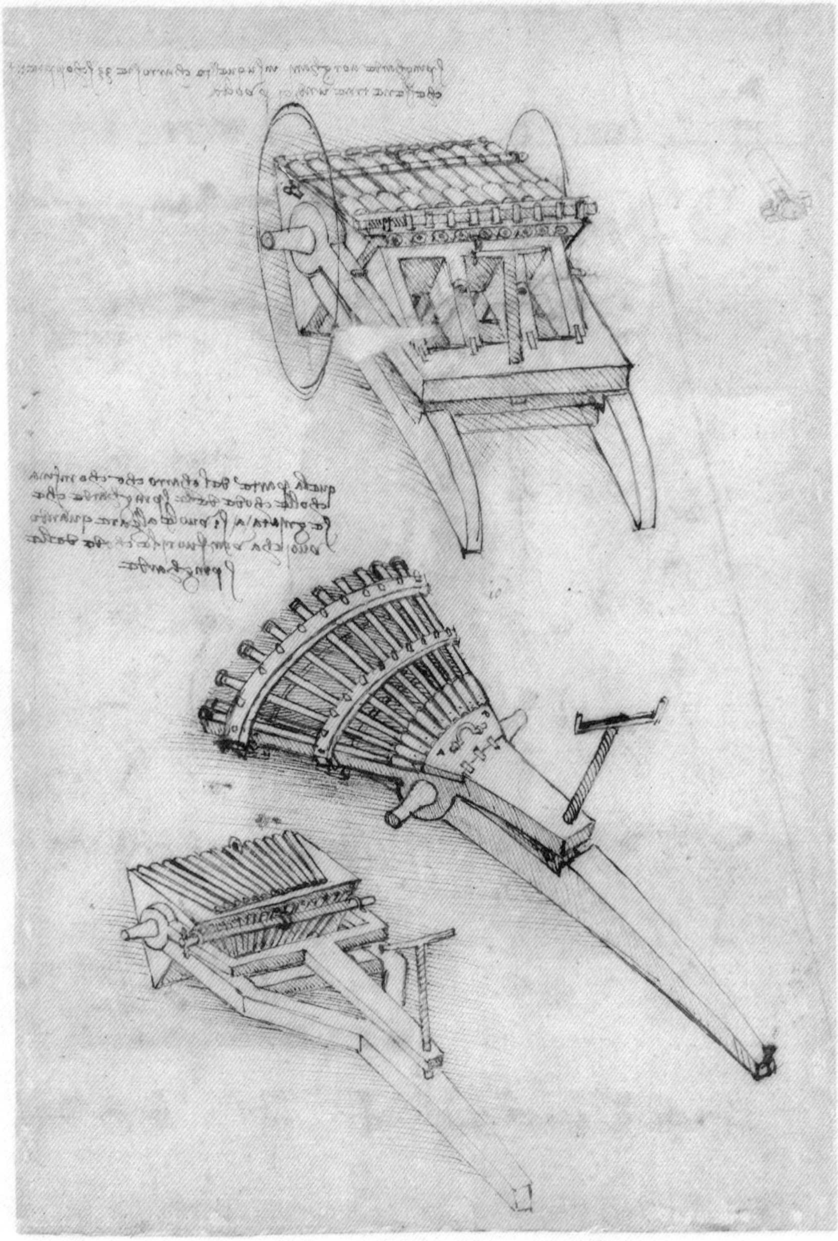

FIGURE 32 | Leonardo da Vinci, *Multi-Barrelled Springald, Known as Organ Springald*. Pen and ink. Codex Atlanticus, fol. 157r. Biblioteca Ambrosiana, Milan © Dea / Veneranda Biblioteca Ambrosiana / Art Resource, NY

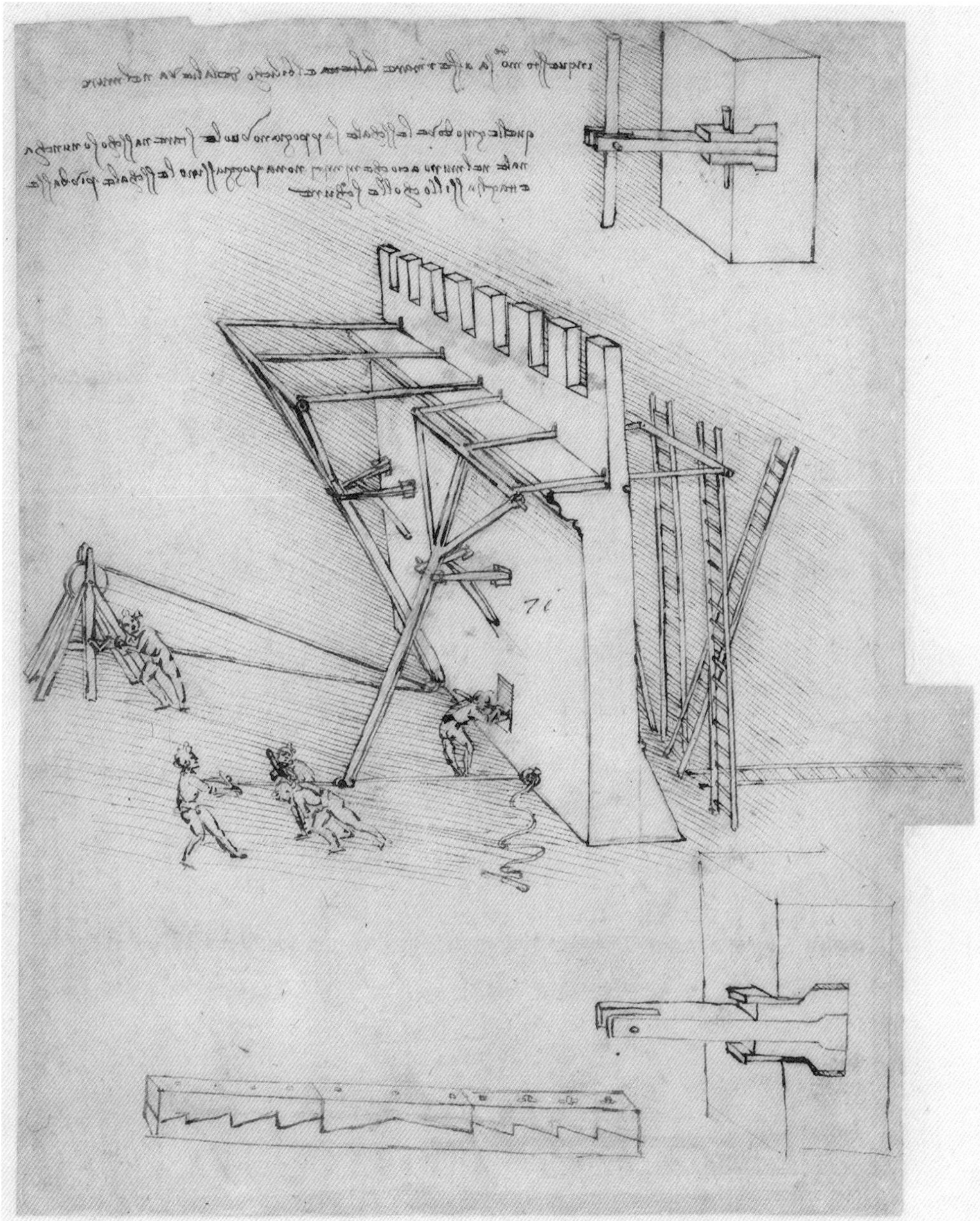

FIGURE 33 | Leonardo da Vinci, *Siege Machine in Defense of a Fortification; Details of Machine*. Pen and ink. Codex Atlanticus, fol. 139r. Biblioteca Ambrosiana, Milan. Photo: Metis e Mida Informatica © Dea / Veneranda Biblioteca Ambrosiana / Art Resource, NY

FIGURE 34 | Leonardo da Vinci, *Portrait of Isabella d'Este*, c. 1500. Black and red chalk, 63 × 46 cm. Musée du Louvre, Paris, mi 753. Photo: Thierry Le Mage © RMN-Grand Palais / Art Resource, NY

FIGURE 35 | Leonardo da Vinci, profile, three-quarter, and frontal studies of a male head, possibly a portrait of Cesare Borgia, 1502. Red chalk, 111 × 284 mm. Biblioteca Reale, Turin, inv 15573. Photo: Sergio Anelli. Mondadori Portfolio/Art Resource, NY

FIGURE 36 | Leonardo da Vinci, a plan of Imola, 1502. Pen and ink, with coloured washes and stylus lines over black chalk, 440 × 602 mm. rcin 912284. Royal Collection Trust/ © HM Queen Elizabeth II 2017

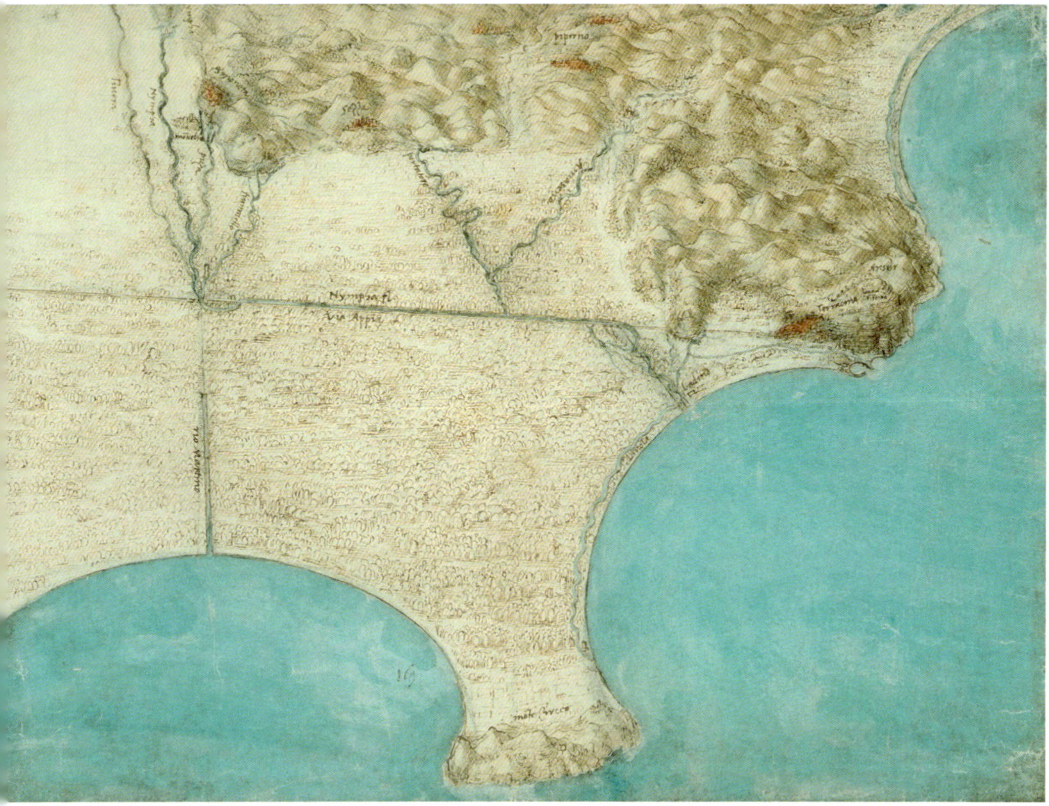

FIGURE 37 | Leonardo da Vinci, *A Map of the Pontine Marshes*, 1515. Pen and ink, wash, blue body-colour, touches of red chalk, over black chalk and stylus, 27.7 × 40 cm. RCN 912684. Royal Collection Trust/ © HM Queen Elizabeth II 2017

FIGURE 38 | Raphael, *Giuliano de' Medici (1479–1516), Duke of Nemours*, 1515, New York, Metropolitan Museum of Art. Jules Bache Collection, 1949 (inv 49.7.12), tempera and oil on canvas, 83.2 × 66 cm.

FIGURE 39 (above and right) | Giorgio Vasari and assistants, *Leo X Appointing Cardinals* and detail of *Giuliano de' Medici*, c. 1556–62. Fresco. Sala di Leone X, Palazzo Vecchio, Florence. Photo Scala / Art Resource, NY

FIGURE 40 | Raphael, *Baldassare Castiglione*, 1514–15 or 1519. Oil on canvas, 82 × 67 cm. Musée du Louvre, Paris, inv 611. Photo: Jean-Gilles Berizzi. © RMN-Grand Palais / Art Resource, NY

post of captain-general of the Florentine forces, and since 1516 had been invested with the title of Duke of Urbino by Leo X, was about to transform Florence, with the encouragement of his mother Alfonsina Orsini and her allies, into a princely state. Thus, they believe, Florence would at last return to play a leading political and military role that would allow for the expulsion of foreign rulers and move Italy closer towards unification.[72]

Could it also be the case that the reason most Machiavelli scholars are convinced that chapter 26 was written for Lorenzo, and not Giuliano as Baron contends, lies in their inability to conceive that in 1513 Machiavelli could have seen Giuliano as the contemporary prince who would, through his prudence and virtue, bring honour to himself and the benefit to the people of Italy? Interestingly, Whitfield believed that chapter 26 was part of the original work written in 1513, but not because of Giuliano, whom he describes as a "nonentity," but rather because he identifies the elevation of the first Florentine, Giovanni de' Medici, to the papal throne as Machiavelli's "unique occasion."[73] Free of bias against Giuliano, the proposition that chapter 26 formed part of the original work intended for him makes the most sense.

In 1513, when Machiavelli saw how Giuliano was gathering together men of the calibre of Leonardo da Vinci to help him consolidate plans for his new state in north-central Italy, and that there was a Medici on the papal throne to support him and underwrite the costs, he must have realized that the time of Cesare Borgia had returned. In chapter 26 Machiavelli once more alludes to Cesare Borgia, who would have succeeded in founding his own state had he not been gravely ill at the same time that his father died. Borgia is not mentioned by name, but most commentators agree that Machiavelli intends his reader, that is, Giuliano, to see Borgia in the following passage: "Some glimmer of light may have shown itself in a single individual, so that it was possible to believe that God had ordained him for Italy's redemption, yet afterwards it was seen how, at the height of his deeds, he was rejected by Fortune."[74]

Did Machiavelli conceive of Giuliano as Italy's redeemer? Did he also use this term because he knew that it would appeal to Giuliano's religious sensibilities? In late 1513, he surely knew, possibly from Leonardo, that Giuliano was about to create a state in Emilia that would be fashioned on Cesare Borgia's example in Romagna. Was this, then, the unique moment? Machiavelli does not mention Giuliano by name as the one who "can cure

[Italy] of those sores that have been festering for so long."[75] But he does place his hopes in the "Illustrious" House of the Medici, with its "fortune and virtue" that is "favoured by God and by the Church, of which it is now prince" (Leo X). He exhorts the Medici to place themselves at the "head of this redemption." The unique occasion that Machiavelli saw, writing in late 1513, with its "extraordinary, unprecedented signs brought about by God," was that Giuliano, "a man newly risen up," who has all the backing of the papacy, can now create a state with new laws and new institutions that would bring him much honour. Chapter 26 comes to a stirring conclusion:

> This opportunity, therefore, must not be allowed to pass by, so that Italy may behold her redeemer after so long a time. Nor can I express with what love he will be received in all those territories that have suffered through these foreign floods; with what thirst for revenge, with what stubborn loyalty, with what devotion, with what tears! What doors will be closed to him? What people will deny him their obedience? What envy could oppose him? What Italian could deny him homage? This barbarian dominion stinks in everyone's nostrils! Therefore, may Your Illustrious House take up this task with the spirit and the hope with which just enterprises are begun, so that under your banner this country may be ennobled, and under your auspices those words of Petrarch may come true:
>
> Virtue will seize arms
> Against frenzy, and the battle will be brief:
> For ancient valour
> Is not yet dead in Italian hearts.[76]

In his pastoral for the ideal ruler, as argued in chapter 4, written ten years earlier at Imola, Machiavelli proclaimed:

> Not merely are you the glory of every shepherd; as all can see, you enrich the forests like every god who inhabits them. No longer is it a grief to you, O forests! that Diana lives in Heaven, nor do you long for Phoebus to return to tend Admetus' herds, nor do you any more call for Hecuba's son, nor Cephalus, nor Atlanta, because with

> this youth you are more happy, more glad. In you I see all the virtues brought together; nor does it seem a marvel, because in shaping you not one god only took part in so great a work ... Juno put in citizen's clothing a soul fit to rule empire and kingdoms, and Saturn gave to you Nestor's years.[77]

When we also remember how, in their *Libellus* of 1513, the two Venetian hermits Querini and Giustiniani hailed Giuliano as a second Leo who would lead an army into battle against the infidels, and how Michelangelo, when he came to carve the statue for Giuliano's tomb in the New Sacristy, gave him the features of his heroic young David,[78] the fearless saviour of his people (Fig. 6), then it becomes quite believable that Machiavelli could, in chapter 26 of *The Prince*, cast Giuliano in the role of Italy's redeemer.

Given Giuliano's particular circumstances in 1514, it could be that he would have wholeheartedly welcomed Machiavelli's book and would have appreciated the advice it contained, whether or not he was ready to commit himself to all of its teachings. In the portrait of Giuliano painted by Raphael in 1515 (Fig. 38), there are hints suggesting that he was willing to accept some of the precepts outlined in *The Prince*, as will be discussed in the next chapter. But first we will discuss his marriage alliance with the House of Savoy and acquisition of a new Emilian state.

Leonardo da Vinci recorded that "The Magnifico Giuliano de' Medici left Rome on the 9th of January 1515, just at daybreak, to take a wife in Savoy."[79] From the outset, Leo X was not in favour of his brother's chosen bride, but, because of Giuliano's insistence as well as pressures from his sister-in-law Alfonsina, who, while jealous of Giuliano's situation, nevertheless wanted the marriage to proceed for the benefits it would bring to her own son Lorenzo and her hopes that he too would secure a royal bride, the pope relented, and he allowed the nuptials to proceed in February.[80] Six months later, the pope expected Giuliano, as a captain-general of the papal troops, to lead his army in a war against Savoy, as part of the pope's anti-French league. Giuliano's conflicted loyalties, as he himself admitted, caused him to fall ill with a severe bout of tuberculosis that led to his death in March 1516.

As the head of the Medici family, Leo X had long considered a dynastic marriage for Giuliano, but perhaps never more than at this time, when he could take full advantage of his exalted position to exact maximum political leverage. Leo's policy was, as Chambers has observed,[81] complex, and, especially during the first few years of his pontificate, it vacillated wildly because he was constantly double-dealing and hedging between the three foreign powers that had vested interests in the Italian peninsula, Spain, France, and the Holy Roman Empire. At the beginning of his papacy, Leo was acclaimed as a bringer of peace and the healer of Italy and Christendom, but his actions suggest that he was every bit a champion of papal authority as had been Julius II. Like his belligerent predecessor, Leo did not shy away from the use of armed force. This was seen, for example, in June 1513 at Novara when the anti-French league, resuscitated by Leo, defeated the army of Louis XII. In early 1514 the pope had appeared to favour Ferdinand of Spain when he decided that the king's niece, Teresa, daughter of the viceroy of Naples, Ramón de Cardona, would make an appropriate bride for Giuliano. Leo knew Cardona well, since his Spanish soldiers had enabled the Medici to return to Florence. With this potential marriage came the understanding that Giuliano would be given estates in the kingdom of Naples,[82] which would presumably cause much less antagonism than the four bitterly contested cities in Emilia, where the Duke of Milan lay claim to Parma and Piacenza and Alfonso d'Este, Duke of Ferrara, claimed Modena and Reggio.

It was apparent, however, that the pope had never consulted with Giuliano regarding a marriage to Teresa. Giuliano's letter of 17 March to his friend and fellow Florentine Giovanni Vespucci, the papal ambassador to the Spanish court, relates how he had another alliance in mind that was "more satisfying" for him and, even though Ferdinand would do everything that the pope wished, Giuliano himself did not want to make an alliance with any of these people, adding that "in fact a marriage with Cardona's daughter was intended for Lorenzo."[83] It appears that Giuliano was already in negotiations with the Duke of Savoy, Charles III, for the hand of his sister Philiberte (1498–1524), half-sister of Louise, the mother of Count François d'Angoulême, the future Francis I (1494–1547).[84] Giuliano preferred an alliance with the House of Savoy to one with Spain because, together with his close allies in Florence, he was anxious to strengthen the traditional ties with the House of Savoy and the kingdom of France so as to ensure the protection of the thriving Florentine mercantile interests in Lyons. Furthermore, as we saw during his exile, he had already forged close personal links with the monarch Louis XII.

Alfonsina Orsini's correspondence shows her great interest in the matter of her brother-in-law's marriage, no doubt because of her own concerns to see her son Lorenzo married into the nobility or, better still, into a royal house.[85] On 9 February 1514, in a letter to Lorenzo in Florence, she reported that Giuliano was very pleased with the prospect of his marriage. Alfonsina believed as well that both Luigi de' Rossi, cousin to Leo and Giuliano, and Cardinal Bernardo Dovizi da Bibbiena were satisfied with the alliance, but that Cardinal Giulio appeared to be neutral on the matter, declining to say either yes or no. The pope's response, she wrote, was a little strange, with just a shrug of his shoulders instead of a definitive answer.[86] She also referred to divisions in the Medici clan,[87] foreshadowing problems to come. A week later, Alfonsina informed Lorenzo that Giuliano had reacted angrily to the pope's suggestion that he marry the daughter of Cardona and had told his brother that, if he did not permit his marriage to Philiberte, he would take no other wife and think seriously of becoming a cleric.[88]

It was probably Claude de Seyssel (c. 1450–1520), Louis XII's envoy in Rome at the time, who proposed the idea of a Medici-Savoyard marriage. This would not only bind the papacy to Savoy, but the projected estates for Giuliano in Naples would make him a not too distant and agreeable neighbour to the Duke of Savoy. Originally a legal scholar from the University of Turin, Seyssel could have met Giuliano during the latter's visits to the Savoy court. Certainly he would have encountered him in 1502 in Bologna, where Seyssel had been sent by Louis XII to represent him in the talks between Valentino and Giovanni II Bentivoglio.[89] Seyssel came to Rome on 24 July 1513 to attend the Fifth Lateran Council and to negotiate a formal end to the schismatic Council of Pisa, instigated by the king. He stayed on in Rome during 1514, where his presence served to counteract the negative influences of the Spanish ambassadors on the new Medici pope.[90] According to Seyssel's biographer, Alberto Caviglia, Giuliano and Seyssel had close relations and met very frequently for "intimate conversations," when, presumably, the two men discussed politics pertinent to Savoy and Florence. This would have been the time for them to start planning for a Savoyard marriage.[91]

Fatini believes that Alfonsina must have pressed Leo X to acquiesce to Giuliano's demands and to conclude the negotiations with the Duke of Savoy because, as he writes, Alfonsina quite sensibly was quick to adapt the situation for her own benefit, being eager for a betrothal between Lorenzo and Cardona's daughter. Moreover, he believes that Leo gave his consent because he was counting on the possibility that Giuliano's marriage to Philiberte would induce Louis XII to give up his rights to Naples, opening the way for Lorenzo, upon his marriage to Cardona's daughter, to receive an estate in the kingdom of Naples.[92] Although he had received word that Louis was assembling troops for an assault on Milan, Leo believed that since the French had suffered defeat at Novara, Louis would think twice before he made a military move in the coming year. Arrangements for Giuliano's marriage were concluded on 14 November 1514, when the pope consented to a dowry of 100,000 ducats, to be paid in several instalments by Jacopo Salviati.[93] Moncallero believes that, because the pope was willing to pay such an enormous sum, he was in favour of the marriage,[94] but the fact that it was Salviati, rather than the pope, who provided the dowry suggests that the French alliance was more in the interests of Florence.

When Louis XII died on 1 January 1515, he was succeeded by his vigorous, young cousin Francis, who, in addition to the title of King of France, also assumed the title of the Duke of Milan; he had inherited the dukedom from his great grandfather, Louis, Duke of Orléans, who had married Valentina Visconti. The Milanese, however, claimed that these French rights to the duchy had been extinguished after the death of Ludovico Sforza. Once again, Milan became the flashpoint in the politics of the Italian peninsula. Perhaps Ferdinand of Spain had it right when he declared that "the accursed state of Milan was the cause, not only of the ruin of Italy, but of all of Christendom."[95] Francis, impatient to avenge the French defeat at Novara and reclaim his duchy, gave his consent to Giuliano's marriage out of respect for his own mother, Louise of Savoy, but also because he believed that his retaking of Milan would fail if he could not count on the support of the pope.[96]

Concerned to give his brother a title before he presented himself to the Savoyard court, the pope appointed Giuliano *gonfaloniere* of the Church on 10 January.[97] From the moment Giuliano set out from Rome on his journey to Savoy, a constant stream of letters to him followed from Pietro Ardinghelli, the pope's secretary, with instructions from the pope and Cardinal Bernardo Dovizi da Bibbiena, who, as Leo's secretary, handled Vatican affairs during the days the pope spent hunting in the woods around the papal lodge at Magliana. A discernible apprehension was evident in the correspondence related to this new alliance with the House of Savoy because the pope adamantly opposed any possibility of a French occupation of Milan. Moreover, while the pope was convinced that Louis XII would not invade Italy, everything indicated that the new king was eager to reclaim the duchy. In a letter dated 23 January, for example, Ardinghelli wrote to inform Giuliano that the pope intended to create a league with the emperor and Spain in order to protect Italy from France, but that Giuliano should not be alarmed, because it would not happen until after his marriage, when, in all likelihood, he would have already returned to Rome.[98] Furthermore, speaking expressly for the pope, Cardinal Bibbiena advised Giuliano not to visit the new king of France, but, instead, he must find an excuse for returning quickly to Rome, such as having to attend urgently to his men at arms and other duties for His Holiness.[99] A letter of 1 February advised Giuliano that it was the pope's wish for him not to lose any time, and that he must rush through the wedding ceremony and consummate the marriage as soon as possible, taking care, of course, to use the appropriate kind and loving words when speaking with the duke.[100] In the same letter, he is informed that Cardinal Bibbiena was most displeased to learn that Giuliano had let it be known that the pope was not inclined to support the league against France. He was admonished not to second-guess the thoughts of the pope and told that, in the future, the cardinal would be more sparing when divulging important information. Giuliano was also reminded that he must "proceed carefully, especially with those who have a passion for the things of France,"[101] counsel that, given his present circumstances, must have been disconcerting for Giuliano to read.

On 5 February, Ardinghelli informed Giuliano that, before leaving for eight days of hunting, the pope had charged Cardinal Bernardo Dovizi da Bibbiena with the task of negotiating the conditions for a league between the pope and the emperor and Spain. Cardinal Bibbiena had spent three continuous days discussing the articles of the alliance. Nominally, the purpose of the league was to defend Christian Europe against the menace of the Ottoman Turks, but the Italian peninsula was also to be safeguarded against the French, and this would include the mutual defence of the sovereignty of the Church over Parma and Piacenza. Bibbiena was able to get the ambassadors of Spain and the emperor's special envoy, Alberto Pio da

Carpi, to agree to give Parma and Piacenza to the pope's nominee, understood to be Giuliano. The Duke of Milan would be compensated with Bergamo, Crema, and Asti. All that remained was for the Duke of Milan and his Swiss allies to give their consent.[102] Ardinghelli also mentioned that the pope was greatly displeased with Giuliano for communicating to the Genoese that his brother was inclined toward the French, adding: "If your Excellency is of the opinion that the pope should be an open or secret friend of France, or at least that he should remain neutral, it would not be out of place if you wrote him a good letter giving him your reasons, but do not say that I gave you this advice, and then I will accompany your letter with some words that occur to me."[103] Ardinghelli is being somewhat disingenuous and raising false hopes in Giuliano, being very well aware of the anti-French attitude of the pope and Cardinal Bibbiena. If Giuliano wrote such a letter, he would have, if anything, only further irritated the pope. Indeed, on the very day Ardinghelli was writing this to Giuliano, Cardinal Bibbiena, "quite convinced that the League would prove to be a powerful check on the French King," sent word to the Spanish nuncio that "'it will be a lesson to Francis I and will teach him to be moderate in this as well as in all other matters.'"[104]

Giuliano's marriage was solemnized at the ducal palace in Turin on 10 February, and shortly after the wedding ceremonies were concluded, Zobi reports, Giuliano made a rapid visit to the royal court in France,[105] where, presumably, Francis I was already expecting him. Fatini writes that Zobi was wrong in believing that Giuliano went to France,[106] perhaps because his own research had revealed that the pope had vetoed just such a visit and Fatini would not have expected Giuliano to disobey his brother. Indications are, however, that a visit to France might have occurred after all. The evidence is a letter Cardinal Bibbiena wrote personally to Giuliano, dated 16 February, which began:

> His holiness has expressed great surprise and dissatisfaction at having heard nothing [of] you during so many days, and complains grievously of your attendants, who have been so negligent, that since your arrival at Nice, no intelligence has been received of your proceedings. The blame of this is chiefly attributed, both by his holiness and myself, to M. Latino [Juvenale, papal secretary], whose province it was to have written. It is no excuse to say, that

> from the remote situation of the place he knew not how to forward his letters, because the expense would have been well laid out in sending a special messenger, who might at any time have proceeded either to Genoa or Piacenza, to inform the pope of that which is dearer to him than any other object – the state of your own health and person.[107]

The fact that the flow of letters was interrupted around the time of the actual wedding and for the few critical days that followed, giving Giuliano enough time to make his journey to France, suggests that this silence may not have been coincidental. Considering Giuliano's circumstances, it could very well be that Louise of Savoy, Philiberte's sister, pressed Giuliano to pay his respects to her son Francis I, a request that may have been difficult to refuse now that he was firmly in the embrace of his French relatives. Perhaps Giuliano mistakenly thought that his brother, who always gave the impression of being indecisive when it came to supporting either France or Spain, could be won over with powerful arguments and be persuaded to side with France, a possibility that Ardinghelli himself had raised in his letter of 5 February.

On 23 February Giuliano was advised that he had been officially appointed governor of Parma, Piacenza, Modena, and Reggio. The members of the anti-French league had agreed to cede the cities of Parma, Piacenza, and Reggio to the pope, who had already separately acquired the rights to Modena from its overlord the emperor for a payment of 40,000 ducats in June 1514.[108] In the same letter Giuliano was informed that a papal bull confirming his new position had been sent to the governments of Parma, Piacenza, Modena, and Reggio.[109] These last letters express some nervousness about Giuliano's travel plans, whether he should return to Rome by sea or by land or first visit Florence as he had planned. By this time, 1 March, the conditions for a league comprising the papacy, the Duke of Milan, Spain, and the emperor against France had been agreed on,[110] and it is quite likely that the pope and Cardinal Bibbiena thought it unwise for Giuliano to make a formal entrance into Florence with his Savoyard bride, fearing, perhaps, that their opponents in the city would be encouraged to seek a separate alliance with the French. Sanudo records that, since his marriage into the House of Savoy, it had become increasingly apparent in Rome that Giuliano had formed a very close attachment to France.[111]

On more than one occasion, Giuliano was advised that he should return to Rome as soon as possible and that it was the preference of the pope and Cardinal Dovizi that he take the sea route rather than travelling overland. He was also instructed to delay his visit to Florence until the summer, when it would be too hot for him to stay in Rome.[112]

Giuliano did heed this advice and returned to Rome by sea, but not before making a few stops along the coast. When he and his new bride reached Livorno in Tuscany, a Florentine embassy of twelve patricians was anxiously waiting, headed by Jacopo Salviati, who had been given orders by the government in Florence to spare no expense in honouring the couple and to offer Philiberte Florentine citizenship.[113] Lorenzo was not managing the affairs of the regime at this time because since September 1514 he had been living in Rome and did not return to Florence until the following May. He had appointed a relative to take his place, the unknown twenty-four-year-old Galeotto de' Medici, who was completely inexperienced at handling the affairs of the state, lacking both the status and the skill required for such a position, though, according to Cerretani, he would prove to be a reliable leader, surprising the Florentines.[114] Resentment about Lorenzo was widespread in the city, and the discontent only increased when it was learned that he was negotiating his Spanish marriage. Jacopo Salviati in particular was angry that Lorenzo was trying to manage the affairs of the state through Galeotto, and he was incensed to learn from Paolo Vettori, who had returned from Rome, that discussions had taken place to make Lorenzo *signore* of Florence.[115] No doubt, during the meeting with Giuliano in Livorno in March, the Florentine delegates were also looking to him to intervene on their behalf to prevent such a move by Lorenzo. The newlyweds finally entered Rome on 31 March.[116] As Fatini writes, "the happiness of the pair was therefore complete but perhaps in the waves of joy that swept over them they were unable to see the threatening clouds that began to gather over their heads, caused by the political machinations of Leo X."[117]

CHAPTER NINE

RAPHAEL'S PORTRAIT OF GIULIANO AS MACHIAVELLI'S NEW PRINCE

Raphael was a successful painter in Urbino, Florence, and Rome, whose very busy workshop received many prestigious commissions from important patrons. His father, Giovanni Santi (d. 1494), had been a courtier at the ducal court of Urbino, devoted to literary pursuits, including playwriting and poetry. His verse chronicle of 2,300 tercets celebrated Duke Federico da Montefeltro, known for his military prowess as well as his promotion of humanism. For the wedding of the duke's son Guidobaldo to Elisabetta Gonzaga, Santi presided as master of ceremonies and dramaturge.[1] His position gave the young Raphael an entrée into one of the most enlightened humanist courts of Italy. Raphael may have met Giuliano, who was a frequent guest of Guidobaldo and Elisabetta, on one of his return visits home. Raphael painted portraits of the couple between 1504 and 1506[2] (Figs. 13 and 14) and in 1507 Duchess Elisabetta gave him a commission to paint *Christ in the Garden of Olives* as a gift for the Camaldolese hermit Don Michele di Ventura Pini, a protégé of Giuliano's father. Shearman has shown that there were close connections between the Urbino court and Camaldoli, where Guidobaldo was a *devotus noster* and his sister Giovanna Feltria della Rovere a *devota nostra*. Apparently in 1507, Baldassare Castiglione visited Don Michele in Camaldoli, suggesting a further context for Giuliano's later close association with the hermitage.[3]

Early in his career at Urbino, Raphael, like his father before him, had opportunity to meet men in Giuliano's circle, including Pietro Bembo and Castiglione, whose portraits he would paint about a decade apart (Figs. 15 and 40). In his *Book of the Courtier*, Castiglione hails Raphael, along with Leonardo and Michelangelo, as a most excellent painter.[4] Interestingly, in light of Olga Pugliese's claim that Castiglione sought verisimilitude when assigning roles in his portrait of the court,[5] Raphael, under the guise of a witticism, criticized the management of the Church, an assessment the artist appears to have shared with Giuliano: "In like manner the painter Raphael replied to two cardinals with whom he was on familiar terms and who in his presence (in order to make him talk) were finding fault with a picture he had painted – in which St. Peter and St. Paul were shown – saying that the two figures were too red in the face. Then Raphael replied at once: 'Gentlemen, you must not wonder at this, for I have made them so quite on purpose, since we must believe that St. Peter and St. Paul are as red in heaven as you see them here, out of shame that their church should be governed by such men as you.'"[6] Such kinship, seemingly established at Urbino, became even closer when the artist and Giuliano found themselves in Rome at the beginning of the papacy of Leo X (Fig. 11).

Documentary evidence strongly suggests that Raphael painted Giuliano's portrait in April 1515, that is, immediately after his return from Savoy. A list, countersigned by Giuliano and approved by the pope, contains members of Giuliano's Roman household, including the name "Rafaello de Urbino." In the list's margin the year 1515 was written down along with the day 28 April.[7] Pietro Bembo mentioned the portrait in a letter to Cardinal Bibbiena written 19 April 1516, just over a month after Giuliano's death.[8] A painting attributed to Raphael and his workshop (Fig. 38), now in the Metropolitan Museum of Art, is likely the original from which several copies were made[9] (Figs. 5 and 39). According to the restorer Angiolo Tricca (1817–1884), an inscription in the lower left corner once read "R.S.M.... V," which may be transcribed as "Raffaello Sanzio M[DX] V,"[10] thus seeming to confirm the above-mentioned list. Fatini suggested that Giuliano commissioned the portrait because he wanted to leave it as a gift for his young wife when he went to war,[11] which he did in early July 1515. Tom Henry postulates that Raphael painted it to commemorate Giuliano's appointment as captain-general of the Church on 29 June, or in conjunction with his marriage to Philiberte and acquisition of the title of Duke of Nemours in January.[12] His beard, "a militaristic, princely attribute,"[13] which he first wore while in France in keeping with fashion, helps to place the portrait more specifically between the end of March and the beginning of July when he was in Rome. He had shaved upon his return to Florence in September 1512, but after moving to Rome at the end of March 1515, he grew it again.[14] As we will shortly see, however, there are elements in the painting that suggest it was intended as an official state portrait for his new principality in Emilia, meant to serve as a reminder of his authority in his absence during his many stays in Rome. The fact that Raphael painted the portrait on canvas, making it easier to transport, and not wood panel as was his usual practice, is a further indication that the portrait was to be sent to his new state.[15]

As previously mentioned, the earliest record of the portrait appears in a letter dated 19 April 1516, sent from Rome by Bembo to Bibbiena, who, as papal legate, was travelling to northern Italy. The cardinal had been staying in Fiesole, just outside Florence, consoling Giuliano at his bedside during the last days of his long illness. When Giuliano died on 17 March, the cardinal resumed his journey, where in Rubiera, between Modena and Reggio, Bembo's letter caught up with him. Bembo refers to a now lost portrait that Raphael had just painted of their friend, the Ferrarese poet Antonio Tebaldeo, which far surpassed in likeness, he writes, a portrait of Baldassare Castiglione and the one that was "dedicated to the excellent and for me always honoured memory of our Duke – may God grant him Salvation,"[16] both of which Bembo attributed to one of Raphael's assistants, rather than the master himself.[17] Francis I had created Giuliano Duke of Nemours in October 1515, following the French victory at Marignano, in compensation for returning Parma and Piacenza to the Duchy of Milan.[18] Bembo's letter does not explicitly identify Giuliano by name, but it is clear that he is alluding to him since, in an earlier letter of 3 April 1516, Bembo thanked Cardinal Bibbiena, who too would commission a portrait from Raphael that year (Fig. 10), for the news concerning Giuliano's death, writing: "I cannot read of the sad death of our good Duke without shedding tears."[19] The only other reference to Giuliano's portrait in the sixteenth century appears in Vasari's *Lives*, where he recorded in the 1550 edition that the work was in Florence in the possession of the heirs of Ottaviano de' Medici, a collector and connoisseur.[20]

Though many art historians, especially in the first half of the twentieth century, have thought that the New York portrait of Giuliano was the original,[21] there is now a general consensus that this work is a contemporary copy (Fig. 38).[22] Meyer zur Capellen believes that irregularities and *pentimenti* suggest that the New York picture was the model for all known copies, but that Raphael only created its concept, leaving the work itself to be painted by his assistants in his workshop, a not uncommon practice at the time because of the heavy demands placed upon Raphael.[23] Henry has attributed the portrait to Raphael and his workshop, citing the picture's compromised condition as reason for lack of scholarly consensus on its origins.[24] Considering that Giuliano was an important member of the Medici family and that they likely knew each other from Urbino, Raphael may indeed have painted the major part of the portrait in his Roman studio before handing it over to his assistants to finish the less important details.

Federico Zeri, who examined the condition of the painting in 1980, recognized the surface as extremely worn, with small losses and retouches throughout, complicating the task of attribution, but he did note that in parts it was very finely painted, even though he was only willing to say that, of the copies, the Met's version was the finest.[25] X-rays of the picture clearly reveal the aforementioned *pentimenti*, alterations made during execution that provide a strong argument for the New York picture as the original, thus contradicting the current consensus and connecting the work's provenance to the heirs of Ottaviano de' Medici, as first mentioned by Vasari. The picture then passed through various collections in Florence and Rome until 1906 when it was sold to Charles Sedelmyer in Paris. From 1907 until 1924, it formed part of the Huldschinsky collection in Berlin, and, through the art dealers Agnew in London and Duveen in New York, it made its way into the collection of Jules S. Bache, finally entering the Metropolitan Museum in 1949.[26] A number of sixteenth-century portraits of Giuliano, all based on this prototype, have survived, dispersed in various collections. Even though in the past there was an attempt to identify the copy in Bellinzona, Switzerland, as the lost original,[27] it is of such feeble quality, as are most of the copies, that the proposal has garnered no support. The New York painting, on the other hand, is recognized as the finest of all extant versions,[28] again pointing to Raphael's authorship.

The reason for the existence of so many copies can easily be explained. All appear to have been painted in the second half of the sixteenth century when Cosimo I de' Medici, created Duke of Florence at the age of eighteen in 1537, began to recognize the propaganda value of portraiture. Cosimo was descended on his father's side from the younger branch of the Medici family, although his mother, Maria, was the daughter of Giuliano's sister, Lucrezia Salviati (Fig. 8). When Cosimo came to power, he was anxious to establish an illustrious lineage for himself that would legitimize his claim to rule. His ancestors from the main Medici line included not only the much-celebrated Lorenzo the Magnificent of the previous century but also two dukes – Giuliano and Lorenzo – and two popes – Leo X and Clement VII. Therefore, Cosimo began to commission portraits of his Medici relatives, living and dead, who could provide him with the proper lineage that was so essential in European courts. This desire for ancestor portraits explains the presence of so many copies of Raphael's portrayal of Giuliano.[29] However, and quite importantly, none of the copies save the Metropolitan Museum version show Castel Sant'Angelo through a window, as seen in the upper right corner of the New York painting.[30] Some have tried to explain the Castel's inclusion as the work of someone other than Raphael, added by an assistant or at a later date.[31] The omission in later copies of the detail, which will be shown to have been part of Raphael's original concept, would be expected because such a symbol of the papacy in Rome would no longer have had much relevance either for the Medici or for Florence in the mid-sixteenth century.

As Meyer zur Capellen demonstrates, Raphael always paid particular attention to the function of portraits, and, of those that he painted during his Roman period, four types are discernible – the state portrait, the clerical portrait, the female portrait, and the friendship portrait.[32] Although Giuliano and Raphael surely knew each other, Giuliano's portrait is certainly not a portrait of friendship. This can be established by comparing it to Raphael's portrait of their mutual friend, Baldassare Castiglione, in the Louvre (Fig. 40), usually dated c. 1514–16.[33] At the time, Castiglione was in Rome serving as the Duke of Urbino's special envoy to the papal court. Unquestionably, it is a portrait of friendship. Castiglione is shown half-length, sitting upright against a plain background, his body turned to the left, hands clasped together in his lap, with his chair drawn up close to the painter, emphasizing their close familiarity. His remarkable blue eyes look steadily across to return the beholder's gaze. A large black *berretta* and full beard frame his head, highlighting the warm flesh tones of his face. An overall expression of calm is reinforced by the softly flowing contours of the rich fabric of his clothes, painted in a subtle orchestration of velvet grays and blacks played off against the creamy white of the pleated chemise. His unwavering gaze overwhelms everything else in the portrait and expresses an extraordinary intimacy with the artist, who, in the act of painting his dear friend's likeness, seems to will into being his eternal presence.

Notwithstanding their significant differences in condition, the gentle, benevolent humanity expressed in the Castiglione portrait is completely absent in that of Giuliano, whose head is also turned towards the front, but here the pupils of his eyes are averted to the right so that no direct eye contact with the viewer is possible. This fact would argue against Fatini's theory that the portrait was painted for Philiberte because, if this were so, we would expect to see some psychological contact with the viewer similar to that found in the Castiglione portrait. Meyer zur Capellen writes that Giuliano's "certain reticence … probably reflects the sitter's nature," and he surmises that "the peculiar impersonal distance noticeable in this portrait … suggests that Raphael was not particularly close to the sitter."[34] Giuliano's lack of human warmth, which could explain why so many doubt Raphael's authorship, makes sense if the picture is seen as deliberately constructed to remind the populace of an absent prince's authority, where a certain aloofness would not only be desirable but also necessary to show him as a man of high station to his subjects in Emilia. Such a posture would, in turn, lend legitimacy to Giuliano's claim to rule. Moreover, as we analyze certain elements in the portrait, it becomes apparent that Giuliano collaborated closely with Raphael on devising an iconography that would explicitly address these political concerns.

Painted with a crisper clarity than the Castiglione, Giuliano's portrait is half-length, his body cropped at the waist, but is he really shown sitting as some have described?[35] Rather, his pose could indicate that he is standing because in the convention for sitting portraits, as was the case with Castiglione, the left arm is usually placed horizontally across the bottom edge above the frame, either resting on the armrest of a chair or on a narrow strip of parapet, whereas Giuliano's left elbow appears to be bent below the actual picture frame. His hands are raised up and resting on what could be the back of a chair, while the right hand holds a folded paper. For this portrait, a standing pose may have seemed more appropriate to emphasize his princely rank. In her influential study of the state portrait, Marianna Jenkins contends that Raphael invented this portrait type during his Roman years, and although the author does not mention Giuliano's portrait, whose neglect in the Raphael literature can be directly linked to doubts concerning the painting's authorship, it conforms to her observation that in Raphael's state portraits the proportions of the figure are purposely enlarged to endow the figure with a "statuesque dignity that is gravely impressive."[36] Giuliano's body is massive and expands to fill the entire foreground, giving him an imposing physical presence. His large head, supported by a curving, elongated neck, dominates the upper third of the canvas, confirming Bartolomeo Cerretani's description of Giuliano as being "tall, pale" and "long-necked."[37] His impassive face is carefully delineated with arched eyebrows and a prominent nose that leads down to his thin, straight, inexpressive lips, which are framed by a trimmed moustache and beard. He is shown wearing an elegant gold-netted cap to keep his hair in place, an excessively large black *berrétta* worn at a stylish angle, and a heavy, fur-lined, olive-green brocaded overcoat with a wide, dark fur collar that exaggerates the pale skin of his neck. Beneath he is wearing a black jacket with a deep square neck and a scarlet doublet with a lapped closing, worn on top of a white linen shirt. While the style of his beard, hat, and overcoat is fashionably French,[38] not surprising given his recent marriage to Philiberte, Giuliano must have instructed Raphael to display his deep attachment to the place of his birth by isolating, at the very heart of the painting, the white and red colours of the Florentine republic.[39]

When one examines Giuliano's hands closely, it becomes evident that the last third of the index finger on the left hand is missing. This minor physical defect was referenced in 1494, in correspondence between Cardinal Farnese in Rome and the Florentine Lorenzo Pucci, who was acting for Giuliano's brother Piero de' Medici. Apparently, Piero was considering the marriage of the fifteen-year-old Giuliano to Laura di Orsino Orsini. The cardinal, whose concern for a healthy lineage was obviously a priority, inquired about young Giuliano, who he had heard had an impediment of the hand. Pucci reassured him by saying that he did not believe there was any impediment or deformity, and even if a small defect did exist, it was not at all apparent.[40] Research has recently revealed that a genetic predisposition for similar joint anomalies of the left hand existed in other members of the Medici family, as demonstrated in the case of Duke Cosimo I de' Medici, whose mother, Maria Salviati, was the daughter of Giuliano's sister Lucrezia. The authors of the study compared three portraits of Cosimo I, two by Pontormo and one by Bronzino, and they all showed a similar deformity of the left hand that could not be explained by distortions of style. Moreover, X-rays taken of Cosimo I's left hand also reveal a deterioration of the joint of the index finger.[41] It is, however, strange that Giuliano is shown with the deformity of his hand because, in the tradition of Renaissance portraiture, especially in the sixteenth century, realism gave way to decorum. It became obligatory to tone down the defects of nature, particularly if the sitter was high-ranking.[42] Why Giuliano wanted Raphael to portray this defect in the index finger is unclear, but perhaps he felt that it was important for his subjects in Emilia to be able to recognize him as their true prince, rather than confusing him with some subordinates.

From the hands in the lower left corner of the canvas, Raphael draws the viewer's eye upwards along a sweeping diagonal over Giuliano's left shoulder through the opening in the curtain, which has been pulled back to reveal a distant view of the Castel Sant'Angelo. Most commentators explain its presence as an allusion to his office of *gonfaloniere* of the Church.[43] We have already noted that, on 10 January, the pope appointed him to this post in order to provide his brother with a suitable title before he arrived at the court of Savoy. On 29 June 1515, however, responding to the imminent threat of a French descent into Italy for the conquest of Milan, Leo X also conferred upon his brother the title of captain-general of the Church in an elaborate ceremony held in St Peter's.[44] While his previous title was purely honorific, his new office of commander of the papal troops carried with it the obligation of military service.[45] The inclusion of the Castel Sant'Angelo, Karla Langedijk writes, allows us to date the portrait to after 29 June,[46] but since we know that Giuliano left Rome on 5 July with his army, heading first for Florence and then for Bologna,[47] he would not have had time to sit for his portrait. Furthermore, if the Castel Sant'Angelo was meant to signify his rank as military commander of the papal army, one would expect to see other emblems of his office, such as the papal standard or the baton of command that Sanudo describes as made of white wood.[48] Nor is Giuliano portrayed wearing armour, as seen, for example, in Michelangelo's portrait of Giuliano as *il Capitano* in the New Sacristy, where the baton is shown (Fig. 6), or later in the sixteenth-century in Vasari's painting on the ceiling of the Sala de Leone X in the Palazzo della Signoria in Florence, showing Giuliano, captain-general of the papal army, dressed in armour, kneeling before Leo X, in the act of accepting the papal flag.

We have argued that it is much more plausible that the portrait was painted in April before Giuliano had been nominated for this military role, but if this was the case, why was the Castel Sant'Angelo included in the background of his portrait? Located on the right bank of the Tiber, the monument was originally built to house the tomb of Emperor Hadrian between 130 and 139 CE. The gigantic tomb was composed of three parts, a massive quadrangular base on which an equally massive cylinder was superimposed that, in turn, supported a smaller cylinder, inspired, according to Cesare D'Onofrio, by ancient wooden funeral pyres that would have been built several storeys high. In the seventh century the mausoleum was dedicated to the Archangel Michael and became known as the "Castellum S. Angeli," and functioned as a military stronghold, papal residence, and prison.[49] In 1492, within a few weeks of Rodrigo Borgia's election to the papacy as Alexander VI, the new pope embarked on an ambitious building program, more extensive than any of his predecessors, including Nicholas V and Sixtus IV. His first priority was to modernize Castel Sant'Angelo by adding four immense octagonal bastions at the four corners of the base that could withstand an artillery attack.[50] When the Castel was under the jurisdiction of Cesare Borgia, who was appointed its *castellan*, he used it to quarter his troops and store weaponry.[51] Before discussing the significance of the Castel Sant'Angelo in Raphael's portrait of Giuliano, there are two other details referencing Alexander VI in the view through the window that should be considered, for they seem to have been included on the instructions of Giuliano.

The first is the clearly visible broad street known at the time as the Via Alessandrina and built by the pope in 1499. This new street, straight and wide, measured four hundred and fifty metres long and led from the gate at the Castel Sant'Angelo to the gate of the Vatican Palace, thus connecting two of the most significant sites in Renaissance Rome. Inaugurated on Christmas Eve at the beginning of the Holy Year 1500, the Via Alessandrina was not built as a new pilgrimage route to celebrate the Jubilee, nor was its intent to demonstrate modern urban planning. Instead it was conceived as a triumphal thoroughfare that would facilitate the movement of armies and artillery, at a time when the overarching concern of the pope was safety and security.[52] Cesare Borgia, as we have already seen in chapter 3, was the first to use the Via Alessandrina when he returned to Rome in triumph on 26 February 1500, following his military victories on behalf of the Church in Romagna. Since we know how much Giuliano admired the duke, the deliberate inclusion of the Via Alessandrina in the view through the window bathed in golden sunlight could be a veiled homage to Cesare, whose deeds Giuliano, as a new prince, wished to emulate.

Indeed, Raphael could have shown the Castel Sant'Angelo from another vantage point or obscured more of the view with Giuliano's coat. Instead, he chose to show a section of Alexander's new road as well as the elevated passageway enclosed within the curving north wall joining the Vatican Palace to the fortress. This walkway was carefully restored and rebuilt by Alexander VI. In times of peril, it guaranteed safe passage between the Vatican Palace and the security of the Castel Sant'Angelo, while the new Via Alessandrina guaranteed the movement of soldiers and artillery.[53] Why would Giuliano wish to include the new street, known to all at the time as the Via Alessandrina, and the curved corridor, if this was not in some way also a tribute to Alexander VI? Could it be that in this portrait Giuliano wished to pay homage not only to Cesare Borgia but also to Alexander VI? We could understand his wanting to recognize Cesare, who had become a role model for him, but why Pope Alexander, especially given the extremely negative connotations attached to the Borgia pope?

In Giuliano's day in certain quarters, perhaps including Pope Leo X, Alexander was in fact admired for his role in strengthening the temporal power of the Church. Machiavelli, for example, in his discussion of ecclesiastical principalities in chapter 11 of *The Prince,* recounted: "Then Alexander VI came to power, and he, more than any of the popes who ever reigned, demonstrated how well a pope could succeed with money and his own troops. With Duke Valentino as his instrument and the French invasion as his opportunity, he achieved all those things that I discussed earlier in describing the actions of the Duke. And although his intention was to make the Duke and not the Church great, nevertheless, what he did resulted in the increase of the power of the Church, which after his death, and once the Duke was ruined, became the heir to his labours."[54] Machiavelli wrote that the power of the Church continued to increase under

Julius II, although he qualified his praise of the Della Rovere pope with an allusion to Julius's constant warfare: "From the ambitions of the priests are born the disorders and the quarrels among the barons."[55] Machiavelli ended chapter 11 by placing his hopes in the new Medici pope and, by extension, in Giuliano: "Therefore, His Holiness Pope Leo has found the papacy extremely powerful. It is to be hoped that, if his predecessors made it great by feats of arms, he will make it extremely great and venerable though his natural goodness and his countless virtues."[56]

If, with his portrait by Raphael, Giuliano presented himself as a new prince, could it be that he wanted to be viewed as a second Cesare Borgia, and that the presence of the Castel Sant'Angelo in the painting signified his will to rule, as the Borgia duke did, with strength of arms? Unfortunately, no text can be seen on the paper Giuliano holds in his right hand. It is tempting to theorize that it represents civil laws and recalls how Borgia appointed the esteemed jurist Antonio Ciocchi del Monte San Savino to be his chief justice of his duchy's Supreme Court, but it could just as easily refer to any number of Giuliano's affairs of state. Whatever its import, in Raphael's portrait, Giuliano fashions himself as the new prince of Parma, Piacenza, Modena, and Reggio who, like Cesare Borgia before him, would bring good government to the subjects of his principality by use of "good laws and good arms." We do not have to look far in order to seek the source for this concept of "good laws and good arms," since it is a central theme in Machiavelli's *Prince*: "We have said above that a prince must have laid firm foundations; otherwise he will necessarily come to ruin. And the principal foundations of all states, the new as well as the old or the mixed, are good laws and good armies. Since good laws cannot exist where there are no good armies, and where good armies exist there must be good laws, I shall leave aside the arguments about laws and shall discuss the armed forces."[57] Machiavelli's great concern was for Giuliano to be strong in arms and, although for him laws and arms were identical, he warns the new prince that the preservation of his power depends on military strength. This could explain why, in his portrait, Giuliano's eyes draw the viewer's attention to the fortress of Castel Sant'Angelo. Machiavelli continues: "A prince, therefore, must not have any other object nor any other thought, nor must he adopt anything as his art but war, its institutions, and its discipline."[58]

In February 1515 rumours began to spread in Rome that, during his brief stopover in Florence on his way to Savoy, Giuliano was planning to engage the services of Machiavelli. As Cardinal Giulio de' Medici made clear in a letter of 14 February, Giuliano was advised not to have anything to do with Machiavelli. When, upon his return to Rome in April, Giuliano commissioned Raphael to paint his portrait, it appears that he wished to present himself as a new prince of the type described and guided by Machiavelli. Could this neglected portrait have historical significance far beyond what was previously thought? Could it, in fact, suggest that Giuliano had not only read *The Prince* but also was willing to follow Machiavelli's precepts with respect to maintaining strength in arms and dispensing justice through good laws? If Giuliano's intention was to show himself as Machiavelli's new prince ready to take possession of his state in Emilia, then the portrait, within a few short months, became obsolete. All Giuliano's plans and wishes, and also the strong desire of Pope Leo X to establish a Medici dynastic state, came to nothing. Francis I invaded Italy and won a decisive victory at the Battle of Marignano on 13–14 September, after which the cities of Parma and Piacenza were restored to the Duchy of Milan, while Modena was given back to the French king's loyal supporter, Alfonso d'Este, Duke of Ferrara.

CHAPTER TEN

DEATH AND BURIAL

My motivation in writing a political biography of Giuliano, the youngest son of Lorenzo the Magnificent, has been to counter the negative criticism aimed at him from the early sixteenth-century until the present day. In previous chapters we saw how ready modern historians have been to dismiss him as an ineffectual non-entity or, even worse, as a reckless, pleasure-seeking degenerate. This attitude of disdain followed him even in death, when one modern commentator wrote, as late as 1991: "By dying, he may have committed his most politically significant act."[1] As the reader of this book will know by now, the above statement is unfair, considering that in his short lifetime Giuliano consistently used his position and good fortune wisely and for the benefit of others. As a youth, he helped to negotiate peace treaties between Cesare Borgia and Giovanni II Bentivoglio, lord of Bologna, thus saving Bentivoglio's state. He gave his support to his two Venetian hermit friends, Vincenzo Querini and Tommaso Giustiniani, in their pursuit to reform the Church, and he offered his protection to the family of Michelangelo and other Florentine republicans who were being mistreated by the newly restored Medici. He almost certainly saved Machiavelli from execution and rescued him from a long sentence in Florence's Stinche prison and, as we have seen, Giuliano's kindness inspired Machiavelli to write *The Prince* for him. Furthermore, Giuliano gave refuge and meaningful employment to the aging Leonardo da Vinci in Rome, sought marriage into the Savoyard ducal family in order to strengthen the traditional Florentine alliance with France and to secure protection for the republic's mercantile interests in Lyons, and, finally, in the last months of his life, while struggling with illness, tried to defend Francesco Maria della Rovere from the pope's nepotistic act of dispossessing the Duke of Urbino in favour of his nephew Lorenzo.

From all of the above we can see that Giuliano's life had political significance for his contemporaries and, as we shall see in this chapter, his death touched nearly everyone in Florence. Was his elaborate funeral, the greatest ever accorded to an individual citizen,[2] intended to celebrate the "restoration of Medici hegemony," as it has been suggested,[3] or did it also represent the universal outpouring of sorrow felt by the citizens of Florence as they marked the passing of a man who had withstood the acrimony of certain Medici supporters and the contempt of his own family in order to preserve the republic and its institutions? This chapter will focus on the last months of Giuliano's life. Although his illness prevented him from participating in the events described, it is important to consider carefully the relationship between the republic and the Medici regime in 1515 because it will undoubtedly help to deepen our understanding of what Giuliano's death meant, not only for the Medici but also for the grateful citizens of the republic.

LEO X AND THE LEAGUE AGAINST THE FRENCH

While King Francis I was making final preparations for his descent into Italy to expunge all memory of the French defeat at Novara, Giuliano, newly appointed captain-general of the papal army, set out from Rome on 5 July 1515, heading first for Florence and then for Bologna, where his troops were expected to join up with the Spanish army and Swiss mercenaries of the anti-French league. On his way he made a detour to Gubbio for an arranged meeting with Francesco Maria della Rovere, Duke of Urbino. Sanudo reports that this visit was in order to persuade the duke to join the pope's military campaign.[4] Leo X needed as many troops as he could assemble for the looming war with France and would have given his approval for this meeting with Francesco Maria, but it is certain that the recruitment of Della Rovere's army to the pope's cause was not uppermost in Giuliano's thoughts. His overriding concern was to reassure the duke that the rumours of a plan by the pope to dispossess him, circulating since February 1515, were groundless. Giuliano wanted the duke to know that he would never consent to such a scheme and that Francesco Maria was as dear to him as a brother. "I have heard, my Lord, that it has been represented to you how the Pope has a mind to take your state from you, in order to give it to me; but this is not true, for on account of the kindness, favour, and benefits I ever have received from your Excellency and your house, I should never consent to it, however much desired by his Holiness, lest other princes of your rank should resolve, in consequence, never again to give such refuge at their courts as was granted to me and mine. Be assured, therefore, that whilst I live, you not only will receive no molestation on my account, but will be ever regarded by me as an elder brother."[5] Giuliano knew that Della Rovere felt the same loyalty toward France as he did and would be very reluctant to take up arms against them. Francesco Maria had spent much of his youth at the court of Louis XII where, at the age thirteen in 1503, the king created him a knight of the Order of St Michael.[6] Since the order's statutes limited the number of companions to thirty-six, this young Italian lord must have greatly impressed the king with his military skills, much in the same way that Cesare Borgia had done in 1499. Becoming a knight of the crown, however, carried with it obligations not to act against the order's sovereign.[7]

In 1508 Julius II had presented Della Rovere with the baton of command as captain-general of the papal troops, an office previously held by his uncle, Duke Guidobaldo of Urbino. This was also the year that Francesco Maria inherited the duchy on Guidobaldo's death. It had been Julius II who had insisted that the impotent and childless Guidobaldo adopt their common nephew Francesco Maria. On 4 August 1513 the new Medici pope renewed the duke's papal appointment as captain-general; however, on 29 June 1515 Leo X removed him from this lucrative and prestigious office without any just cause. Giuliano was keenly aware that this slight would wound Francesco Maria's pride, only increasing his sense of vulnerability.[8] Sanudo records that in Gubbio the duke wished to take Giuliano with him to Urbino, but messengers sent by the pope persuaded him to return to the road for Rome by way of Viterbo.[9] Did the duke try to counsel Giuliano not to proceed with his troops to Bologna and fight a war that neither he nor Giuliano wanted? On 14 July the pope finally made public his decision to join the anti-French coalition in response to the refusal of

Francis I to cede his rights over Parma, Piacenza, or Naples.[10] Yet, as events transpired, neither the duke nor Giuliano had committed to the league. Della Rovere, ignoring the pope's direct orders to march with his troops to Bologna, began negotiating at the end of July directly with the French for protection.[11] At the same time, Giuliano contracted an unrelenting and debilitating fever, and on 8 August his nephew Lorenzo took his place as commander of the papal troops.[12]

Lorenzo had returned to Florence in the middle of May 1515 after an eight-month absence in Rome, accompanied by two of his closest advisers who formed part of a tight circle of privileged *amici*, his brother-in-law Filippo Strozzi and his friend Francesco Vettori. Both men, Florentine patricians, aided and abetted Lorenzo in his ambition to aggrandize himself and gain seigniorial power in formerly republican Florence.[13] Lorenzo took advantage of Vettori's long experience in dealing with the councils of the Florentine government to alter drastically the relationship between the Medici and the citizens of Florence. In April, even before returning to the city, Vettori had communicated to the Otto di Pratica (an executive council responsible for foreign policy that replaced the Dieci) that it was the pope's wish, as part of his preparations for war, that they raise a contingent of 500 men at arms as soon as possible, thus giving the Otto new authority to recruit soldiers; at the time, however, there was no mention of who would command these soldiers.[14] During the meeting of the Council of Seventy that took place in Florence on 23 May, it was recommended that Lorenzo be appointed captain-general of the Florentine army. Serving on the Council of the Seventy, Vettori not only voted in favour of this motion but also urged that it should be carried out as soon as possible. Moreover, having been elected to the Otto four days prior, Vettori took part in the deliberations of 6 June, when the body voted, with every semblance of legality, to elect Lorenzo captain of the Florentine forces, effective immediately.[15] In this way, the vote taken in the Otto di Pratica circumvented the law that prohibited Florentine citizens from occupying the office of captain-general. This law, enacted in the early days of the commune, was intended to prevent any one citizen having authority over other citizens of the republic.

The dangers inherent in Lorenzo's audacious act were apparent to all, as Trexler points out, because Lorenzo was not only a citizen but also the nephew of the most powerful man in Christendom.[16] Furthermore, he would hardly have taken such a far-reaching step without the prior approval of the pope. Even if the magistrates had wanted to object, Vettori's presence on the council would guarantee Lorenzo a unanimous vote. He was offered the command of 250 soldiers for a period of three years with a possible one-year extension, immunity from prosecution for his officers and soldiers, and a generous yearly stipend of 35,000 gold ducats, an amount that was raised to 37,000 in the deliberations of the Otto on 3 July.[17] Devonshire Jones believes that Vettori could have been responsible for the decision to increase the captain's salary.[18] Francesco would have known from his time in Rome serving as the Florentine ambassador that Lorenzo was a notorious spendthrift and chronically short of money.[19] The Medici account book of the year 1515 makes clear that he spent large amounts on his personal attire. In 1515 alone his wardrobe purchases show that he dealt with at least forty-seven different persons or companies to supply his clothes, ordering, for example, fifty garments of more than seventeen different types.[20] Most importantly, however, in the summer of 1515, Lorenzo gave Filippo Strozzi control of the Depository of the Signoria and the Otto di Pratica so that he could simultaneously enrich himself while watching over the commune's expenses.[21]

Even though the pope had sanctioned Lorenzo's actions in Florence, and Giuliano's sister-in-law Alfonsina was ecstatic about her son's enhanced status, the opposition in Rome was fierce, particularly from Giuliano but also from Cardinal Bernardo Dovizi da Bibbiena. Benedetto Buondelmonti's letters from Rome to his friend Filippo Strozzi reveal that Bibbiena was afraid that Lorenzo's growing power and increased prestige would make him superior to Giuliano and that with his new military command there would be nothing to stop him and his supporters from disposing of Florence as he wished.[22] Paolo Vettori, showing how little he thought of Giuliano, said to Buondelmonti that "it was natural that Giuliano should resent Lorenzo's increased prestige, for Giuliano would be deserted by his followers."[23] Buondelmonti also reported how well disposed Paolo Vettori was to Lorenzo and "how grateful he was for what Lorenzo had done for him and his brother."[24]

Reactions in Florence to Lorenzo's assumption of new powers were subdued, probably because, as Cerretani writes, the enemies of the Medici family were afraid, "although their friends thought that it was a good thing because they said it was better to give the money to one of us than to other foreign *condottieri*."[25] Cambi reported that many citizens were convinced that Lorenzo, who was raised outside Florence and therefore did not understand the republic, aspired only to dominate the city with his ambition and avarice.[26] Nerli writes that Lorenzo's new title allowed him to dissociate himself from the old style of Medici rule, putting on lordly airs and neglecting the business of consultation.[27] Young Niccolò Guicciardini, who has already been mentioned as an early reader of Machiavelli's *Prince*, wrote several years later that Lorenzo, by becoming the captain-general of the Florentine militia, "deprived the city of whatever authority and force remained to it and conferred so much honour upon [Lorenzo] that it seems one could not legitimately contradict his will and actions."[28] Lorenzo soon came to dress in gold brocade and everywhere in the city he was addressed as "lord" (Fig 12).[29]

When Giuliano arrived in Florence for a stopover at the beginning of July, ostensibly to raise additional soldiers before making his way with the papal army to Bologna and Lombardy to engage with the French, Nerli writes that his presence in the city aroused the jealousy of Lorenzo and his mother.[30] Lorenzo's fears of being upstaged were increased no doubt because of Giuliano's exalted status as commander of the papal troops and having become the uncle of the king of France. Fatini writes that Lorenzo was irritated because his own marriage with the daughter of the Spanish viceroy Cardona had been put on hold owing to the imminent war.[31] But Lorenzo was beginning his own ascendancy in Florence and was well on his way to transforming the republic into a principate, where he could become an absolute ruler. This was an ambition that Giuliano had tried to curb in 1513, as we saw in chapter 5, by writing his nephew a set of instructions, ostensibly on behalf of the pope but not without his own thoughts on how to govern the republic properly. Soon after arriving in the city, Giuliano most likely became deeply disillusioned with the unfolding events, first with his brother's decision to join the anti-French coalition and then with the pope's condoning of Lorenzo's blatant violation of the Florentine constitution. Lorenzo and his group of *palleschi* friends were probably not too upset at the news of Giuliano's fever. This would have been especially true of Alfonsina Orsini, who had moved to Florence from Rome in early June to take over the reins of government during her son's expected absence with the Florentine army.[32] She had always opposed Giuliano for supporting the popular government and had treated him with disdain because of his close friendship with Jacopo Salviati, her son's harshest critic. As Lorenzo's fortune increased in the city, Giuliano began his slow decline into a severe and prolonged bout of pulmonary tuberculosis, leading to his death in March 1516.

The pope's secretary, Ardinghelli, addressed a letter to Giuliano in Florence on 20 July, hoping to comfort him in his illness with the assurance that his strength would be renewed after a few days of rest and recuperation.[33] Ardinghelli also expressed the hope that his "poco suo male" would not be long-lasting and thus interrupt the pope's plans.[34] However, he continued, "if the fever persists, God forbid, and it is the time that you should be in Lombardy, it might be necessary to take you in a litter to convalesce on the way, because His Holiness does not want to do anything without you being present."[35] Ardinghelli's letter addressed to Giuliano's friend, Giovanni Vespucci, on 27 July, advised him that the pope was creating his cousin Cardinal Giulio de' Medici, who would be arriving with new orders, to be legate with the papal troops, and also that the pope expressly forbade Lorenzo, who was eager to leave for Bologna at the head of the Florentine army, from leaving the city, noting that it would be difficult for Lorenzo to disobey the orders of a legate. The pope was anxious that, with Lorenzo and his soldiers gone from the city, the anti-Medici faction with their pro-French leanings would rise up and overthrow the regime. In his letter, Ardinghelli took note of the news that Giuliano's health was showing a strong improvement and hoped that in a short period of time he would be ready to ride with his troops. If tomorrow this improvement was confirmed, he wrote, the pope would not proceed with the appointment of a legate.[36] Ardinghelli's next letter to Giuliano, on 30 July, was no doubt distressing for him to read because the secretary asked him to write immediately to the Duke of Urbino and warn him that the pope's patience had reached its limits, and that if Della Rovere did not march at once in the service of the Holy Church, he would be a "ruined man." If Giuliano loves and wants to protect him, Ardinghelli continued, he should write to him straight away and "tell the duke not to delay any further."[37]

On 20 August Giuliano sent his own emissary, Raffaello Girolami, to Turin with a set of secret instructions for his brother-in-law, the Duke of Savoy. He asked the duke to mediate between the pope and the king of France "before everything gets out of hand and the wound becomes incurable."[38] Giuliano was conflicted about his own situation, readily admitting that he believed a major part of his infirmity was caused by his great sorrow in not seeing unity between the pope, whom he dutifully served, and the king, with whom he now shared ties of kinship. He was confident, he told the duke, "if an accord follows, the happiness he will feel will be salutary medicine for all his indispositions."[39] The instructions set out the pope's conditions: first, Parma and Piacenza would remain in the possession of the pope; second, a peace must be concluded between France and Spain because the constant wars between Christians not only interrupted the universal peace but also the holy crusade against the Turks; third, the king must renounce the kingdom of Naples in favour of the Holy See or of a third party agreeable both to the pope and the king; and finally, the pope would not permit, under any circumstances, the same sovereign to govern the head and tail of the Italian peninsula, *del capo e de la coda di Italia*, Milan and Naples.[40] Sadly, Giuliano would have known that these conditions would not be acceptable to the zealously ambitious French king, whose huge army was at that very moment crossing the Alpine passes, and that a war between the pope and his wife's family, the traditional defenders of the Florentine republic, would now be unavoidable.

The Duke of Savoy did indeed mediate between the two parties, but only after the defeat of the Swiss and Spanish coalition at the battle of Marignano, which took place over two days, on 13 and 14 September. Lorenzo, as commander of both the papal and Florentine forces, did not participate in the battle because his armies were ordered not to advance farther north than the border of the Papal States of Parma and Piacenza at the Po River. Perhaps Lorenzo was, in his reticence to commit his troops, restrained not only by the Florentines but also by memories of his father, fearing that, if the French were victorious, he would be overthrown by the citizens of Florence, as had happened during the invasion of Charles VIII in 1494. The peace treaty negotiated by the Duke of Savoy and the papal ambassador Canossa was concluded on 17 September but received ratification only a month later, because the pope was still holding out in the hope of reaching better terms.[41] Leo was forced to cede Parma and Piacenza, which were once more united with Milan, and, in exchange for an exile in France on generous terms, the young Massimiliano Sforza gave up his rights to the duchy. For his part, Francis I committed to buy all the salt necessary for his duchy from the salt mines of Cervia, a considerable income for the papal treasury,[42] and he promised protection for the Papal States, the republic of Florence, and all members of the house of the Medici.[43] In November 1515 the king issued letters in Milan conferring on Giuliano and his wife, Philiberte of Savoy, the rank of French princes and granting them the Duchy of Nemours "in consideration of the new alliance concluded between Francis I and Pope Leo X."[44] Francis I expressed the wish to meet with the pope personally, and at first it was thought that Florence should be the venue for such an encounter. This was quickly changed to Bologna, however, even though it would entail a longer and more arduous journey for the pope, because both Cardinal Giulio and Lorenzo feared that the presence of the French king in the city might stimulate in its citizens a nostalgia for the republic and, furthermore, that there was the danger that their opponents might seek a separate accord with the French king. The official signing of the peace treaty took place in Bologna between 11 and 14 of December 1515.[45]

POPE LEO X'S ENTRY INTO FLORENCE

Leo X's entry into Florence on 30 November was planned to take place prior to his meeting with Francis I in Bologna. The fact that a reigning pope was to make a triumphal entry into the city of his birth had tremendous religious significance for the entire population, but at the same time the political dimensions of such a visit were not lost on the citizens. Everyone recognized that the supreme authority, and therefore the destiny of the city, was inexorably tied to that of the papacy in Rome, where all decisions concerning the republic were made, turning Florence into merely a satellite of the papacy.

The *entrata* of Pope Leo X, who was also the effective sovereign of Florence, resonated in the city, and the event was recorded in numerous descriptions.[46] In a procession that lasted seven hours, the pope was carried through the streets of Florence, sitting under a baldachin decorated with brocaded panels bearing the papal arms. The procession wove its way along a course of more than three kilometres in length,[47] making stops at each of twelve triumphal arches, modelled on those of imperial Rome, spanning the streets and bridges along the ceremonial route. Florence was fortunate in being blessed with an abundance of talented artists who were put to work to decorate these wooden constructions with Roman-inspired inscriptions, classical architectural motifs, and illusionistic sculpture that ingeniously combined dynastic and papal imagery.

Further allusions to imperial Rome were seen in a series of copies of Roman monuments, such as a colossal equestrian statue in Piazza Santa

Maria Novella and representations of Trajan's column and the Castel Sant'Angelo, as well as a colossal statue of Hercules placed beneath the Loggia dei Lanzi across from Michelangelo's *David*, who stood guard outside the entrance to Palazzo della Signoria.[48] Cox-Rearick has suggested that the fundamental message of the *entrata* was that of a hero's triumphal return, and that the pope was hailed as "an agent of peace and reconciliation," a theme that was to become fundamental to his personal imagery. She also suggests that the sequence of Roman arches decorated with columns and obelisks expressed the theme of "Florence as a new Rome under Leo."[49] The return of the pope to Florence, however, was a moment no less crucial for the consolidation of the Medici power in the city, where, enshrined in the rituals of the triumphal entry, the pope's visit could also be viewed as the highest representative of the Medici family "taking possession" of the city itself.[50]

Knowing how unprecedented this event was for the citizens of Florence, and also given the existing political tensions in the city, where many citizens felt antagonistic toward the Medici regime for having lost their popular government, it is surprising to learn that the pope took a decision, made public in a papal brief dated 4 November 1515, to give his sister-in-law Alfonsina Orsini full responsibility for overseeing the huge undertaking of putting on the *entrata*. In his papal brief, Leo X exhorts her to "make every effort and industry, strength of mind and spirit … to ensure that he and his entourage would be adequately provided for as befits his princely status."[51] By appointing Alfonsina, the pope was not only publicly recognizing her as the unofficial ruler of the republic but also at the same time exposing his own deep mistrust of the *ottimati* and the elected representatives of the government. Tomas suggests that Lorenzo might have become jealous of his mother's commission and "piqued at being excluded from involvement in the preparations and all decisions."[52] However, it is certain that, among the city's officials, the pope's decision to appoint Alfonsina, a woman and a foreigner, to perform this central role would have been seen as an insult, provoking widespread resentment among the city's officials.

The papal master of ceremonies, Paride de' Grassi, may have first encountered this animosity at the gate of San Piero Gattolini,[53] where sixty liveried youths, sons of office-holding citizens, and a delegation from the Florentine Signoria, including the *Gonfaloniere* Niccolò Ridolfi, waited to greet the pope on his arrival. Part of the wall of the outer gate and its portcullis had been dismantled and placed on the ground in a symbolic gesture of submission. This was done, Trexler explains, as a substitute for giving the keys of the city to the pope. When de' Grassi demanded that the city bestow its keys upon Leo X, he was told that the republic's practice had always been to tear down the gates for popes but never to give its keys.[54] Ciseri writes that this architectural modification was also a necessity to widen the passageway for such a large procession to proceed.[55]

Another point of friction at the Porta San Piero Gattolini involved three principal magistrates, Jacopo Salviati, Roberto Acciaiuoli, and Lanfredino Lanfredini. According to de' Grassi's account, the magistrates claimed equality with the cardinals and wanted to proceed on horse rather than on foot, but the pope's master of ceremonies overruled them. Apparently they appealed to the pope, who upheld de' Grassi's decision.[56] Landucci provides a vivid picture of the *entrata*, describing how the pope was accompanied by "numerous infantry, and amongst them the papal guard, consisting of many German soldiers, in a uniform with which they wore two-edged axes in the French fashion. Besides these, many mounted bowmen and musketeers, all belonging to his guard."[57] Following Leo X were eighteen cardinals, archbishops, bishops, foreign ambassadors, and the entire papal court. Describing in great detail all the theatrical *apparati* that had been hurriedly constructed throughout the city, Landucci writes that "the grandeur of it was incredible."[58] Although it would certainly seem that Alfonsina had risen to the occasion, Landucci, nonetheless, was highly critical: "We had more two thousand men at work, as it was estimated, for more than a month ... all for things of no duration; when a splendid temple might have been built in honour of God and to the glory of the city."[59] He also bitterly lamented the wholesale destruction in parts of the city, caused "without discretion," to widen streets and provide additional accommodations for papal courtiers, "which displeased many." Landucci was not the only one to resent the expense and extravagance, since the chronicler Piero Parenti voiced similar objections to the papal visit, saying how displeased everyone was, especially those whose houses had been requisitioned by the Signoria and "Madonna Alfonsina" to provide free lodging to members of the papal court. The walls of the house where the cardinal of Siena and his retainers were staying, he wrote, were scrawled with hostile slogans, and the authorities had threatened severe punishment for those found responsible.[60]

Trexler points to a number of instances when the priors seem to have adopted a policy of "ritual distancing" in an attempt, he says, "to counter the irresistible charisma of the Medici pope."[61] Given the widespread indignation among the magistrates, however, more likely their aloofness was an outward display to register their displeasure. The distancing upset many of the Curia, especially Paride de' Grassi, and manifested itself in various ways, for example, when the Signoria were unwilling to accompany the pope to the Medici parish church of San Lorenzo but went straight to the church instead, awaiting his arrival there, or when they refused de' Grassi's order to tip their caps and stand when the cardinals passed. Apparently, de' Grassi became "enraged by the insupportable misery with which the Florentine *popolo* persecuted members of the papal curia, as if they were enemies."[62] Perhaps the Florentine magistrates could derive some small measure of satisfaction, as they watched the papal procession, from knowing that he had suffered the humiliation of losing territory in the Papal States and was now on his way to Bologna, where his reception would be "just the opposite of that at Florence: no decorations, no acclamations,"[63] to sign a concordat with Francis I which would recognize the supremacy of the pope's authority over the church in France but leave ecclesiastical nominations, and thereby the real power, in the hands of the king.[64]

The hostility felt toward Leo X and the regime only intensified when the pope, returning to Florence on 22 December, decided to remain in the city for two months, only taking his leave on 18 February. Cambi wrote that the papal presence in the city did not benefit anyone because the inconvenience and great expense was a burden on those who had been ordered by the commune to provide free accommodation for such a large retinue of cardinals and other courtiers, a complaint, as we have seen, that was echoed by Parenti.[65] Even Cerretani objected to the disruption caused by these visitors, who, he wrote, "everyone dislikes," reporting that there was also a steep rise in the price of grain.[66] That Leo X was extremely unpopular when he visited Florence in 1515 is confirmed in a poem disseminated in Florence that laments how evil has proliferated under the Florentine pope:

> Panders controlled Sixtus, catamites Julius;
> a buffoon has control of vain Leo …
> Liberty is lost after this, Florence,
> for a woman of the Orsini blood is your sole ruler.
> Lo, Florence as a suppliant before the altar often begs
> to become famed by the miter of the pontiffs.

She has her prayer granted: every kind of evil has increased;
her citizens everywhere bear great burdens.
Our native laws and magistrates are carried off by the hour;
ambition, self-indulgence, and harsh tyranny are upon us."[67]

When the pope returned to Florence after his meeting with Francis I, word quickly spread that he had made a decision to depose the Duke of Urbino. Anticipating that this would most likely be the outcome of the meeting between the pope and the French king, Della Rovere had sent his envoy Baldassare Castiglione to Bologna to appeal to the king on his behalf, as a knight of the Order of St Michael, its sovereign head. While the king was reluctant to give his consent and spoke warmly of Della Rovere, Leo was obdurate on the matter of deposing Francesco Maria. Contemporary sources, most notably Paolo Giovio, the contemporary historian and papal official, in his biography of Leo X, claim that Lorenzo and his overly ambitious mother pressured the pope to invest Lorenzo with the duchy; in fact, however, the idea originated with Leo X and Cardinal Giulio de' Medici,[68] who were even more determined to create a Medici hereditary state now that the pope had been forced to surrender Parma and Piacenza. The acquisition of Urbino, an undertaking opposed by Giuliano, appeared to be valid for dynastic reasons because by making Lorenzo the new duke it would guarantee a Medici hereditary state that would be secure, stable, and independent of the factional strife in Florence.[69] The French king, as Clough has argued, needed the pope's cooperation if he was to realize his ambitions in the peninsula, and since the king's prime objective was to ensure that Leo X honoured the Bologna agreement, especially those aspects of the negotiations that were concerned with the ecclesiastical affairs of the French kingdom, Della Rovere was deemed expendable.[70]

Sanudo records how Giuliano pleaded with the pope not to harm the duke or take his state away from him because the duke had been so helpful to the Medici and taken them in when they were exiled from Florence.[71] He also reports that the pope refused to make any promises to his brother because Lorenzo was pressing him to take Urbino.

FRATESCHI, THE MEDICI, AND SAN MARCO

When Giuliano died on Monday 17 March, his body was carried down to Florence from the hills of Fiesole where his doctors had recommended he be taken in the last weeks of his life for "better air."[72] According to both Cambi and Masi, our chief sources, the next day, Tuesday, he was laid to rest in a chapel in the Church of San Marco. Masi wrote that he did not believe there was anyone in Florence who did not go to see him, all of whom broke down in tears.[73] The decision to take Giuliano to San Marco, the original centre of Savonarola's movement, must have reflected Giuliano's own last wishes, which were not necessarily those of his brother the pope or his cousin Cardinal Giulio de' Medici, archbishop of Florence. In previous chapters we have seen how Giuliano had gravitated toward the *frateschi*, not only because of his sympathy for their republican politics and for their desire for radical religious reform but also because the head of the *frateschi* faction in Florence was his brother-in-law Jacopo Salviati married to his sister Lucrezia. The Medicean authorities, however, had become very wary of the friars in the convent of San Marco, who, as supporters of Savonarola's popular government, were accused of being disruptive, fomenting discord, and undermining the Medici's hold on the state. In fact, since the Boscoli-Capponi Conspiracy of 1513, the convent of San Marco had come under increasing scrutiny and suspicion, and Cardinal Giulio de' Medici, determined to stamp out any subversive political activity, undertook the precautionary measure of planting an informer within its walls.[74] At the same time, in a move that was unprecedented and bitterly resented by the friars of San Marco, he contravened their privileges and immunity by obtaining from Leo X the right for himself or his vicar to conduct visitations of the convent whenever they saw fit.[75] The aim, as Polizzotto points out, "was to isolate and neutralize San Marco by keeping it under surveillance and by publicizing the fact so as to discourage individual or institutional association with the convent."[76] The Medici were also increasingly aware of the political significance of a flood of Savonarola-inspired prophecies that appeared in the city at the beginning of the sixteenth century, together with a seemingly endless stream of other would-be prophets who were preaching in the streets and churches, all calling for an imminent chastisement of the wicked and a renovation of the Church. The chronicler Luca Pitti wrote that "everyday there arose monks, nuns, and peasants all prophesying a flagellation and renovation of the Church and they were listened to by all those with troubled souls."[77] Implicit in these prophecies was a criticism of Medici politics, so that, by flocking to hear these prophets, the citizens of Florence were in fact signalling their opposition to the Medici.[78]

One such prophetic tract, first published by Olga Pugliese in 1985, relates specifically to Giuliano and provides a valuable insight into *fratesco* thinking in 1515. The one-page text was written in the hand of the acclaimed Florentine poet and ardent disciple of Savonarola, Girolamo Benivieni (1453–1542), who first came to prominence in Florence in the circle of humanists and poets surrounding Lorenzo the Magnificent.[79] Benivieni wrote a defence of the friar's prophetic revelations, and he was also in contact with the Camaldolese hermits Vincenzo Querini and Tommaso Giustiniani; more significantly, he was a particularly close and lifelong friend of Jacopo Salviati. Benivieni, therefore, almost certainly would have personally known Giuliano.[80] His prophecy claimed: "When the sun after 1515 shall have rolled on for six months then there will be brought to the Italians dangers worse than earlier ones." A French monarch, described as another "Hercules," would attack Italy with a large army, "not, as many believe, against the rights of the Church, but on behalf of the Church's rights":

> After the capture of the city of the fraudulent he will enter F[lorence], and there after committing a great slaughter of the citizens, he will subject it to his rule for 120 days. But afterwards that gentle Duke whom some impious people expelled will be restored to his own command. In the meantime he will devastate all Italy and provide good government to cities. Moreover, he who is called the Supreme Pontiff, hearing these things will breathe out his soul because of his strong grief. And a Shepherd of such great sanctity will be created who will look upon all the things done by the King of the French with a heavenly blessing.[81]

Benivieni's prophecy seems to have been written during the time that Leo was visiting Florence in December, that is, six months after the invasion by Francis I. It expressed the hope that a leader, presumably Giuliano, "whom some impious people expelled," a reference to his removal as the head of the government of Florence in 1513 by Leo and Cardinal Giulio, "will be returned to his command." Since the prophecy called for the pope's imminent demise, it represented a dramatic loss of faith in the Medici pope and stood in sharp contrast to Benivieni's adulatory poem composed two years earlier, titled *Frottola pro Papa Leone in renovatione ecclesiae* (A *frottola* for Pope Leo on the Renovation of the Church), in which he celebrated Leo X's accession to the papacy and described him as God's conquering Lion from Judah who would put to flight all the wolves that were tormenting the city of St Peter.[82] As Weinstein has observed, "Benivieni rejoiced that the seed had been sown in Florence. From her the new fruit would come forth, all would be united in a single sheepfold under one shepherd."[83] Like so many Florentines, Benivieni had been optimistic about the election of Cardinal Giovanni de' Medici, believing that he would usher in an Age of Gold and revive the magnificence of Lorenzo, the pope's revered father. Three years on, however, the hope was turning into despair. The negative view of Leo X expressed in Benivieni's prophecy was no doubt directly linked to the papal brief issued on 17 April 1515 that was intended to eradicate the influence of Savonarola in the city once and for all. Savonarola was condemned as a heretic and a schismatic, and his doctrines as diabolical. All prophetic speculation was prohibited. The prohibitions against *frateschi* were severe and wide-ranging, as recorded at the time by Cerretani,[84] Cambi,[85] and other chroniclers, since anyone "possessing or venerating images, clothing, bones, or writings belonging to persons condemned as heretics and schismatic was himself to be adjudged a heretic and schismatic and therefore excommunicated. All such objects and writings were to be surrendered up to the Archiepiscopal Curia within a fortnight."[86] A great many Florentines were sympathetic to the friar's cause because, as we have seen in previous chapters, Savonarola had initiated and championed the popular Florentine government. It is perhaps not surprising, therefore, that in the year 1515 support for the Medici regime reached a lower point than at any other time between 1512 and 1527.[87]

BURIAL

Early on Wednesday morning, 19 March, Giuliano's body was moved to San Giovannino, a church not far from San Marco, situated across from the Medici palace in the Via Larga. From there it was placed on a catafalque and set in the middle of the street in front of the palace, draped in brocaded curtains bordered in black. The street was completely filled with two tiers of church benches, occupied by the secular and ecclesiastical representatives of the city and other Florentine dignitaries, including members of all the Florentine guilds, and it took two hours before all the citizens were seated for the ceremony. Cambi and Masi both comment that this was the greatest funeral ever staged for a citizen of the republic, while Strocchia writes that the sheer size of the funeral cortège far outstripped that of Leo X's *entrata*.[88] The logistical problems of organizing such a large gathering became apparent when the many priests, friars, monks, and clerics who had gathered to march at the head of the procession completed the entire route through the city streets and entered the Basilica of San Lorenzo, where the requiem Mass was to be held, before Giuliano's catafalque had even moved from its starting point in the Via Larga.[89]

As Fatini rightly observes, neither Lorenzo nor Alfonsina would have participated in the general mourning over Giuliano, for they had always been fiercely jealous of him, especially because he had enjoyed widespread popularity among the citizens of Florence. Furthermore, he had been an outspoken critic of Lorenzo's despotic act in assuming the captaincy of the Florentine forces. Even more crucially, however, right up to the point of his death, he had bitterly opposed Lorenzo's ambition to make himself Duke of Urbino. The day after Giuliano died, a bull of excommunication was issued, dated 18 March, that divested Della Rovere of all his papal vicariates and the title of duke.[90] Giuliano had kept his promise "that whilst I live, you … will receive no molestation on my account," but his fraternal care for Della Rovere could not even last until his burial.[91]

In Cerretani's account of Giuliano's funeral, he wrote that, when everyone was seated in the Via Larga, Lorenzo, wearing a Spanish cloak, came out of the Medici palace together with Philiberte and other family members.[92] Piero Parenti contradicts Cerretani and records that Lorenzo had left Florence for Rome in a great hurry the day before the funeral, that is, on 18 March. Parenti wrote that he did not know the reason for Lorenzo's sudden departure, only that it was very abrupt.[93] Verdi believes he went to Rome with the understanding of the pope in order to receive the titles of Duke of Urbino and prefect of Rome.[94]

Judging by the actions of Leo X, the pope did not seem to have been particularly moved by his younger brother's death. As we have seen, there were many instances when the political differences between the two became apparent. Giuliano was removed against his will from his position as head of the Florentine government in favour of his autocratic nephew because Leo X and his cousin Giulio disapproved of Giuliano's conciliatory politics, especially toward the *frateschi*. Giuliano's strong attachment to the French crown also ran counter to the pope's political strategy of forging an alliance with Spain. Of all their differences, however, perhaps none was so glaring as Giuliano's open and very public criticism of the pope's plan to usurp the Duchy of Urbino from his "brother" Francesco Maria. When news of Giuliano's death reached Rome, we learn from Paride de' Grassi that Leo was not in favour of celebrating a public funeral Mass there. This choice must have struck his master of ceremonies as strange because he made a special note of it in his diary, reporting that many Florentines and Medici relatives in Rome thought that, since Giuliano was a full brother of the pope and captain-general of the papal army, there ought to be a public display of mourning with solemn funeral ceremonies. De' Grassi wrote that the pope did not think that even his own family had reason to hold a public funeral Mass in Rome for Giuliano, and he would only allow those who were deeply moved by private feelings to arrange a private Mass.[95]

In Florence the humanist scholar and Florentine chancellor Marcello Virgilio Adriani (1464–1521) delivered the official eulogy to the citizens assembled in the Via Larga.[96] Adriani had succeeded Bartolomeo Scala in 1498 at the same time that Machiavelli entered the Florentine chancery, but, unlike Machiavelli, Adriani was able to survive in his position until his death in 1521. He would have known Giuliano personally, working closely with him after the return of the Medici in 1512, and, more importantly, he would have been fully aware of Giuliano's attempt to reconcile with the enemies of the regime, not wishing to impose an autocratic government under the Medici. This could explain McManamon's observation that Chancellor Adriani "used his funeral oration [for Giuliano de' Medici] to trace his ideals for the Florentine republic in 1516,"[97] knowing that these views closely conformed to those of Giuliano. Adriani commended the citizens of Florence for wisely regulating their citizen assembly, where "all men were allowed to seek out with confidence that which corresponded to their own virtue," such as "marriages, appointments, offices, associations," so long as they "adhered to the fellowship and society of *res publica* (and a thing characteristic of equal freedom) were commanded by means of election, and by annual magistracies turn-by-turn," through which "their achievements have advanced in magnitude and glory, and power has been added to the glory of deeds."[98]

Adriani then spoke at length about the history of the Medici family, beginning with the virtues of Cosimo the Elder, "the greatest jewel" of the family,[99] who, because of his generosity, was responsible for many building projects in the city – libraries, monasteries, and churches, restored or newly built – which earned him the epithet of founder and pious restorer of temples (Fig. 22). He had equally exalted praise for Giuliano's father, Lorenzo, who was granted the title of "Magnificent" because of the grandeur of his accomplishments in fine arts, music, and in poetry, but also in diplomacy. He helped many kings and princes throughout Italy with advice, resources, and weapons; to some he was of service, others he enriched, and on some he bestowed kingdoms (Fig 24).[100]

The most striking feature of Adriani's oration is that Leo X and his nephew Lorenzo are barely mentioned. Adriani made only an oblique reference to Giuliano's brother by expressing the hope that the virtue that had carried Leo X to eminence would bring everything back to the tranquility everyone longed for in the current difficult times and amidst the extreme violence of military campaigns.[101] As for Lorenzo il Giovane, here too Adriani's reference was somewhat indirect. He hoped that Giuliano would remain a presence for his nephew, who "while he was alive had wished to guide with no less Fortune and earthly Gloria [than his own]."[102] Adriani brought his oration to a close by exhorting his fellow citizens of Florence to escort Giuliano to his burial

> Go therefore, and with that *humanitas* with which he alive was accustomed to lead your *res publica* and his fatherland, with that *humanitas civis* which was in him, with that wisdom which was his father's, with the *consilium* which was ancestral and native, and with the *pietas* finally that was unique to him … follow what remains of him left to us, beseeching God Almighty with your prayers and tears, that he, although now in a better place, might wish to be with you everywhere … Go therefore you citizens of the whole *res publica* who have come hither, and remember forever that this man was an outstanding Dux of your city and *res publica* under whose auspices everything was forever happy and famous.[103]

It took Giuliano's funeral cortège five hours to make its way through the streets of Florence, following the same route as the pope's *entrata* only three and a half months prior, when, as Cambi observed, Leo had come to Florence in great triumph. Today, he wrote, the body of his blood brother was carried by the same route and the whole city that had come to see the living pope now assembled to watch the Giuliano's cortège pass.[104] Perhaps it was the intention of the organizers of the funeral to have the cortège retrace the same steps, so that all citizens of Florence would be able to reflect on the lives of these two Medici brothers. Even more significantly, however, perhaps they wanted to use this occasion to reclaim the republican identity of the Florentine state.

NOTES

INTRODUCTION

1 Casa Buonarroti, Florence, Inv. 10a. Translation by C. Gilbert, "Medici Chapel," 402–4. The full passage reads: "El cielo e la terra / el di e la nocte parlano e dichono noi abiamo chol nostro veloce chorso chondu / cto alla morte el ducha giuliano e ben giusto ch e' ne facci vendecta chome fa / e la vendecta e questa ch' avendo noi morto lui lui chosi morto a ctolta la / luce a noi e chogli ochi chiusi a serrato e nostri che non splendono più so / pra la terra ch' arrebbe di noi dunche fatto mentre vivea?" De Tolnay and Squellati Brizio, *Michelangelo e i Medici*, 83.

2 The New Sacristy was also to contain a double wall tomb for Lorenzo the Magnificent (d. 1492) and his murdered brother Giuliano (d. 1478), but these were never built. Both are buried in a plain sarcophagus placed against the chapel's entrance wall opposite the altar.

3 Gilbert, "Medici Chapel," 405.

4 De Tolnay, *Michelangelo: Medici Chapel*, 73.

5 Gilbert, "Medici Chapel," 405.

6 Hibbard, *Michelangelo*, 146.

7 "... die unbedeutenden Sprossen eines schnell entarteten Geschlechtes." Steinmann, *Das Geheimnis der Medicigräber Michelangelos*, 50.

8 "E il suo spirito, fiaccato dagli esaurimenti della lussuria, si rifugiava nel misticismo, nelle pratiche della religione e dei sortilegi, preso anche spesso da un sentimento di tedio della vita, che parve arrivasse fino al pensiero del suicidio. L'ingenita dolcezza dell'indole, l'erotismo ed il misticismo, che lo disgustavano di ogni cosa, che lo rendevano quasi impotente a qualsiasi operare, e lo facevano alieno d'ogni ambizione ed insofferente d'ogni pratica pubblica." Nitti, *Leone X*, 26.

9 "inetto o piuttosto poco curante, per indole, degli affari, si tuffò con foga e con politica medicea nei piaceri, specialmente nelle voluttà d'amore, dissipando il tempo el la salute nei suntuosissimi banchetti che i privati gli offrivano ... e il cui poeta era il giovane Jacopo Nardi, dandosi ad orgie tali." Cian, *Musa Medicea*, 7.

10 Pastor, *History of the Popes*, 7:90.

11 Pieraccini, *Medici di Cafaggiolo,* 1:217.

12 Hale, *Florence and the Medici*, 98.

13 "Fu questo uno dei numerosi e fuggevoli amori che caratterizzarono la vicenda biografica del [Giuliano], il quale, specialmente negli anni di esilio, appare in bilico tra una raffinata indolenza, a tratti venata di impulsi mistici, e una sensualità esasperata." Tabacchi, "Giuliano de' Medici," 86.

14 Fatini, "Giuliano de' Medici," vii–xcvii.

15 "Non si deve cadere però nell'errore di ritenere il [Giuliano] una figura irrilevante." Tabacchi, "Giuliano de' Medici," 86–7.

16 Kent, *Friendship, Love, and Trust*. See also review by Jurdjevic, 960–2.

17 Versions of Raphael's portrait, painted at the time of Giuliano's engagement to Philiberte, are in collections in New York, Florence (Uffizi), Northumberland (Alnwick Castle), and Turin. The Metropolitan Museum of Art currently lists its version as an early copy after Raphael. The painting has been attributed to Raphael himself and also as a copy after his lost original. In 2012 the painting was exhibited as a damaged original by Raphael with workshop assistance. Henry and Joannides, eds., *Late Raphael*, 262–6, 269, 287, 292, 294.

18 "La presa di Prato e il successivo saccheggio da parte delle truppe spagnole indussero i Fiorentini a togliere il loro appoggio al gonfaloniere Pier Soderini e, il 1° sett. 1512, [Giuliano] entrò trionfalmente in città con il fratello." Tabacchi, "Giuliano de' Medici," 86.

19 Letter dated 9 February 1514 from Alfonsina Orsini to Lorenzo de' Medici. ASF, MAP, 114, fol. 51. "Da una banda è il Magnifico [Giuliano], [Bernardo Dovizi da Bibbiena, Cardinale di] S.ta Maria in Portico, M. Luigi [de Rossi], la Contessina [Ridolfi], et Mona Lucretia [de' Medici]; da l'altro canto el Cardinale [Giulio] de' Medici, Lorenzo de' Medici, io, Mona Magdalena, et Cardinale Cibo, el Signore Francesco [Cibo], et ciascuno degli altri adherenti." Tommasini, *Vita e Scritti di Machiavelli*, 2.2:993.

20 Butters "Machiavelli and the Medici," 64–79.

21 Atkinson and Sices, eds., *Machiavelli and His Friends*, 308, and commentary on letter from Francesco Vettori to Niccolò Machiavelli, Rome, 21 April 1513, 501n.9. See also Tabacchi ("Giuliano de' Medici," 87), who notes a shift in Machiavelli's dedicatory intentions from Giuliano to his nephew Lorenzo: "A lui Machiavelli, nel corso dell' anno, propose di dedicare *Il principe*, ma di fronte alla freddezza con cui fu accolta l'offerta, si orientò su Lorenzo di Piero de' Medici."

22 Letter dated 18 March 1513. Atkinson and Sices, eds., *Machiavelli and His Friends,* 222.

23 Butters, "Machiavelli and the Medici," 67.

24 Guasti, ed. "I Manoscritti Torrigiani," 231; idem, *I Manoscritti Torrigiani*, 67.

25 Though the Metropolitan Museum currently lists the portrait as "Copy after Raphael," there has been a return to the idea of accepting the portrait as a

damaged autograph work with workshop assistance. Henry, "Raphael and Workshop," 262. See also n.17 above.

26 Giuliano was appointed captain-general of the papal troops in 1515, and in the same year Lorenzo was given the captaincy of the Florentine troops. Grimm, *Life of Michael Angelo*, 1:447–51.

27 Weinberger, *Michelangelo the Sculptor*, 1:338.

28 Hibbard, *Michelangelo*, 147.

29 Trexler and Lewis, "New Light on Medici Chapel," 93–123; Trexler, "Michelangelo's New Sacristy," 101–17.

30 Bambach, "Leonardo and Raphael," 28.

31 Weinberger, *Michelangelo*, 1:321.

32 Hibbard, *Michelangelo*, 147. For a differing interpretation that this object is not a casket or box but rather a smoothed ashlar block decorated with a mask that symbolizes the artistic process, see Giuliani, "Kästchen oder Quader?" 334–57.

CHAPTER 1

1 "Solo una speranza restava che parve che ognuno confortassi, questo era che lo spirto d'esso pareva entrato nel corpo del figl[i]olo suo Piero in questo primcipio." Cerretani, *Storia Fiorentina*, 185.

2 F. Guicciardini, *History of Florence*, 80–1.

3 F. Guicciardini, *History of Italy*, 36; idem, *Storia d' Italia*, 1:57.

4 Najemy, *History of Florence*, 369.

5 "perché per essere mio figluolo non se' però altro che cittadino di Firenze, come sono ancor loro." L. de' Medici, *Lettere*, 8:70; F. Kent, "Lorenzo de' Medici and Oligarchy," 50.

6 Kent, "Lorenzo de' Medici and Oligarchy," 44.

7 F. Guicciardini, *History of Italy*, 36; idem, *Storia d' Italia*, 1:57.

8 F. Guicciardini, *History of Florence*, 84.

9 Bullard, *Lorenzo il Magnifico*, 37; Cerretani (*Storia Fiorentina*, 197) reports that the city had spent more than 50,000 gold florins on Sarzana.

10 Rubinstein, *Government of Florence*, 267–9.

11 Landucci, *Florentine Diary*, 62.

12 Najemy, *History of Florence*, 414–50.

13 Cardinal de' Medici was taken prisoner by the French but escaped during his transportation to France disguised as a soldier. See Chambers, *Popes, Cardinals and War*, 127.

14 See Bernardo Dovizi's letter to Cardinal de' Medici dated 14 March 1512 in Dovizi, *Epistolario*, 1:472.

15 Pitti, *Istoria Fiorentina*, 107; Pesman Cooper, "Caduta di Piero Soderini," 227.

16 Shaw, *Julius II*, 291–2; Minnich, "Role of Schools of Theology," 83–4; idem, "Images of Julius II," 79–90, esp. 80.

17 Pesman Cooper, "Caduta di Pier Soderini," 225–60, esp. 230.

18 Fatini, "Giuliano de' Medici," xxxiv.

19 Pesman Cooper, "Caduta di Pier Soderini," 230.

20 Shaw, *Julius II*, 305.

21 The number of victims varies greatly in contemporary sources, and the lower figures may, as Pasquale Villari suggests, have been more advantageous for the Medici and thus underreported by sympathetic writers (Villari, *Niccolò Machiavelli*, 1:626). Jacopo Modesti, an eyewitness, put the number as high as 5,560 (Modesti, "Miserando sacco di Prato," 102). Francesco Vettori, Florentine diplomat and strong Medici supporter, tellingly puts the number as low as 500 (Vettori, "Sommario della Storia d'Italia," 142). The Florentine ambassador, Roberto Acciaiuoli, reported on 24 September that "meglio che V^{m} persone d' ogni sorte" had perished (Gattoni da Camogli, *Leone X*, 38n.72).

22 J. Guicciardini, "Letter to Francesco Guicciardini," 1:223–9; Pesman Cooper, "Caduta di Pier Soderini," 252–3.

23 Nardi, *Istorie di Firenze*, 1:432.

24 See, for example, Polizzotto, *Savonarolan Movement in Florence*, 239.

25 Cerretani, *Storia Fiorentina*, 444; Stephens, *Fall of Florentine Republic*, 59.

26 See Bernardo's letter of 5 September to his brother Pietro Dovizi in Venice in Sanudo, *Diarii*, 15:57–8.

27 Stephens, *Fall of Florentine Republic*, 59.

28 Cerretani, *Storia Fiorentina*, 444; Pitti, *Istorie Fiorentina*, 112.

29 Cotton, "Il Lucco del Poliziano," 353–68. A portrait of Lorenzo the Magnificent wearing the *lucco* appears in Domenico Ghirlandaio's fresco of the *Confirmation of the Franciscan Rule by Pope Honorius III*, 1483–86, in the Sassetti Chapel, Santa Trinità, Florence.

30 Cerretani, *Storia Fiorentina*, 444. The Medici bank had been founded by Giovanni di Bicci (1360–1429), who had two sons, Cosimo the Elder (1398–1464), progenitor of the senior line, and Lorenzo (1395–1440), founder of the cadet branch of the Medici. The senior line came to an end in the 1530s but the cadet branch predominated from 1530s until its extinction in the 1730s.

31 F. Guicciardini, *History of Florence*, 73.

32 A. Brown, "Lorenzo and Public Opinion," 71; idem, "Revolution of 1494," 17–20.

33 "in modo che Piero tenttò … ma per mezzo di chancellieri, tre ghonfalonieri a la fila di fare tagl[i]are la testa a cimque di loro et de' primi de la ciptà, e quail richusorno farllo sanza intendere Piero proprio et gl'huomini de lo stato." Cerretani, *Storia Fiorentina*, 191.

34 Parenti, *Storia Fiorentina*, 1:150.

35 Pitti, *Istoria Fiorentina*, 111.

36 Nerli, *Commentari*, 112; Devonshire Jones, *Francesco Vettori*, 67.

37 Weinstein, *Savonarola and Florence*, 129.

38 Weinstein, "Myth of Florence," 41.

39 Weinstein, *Savonarola and Florence*, 142–5.

40 Polizzotto, *Savonarolan Movement in Florence*, 19.
41 Ibid., 13.
42 F. Gilbert, "Venetian Constitution," 465.
43 Finlay, "Immortal Republic," 931–44.
44 Bracciolini, "In Praise of the Venetian Republic," 138.
45 Weinstein, *Savonarola and Florence*, 248; Butters, *Governors and Government*, 23.
46 Savonarola, *Selected Writings*, 161.
47 Ibid., 162.
48 F. Gilbert, *Machiavelli and Guicciardini*, 9.
49 Pesman Cooper, "Florentine Ruling Group," 71–129, esp. 72–4, 90; Polizzotto, *Savonarolan Movement in Florence*, 25; Najemy, *History of Florence*, 381–9.
50 F. Gilbert, "Venetian Constitution," 477; Rubinstein, *Palazzo Vecchio*, 40–3.
51 See Angelo Poliziano's letter to his friend in Milan, Jacopo Antiquario, dated 18 May 1492, in which he describes the death of Lorenzo. The letter is published in Godman, *From Poliziano to Machiavelli*, 15.
52 Ridolfi, *Life of Girolamo Savonarola*, 50–1.
53 Nardi, *Istorie di Firenze*, 2:32.
54 Polizzotto, *Savonarolan Movement in Florence*, 216.
55 F. Guicciardini, *History of Florence*, 219.
56 Pesman Cooper, "L'elezione di Piero Soderini," 161–3.
57 Pesman, "Machiavelli, Soderini, and the Republic," 50.
58 Guicciardini, *History of Florence*, 229; Butters, *Governors and Government*, 45.
59 F. Gilbert, "Venetian Constitution," 484.
60 Butters, *Governors and Government*, 174.
61 F. Gilbert, "Venetian Constitution," 485.
62 "La quale provisione si vinsse ne' primi luoghi al primo, e dubitando non pasaxi in consiglio e primi della ciptà preghando constrinxono G[i]uliano de' Medici che stava im palazo a preghare la si vincessi gl'homini del consiglio." Cerretani, *Storia Fiorentina*, 444. See also Stephens, *Fall of the Florentine Republic*, 60.
63 "et perché in Consiglio se ne dubitava, Jacopo Salviati e Lanfredino et altri spinsono Giuliano nella corte del palazzo a confortare mentre si ragunava il Consiglio grande, a credere e confortare la si vincessi." Cerretani (Berti, ed.), *Dialogo della Mutatione*, 32–3.
64 Devonshire Jones, *Francesco Vettori*, 67.
65 Cerretani (Berti, ed.), *Dialogo della Mutatione*, 33.
66 Pesman, "Machiavelli, Soderini, and the Republic," 52.
67 F. Guicciardini, *History of Italy*, 263; idem, *Storia d' Italia* 2:1087.
68 Butters, *Governors and Government*, 167.
69 Ibid., 179.
70 Ibid., 181.
71 Cerretani, *Ricordi*, 282, 284; idem, *Storia Fiorentina*, 445–6; Cerretani (Berti, ed.), *Dialogo della Mutatione*, 33–4; Devonshire Jones, *Francesco Vettori*, 69.

72 “e così Ramazotto, che venne con mille fanti, fece il simile per sbigottire quelli che pensavono havere disegniato e colorito che non si facessi nulla.” Cerretani (Berti, ed.), *Dialogo della Mutatione*, 34.

73 “In tra i quali, Jacopo Salviati e Lanfredino Lanfredini lo consigliarono a non alterare in modo alcuno il Gran Consiglio, per l’affezione che ci aveva l’universale e tanti cittadini, onorati, per diciotto anni da quello, dimostrando la debolezza della parte pallesca, esausta per tanti anni di uomini e di facoltà, e di prudenza non molta: chè, quando per satisfarle, volesse fondarvi su interamente lo stato e la sicurtà sua, si farebbe ministro dell’ avarizia e della loro violenza; ma, compiacendosi nella presente riforma, sarebbe sicura e grande la casa sua, amata ed esaltata da tutti quanti: da popolo, confermandogli il suo Consiglio, dalli Ottimati, per la contentezza della nuova riforma.” Pitti, *Istorie Fiorentina*, 113.

74 Nerli, *Commentari*, 115.

75 Cambi, *Istorie*, 2:323; Coyle and Cummings, *Music for Medici Festivals*, 11–12, 174n.4.

76 Pitti, *Istorie Fiorentina*, 114. These descriptions run counter to Cardinal de’ Medici’s own report to Piero Dovizi in Venice, brother of his secretary Bernardo, dated 16 September, when he says that he entered the city accompanied by “da gran moltitudine de primarii citadini de questa città, intrassemo in essa honorificentissimamente.” See Sanudo, *Diarii*, 15:101.

77 F. Guicciardini, *History of Italy*, 265; idem, *Storia d’ Italia*, 2:1089.

78 Landucci, *Florentine Diary*, 261; Cerretani (Berti, ed.), *Dialogo della Mutatione*, 39–40; Pitti, *Istoria Fiorentina*, 114–15.

79 “Giuliano armato d’arme bianche con buona compagnia comparse in su la sala, al quale que’ cittadini strettamente si racomandavano. Fu alcuni di noi che vollono vendicarsi con qualche particulare, il che con gran diligentia fu da Giuliano medicato, di sorte che non si fe’ male a persona, salvo che il palazzo, maxime il resto della munitione e parte dell’ argenterie andò male per le mani de’ soldati.” Cerretani (Berti, ed.), *Dialogo della Mutatione*, 39–40.

80 “In the Medici household a plot was prepared by the Cardinal; on the 16th of September Giuliano and some conspirators entered the Palazzo with hidden weapons, and at a given signal the square filled with soldiers and populace, and the Palazzo was quickly occupied. *Palle! Palle!*” Ridolfi, *Life of Niccolò Machiavelli*, 130. See also Stephens, *Fall of the Florentine Republic*, 63; Butters, *Governors and Government*, 183; and Najemy, *History of Florence*, 424.

81 F. Guicciardini, *History of Italy*, 266; idem, *Storia d’ Italia*, 2:1090; Nardi, *Istorie di Firenze*, 2:5; Nerli, *Commentari*, 116.

82 “E per far questo, a dì 16 del presente andò la matina el magnifico Juliano in palazo per consultar i casi de la cità, e si meteno insieme tutti li amici et armata mano ci trovamo in palazo et quello pigliamo et con parole grande ci voltassemo al Magnifico facendoli intendere che quello era il giorno per il quale lui havea a ordinare uno stato a suo modo, et che volevamo si facesse per *omni modo*

parlamento, et lui si acostasse a la voglia di tutti nui altri giovani soi amici." Sanudo, *I Diarii*, 15:141.

83 Though Atkinson and Sices hesitate to identify the letter's recipient definitively, Brian Richardson has argued that it was Isabella d'Este. Richardson, "Lettera a una Gentildonna," 271–6; Atkinson and Sices, *Machiavelli and His Friends,* 495n.1.

84 Atkinson and Sices identify the captain as the Bolognese Melchiorre Ramazzotti (or Melchiorre di Ramazzotto), a *condottiere* hired by the Medici. Atkinson and Sices, *Machiavelli and His Friends*, 216–17, 496n.18.

85 Nardi, *Istorie di Firenze*, 2:5.

86 The full inscription read: "Se questo popolar consiglio, e certo / Governo, popol, della tua cittate / Conservi, che da Dio t' è stato offerto, / In pace starai sempre e 'n libertate. / Tien, dunque, l'occhio della mente aperto, / Chè molte insidie ognor ti fien parate; / E sappi che chi vuol far parlamento / Vuol torti dalle mani il reggimento." Villari, *Storia di Girolamo Savonarola*, 1:312n.1; for translated section see: Najemy, *History of Florence*, 390.

87 Cerretani (Berti, ed.), *Dialogo delle Mutatione*, 45–6.

88 Nerli, *Commentari*, 116–17; Stephens, *Fall of the Florentine Republic*, 68.

89 Butters, *Governors and Government*, 189–90.

90 F. Guicciardini, *History of Italy*, 266; idem, *Storia de' Italia*, 2:1091. See also Rubinstein, "Dalla Repubblica al Principato," 1:162.

91 Najemy, *History of Florence*, 426–7.

92 Malanima, "Bartolomeo Cerretani," 23:806.

93 Cerretani, *Storia Fiorentina*, x.

94 Malanima, "Bartolomeo Cerretani," 806–7.

95 Cerretani, *Ricordi*, 284.

96 Cerretani, *Storia Fiorentina*, 445–6; Cerretani (Berti, ed.), *Dialogo della Mutatione*, 33–4.

97 Najemy, *History of Florence*, 422–4.

98 "Qui ci dividemo noi capo della mutatione, perché una parte non volevano altro che levar Piero Soderini, un'altra parte, fra' quali ero io, volevamo fare nuovo stato, e capo e Medici." Cerretani (Berti, ed.), *Dialogo della Mutatione*, 31–2; Malanima, "Bartolomeo Cerretani," 808.

99 Apparently Cerretani was unaware that his name had been put forward. This confusion resulted, according to Mordenti, because on other occasions Bartolomeo had begged Lorenzo for an office. Cerretani (Mordenti, ed.), *Dialogo della Mutatione*, xv–xvi.

100 Felix Gilbert, for example, writes that he finds Cerretani's *Dialogo* "the best narrative source for the period of the Medici restoration." See F. Gilbert, *Machiavelli and Guicciardini*, 133n.53.

101 Ibid., 131.

102 Butters, *Governors and Government*, 180.

103 Stephens, *Fall of the Florentine Republic*, 60.

104 Silvano, *Firenze nel Primo Cinquecento*, 23.

105 "Giuliano (che era, inoltre, uomo più interessato alle lettere che alle armi, e scarsa inclinazione e attitudine aveva fino ad allora mostrato – e avrebbe mostrato anche in séguito – per le questioni di governo)." Bausi, *Machiavelli*, 202.

CHAPTER 2

1 Fatini, "Giuliano de' Medici," xiii.

2 Najemy, *History of Florence*, 275–7.

3 Fatini, "Giuliano de' Medici," xiii–xiv; Gullino, "Girolamo Lippomano," 65:235.

4 Fatini, "Giuliano de' Medici," xv; Tabacchi, "Giuliano de' Medici," 85. Since one of his poems carries the title "In Milano di luglio 97," it is possible he left Milan at a later date. G. Medici, *Poesie*, 20.

5 D. Brown, *Virtue and Beauty*, 142–6.

6 Pincus, "Bembo's Portrait of Dante," 61–94.

7 King, *Venetian Humanism*, 9.

8 Lackner, "Camaldolese Academy," 23–4.

9 Ficino, *Letters*, 2:25; King, *Venetian Humanism*, 13.

10 For a discussion of Bembo's collection, see Danzi, *Biblioteca del Cardinal Pietro Bembo*.

11 Ibid., 9.

12 Giannetto, *Bernardo Bembo*, 143.

13 F. Gilbert, "Venetian Constitution," 474.

14 Cian, "Per Bernardo Bembo," 354–5; Giannetto, *Bernardo Bembo*, 147.

15 Giannetto, *Bernardo Bembo*, 149.

16 F. Gilbert, "Venetian Constitution," 474–5.

17 Cian, "Per Bernardo Bembo," 359.

18 Sanudo, *Diarii*, 11:519. In October 1510 Giuliano was apparently in Venice to have his eyes treated.

19 Cian, *Musa Medicea*, 15.

20 Giannetto, *Bernardo Bembo*, 212.

21 "intensi desideri era di vedere la casa de' Medici nel primiero stato." Cian, *Musa Medicea*, 51n.41.

22 F. Gilbert, *Machiavelli and Guicciardini*, 77–8.

23 Dionisotti, "Pietro Bembo"; Kidwell, *Pietro Bembo*, 220.

24 Kidwell, *Pietro Bembo*, 223.

25 Ibid., 164–6.

26 Bembo, *Prose e Rime*, 31.

27 Ibid., 73–309.

28 Kidwell, *Pietro Bembo*, 223.

29 Cian, *Musa Medicea*, 15.

30 "Io non so già quello che io della credenza di messer Ercole mi debba credere il quale io sempre, Giuliano, per uomo giudiciosissimo ho conosciuto." Bembo, *Prose e Rime*, 83.

31 Fatini, "Giuliano de' Medici," xxvii–xxviii.
32 Massa, *L'eremo*, 15–17; Ross, "Gasparo Contarini and His Friends," 192–232; Bowd, "Swarming with Hermits," 16–25.
33 Bowd, *Reform before the Reformation*, 39.
34 Ibid., 34; idem, "Swarming with Hermits," 19.
35 Bowd, *Reform before the Reformation*, 37–40.
36 Bembo, *Prose e rime*, 313–504. For an excellent synopsis in English of Bembo's little-read treatise on love *Gli Asolani*, see Kidwell, *Pietro Bembo*, 99–112. See also Raffini, *Ficino, Bembo, Castiglione*, 67–74; and Bolzoni, *Il Cuore di Cristallo*.
37 Nardi, *Istorie*, 2:32.
38 "si ripetono con una monotonia esasperante." Fatini, "Giuliano de' Medici," cxxi.
39 "lo distrassero dalle penose incertezze dell'esilio e dall'amarezza dei vani tentativi fatti per ritornare in patria." Ibid.
40 "Nessuna però di quelle donne e di quegli amori riuscí a imprimere nella fantasia poetica di lui una nota personale o un accento di vera passione, anche se si parla quasi sempre di amore non corrisposto, di attesa delusa, di speranza lungamente vagheggiata. Tutta queste donne diventano uguali nel suo canto, che al pari di quello degli altri rimatori si svolge intessuto con le solite immagini del fuoco che brucia il suo cuore, delle lacrime che lo dissolvono in ghiaccio, del dolore che lo avvicina gioiosamente alla morte, della morte che è l'unico suo diletto." Ibid., cxxi.
41 Bowd, "Swarming with Hermits," 19n.42.
42 Fosi and Rebecchini, "Ippolito de' Medici," 73:99–104; Rebecchini, *Ippolito de' Medici tra Firenze e Roma*.
43 Weinstein, *Savonarola and Florence*, 362–3.
44 Polizzotto, *Savonarolan Movement in Florence*, 149–53.
45 Lackner, "Camaldolese Academy," 30–2.
46 Ibid., 16–17.
47 Ibid., 42.
48 Bowd, *Reform before the Reformation*, 61–3.
49 Ibid., 70.
50 Alberigo, "Sul *Libellus ad Leonem X*," 350. A symbol of the enduring relationship between the Camaldolese and the Medici, generation after generation, is the cell that Piero the Gouty de' Medici had built at the hermitage of the Camaldoli in 1463. In 1468 he donated a gold altar plate for the cell out of gratitude for the intercession of St Romauld in the recovery of his wife, Lucrezia Tornabuoni, in 1468. See Caby, *Les Camaldules en Italie*, 582–3.
51 Massa, *Manoscritti del Paolo Giustiniani*.
52 Bowd, *Reform before the Reformation*, 114.
53 F. Gilbert, "La bolla 'Apostolici Regiminis,'" 986–7.
54 Bowd, *Reform before the Reformation*, 116.
55 Ibid., 117.
56 Woodhouse, *A Reassessment of* The Courtier, 8–18.

57 Cian, *Baldassar Castiglione*, 193.
58 Castiglione, *Il Cortegiano*, 549–71; Cartwright, *Perfect Courtier: Baldassare*, 1:160–1.
59 For Medici marriages, the average was a dowry of 12,000 ducats. See Tomas, *Medici Women*, 131.
60 Ibid., 255–64.
61 Ibid., 264.
62 Ibid.
63 Castiglione, *Book of the Courtier*, 17–18.
64 Ibid., 221–2.
65 Ibid., 222.
66 Pugliese, *Castiglione's* Book of the Courtier, 84.
67 Ibid., 87.
68 Ibid., 34; and Irene Iarocci, "Camillo Paleotti."
69 Piero Floriani, *I Gentiluomini Letterati*, 56–7; Pugliese, *Castiglione's* Book of the Courtier, 86.
70 Pugliese, *Castiglione's* Book of the Courtier, 87.
71 Cian, *Baldassar Castiglione*, 288–9.
72 Gattoni, *Leone X*, 158.
73 Cian, *Baldassar Castiglione*, 60–1.
74 Ibid., 67. On the subject of the *Cortegiano* and Leo's war with Urbino, see also Jungić, "Raphael at Bologna," 580–99, esp. 591–4.
75 Dennistoun, *Memoirs of the Dukes of Urbino*, 2:361; Cartwright, *Perfect Courtier*, 1:400.
76 Fatini, "Giuliano de' Medici," lxxxix.
77 Gattoni, *Leone X*, 158.
78 Sanudo, *Diarii*, 22:456. Following the death of Lorenzo in 1519, Francesco Maria was able to recover his duchy.
79 Minnich, "The Fifth Lateran Council," 189.
80 Massa, *I Manoscritti del Paolo Giustiniani*, cxvii. For the *Libellus*, see Bowd, *Reform before the Reformation*, 136–65; Alberigo, "Sul *Libellus ad Leonem X*," 349–59; idem, "Reform of the Episcopate," 139–52.
81 Bowd, *Reform before the Reformation*, 163.
82 Ibid., 164.
83 Ibid., 180.

CHAPTER 3

1 Anderson, "Altobello Melone, *Portrait of a Gentleman*," 186.
2 John Najemy has taken issue with assessments of Borgia as Machiavelli's ideal prince, arguing instead that he "is the negative model of the new prince who depends on the arms of others, inevitably fails, and blames fortune misconstrued as malicious fate." Najemy, "Machiavelli and Cesare Borgia," 539.
3 Rowland, *Culture of the High Renaissance*, 43. See also De Matteis, "Alessandro VI," 1:85–97.

4 Rowland, *Culture of the High Renaissance*, 45.
5 Ibid., 42–3.
6 Strathern, *Da Vinci, Machiavelli, and Borgia*, 63.
7 Dated 26 June 1502: "Questo Signore è molto splendido e magnifico." Machiavelli, *Legazioni*, 2:247. For a contrary interpretation of Machiavelli's use of "splendido," possibly sarcastically, see Najemy, "Machiavelli and Cesare Borgia," 540n.3.
8 Machiavelli (Bondanella, ed.), *Prince*, 24, 29.
9 Ibid., 25. For the contrary view that Borgia was not Machiavelli's "ideal prince" but rather an exemplar of failure and limited legacy, "a flash in the pan, no more than a noisy footnote to history," see Clifford Orwin, "Riddle of Cesare Borgia," 157–8, 189n.5. Orwin follows Najemy ("Machiavelli and Cesare Borgia," 555), who argues that "Machiavelli's Borgia emerges as another unarmed, or at least poorly armed failure … *The Prince* is a study of *failed* princes and of the many ways they fail."
10 Sanudo, *Diarii*; and idem, *Cità Excelentissima*.
11 "Or apropinquato, fo dimandato si dovesse render perchè il magnifico Juliano vi era ivi. Et li custodi, inteso, volseno vederlo, et *immediate* li aperseno le porte cridando: *Marco, Marco, Palle, Palle*, ch' è il Cognome de' Medici." Sanudo, *Diarii*, 1:1109. See also Fatini, "Giuliano de' Medici," xvi.
12 Fatini, "Giuliano de' Medici," xvii–xix. Six months later, Paolo Vitelli, accused of treason on the grounds that he had colluded with Piero de' Medici during the siege of Bibbiena, was beheaded in Florence.
13 "Vene Piero et Juliano di Medici, et Piero parlò molto longamente facendo vari discorsi, et era venuto il tempo desiderato, et volea andar uno di lhoro, zoè Juliano in Franza; per tanto pregava la Signoria lo ajutasse presso il re." Sanudo, *Diarii*, 2:1199.
14 To satisfy the pope's next dearest wish, the king promised that, as soon as Milan was in his possession, he would provide Cesare with enough French troops for the conquest of the Romagna, enabling the Church to reassert papal control over the rebellious vicariates. Finally, the king agreed to give his own niece, Charlotte d'Albret (1480–1514), as a bride for Cesare, in exchange for a cardinal's hat for her brother Amanieu (d. 1520). Cesare signed the marriage contract in France on 19 May 1499. Sacerdote, *Cesare Borgia*, 254–6, 286–90; Baumgartner, *Louis XII*, 79.
15 Sacerdote, *Cesare Borgia*, 269; Hozier and Popoff, eds., *Chevaliers de L'Ordre de Saint-Michel*, 1:107–10.
16 Cartwright, *Baldassare Castiglione*, 1:20.
17 Along the Via Emilia were principalities ruled by vicars who refused to recognize the pope as their overlord, claiming in effect full sovereign rights, refusing to pay the papal census, and perhaps also conspiring to create a league of their own and take up arms against the Church. Alvisi, *Cesare Borgia*, 63; Angiolini, "La Politica dei Borgia," 154; Woodward, *Cesare Borgia*, 149–54.

18 Sacerdote, *Cesare Borgia*, 341–54; Ady, *The Bentivoglio of Bologna*, 85.
19 Alvisi, *Cesare Borgia*, 72.
20 Sforza held the city until 10 April whereupon the Swiss betrayed him; he was captured and imprisoned in France where he died on 27 May 1508. See Sacerdote, *Cesare Borgia*, 358.
21 Burchard, *At the Court of the Borgia*, 179–82; Alvisi, *Cesare Borgia*, 89–90; Woodward, *Cesare Borgia*, 170–2.
22 "Come domino Juliano di Medici passò di lì con cavali 12, va a Roma; et chome ha inteso la nova dil prender dil signor Lodovico, à buto apiacer." Sanudo, *Diarii*, 3:235.
23 They had been travelling for nine months in northern Europe. They visited the Emperor Massimiliano of Augsburg at Ulmo and were guests of the Archduke Philip in Flanders, but they decided not to go to England. In France the group was arrested in Rouen where they were forced to wait until Piero de' Medici in Venice offered Louis XII the necessary guarantees for their freedom. See Pellegrini, "Leone X," 64:513–14.
24 Woodward, *Cesare Borgia*, 32; Sacerdote, *Cesare Borgia*, 89; Mallett, *The Borgias*, 98.
25 Kolsky, "The Courtier as Critic," 165.
26 Calitti, "Pier Francesco Giustolo."
27 Alvisi, *Cesare Borgia*, 98. On the Roman Academy, see Rowland, *Culture of the High Renaissance*, 10–25.
28 Bowd (*Reform before the Reformation*, 39) sees this compliment as stretching credulity.
29 Alvisi, *Cesare Borgia*, 100–3; Sarcedote, *Borgia*, 547–8. On Serafino, see Rowland, *Culture of the High Renaissance*, 92–101.
30 "Perché hai Serafin, Morte, offeso tanto?" Giuliano de' Medici, *Poesie*, 75.
31 Achillini, *Collettanee grece, latine e vulgari*. Vincenzo Colli, called Calmeta, secretary to Beatrice d'Este Sforza, wrote a biography of Serafino published in this volume. See Calmeta, *Prose e Lettere*, 60–77.
32 His loyal Spanish captains led the army, together with some notable Italian *condottieri*, including the barons Giulio and Paolo Orsini of Rome and Paolo's son-in-law, Vitellozzo Vitelli, lord of Città di Castello, who was celebrated for his artillery expertise and thus commanded a train of twenty-one cannon for Borgia. Alvisi, *Cesare Borgia*, 124; Mallett, *The Borgias*, 165.
33 Sacerdote, *Cesare Borgia*, 403.
34 The vastly unpopular Giovanni Sforza, knowing that the people of Pesaro would not resist, fled by ship to Ravenna, so that when Valentino's army arrived, the people surrendered peacefully. Hated in Rimini for his oppressive misrule, Pandolfo Malatesta extorted a huge payment of 10,000 ducats from his frightened subjects on the condition that he would go quietly, which he did, thus leaving the townspeople of Rimini to welcome Valentino. Sacerdote, *Cesare Borgia*, 410–11; Mallett, *The Borgias*, 166.

35 Sacredote, *Cesare Borgia*, 414–18.

36 Alvisi, *Cesare Borgia*, 145; Sacerdote, *Cesare Borgia*, 420–1; Mallett, *The Borgias*, 166–7.

37 "Manda letere di Juliano di Medici. Scrive da Bologna qui a Piero di Bibiena, che saria hora tempo far fati contra Fiorenza." Sanudo, *Diarii*, 3:496. See also 3:474.

38 Roscoe, *Life and Pontificate of Leo the Tenth*, 1:209.

39 "et speravano intrar in Fiorenza, e mancha molti soi contrarij; poi Medici è in gracia dil papa." Sanudo, *Diarii*, 3:942.

40 "Juliano andò a Roma, chiamato dal cardinal per saper nove di Fiorenza dil turcho, qual, li è stà ditto, saperà *etc*." Ibid., 3:906.

41 "credendo Juliano di Medici fusse lì a Bologna; prega esso conte queste cosse siano secrete." Ibid., 3:987.

42 "Faenza è in gran pericolo, et il ducha tien sia spazato. Et Piero di Medici, stato a Pisa, è partito e andato dal ducha Valentinoys, chiamato, è perhò si tien le cosse di Toschana habi a far novità." Ibid., 3:1019.

43 "Giuliano de' Medici era partito di Roma et venuto ad Bolognia per conto di questa impresa et seco uno homo del Card.le Orsino." Buonaccorsi, *Diario*, 101.

44 "Lorenzo e Zulian di Medici par siano per intrar, con l'ajuto dil ducha; et li Strozi e Nerli hanno fato provision di arme in caxa lhoro." Sanudo, *Diarii*, 3:1293.

45 Sacerdote, *Cesare Borgia*, 421.

46 "come Zuliano era lì in caxa sua, et monsignor di Trans è stato lì, e have commission dil re, de dirli non ajuti Faenza, e lassi tuorla al ducha Valentino." Sanudo, *Diarii*, 3:1313.

47 "Come monsignor di Trans, orator dil *roy*, è stato a Faenza per tratar acordo. Faventini non lo hanno voluto aldir; et vi fu con lui Juliano di Medici." Ibid., *Diarii*, 3:1319.

48 Ady, *The Bentivoglio of Bologna*, 147.

49 Ibid., 147–8.

50 "e sono ritornati lì a Bologna con mal animo; sì che Faenza non vol acordo." Sanudo, *Diarii*, 3:1319.

51 "e che vene lì uno corier, e li portò danari senza dir chi li mandi; si judicha fusseno fiorentini, e questo perchè Juliano di Medici sta *continue* con il ducha Valentino." Ibid., 3:1374.

52 "et Juliano è andato in Franza, si dice *etiam* il cardinal di Medici, per parlar al *roy* acciò sij col voler dil ducha Valentino." Ibid., 3:1401.

53 "A dì decto partì Giuliano de' Medici da Bolognia et in poste andò ad trovare la M.tà del Re per ordine del Papa et di Mons. di Trans." Buonaccorsi, *Diario*, 102.

54 F. Guicciardini, *History of Florence*, 199.

55 Ibid., 185, 198–9.

56 Ibid., 199.

57 Sacerdote, *Cesare Borgia*, 427–9; Mallett, *The Borgias*, 167; Woodward, *Cesare Borgia*, 206–7. Woodward writes that Astorre was allowed the freedom to go anywhere he wished but remained with Cesare because "captivated by the

personality of his conqueror, he preferred to take service with Cesare as one of the group of young captains who followed the fortunes of the Duke." Mallett believes he was held under duress. In July he was imprisoned in Castel S. Angelo and strangled a year later in June 1502. Caterina Sforza was also imprisoned in the Castel S. Angelo, but she escaped Astorre's fate by signing away her rights and was allowed to retire to Florence. See Mallett, *The Borgias*, 168.

58 Alvisi, *Cesare Borgia*, 159–61.

59 Sacerdote, *Cesare Borgia*, 444–5; Ady, *The Bentivoglio of Bologna*, 6.

60 Alvisi, *Cesare Borgia*, 179.

61 Ibid., 180; Cavicchi "Girolamo da Casio," 4.

62 Ady, *The Bentivoglio of Bentivoglio*, 143.

63 Sacerdote, *Cesare Borgia*, 450–1.

64 Woodward, *Cesare Borgia*, 212.

65 F. Guicciardini (*History of Florence*, 194) says it was Piero but certainly it was Giuliano. See Alvisi, *Cesare Borgia*, 188; Sacerdote, *Cesare Borgia*, 451–2.

66 Alvisi, *Cesare Borgia*, 188.

67 Fatini, "Giuliano de' Medici," xxi.

68 Alvisi, *Cesare Borgia*, 190.

69 Nerli, *Commentari*, 87; Sacerdote, *Cesare Borgia*, 452.

70 "che si rimettesse in Fiorenza Piero de' Medici, ovvero si fermasse uno stato tale, che ei potesse esser sicuro di tutto quello che esso risolveva seco, e sapesse che le promesse s'avessero fermamente ad osservare." Nardi, *Istorie*, 1:204.

71 Sacerdote, *Cesare Borgia*, 451; Mallett, *The Borgias*, 169.

72 Landucci, *Florentine Diary*, 178–9.

73 Sacerdote, *Cesare Borgia*, 453–5. Valentino was given a *condotta* of 300 men-at-arms for a period of three years at 36,000 ducats to be paid annually. A year later Borgia would claim, in a conversation with Machiavelli that took place in Imola in October, that he had entered Florentine territory because he could not refuse his captains, Vitellozzo and the Orsini. He assured Machiavelli that the Medici were never mentioned in any discussion; furthermore, Cesare claimed he never wanted Piero to come into his camp. See dispatch of 7 October 1502 from Machiavelli to the Ten of Liberty, in Machiavelli, *Legazioni*, 2:336–7; A. Gilbert, ed., *Machiavelli: Chief Works and Others*, 1:121–3. But Borgia's situation in October 1502 had deteriorated and, in a position of weakness, he was now seeking an alliance with Florence because Vitellozzo and the Orsini had rebelled and had joined a league with other malcontents to oppose him.

74 Sacerdote, *Cesare Borgia*, 444.

75 Sanudo, *Diarii*, 4:70; Fatini, "Giuliano de' Medici," xxi.

76 Sanudo, *Diarii*, 4:75.

77 According to Fatini, we lose track of Giuliano for some time. Fatini, "Giuliano de' Medici," xxi.

78 Nardi, *Istorie*, 1:224.

79 Woodward, *Cesare Borgia*, 236–8.
80 Ridolfi, *Life of Machiavelli*, 49. "Questo governo non mi piace e non mi posso fidare di lui; bisogna lo mutiate e mi facciate cauto della osservanzia di quello mi promettessi; altrimenti voi intenderete presto presto che io non voglio vivere a questo modo, e se non mi vorrete amico, mi proverrete inimico." Machiavelli, *Legazioni*, 2:240. For an alternate interpretation of the June dispatches, including the possibility that Machiavelli was not their author, see Najemy, "Machiavelli and Borgia," 540–1.
81 Ridolfi, *Life of Machiavelli*, 50. "Questo signore è molto splendido e magnifico; e nelle armi è tanto animoso che non li paia piccolo; e per gloria e per acquistare stato mai si riposa, né conosce fatica o periculo. Giugne prima in un luogo che se ne possa intendere la partita donde si leva; fassi benevolere a' suoi soldati; ha cappati e' migliori uomini d'Italia. Le quale cose lo fanno vittorioso e formidabile, aggiunto con una perpetua fortuna." Machiavelli, *Legazioni*, 2:247.
82 Sanudo, *Diarii*, 4:424.
83 F. Guicciardini, *History of Florence*, 227–9. In December 1502 Guidobaldo was forced once again to capitulate to Valentino, although he was able to recover his state in August 1503, following the death of Alexander VI.
84 Ibid., 230.
85 Ridolfi, *Life of Niccolò Machiavelli*, 55.
86 Woodward, *Cesare Borgia*, 255–6.
87 "uomo dottissimo e di ottima vita." Machiavelli, *Legazioni*, 2:470.
88 For more on Cardinal Antonio Maria Ciocchi Del Monte, see Minnich, "Official Edition of Fifth Lateran Council," 3:2–14.
89 F. Guicciardini, *History of Florence*, 244.
90 Machiavelli (Bondanella, ed.), *Prince*, 27.
91 F. Guicciardini, *History of Florence*, 194.
92 Sacerdote, *Cesare Borgia*, 514.
93 Ady, *The Bentivoglio of Bologna*, 6.
94 Sacerdote, *Cesare Borgia*, 567.
95 Giuliano Fantaguzzi, in his chronicle *Chaos*, lists all the projects that Cesare wanted for the capital of his state: "volea fare a Cesena: palazo, canale, rota, studio … piaza in forteza, agrandare Cesena, fontana in piaza, duchessa, corte a Cesena, fare el porto Cesenatico." See Londei, "Progetti Leonardiani di Macchine Scavatrici," 57.
96 Sacerdote, *Cesare Borgia*, 567.
97 Ibid., 591.
98 Ibid., 592.
99 Ady, *The Bentivoglio of Bologna*, 127.
100 Ibid.
101 Woodward, *Cesare Borgia*, 323–4.
102 Machiavelli (Bondanella, ed.), *Prince*, 29.

103 "el Cardinale gli aveva detto che 'l Duca gli pareva uscito del cervello, perché non sapeva lui stesso quello si volessi fare, sí era avviluppato e irresoluto." Machiavelli, *Legazioni*, 3:357; Mallett, *The Borgias*, 220–1.

CHAPTER 4

1 Atkinson and Sices, *Machiavelli and His Friends*, 264; Connell, "Machiavelli's Letter to Vettori," 93–127.
2 Butters, "Machiavelli and the Medici," 64.
3 Najemy, *Between Friends*, 91.
4 Martelli, "Preistoria (Medicea) di Machiavelli," 377.
5 Ibid., 383–6; Machiavelli, *Scritti*, 242–4.
6 Martelli, "Preistoria (Medicea) di Machiavelli," 392; Najemy, *Between Friends*, 91n.76. Antonio Corsaro and Nicoletta Marcelli do not unequivocally accept that Giuliano was the dedicatee. Machiavelli, *Scritti*, 206–7n.27, 242n.2.
7 Gilbert, *Machiavelli: Chief Works*, 1:97–100.
8 Martelli, "Preistoria (Medicea) di Machiavelli," 391–3. See also Marcelli's notes in Machiavelli, *Scritti*, 206–12.
9 Dionisotti, *Machiavellerie*, 64–6.
10 Gilbert, *Machiavelli: Chief Works*, 1:99, line 91.
11 "In effetti, soprattutto in considerazione dei vv. 91-93 (nei quali si celebrano le virtú militari del destinatario), non vedo come la persona cui Machiavelli si rivolge possa essere altra da quella di Lorenzo duca d' Urbino: il che, pertanto, ci respingerebbe agli anni compresi fra il 1514 e il 1518." Martelli, "Firenze," 130n.15. Those who agree with Martelli's reassessment that Hyacinth should be read as Lorenzo, and not Giuliano, include Francesco Bausi and Nicoletta Marcelli. Bausi, "L' 'occasione' del 1518," 201–3; Machiavelli, *Scritti*, 207–12.
12 Butters, *Governors and Government*, 265.
13 Martelli and Bausi, "Machiavelli e Guicciardini," 273–6.
14 Najemy, *Between Friends*, 91n.76. See also Machiavelli, *Scritti*, 242.
15 Machiavelli, *Scritti*, 205–12. Francesco Bausi had also proposed that the poem was meant for Lorenzo in 1987. Bausi, "L' 'occasione' del 1518," 201–3.
16 Luigi Blasucci, Rinaldo Rinaldi, and Corrado Vivanti maintain that Martelli was correct in his first assessment of the poem and therefore interpret Hyacinth as Giuliano. Giuseppe Gigli and Ezio Raimondi leave the question open. Machiavelli, *Scritti Letterari*, 417; Machiavelli, *Opere*, 3:ix and 739–40; idem, *Opere Poetiche*, xxiv–xxv; idem, *Opere di Niccolò Machiavelli*, 1282; Machiavelli, *Scritti*, 208.
17 "La bocca e le parole / son l'arco e le saette che tu hai: / non è uom sotto il sole / che nol ferisca quando tu le trai." Machiavelli, *Opere*, 3:3; Machiavelli, *Scritti*, 243.
18 Gilbert, *Machiavelli: Chief Works*, 1:98.
19 Ibid., 99.
20 "Marte feroce onde tu piú riluci, nel generoso petto un core incluse simile a Cesar, duca alli altri duci." Machiavelli, *Opere*, 3:6; Machiavelli, *Scritti*, 269–70.

21 "Ferocious Mars – by contrast you shine more / Put in your valiant breast a heart that Caesar / Would envy, just as any emperor." Machiavelli, *Lust for Liberty*, 35. "Fierce Mars, that you might shine the more, within your noble / breast enclosed a heart like that of Caesar the general, like / those of all the generals." Gilbert, *Machiavelli: Chief Works*, 1:99, lines 91–3.

22 Machiavelli, *Scritti*, 270.

23 "E tanto è più detestabile Cesare, quanto più è da biasimare quello che ha fatto, che quello che ha voluto fare un male." Machiavelli, *Discorsi*, 27; idem, *Discourses on Livy*, 32.

24 "Cesare; il quale fu primo tiranno in Rome; talchè mai fu poi libera quella città." Machiavelli, *Discorsi*, 64; idem, *Discourses on Livy*, 80.

25 Machiavelli (Bondanella, ed.), *Prince*, 24–30.

26 Gilbert, *Machiavelli: Chief Works,* 1:100, lines 121–4.

27 Ibid., 100.

28 Atkinson and Sices, *Machiavelli and His Friends*, 214–17; Najemy, *Between Friends*, 91.

29 "moderatamente ossequioso verso i nuovi 'patroni *suoi*.'" Dotti, *Machiavelli Rivoluzionario*, 225.

30 Ridolfi, *Vita di Machiavelli*, 498–9n.29; Machiavelli, *Lettere*, 354.

31 Richardson, "Lettera a una Gentildonna," 271–6. See also Gaeta, who agrees that the addressee is neither Alfonsina Orsini nor Clarice de' Medici. He also rejects Lucrezia Salviati and Contessina Ridolfi as potential candidates, proposing that it could be Isabella d'Este. Machiavelli, *Lettere*, 3:354n.1.

32 Both letters are published in Cartwright, *Isabella d'Este*, 1:67–8.

33 Richardson, "Lettera a una Gentildonna," 274.

34 Atkinson and Sices, *Machiavelli and His Friends*, 216.

35 Richardson, "Lettera a una Gentildonna," 274.

36 Atkinson and Sices, *Machiavelli and His Friends*, 216. Atkinson and Sices (496n.15) note that Machiavelli omits his own part in Soderini's departure, wherein he acted as his agent to ensure his safe passage through Tuscany.

37 Ibid., 217.

38 Machiavelli, *Lettere*, 3:354n.1; Inglese, review of *Opere*, 271–80; and Atkinson and Sices, *Machiavelli and His Friends*, 495n.1.

39 "e certo non era ben visto dai Medici." Bausi, *Machiavelli*, 70n.138.

40 Ibid., 70–1.

41 "Nei mesi di settembre e ottobre 1512 Niccolò rimase formalmente al suo posto, ma non svolse alcun compito e non scrisse una sola lettera ufficiale; per colui che era stato l'uomo di fiducia e il primo collaboratore di Piero Soderini, e che (a quanto sembra) nel corse delle sue missioni non aveva risparmiato frecciate ai Medici in esilio, il destino era ormai segnato." Bausi, *Machiavelli*, 73. See also Ridolfi, *Life of Machiavelli*, 131; Atkinson and Sices, *Machiavelli and His Friends*, 196.

42 Both works are published in F. Vettori, *Scritti Storici e Politici*.

43 See especially Najemy, *Between Friends*.

44 "e particolarmente Paol Vettori, che con grande astuzia, e molto artifiziosamente mostrava d'osservare il Gonfaloniere, il quale andava godendo il beneficio del tempo, perchè temeva assai d'un' altra più gagliarda parte, la quale segli opponeva più vivamente in tutte le pubbliche, e private faccende." Nerli, *Commentari*, 98; Butters, *Governors and Government*, 62.

45 F. Guicciardini, *History of Italy*, 263.

46 G. Niccolini, *Filippo Strozzi*, xxix, xxx.

47 Nardi, *Istorie*, 1:428.

48 Devonshire Jones, *Francesco Vettori*, 58. In a letter to Paolo dated 5 August 1513, Francesco Vettori tells his brother that he needs to show that he had just cause for his actions against Soderini in August 1512, because the *gonfaloniere* had tried to ruin him by involving him in this iron foundry. See Hughes, "Francesco Vettori," 572.

49 Nardi, *Istorie*, 2:10; letter to Luigi Guicciardini to Francesco Guicciardini dated 6 November 1512, in F. Guicciardini, *Lettere*, 1:281.

50 Najemy, *History of Florence*, 425.

51 The memorandum was discovered among Strozzi Papers in the Florentine Archives by Rudolf von Albertini in 1955. P. Vettori, "Ricordi," 357–9.

52 "Li antecessori vostri, cominciandosi da Cosimo e venendo infino a Piero, usorno in tenere questo Stato piú industria che forza. A voi è necessario usare piú forza che industria, perché voi ci avete piú nimici e manco ordine a saddisfarli; però a voi bisogna, non ve li potendo riguadagnare, che voi stiate ordinate che gli abbino paura a nuocervi." P. Vettori, "Ricordi," 357; idem, "Memorandum," 2:239.

53 "e' non passano sei mesi da oggi, che vi parrà essere piú sicuri in Firenze che se voi avessi un esercito di Spagnuoli a Prato in favore vostro." P. Vettori, "Ricordi," 357; idem, "Memorandum," 239.

54 Butters, *Governors and Government*, 105.

55 Pocock, *The Machiavellian Moment*, 200.

56 Machiavelli, *Art of War*, 17; Machiavelli (Vivanti, ed.), *Opere*, 1:541.

57 Martelli and Bausi, "Politica, Storia e Letteratura," 255. On Machiavelli and the Florentine militia, see Bayley, *War and Society*, 240–84.

58 Albertini, *Firenze*, 23.

59 "come Juliano si abbi a maneggiare e a chi abbi a chiedere cosí delle cose drento come di quelle di fuora … se questa cosa non si piglia bene, ne potrebbe nascere confusione e danno … nascerà in Juliano mille dificultà, le quali Juliano per sé non potrà bene risolvere non s'intendendo per ancora delle cose nostre: di che ne potrebbe nascere scandoli gravissimi." P. Vettori, "Ricordi," 357–8; idem, "Memorandum," 240.

60 P. Vettori, "Ricordi," 358; idem, "Memorandum," 240. See also Hörnqvist, "Approaching the Medici," 400–1.

61 "togliendo di quelli che vogliono correre la fortuna della Casa vostra." P. Vettori, "Ricordi," 358. Unfortunately, Russell Price (P. Vettori, "Memorandum,"

240) employed modern Italian usage in his translation of this passage, leading to a significant distortion of Vettori's meaning: "being careful to exclude any who are fair-weather supporters of your family."

62 Hörnqvist, "Approaching the Medici," 406–10.

63 This mistrust led to the total suppression of the *frateschi* in 1514. See Polizzotto, *Elect Nation*, 274–90.

64 "perché Jacopo Salviati / cogniato loro operò molto poco nella lor tornata; dipoi non attese mai ad altro che rintrodurre e tener viva la parte del frate, di chi e' fu sì divoto et riuscivagli rispetto al mal getto della balìa. Di che moltissime volte fumo tra noi insieme et disperavaci, perché vedevamo risucitare, ma destramente, quella parte." Cerretani (Berti, ed.), *Dialogo della Mutatione*, 48–9.

65 "Voglio che impari da Jacopo Salviati, el quale, chome si truova in luogho dove sieno amici de' Medici, monstra tutte le actione sua dal 1494 in qua esser sute per rimetterli in casa, e tutto quello ha operato comenta e tira a questo fine. Quando è chon quelli che sa che sono inimici de' Medici e che piaceva loro il vivere passato, monstra haver voluto sempre tener fermo quel governo e mai haver havuta altra intentione." See Francesco's letter of 5 August 1513 in Hughes, "Francesco Vettori," 571–2.

66 Devonshire Jones, *Francesco Vettori*, 86.

67 Nerli, *Commentari*, 120–1.

68 Hurtubise, *Une Famille-Témoin*, 138.

69 Ibid., 137.

70 Landucci, *Diary*, 263; letter from Pandolfo de' Conti to Francesco Guicciardini dated 13 November 1512, in F. Guicciardini, *Lettere*, 1:293.

71 Devonshire Jones, *Francesco Vettori*, 96–7.

72 Stephens, *Fall of the Florentine Republic*, 66.

73 Black, "Machiavelli," 71–99, esp. 85.

74 "Esequirle in tutto a casa, vi sarebbe di troppo carico; exequendole in palazzo, bisogna l'exequischino e Dieci, perché la Signoria fu sempre il bastone e none il cervello dello Stato." P. Vettori, "Ricordi," 358; idem, "Memorandum," 240–1.

75 "Al presente, la Cancellerie de'Dieci con quella della Signoria è confuse, perché mess. Marcello serve nelle lettere a'Dieci, e il Machiavello serviva alle lettere didrento inanzi che andassi all'Ordinanza." P. Vettori, "Ricordi," 358–9; idem, "Memorandum," 241.

76 Hörnqvist, "Approaching the Medici," 401n.9.

77 "le faccende di Stato si maneggino a'Dieci, bisognerebbe che Juliano, ogni dí almeno una volta, si ragunassi co'X, e avessi seco parte di quelli cittadini deputati per suo consiglio; e quivi si deliberassi le risposte agli oratori e tutto quello che lui iudicassi che fussi necessario; e avessi uno cancelliere che stessi a'Dieci bene pratico delle cose di drento e di fuora, el quale scrivesi ancora lui in nome di Juliano alli oratori quelle cose che fussino a proposito dello Stato vostro particulare, né disforme o contrarie a quello che si fussi deliberato." P. Vettori, "Ricordi"; idem, "Memorandum," 241.

78 "E quando voi vi abbattessi a questo istrumento che fussi pratico o fidato, e' sarebbe in questo principio per lo Stato vostro un'ottima cosa, perché la è cosí necessaria come cosa che voi ordiniate." P. Vettori, "Ricordi," 359. Unfortunately, Price again mistranslates this passage, using modern conventions for "abbattessi" and thus significantly changing Vettori's meaning: "Moreover, if you should remove an experienced and trusted man, that would be an excellent beginning for your rule, because it is essential that it should be seen as ordered by you." P. Vettori, "Memorandum," 241. See also n.61 above.

79 Najemy, "Controversy surrounding Machiavelli's Service," 102.

80 While most scholars give the date as 7 November, the correct date, as confirmed by Martelli, is 6 November: "In margine al secondo dei due ricordi…sempre di pugno del Buonaccorsi, si legge: 'A di 6 di novembre 1512, sendosi rinnovato lo stato, fui casso di cancelleria insieme con Niccolò Machiavelli.' È appena il caso di ricordare che la data della rimozione di Niccolò Machiavelli dall'ufficio verrebbe, a starcene alla testimonianza del Buonaccorsi, anticipate d'un giorno." Martelli, "Preistoria (Medicea) di Machiavelli," 388n.1.

81 Hörnqvist, "Approaching the Medici," 399–417.

82 Black, "Machiavelli," 95.

83 Ibid., 99.

84 Najemy, "Controversy surrounding Machiavelli's Service," 115–17.

85 Black, "Machiavelli," 96.

86 Devonshire Jones, *Vettori*, 104 and n.130.

87 Dotti, *Machiavelli Rivoluzionario*, 228. Machiavelli was forced to suffer a further indignity by having to appear several times before a special commission of inquiry in the palace, the mandate of which was to investigate whether he had embezzled any of the funds allotted to the Ordinanza.

88 Black, "Machiavelli," 96.

89 Guasti, "Una Scrittura di Niccolò Machiavelli," 182–5. An autograph copy is conserved in the Florentine State Archives. ASF, *Manoscritti Torrigiani*, V, XXV 13, and *Carte Strozziane*, ser. 2, 86, fol. 35, as noted in Ridolfi, *Life of Machiavelli*, 131, 289n.39. See also Tommasini, *La Vita e Gli Scritti*, 1:600.

90 Bausi, *Machiavelli*, 71n.142.

91 "come e' sarebbe bene scoprire e difecti di Piero Soderini per torli reputatione nel populo." Machiavelli, "Ricordo a' palleschi 1512," 183. Peter Constantine translates *Ai Palleschi* as "To the Medici Faction," interpreting it as "a desperate attempt by Machiavelli to regain some of his standing." See Machiavelli, *The Essential Writings*, 375.

92 Ibid., 376.

93 Ibid., 375.

94 Ibid., 376.

95 Ibid., 377.

96 Marchand, *Niccolò Machiavelli*, 296–309, esp. 301–4; Machiavelli, *L'arte della Guerra*, 580.

97 Black, "Machiavelli," 96.
98 Najemy, "Controversy Surrounding Machiavelli's Service," 102.
99 Najemy, *Between Friends,* 91–2.
100 Machiavelli, *Il Principe*, 13.
101 "insistendo soprattutto sul fatto che il pericolo non viene ormai piú da Piero Soderini, ma dagli ottimati, i quali, con il consueto ambiguo comportamento, sperano di restaurare l' 'ordine vecchio', ossia il governo oligarchico." Bausi, *Machiavelli*, 71.
102 "che Machiavelli, in coerenza con le sue idee, esortasse i Palleschi ad unirsi con gli estimatori del vecchio regime soderiniano per far fronte comune a una 'dittatura' ottimatizia ostile ad entrambe le parti." Dotti, *Machiavelli Rivoluzionario*, 226.
103 Butters, "Machiavelli and the Medici," 66.
104 Niccolini, *Filippo Strozzi*, xxxi.
105 F. Guicciardini, *History of Italy*, 265.
106 Marchand cites Guicciardini, who recorded that Julius II in early November was angry with Cardinal Giovanni de' Medici for appearing to lean more to the Spanish than to himself and that he had "concocted new plans and new plots to alter the state of things in Florence." Machiavelli, *L'arte della Guerra*, 580. See also F. Guicciardini, *History of Italy*, 271.
107 F. Guicciardini, *History of Florence*, 226.
108 Butters, *Governors and Government*, 59.
109 Ibid., 63.
110 Guicciardini, *History of Florence*, 258.
111 Butters, *Governors and Government*, 217.
112 "Piero Soderini arrivò qui quatro dì sono. Venne a vicitarci, ch'ero in chasa Jacopo, et dice vole finire e' dì sua qui et havere mandato per la moglie." Francesco Vettori in a letter of 13 May 1513 addressed to Paolo Vettori. Hughes, "Francesco Vettori," 557.
113 "Giuliano de Medici manddò a la sorella di Piero Soderini a ringratialla che il chardinale Soderini suo fratello haveva facto quello che gl'aveva potuto per farllo papa, et che loro lo richonosceva, et dicevasi che il papa haveva mandato per Piero Soderini, e che tornerebbono tutti." Cerretani, *Ricordi*, 301–2.
114 "che questo Stato non ha per nimico Piero Soderini, ma sì bene l'ordine vechio." Machiavelli, "Ricordo a' Palleschi 1512," 184; idem, *Essential Writings*, 376.
115 F. Guicciardini, *History of Florence*, 260.
116 Ibid., 259.
117 Ibid., 259, 297.
118 Nerli, *Commentari*, 107. See also F. Gilbert, "Bernardo Rucellai," 217–47, esp. 231–2.
119 "ma tu restavi chon non molti parenti et quelli mali disposti et male contenti di te, chi rispecto a Piero Soderini et chi al parlamento, perchè li altri dua [Baccio Valori and Antonfrancesco degli Albizzi] dal parlamento furono alieni et che li

non li volevo nominare nessuno." Letter of August 5 from Francesco Vettori to Paolo Vettori, in Hughes, "Francesco Vettori," 572. See also Butters, *Governors and Government*, 218.

120 "Io non manchai di dire all'arcivescovo (Giulio de' Medici) nella sua partita che era necessario ti pigliassi in protectione et che di voi tre che ... nessuno era più odiato dal loro e dalli amici di te e nessuno portava più pericolo." Hughes, "Francesco Vettori," 572. See also Butters, *Governors and Government*, 218.

121 "et in spetie questi che puttaneggiono infra el popolo et e Medici, hanno bene per nimico Piero, et vorrebbollo scoprire tristo per levarsi quello carico ch'egli hanno con el popolo di averlo inimicato." Machiavelli, "Ricordo a' Palleschi 1512," 185.

CHAPTER 5

1 "Da una banda è il Magnifico [Giuliano], [Bernardo Dovizi da Bibbiena, Cardinale di] S.ta Maria in Portico, M. Luigi [de Rossi], la Contessina [Ridolfi], et Mona Lucretia [de' Medici]; da l'altro canto el Cardinale [Giulio] de' Medici, Lorenzo de' Medici, io, Mona Magdalena, et Cardinale Cibo, el Signore Francesco [Cibo], et ciascuno degli altri adherenti. Altro non ho che dirti, salvo che noi siamo più, et più savij." Alfonsina to Lorenzo, published in Tommasini, *La Vita e Gli Scritti*, 2: 993; Tomas, *Medici Women,* 133.

2 Ridolfi, *Life of Machiavelli*, 163.

3 Clough, "Clement VII and Francesco Maria," 81.

4 Gar, "Instructione al Magnifico Lorenzo," 299–306.

5 Gar, "Documenti," 296, 299n.1.

6 Villari, *Machiavelli*, 2:39; Stephens, *Fall of the Florentine Republic*, 80; Albertini, *Firenze*, 25; Silvano, "*Vivere Civile*," 35. See also Bullard, *Filippo Strozzi and the Medici*, 39.

7 "Lorenzo, figliolo carissimo ... mi è parso in questo poco tempo che io a Firenze sono dimorato, ricordarti tucto quello che secondo me sia utile et necessario a quel governo, per facilitarti el discorso, et darti via da poter più sottilmente et meglio pensare a la salute et perseveratione de la patria nostra." Gar, "Instructione al Magnifico Lorenzo," 299.

8 "Et solum ho facto questo per satisfare al comandamento de la Santità di N. S." Ibid., 306.

9 Najemy, *History of Florence*, 427.

10 Tomas, *Medici Women*, 130–1.

11 "come spesso accadde, el di dipoi, con buon modo et con qualche buona parola m'ingegnavo remediare al tucto." Gar, "Instructione al Magnifico Lorenzo," 302.

12 Albertini, *Firenze dalla Repubblica al Principato*, 25.

13 "Circa al Gonfaloniere di Iustitia, bisogna haver grande advertenza et cura, per esserli attribuita reputatione sopra tucti li Signori, anco che in facto quanto lor possi in auctorità." Ibid., 300.

14 "ti debbi guardare di non offendere le case in dare la dignità a quelli di manco tempo, lassando quelli a chi prima si venisse; et guarda a le case le quali son consuete haver lo stato." Ibid., 301.
15 "da Giovan Batista Ridolfi in fuora, non fussi in Firenze uomo che lo aggua-gliassi." F. Guicciardini, *Scritti Autobiografici e Rari*, 71.
16 "Questo officio [potestà] feci fare io a Ser Francesco di Arezzo ad ogni magistrato, quando entrava in nome mio, in tutto il tempo ch'io dimorai a Firenze; et questo costume tenne sempre in quel governo il padre mio e'l tuo poi." Gar, "Instructione al Magnifico Lorenzo," 306.
17 Kent, "Lorenzo de' Medici and Oligarchy," 53.
18 F. Guicciardini, *History of Florence*, 75; Najemy, *History of Florence*, 361–9.
19 "El Magistrato de' Dieci, per essere di maggiore consideratione la electione et più reputato l'offitio, ha bisogna di altra sorte di homini, cioè sufficienti et reputati, perchè quivi si deliberano tucte le cose grandi: qui si può mettere qualcuno quando non fusse confidente, purchè la sufficientia et li meriti vi sieno." Gar, "Instructione al Magnifico Lorenzo," 303.
20 "A me non occorreria meglio che Iacopo Salviati e'l Lanfredino." Ibid., 303–4.
21 Letter from Alfonsina to Lorenzo dated 9 February 1514 in Tommasini, *La Vita e Gli Scritti*, 2:992–3.
22 Kent, "Lorenzo de' Medici and Oligarchy," 48.
23 Letter from Lorenzo to Cardinal Giulio, 27 October 1513, in Tommasini, *La Vita e Gli Scritti*, 2: 977–8.
24 Butters, *Governors and Government*, 237.
25 "Et in verità Lei n'è stata tenuta d'un poco cervello dal Papa, dal Cardinale ... et da ciascuno che vi si trovò, et anche v'era forestieri: et non ebbe riguardo nessuno." Letter from Alfonsina to Lorenzo dated 9 February 1514 in Tommasini, *La Vita e Gli Scritti*, 2:993.
26 Letter from Lorenzo to Alfonsina dated 14 February 1514. Ibid., 2:994.
27 Herlihy et al., *Online Tratte*.
28 "Io ho sempre tenuto Ser Zanobi, el quale continuamente mi referiva et teneva ragguagliato d'ogni deliberation che ne lo officio si faceva." Gar, "Instructione al Magnifico Lorenzo," 301.
29 Gar, "Instructione al Magnifico Lorenzo," 301–2; Butters, *Governors and Government*, 205.
30 Gar, "Instructione al Magnifico Lorenzo," 303.
31 A. Brown, "Lorenzo and Public Opinion," 61–85, esp. 83.
32 "perché Giuliano era guidato e non bene. E gl'Otto che erono entrati il gennaio havevono tolto l'arme agli amici e nemici indistintamente, di sorte che non si vedeva chi havessi vinto, et noi stavamo di malissima voglia dubitando di quello avenne, che tanta negligenzia non partorissi male per noi, come fu pres[s]o." Cerretani (Berti, ed.), *Dialogo della Mutatione*, 52.
33 Gar, "Instructione al Magnifico Lorenzo," 305.
34 Butters, *Governors and Government*, 240.

35 A. Brown, "Public and Private Interest," 103–65, esp. 134.

36 Butters, *Governors and Government*, 203.

37 "Del chaso de' Medici, io non ò mai parlato contra di loro chosa nessuna, se non in quel modo che s'è parlato generalmente per ogn'uomo, come fu del caso di Prato; che se lle pietre avessin Saputo parlare, n'arebbono parlato." Letter to his father in Florence from Rome, October 1512, in Buonarroti, *Complete Poems and Selected Letters*, 212. See also idem, *Il Carteggio*, 1:139.

38 "De' sessanta ducati che voi mi dite avere a pagare, mi pare chosa disonesta e ònne avuto gran passion." Buonarroti, *Complete Poems and Selected Letters*, 213; idem, *Il Carteggio*, 1:140.

39 "Io scriverrò dua versi a Giuliano de' Medici, e' quali saranno in questa; leggietegli, e sse e' vi piace di portrargniene, portargniene, e vedrete se gioverrano niente." Buonarroti, *Complete Poems and Selected Letters*, 213; idem, *Il Carteggio*, 1:140.

40 Elam, "Lorenzo de' Medici's Sculpture Garden," 41–83, esp. 51, 58–61.

41 "Se non gioverrano, pensate se si può vendere ciò che noi abbiàno; e andreno a abitare altrove." Buonarroti, *Complete Poems and Selected Letters*, 213; idem, *Il Carteggio*, 1:140.

42 Wilson, *Life and Works of Michelangelo*, 186.

43 Buonarotti, *Il Carteggio Indiretto*, 41.

44 "Giuliano non poteva soportare e disagi de l'udientie, delle pratiche et ogni fatico lo metteva in su letto. Desiderava vita solitaria, pacifico et bonario, il che lo faceva inclinare a tutte le chieste, di modo che non poteva mantenere il motto e per mantenderlo seguiva alle volte molti disordini e non piccoli. Messer Giulio era di bella presenzia ... savio, di somma gravità e patientia, di poche et rare parole, d'ingegno grande, iuditio buono et universale, sollecito, patiente d'ogni disagio, cauto et costumato, et di buona iustitia et religione: il che aiutava assai il mancar di Giuliano." Cerretani, *Dialogo delle Mutazione*, 48.

45 Nardi, *Istorie di Firenze*, 1:163–4; Bayley, *War and Society*, 243.

46 F. Guicciardini (*History of Florence*, 171–3) was among those who thought he was innocent.

47 Landucci reports that his head was stuck on a spear and displayed from one of the windows of the palace with a lighted torch beside it for all to see. Landucci, *Diary*, 162.

48 Rendina notes that Paolo Vitelli was guilty because there are documents that prove Paolo was in contact with the Venetians to restore the Medici to Florence. Rendina, *I Capitani di Ventura*, 481–7, esp. 482.

49 Nardi, *Istorie di Firenze*, 2:18.

50 "perciò che detto Giuliano, per assicurarlo, benignamente gli promise sopra la sua fede, che egli non sarebbe offeso di cosa alcuna, e cosi gli fu osservato." Ibid.

51 Arrighi, "Giacomini Tebalducci, Antonio," 173–9; Nardi, *Vita di Antonio Giacomini*; Pitti, "Sulla Vita di Antonio Giacomini," 75–270.

52 Pitti, "Sulla Vita di Antonio Giacomini," 264–6.

53 Hale, *Machiavelli and Renaissance Italy*, 14.

54 Bayley, *War and Society*, 247, 253.

55 The Decennali as a whole cover Florentine history from 1494 to 1509. Machavelli wrote the first, recounting the decade from 1494 to 1504, in 1504. The second, which continues through 1509, is presumed to be unfinished. A. Gilbert, *Machiavelli: Chief Works*, 3:1444.

56 Ibid., 3:1458, lines 34–45.

57 See Jacopo Guicciardini's letter of 8 January 1513 to his brother Francesco in Spain in F. Guicciardini, *Le Lettere*, 1:325.

58 "In fact, it is in every possible way most harmful and dangerous for both the House of Medici and its government, as it removes the muzzles from many mouths that will surely and most readily bite them." Machiavelli, *Essential Writings*, 377.

59 F. Guicciardini, *History of Florence*, 69.

60 Machiavelli, *Florentine Histories*, 8.36, p. 361.

61 Ventrone, "Lorenzo's *Politica Festiva*," 105–16, esp. 114–15.

62 Newbigin, "Piety and Politics," 17–41, esp. 23; Trexler, *Public Life in Renaissance Florence*, 451–2.

63 Cerretani (Berti, ed.), *Dialogo delle Mutatione*, 47–8, 52.

64 Poliziano, *Stanze*, x. For a discussion of the association of Laura and laurel in Petrarch's *Canzoniere*, see Braden, *Petrarchan Love*, 8–15.

65 Langedijk, *Portraits of the Medici*, 1:40n.4. For the significance of the personal devices used by Giuliano and Lorenzo, see Cox-Rearick, *Dynasty and Destiny*, 15–27.

66 Gombrich, *Norm and Form*, 31.

67 Vasari, *Lives*, 3:237–9. See also Coyle and Cummings, *The Politicized Muse*, 15–41.

68 For a discussion of the works of art commissioned for the festival, see Shearman, "Pontormo and Andrea del Sarto," 478–83.

69 Vasari, *Lives*, 3:239. This promise did not extend to the golden boy, the *putto dorato*, who was the son of a baker, because a few days later he died from exposure to the February cold and also perhaps to the toxic effects of the gold paint.

70 Cerretani (Berti, ed.), *Dialogo delle Mutatione*, 52.

71 "Volan' gli anni, i mesi, e l'hore / Questa Ruota sempre gira, / Chi sta lieto, e chi sospira, / Ogni cosa al fin poi muore." Langedijk, *Portraits of the Medici*, 1:42.

72 Machiavelli ridicules this same Dazzi in a poem he sent to Giuliano while in prison. See chapter 6.

73 Syson and Thornton, *Objects of Virtue*, 114.

74 Scher, "Renaissance Portrait Medal," 1–9.

75 "'cum summa atqua amplissima beneficia in rem publicam florentiam bello et pace contulerit, semperque patriam suam omni pietate conservaverit ... diligentiaque gubernarit pro eius maximis virtutibus beneficia et pietas.'" Quoted and translated by D. Kent, *Cosimo de' Medici*, 376, 491n.35.

76 The abbreviation P.P.P. has also been interpreted as Princeps Pater Patriae. A second version shows slight differences in Cosimo's cap and collar and is inscribed COSMUS MEDICES DECRETO PVBLICO P[ATER] P[ATRIAE]. Impressions of the medal illustrated can be found in the collections of the Victoria and Albert Museum (Salting bequest, A.284–1910) and the National Gallery Washington (Samuel H. Kress Collection, 1957.14.839). Hill, *Corpus of Italian Medals,* 1:236–7; 2:147, nos. 909–10; Hill and Pollard, *Renaissance Medals*, 47–8, nos. 245–6; Pollard, *Renaissance Medals*, 1:296, no. 279.

77 D. Kent, *Cosimo de Medici*, 375.

78 An impression of the medal can be found in the National Gallery Washington (Samuel H. Kress Collection, 1987.34.2.a). Hill, *Corpus of Italian Medals,* 1:247, 2:150, no. 926; Pollard, *Renaissance Medals*, 310, no. 291.

79 Pollard, "Niccolò Fiorentino," 132–4.

80 "E tu, ben nato Laur, sotto il cui velo Fiorenza lieta in pace si riposa." Poliziano, *Stanze*, 3. See also Cox-Rearick, *Dynasty and Destiny*, 19.

81 Hill, *Corpus of Italian Medals*, 1:228; 2:141, no. 881; Hill and Pollard, *Renaissance Medals*, 46–7, no. 240; Langedijk, *Portraits of the Medici*, 1:56 and 2:1055–6, no. 16; Cox-Rearick, *Dynasty and Destiny*, 24–5; Pollard, *Renaissance Medals*, 292, no. 276.

82 Fatini, "Giuliano de' Medici," xli.

83 *Giuliano II de' Medici* (reverse) MAG[nus] IVLIANVS MEDICES; *Rome Holding a Figure of Victory* (obverse) C[onsensu] P[opuli] ROMA, 1513, copper alloy, 3.41 cm, 19.49 g, Samuel H. Kress Collection, 1957.14.835; Hill, *Corpus of Italian Medals*, 1: 230, nos. 887–9; Hill and Pollard, *Renaissance Medals*, 47, no. 241; Langedijk, *Portraits of the Medici*, 1:56; Pollard, *Renaissance Medals*, 293, no. 277.

84 Hill, *Corpus of Italian Medals,* 228; Hill and Pollard, *Renaissance Medals*, 47; Pollard, *Renaissance Medals*, 292.

CHAPTER 6

1 Ridolfi, *Life of Machiavelli,* 135.

2 For example, see most recently Butters, "Machiavelli and the Medici," 67; Najemy, *History of Florence*, 426–7; Marchi, *Testi Cinquecenteschi sulla Ribellione Politica*, 25; Simonetta, *Volpi e Leoni*, 89–91.

3 Nardi, *Istorie*, 2:20–1.

4 "Erano i descritti in quella listra disegnati per valersene nell' assicurazione, e dopo il fatto; ma non già, come poi si conobbe nell' esame, perchè i descritti in quella listra avessero colpa nella congiura, nè manco si conobbe, ch' egli avessero scienza alcuna de' disegni d' Agostino, e di Pietropagolo ... e sene fosse aperto seco più che non gli era di bisogno, e così venne subito quella listra nelle mani de' Medici." Nerli, *Commentari*, 123.

5 "1513: In Firenze questo nuovo modo di governo era a molti insopportabile. E congiurorono Agostino Capponi e Pietropaulo Boscoli di amazzare Giuliano de' Medici." F. Vettori, "Sommario della Storia d'Italia," 147.

6 In what seems to have been a prelude to the alleged conspiracy, Landucci records that on 24 January two men were banished from Florence for five years: the first, Martino dello Scarfa, was additionally heavily fined for being hostile toward the Medici; the other, Piero, a mace-bearer, who Landucci says "was a foolish man, and apt to chatter thoughtlessly," was put to torture on the rack because he spoke against the government. Landucci, *Diary*, 265–6.

7 "E tutti furono essaminati; ma solo furono trovati in colpa notabile Agostino e Pietropaulo i quali dalli Otto furono condannati a morte." F. Vettori, "Sommario della Storia d'Italia," 147.

8 Nardi, *Istorie*, 2:21.

9 "io ho sempre tenuto Ser Zanobi, el quale continuamente mi referiva et teneva ragguagliato d'ogni deliberation che ne lo officio si faceva." Gar, "Instructione al Magnifico Lorenzo," 301. See chapter 5.

10 "sono presi et non si ritrahe per insino ad hoggi che hieri si scoperse se non una mala intentione o qualche pratica contro di noi, ma sono homini benché nobili di debole qualità et senza fondamento alcuno et senza pericolo dello stato quando ben fusse loro riuscito el disegno." Luzio, "Isabella d'Este," 107.

11 "Idio sia ringratiato, le cose sono procedute quiete con reputatione et unione senza novità o alteratione alcuna: et di questo caso ne resulterà tucto beneficio nostro." Ibid.

12 "non si è ritracto se non una mala intentione con poco ordine, senza fondamento o coda, et senza pericolo de lo Stato, quando fusse ben loro reuscito el disegno, che haveamo pensato fussi in su la morte di Nostro Signor et ne la absentia del reverendissimo Legato." Sanudo, *Diarii*, 15:573.

13 Ibid.

14 The full list included, in this order: Niccolò Valori, Agostino Capponi, Pierpaolo Boscoli, Giovanni Folchi, Ludovico Nobili, Francesco Serragli, Machiavelli, Andrea Marsuppini, Piero Orlandini, Daniele Strozzi, Cechotto Tosinghi, and "el prete de' Martini." Ibid., 574.

15 "Onde i detti Agostino Capponi e Pietro Pagolo Boscoli furono condannati alla morte, si che nel seguente dì dalla partita del reverendissimo cardinale de' Medici da Fiorenza, per andare alla creazione del nuovo papa, ne fu fatta la esecuzione [il 23 di febbraio]." Nardi, *Istorie*, 2:21n3.

16 "e il Magnifico probabilmente avrebbe chiuso quell'incidente con un gesto di umana benevolenza; ma Lorenzo, Giulio e forse lo stesso Cardinale, che non era piú in Firenze, non lo consentirono, perché si credette opportuno un immediato esempio di severità ad ammonimento di tutti." Fatini, "Giuliano de' Medici," xliii.

17 Valori, *Vita di Lorenzo de' Medici*, 34.

18 Robbia, "Recitazione," 283–312. See also the English translation in Frazier, "Luca Della Robbia's Narrative," 293–326. Frazier (293) is also skeptical about the conspiracy: "The material evidence for the plot was, at any rate, flimsy and possibly fabricated." For a further discussion of the "Recitazione," see Trexler, *Public Life in Renaissance Florence*, 198–205.

19 "tirato da una gran pietà di consolare quanto potevo Pietro Pagolo, col quale io tenevo gran famigliarità." Robbia, "Recitazione," 283; Frazier, "Luca Della Robbia's Narrative," 302.
20 Frazier, "Luca Della Robbia's Narrative," 295.
21 "sappia ciascheduno che leggerà il presente ricordo, che li può prestar fede come a cosa vera e senza passione recitata; perché mi farei non poca conscienza di scriver bugie, massime in tal materia, che, s'io non m'inganno, assai appartiene alla cristiana religione." Robbia, "Recitazione," 284–5; Frazier, "Luca Della Robbia's Narrative," 303.
22 "E perché sapevo era di singolare ingegno e di buone lettere, e aveva assai nervo ne'suoi discorsi." Robbia, "Recitazione," 284; Frazier, "Luca Della Robbia's Narrative," 302.
23 Albertini, *Firenze*, 71.
24 "Deh! Luca, cavatemi della testa Bruto, acciò ch'io faccia questo passo interamente da cristiano." Robbia, "Recitazione," 289–90; Frazier, "Luca Della Robbia's Narrative," 307.
25 "io muoio volontieri, ancorchè innocente." Robbia, "Recitazione," 299; Frazier, "Luca Della Robbia's Narrative," 315.
26 Frazier, "Luca Della Robbia's Narrative," 319.
27 "Così *etiam* m'entrò in Agostino Capponi, dolendosi che lui era stato alquanto precipitoso nel conferir tal congiura; e però nell' examina l'aveva un poco carico. E dissemi: Parv' egli ch' io gli chiegga perdono ora? Et io: Confessatevi prima a Dio, e di poi gli chiederete perdonanza." Robbia, "Recitazione," 289. Frazier ("Luca Della Robbia's Narrative," 307) translates the passage as: "In the same way also he began to talk to me about Agostino Capponi, lamenting that he [Capponi] had been a little hasty in drawing up that conspiracy, and nevertheless that in the interrogation he [Boscoli] had burdened him with it somewhat." This passage implies that Capponi was party to the conspiracy but does not take into account the fact that later Boscoli begged forgiveness from Capponi especially for having "offended against him in the interrogation."
28 Frazier, "Luca Della Robbia's Narrative," 307.
29 "Io vi chieggo perdonanza di ciò che mai v'avessi offeso in questa vita; e massime ch'io v'ho offeso nell'examina." Robbia, "Recitazione," 303; Frazier, "Luca Della Robbia's Narrative," 319.
30 Baker's study of political executions and the Medici after their restoration in September 1512 establishes that there was an increase in political executions in the city, indicative of the changing nature of the state as Florence moved toward a Medicean principality. See Baker, "For Reasons of State," 444–78, esp. 460.
31 "e così fu fatto." Robbia, "Recitazione," 289.
32 Nardi (*Istorie*, 2:22) writes that the fact that Valori's nephew, Bartolomeo Valori, was one of the *palleschi* who, together with Paolo Vettori and others, had entered the Palazzo della Signoria and forced the *gonfaloniere* to resign may have helped to prevent his execution. See also Jurdjevic, *Guardians of Republicanism*, 98–9.

33 "E di più detto Pier Paulo fu mandato a dirmi inconsideratamente e quasi non sapessi quello si voleva dirmi. Le sue parole formale furono, dopo altri ragionamenti e domestici: 'Orsù Niccolò, il papa si muore, che facciamo noi? E' si spaccerebbe anche Giuliano de' Medici; egli era poche sere sono con poca compagnia molti tardi.'" Valori, *Ricordanze*, 134, fols. 17v–18v, qtd. in E. Niccolini, *Lorenzo de' Medici*, 33.

34 "in su la quale messono me, più alieno da ogni novità che uomo fussi in questa città, carico di famiglia, massime di fanciulle grande, benestante e perché avuti tanti offici et onori che io n'ero sazio, e tutto volto alla quiete." E. Niccolini, *Lorenzo de' Medici*, 33.

35 "Io cognobbi l'importanza delle parole e subito gli soggiunsi: 'Or non sai tu quanto questa città aborrisce dal sangue? Fa che mai più intenda ragioni di cose simile prima perché mai mi piacque la violenza, appresso perché non erano uomini da simili faccende, in ultimo perché la morte di Iuliano non faceva effetto alcuno rimanendo il Cardinale, che fu poi Papa Leone X, Lorenzo figliuolo di Piero e messer Iulio figliuolo naturale di Giuliano di chi si parlava.'" Ibid., 33.

36 "E così si partì da me tutto quieto e, niente di meno, la sera fu preso e con tormenti essaminato: disse di avermi conferito questo ragionamento e la risposta gl'avevo fatto. E, niente di meno, mandorono a mezza notte per me come se io avessi confortato e non isconfortato: mi tennono stretto e il Magistrato delli Otto mi essaminò in sulla fune e mai ebbono altro perché così era la verità." Ibid., 33.

37 Jurdjevic, *Guardians of Republicanism*, 64.

38 Arrighi, "Giovanni Folchi," 531–2.

39 Machiavelli had dedicated his poem "Dell'ingratitudine" (of uncertain date) to Giovanni Folchi. See Machiavelli (Vivanti, ed.), *Opere*, 3:38–42. For an English translation, see A. Gilbert, *Machiavelli: Chief Works*, 2:740–4.

40 ASF, Archivio Mediceo avanti il Principato, lxxxix, no. 38, published in Stephens and Butters, "New Light on Machiavelli," 54–69, esp. 67.

41 Ibid., 67.

42 De Grazia, *Machiavelli in Hell*, 36.

43 Frazier, "Luca Della Robbia's Narrative," 309.

44 Ibid., 316.

45 "Io ho, Giuliano, in gamba un paio di geti, / e sei tratti di fune in su le spalle; / l'antre miserie mie vi vo' contalle, poi che cosí si trattono e poeti. / Menon pidocchi questi parieti, / golfi e paffuti che paion farfalle, / non fu mai tanto puzzo in Roncisvalle, / o là in Sardigna tra quegli albereti, / quanto è nel mio sí delicato ostello. / Con un romor che par proprio che in terra / folgori Giove tutto Mongibello, / l'un s'incatena, quell'altro si sferra; / combatte toppe, chiave e chiavistello; un altro grida: 'Troppo alto da terra!' / Quel che mi fe' piú guerra / fu che dormendo presso alla aurora, / cominciai a sentire: 'Pro eis ora.' / Ma vadino in buona ora, / purché vostra pietà ver' me si volga / ch'al padre e al bisavol fama tolga." De Grazia, *Machiavelli in Hell*, 34–7; Machiavelli, *Scritti*, 277–80; Machiavelli (Vivanti, ed.), *Opere*, 3:8–9.

46 Letter to Francesco Vettori of 18 March 1513, in Atkinson and Sices, *Machiavelli and His Friends*, 222.

47 Scarpa, "Sonnetti dal Carcere," 139–60, esp. 148.

48 "come io non sono il Dazzo ma sono io." Machiavelli (Vivanti, ed.), *Opere*, 3:8–9; Machiavelli, *Scritti*, 280–2.

49 "Erano i capi di questa intelligentia Agostino Capponi e Piero Pagolo Boscoli, giovani, benchè di buona casa, senza reputatione, o seguito, o facultà, et havien conferito più volte insieme di levarci da terra, consentito et deputato el luogo et facto una lista di parechii giovani che credevano fussin malcontenti di noi, et andaronli tentandoli. Riscontrorno in Nicolò Valori et Giovanni Folini i quali prestorno orechie, et interogati più volte de' modi ad far novità, et aperto l'animo loro, visi a dui, li porno drento. De' primi due, Agostino et Pietro Paulo *supplicium capitis sumptum est*." Sanudo, *Diarii*, 16:26.

50 "Nicolò et Giovanni son confinati nel fondo de la torre de la rocha de Volterra per due anni … Alcuni altri, per aver qualche participatione, come Francesco Seragli, Pandolpho Biliotti, Dutio Adimari, Ubertino Bonciani, son confinati per parechi anni nel contado in diversi luoghi; li altri, che non erano in dolo, son rilassati a buon sodamento." Sanudo, *Diarii*, 16:26.

51 Cerretani, *Ricordi*, 300.

52 Ibid., 301; Cambi, *Istorie*, 22, 8; Butters, *Governors and Government*, 211. Cerretani (*Ricordi*, 300) writes that even Piero Soderini and his brothers were pardoned and allowed to return to Florence, adding this was because Piero Soderini's brother, Cardinal Francesco Soderini, had offered Medici his vote and the votes of two other cardinals, plus 40,000 florins as well.

53 Villari, *Machiavelli*, 2:33.

54 Ridolfi, *Life of Machiavelli*, 291n.19.

55 De Grazia, *Machiavelli in Hell*, 40; Najemy, *Between Friends*, 95; Dotti, *Machiavelli Rivoluzionario*, 240; Bausi, *Machiavelli*, 74; Connell, *Prince*, 17; Atkinson, "Niccolò Machiavelli: A Portrait," 22.

56 Atkinson and Sices, *Machiavelli and His Friends*, 221, 497n.2.

57 Landucci, *Diary*, 267. It is interesting to note that Landucci also says that the Otto issued a decree that warned that *frateschi* were not to be insulted on pain of death, an order no doubt given to the Otto by Giuliano.

58 Atkinson and Sices, *Machiavelli and His Friends*, 221.

59 Letter dated 26 June 1513, ibid., 239.

60 If, as it seems quite likely, the cardinal concocted the conspiracy, this will not be the last time he took such an extreme, politically motivated step. In 1517 a conspiracy to assassinate him in Rome was uncovered that led to the arrest of five cardinals. Giovanni Battista Picotti was the first historian in the early twentieth century to assert that Leo X had fabricated a plot against his own life as a pretext to rid himself of his enemies, extort huge sums of money from the accused, which he needed to continue his war with the Duke of Urbino, and

prepare the way for an unprecedented enlargement of the Sacred College by the appointment of neutral or pro-Medicean cardinals. See Picotti, "La Congiura dei Cardinali," 249–67. In a study of a portrait of one of the accused, Cardinal Bandinello Sauli, painted by Sebastiano del Piombo in 1516, the writer of this book, having reviewed all the known facts and surviving documents, came to the same conclusion that a conspiracy had never taken place. See Jungić, "Prophecies of the Angelic Pastor," 345–70. More recent research supports this view; see Lowe, "Political Crime of Conspiracy," 193–8, and idem, "Alleged Cardinals' Conspiracy," 53–78.

61 Villari, *Niccolò Machiavelli*, 2:33.

62 Atkinson and Sices, *Machiavelli and His Friends*, 222, 498n.4.

63 Najemy, *Between Friends*, 71–94. During the whole correspondence, Machiavelli never seems to lose hope that one day Vettori would help him secure employment with the Medici, either in Florence or in Rome, but in the meantime he had the consolation of discussing politics in his letters to Vettori that gave him so much pleasure. Vettori, however, while continually making excuses for not being able to help him, appears to have used the opportunity of writing to Machiavelli partly as a means to elicit the former secretary's assessments of the political events of the day, perhaps to enhance his own role as Florentine ambassador at the papal court. In his letter of 21 April 1513, he says as much when he writes: "I shall agree with your judgment because, to tell you the truth without flattery, I have found it more sound in these matters than that of any other man that I have spoken with." See Atkinson and Sices, *Machiavelli and His Friends*, 231, 502n.15.

64 "e non li domandai altra grazia che la liberazione vostra, la quale ho molto caro fussi seguita prima." Francesco Vettori to Machiavelli, 15 March 1513, in Machiavelli (Vivanti, ed.), *Opere*, 2:236; Atkinson and Sices, *Machiavelli and His Friends*, 221, 497–8n.2. Najemy (*Between Friends*, 96) translates the conclusion of this sentence as: "which I dearly wish had happened sooner."

65 Ridolfi, *Life of Machiavelli*, 141.

66 Bullard, *Filippo Strozzi*, 86–7.

67 Atkinson and Sices, *Machiavelli and His Friends*, 222.

68 Ridolfi, *Life of Machiavelli*, 138.

69 Paolo Vettori's name appears in the deposition made by Giovanni Folchi: "Et che sfuggiva i ragionamenti di detto Nicholò [Machiavelli], domandato perchè, dixe perché Pagholo Vectori lo adverti che lui non usassi con Duccio, et lui dix 'et io non userò achora col Machiavello." "Et Pagolo li dixe 'Nè cotesto non dà noia." Stephens and Butters, "New Light on Machiavelli," 67.

70 Ridolfi, *Life of Machiavelli*, 161.

71 Butters, *Governors and Government*, 207.

72 Atkinson and Sices, *Machiavelli and His Friends*, 228, 501n.9. Machiavelli seems optimistic about his own prospects, writing: "So if my case is managed with

some skill, I cannot believe that I shall not succeed in being put to some use, if not on Florence's behalf, at least on behalf of Rome and the papacy; in which case I should be less mistrusted."

73 Stephens, *Fall of the Florentine Republic*, 81.

74 Fatini, "Giuliano de' Medici," xlv.

75 In March 1514, for example, Alfonsina complained bitterly that Giuliano was much worse than his model, Cesare Borgia. Simonetta, *Volpi e Leoni*, 103–5.

76 Cerretani (Berti, ed.), *Dialogo delle Mutatione*, 56; Pitti, *Istoria Fiorentina*, 118; Stephens, *Fall of the Florentine Republic*, 83.

77 Stephens, *Fall of the Florentine Republic*, 83.

78 Butters, *Governors and Government*, 219.

79 "Non fu piccola disputa se Giuliano o Lorenzo doveva venire a governare Firenze. Ultimamente Giuliano, sendo infastidito e sbigottito, lasciò questo carico a Lorenzo." Cerretani (Berti, ed.), *Dialogo delle Mutatione*, 57.

80 Cited in Devonshire Jones, *Francesco Vettori*, 76 and n.121.

81 "Giuliano pensava a grandezza eccessiva ... il re Fernando dicea: 'Poiché Giuliano ha lasciato lo stato di Firenze, che è sì bella cosa, bisogna che abbi fantasia a cose maggiori, che non può essere altro che il Regno di Napoli.'" Vettori, "Sommario della Storia d'Italia," 152, 156.

82 "perché in Firenze era necessitato a vivere con mille rispetti et a Roma non ne avea avere uno al mondo." Ibid., 152.

83 Ibid., 152–3.

84 Butters, *Governors and Government*, 219.

85 "Perciò desiderava in cuor suo di passare da Firenze a Roma, dove, intanto, poteva godersi, nel lusso, negli svaghi mondani e nella popolarità che con la sua magnificenza si sarebbe guadagnata, i benefici del Papato e prepararsi a svolgere le sue innate attitudini di Principe mecenate." Fatini, "Giuliano de' Medici," xlvii.

86 "Parliamo con voi liberamente ogni cosa e sanza riserva, parendoci farlo con noi stessi e come vedrete molte cose habbiamo taciute con li ambasciadori." Devonshire Jones, *Francesco Vettori*, 95n.69.

87 Nerli, *Commentari*, 129.

88 Butters, *Governors and Government*, 221 and n.205.

89 "Pagolo mio, anchora che nel tornare ricevessi danno e vergogna, tornavo volentieri, perchè questi governi io non li intendo e se son ricordati e' buoni, non sono acepti, e pare che li huomini voglino mettere loro paura. E ieri pure fui con Juliano sopra e' collegi, e conobbi non hebbe caro certe parole li dixi, e par loro essere troppo sicuri." Letter to Paolo dated 13 May 1513, in Hughes, *Francesco Vettori*, 556–7.

90 "Non monstrare le lettere che io ti scrivo, perchè qui è stato scripto che tu parli molto largo delle chose di qua e che le di' a ogni huomo chome si ti fussi ritrovato a tutti e secreti: e questo è suto scripto a Jacopo, non so già da chi, credo da Matteo. E tu di' che lo scrivere mio ci nuoce, di che non dubitare: guardato pure

dal parlare, che io non scriverrò mai chosa se non chon quelle cautele si richerchano." Hughes, *Francesco Vettori*, 557.

91 Vettori's letter of 16 May to Paolo, in Hughes, *Francesco Vettori*, 559.

92 Atkinson and Sices, *Machiavelli and His Friends*, 261.

93 Hughes, *Francesco Vettori*, 555.

94 Letter dated 26 July 1513. Ibid., 570.

95 "Con Juliano non c'è ordine delle palle, perchè lui è uno spenditore tanto grande che sempre ha haver bixogno per sè, e io per me non viddi mai huomo stimare manco e danari di lui, e se fia gran signore chi li sarà intorno n' harà più che per sè." Hughes, *Francesco* Vettori, 577.

96 "El Cardinale de' Medici mi domandò hieri molto strectamente, se io sapevo che V. Excellentia havessi preso a' servitii sui Nicolò Machiavelli; et respondendoli io, che non havevo notitia nè lo credevo, Sua Signoria reverendissima mi dise queste formali parole: Anchora io non lo credo; *tamen*, perchè da Firenze ce ne è adviso, io li Ricordo che non è il bisogno suo, nè il nostro. Questa debbe essere inventione di Paulo Vectori, come fu farlo andare ad desinare con Martino Scarfi. Scriveteli per mia parte, che io lo conforto ad non si impacciare con Nicolò; et questo non dico per insegnarli quello habbi ad fare, ma mosso da lo amore ec." Guasti, *I Manoscritti Torrigiani*, 67.

97 Even with Vettori's vastly increased influence with the Medici and his close friendship with Lorenzo, Vettori still did nothing to help Machiavelli, who was forced to live in poverty and obscurity on his farm at Sant'Andrea in Percussina.

98 Pieraccini, *Medici di Cafaggiolo*, 1:283.

99 Devonshire Jones, *Frances Vettori*, 89.

CHAPTER 7

1 Nardi, *Istorie*, 2:32; Laurenza, *Leonardo nella Roma*, 25–6, 40–1, and figs. 20 and 21.

2 Sanudo, *Diarii*, 15:357; Fatini, "Giuliano de' Medici," xlix.

3 Vecce, *Leonardo*, 304.

4 Shaw, *Julius II*, 196. For a discussion of Pinturicchio's frescoes in the Borgia apartment, see Rowland, *Culture of the High Renaissance*, 46–53.

5 For a recent study of Leonardo's Roman activity, see Bambach, "Leonardo and Raphael," 26–37.

6 Vasari (De Vere, trans.), *Lives*, 1:638

7 Bambach, "Leonardo and Raphael," 26.

8 Vasari (De Vere, trans.), *Lives*, 1:638; qtd. also in Bambach, "Leonardo and Raphael," 32.

9 In his role as datary, Turini was in charge of the office that oversaw papal benefices. Bambach, "Leonardo and Raphael," 32, 35.

10 Altieri, *Giuliano de' Medici*, 20; Fatini, "Giuliano de' Medici," xlix–l. See also Mitchell, *Italian Civic Pageantry*, 119–24.

11 "Poi con magnifica et honorata compagnia dargli un sontuoso e splendido pranzo, con grata dimostratione di publica letitia, applicando tal solennità, alli

Natali di Roma et intitolarla le PALILIE, per essere se dir si puote rinata Roma, *cioè liberata da Sua Santità d'affanno, e di miseria e dato principio e modo di più felice vita con grandissima speranza di migliore conditione.*" Altieri, *Giuliano de' Medici*, 25–6.

12 Connell, *Prince*, 18.

13 Shaw, *Julius II*, 306.

14 "le ragion de la Chiesa sono tante vecchie che è vergogna ad parlane." Chambers, *Popes, Cardinals and War*, 127.

15 Ibid.

16 Ibid., 128.

17 Minnich, "Images of Julius II," 87.

18 Shaw, "Papacy and European Powers," 113.

19 Letter dated 12 July 1513 in Atkinson and Sices, *Machiavelli and His Friends*, 242, 507n.1.

20 Prodi, "Relazione Diplomatiche," 437–94, esp. 447.

21 Atkinson and Sices, *Machiavelli and His Friends*, 242, 507–8n.2.

22 "perché nacque da una estraordinaria ed estrema malignità di fortuna." Machiavelli (Vivanti, ed.), *Opere*, 1:134; Machiavelli (Bondanella, ed.), *Prince*, 25.

23 Mallett, *The Borgias*, 215–20.

24 Pellegrini, "Leone X," 515; Fatini, "Giuliano de' Medici," lii.

25 Luzio, "Isabella d'Este" 121–3; Fatini, "Giuliano de' Medici," liii.

26 "El magnifico Juliano di Medici … si vol far signor di Modena, Rezo, Parma e Piasenza; sichè questo Papa è pezo cha papa Julio." Sanudo, *Diarii*, 16:519.

27 Fatini, "Giuliano de' Medici," lvii.

28 See the "Orazione funerale di M. Benedetto Varchi, fatta e recitata da Lui publicamente nell'esequie di Michelangelo Buonarroti in Firenze nell Chiesa di San Lorenzo," cited in Cermenati, "Leonardo a Roma," 317–18. Further evidence of intimacy is seen in the coded letters of Cardinal Bernardo Dovizi, the pope's most influential adviser, who always substituted Giuliano's name for that of Leonardo. See Moncallero, *Il Cardinale Bernardo Dovizi*, 402.

29 Beatis, *Travel Journal*, 132; Kemp, *Leonardo: Marvellous Works*, 261. Some have taken Antonio's remarks to indicate that the *Mona Lisa* was not the wife of Francesco del Giocondo but one of Giuliano's mistresses. This speculation has been put to rest by Schlecter's discovery of marginal notes by Agostino Vespucci recording Leonardo's work on a portrait of Lisa Del Giocondo, confirming Vasari's identification. Vasari (Hinds, trans.), *Lives*, 2:164; Dorfman, "'Mona Lisa': Case Closed," 39.

30 Bambach, "Leonardo and Raphael," 32–3, 37nn.43, 44.

31 This would also account for the otherwise anomalous feature of the delicate veiled glazes Leonardo applied to *Mona Lisa*, a technique that was a characteristic only of his late style. Kemp, *Leonardo: Marvellous Works*, 261–2. For the most recent discussion of the works of art Leonardo undertook for Ludovico il Moro, see Syson, *Leonardo da Vinci*, 13–53.

32 Ibid., 162, 173.

33 Kemp believes that the unidentified portrait known as *La Belle Ferronière* could be Lucrezia Crivelli, another mistress of Ludovico, c. 1495. See Kemp, *Leonardo: Marvellous Works*, 187.
34 Richter, *Literary Works of Leonardo*, 2:396.
35 Ibid., 397.
36 Ibid.
37 Galluzzi, *Renaissance Engineers*, 47.
38 Richter, *Literary Works of Leonardo*, 2:398.
39 Leonardo's papers are now bound in various manuscripts and dispersed among a number of libraries in Europe and North America. Nathan, "Engineering and Machinery Studies," 372.
40 Galluzzi, *Renaissance Engineers*, 46.
41 In addition to his interest in mechanical and military engineering, Leonardo studied anatomy, physiology, botany, zoology, geology, geography, meteorology, astronomy, optics, hydrodynamics, aerodynamics, acoustics, cartography, and much more, including the arts of painting, sculpture, and architecture; it is clear from his notes that he intended to write treatises on many of the aforementioned subjects. Reti, "The Engineer," 125.
42 *Codex Atlanticus*, fol. 157r., Biblioteca Ambrosiana, Milan.
43 Ibid., 139r.
44 Marani, "Leonardo, Fortified Architecture," 303.
45 Marani, *L'Architettura Fortificata*.
46 Ibid., 12.
47 Vecce, *Leonardo*, 187–8. The sketch measuring 63 × 46 cm is in the Cabinet des Dessins, Musée du Louvre, Paris.
48 Pedretti, *Literary Works of Leonardo*, 2:196–9; Vecce, *Leonardo*, 188–91.
49 Isabella wanted something for her *studiolo*, or, if that was not possible, a "little picture of Madonna." She also wanted another sketch of the charcoal portrait he had made of her, since her husband, Francesco Gonzaga, had given the original sketch away. Letter from Isabella d'Este to Fra Pietro da Novellara, 27 March 1501, in Chambers, *Patrons and Artists*, 144–5.
50 Letter from Fra Pietro da Novellara to Isabella d'Este, 3 April 1501, ibid., 145–6.
51 Letter from Fra Pietro da Novellara to Isabella d'Este, 14 April 1501, ibid., 146.
52 Kemp, *Leonardo: Marvellous Works*, 203.
53 Ibid., 218.
54 Vecce, *Leonardo*, 209.
55 Kemp, *Leonardo: Marvellous Works*, 95. For Leonardo's annotated copy, see Mariani, *Francesco di Giorgio*.
56 Vecce, *Leonardo*, 209–10.
57 Valentiner writes: "The view from the front makes it comprehensible that Cesare was regarded as the most handsome man in all of Italy." Valentiner, "Leonardo as Verrocchio's Coworker," 60n.32. Clark refers to Borgia's "exquisitely curled, blond beard" and the "curiously northern look which distinguished all

the Borgias." Clark, *Leonardo da Vinci*, 109. Bambach sees a resemblance of the head to portrait medals of Cesare. Bambach, *Leonardo da Vinci*, 505n.4. Zöllner accepts that Leonardo's portrait heads are of Cesare. Zöllner, *Leonardo*, 277.

58 Clayton, *Leonardo: Divine and Grotesque*, 13.

59 "mai si riposa, né conosce fatica o periculo." Machiavelli, *Legazioni*, 2:247.

60 Vecce, *Leonardo*, 210.

61 Pedretti, *Disegni di Leonardo*, 11.

62 Reti, "Leonardo," 336–7; Vecce, *Leonardo*, 212.

63 Pedretti, ed., *Documenti e Memorie*, 165–7.

64 Manuscript L, compiled between the years 1497 and 1503, has 94 folios mostly devoted to the period of his service to Cesare Borgia, above all pertaining to his journeys to the Marches and in the Romagna. See Marinoni, ed., *Il Manoscritto L*.

65 Mallett, *The Borgias*, 191.

66 Reti, "Leonardo," 350–2; Marani, *L'Architettura Fortificata*, 49–63.

67 Reti, "Leonardo," 352–64. See also Londei, "Progetti Leonardiani di Machine Scavatrici," 55–71.

68 Woodward, *Cesare Borgia*, 255.

69 For a full discussion of Leonardo's cartography for Borgia, see Reti, "Leonardo," 343–9. See also Clayton, *Leonardo: A Curious Vision*, 94–8.

70 "Giugne prima in un luogo che se ne possa intendere la partita donde si leva." Machiavelli, *Legazioni*, 2:247.

71 The drawing is in the Royal Library at Windsor (12284). See Kemp, *Leonardo da Vinci*, 176.

72 Marinoni, "La pianta di Imola," 77.

73 Machiavelli (Bondanella, ed.), *Prince*, 51.

74 Kemp, *Leonardo: Marvellous Works*, 223–5; Clayton, *Leonardo: A Curious Vision*, 100–5.

75 Whatever remained of Leonardo's fresco was covered over by Giorgio Vasari's mural in the 1560s. Kemp, *Leonardo: Marvellous Works*, 226–40; Rubinstein, "Machiavelli and Mural Decoration," 275–85.

76 Michelangelo, commissioned to paint the *Battle of Cascina* on the opposite wall, commemorating the Florentine Victory over the Pisans in 1364, only got as far as a preliminary cartoon.

77 Vecce, *Leonardo*, 435.

78 "Partii da Milano per Roma addí 24 di sectembre 1513 con Giovanfrancesco de Melzi, Salaí, Lorenzo e il Fanfoia." Leonardo qtd. in Vecce, *Leonardo*, 305.

79 Ibid.

80 Pedretti, *Leonardo & Io*, 462.

81 Atkinson and Sices, *Machiavelli and His Friends*, 264.

82 Coffin, *The Villa*, 69–87. See the drawing of the villa on the Vatican Hill by Van Heemskerk in Pedretti, *Leonardo da Vinci's Architectural Studies*, 83, Fig. 43.

83 Villata, ed., *Leonardo da Vinci*, 244–5.

84 "finjta addj 7 dj luglio a ore 23 a beluedere nello studjo fattomj dal magnjficho 1514." Pedretti, *Literary Works,* 2:322. The twenty-fourth hour corresponds to half an hour after sunset.
85 Fatini, "Giuliano de' Medici," lxii.
86 Laurenza, *Leonardo nella Roma*, 8–14, 28–30.
87 Fatini, "Giuliano de' Medici," lxii.
88 Pedretti, *Literary Works*, 2:303.
89 Sanudo, *Diarii,* 18:278, 292, 293, 313, 342.
90 In March 1514 Sanudo recorded that, according to Bernardin di Prosperi, secretary of the Duke of Ferrara, the pope wanted to take Ferrara and give it to Giuliano. See Sanudo, *Diarii*, 18:9.
91 Luzio, "Isabella d'Este," 146–7; Fatini, "Giuliano de' Medici," lx; Cartwright, *Isabella d'Este*, 2:110–11.
92 Vitruvius, *Architecture in Ten Books*, Book 1, chapter 4, 17.
93 Solmi, *Scritti Vinciani*, 324.
94 Zöllner, *Leonardo*, 344.
95 Solmi, *Scritti Vinciani*, 328; Fatini, "Giuliano de' Medici," lxii.
96 The Pontine Marshes were finally completely drained during the time of Mussolini in the twentieth century. See Sallares, *Malaria and Rome*, 4–5.
97 Codex Atlanticus, fol. 87r. Dupré, "Leonardo's Drawings of Mirrors and Machinery," 211–36, esp. 218.
98 "ricordati delle saldature con che si saldo la palla dj Sancta Maria del Fiore." Pedretti, *Literary Works*, 2:20.
99 Ibid.
100 "djmandasi sella piramjde di chondensa a ridurre tanta potential nu. sol punto essella si fa piu densa chellaria chella sostiene / chon questo si fara bollire ognj chaldara dj tintoria – e da questa sara scaldata vna pessciera perche sempre vi sara acqua che bollira." *Codex Atlanticus*, fol. 371v, Pedretti, *Literary Works*, 2:19.
101 Pedretti, *Leonardo: Engineer and Architect*, 12; idem, *Leonardo: Le Macchine*, 20.
102 Kemp, *Leonardo: Marvellous Works*, 328.
103 "Gli eventuali usi militari, inoltre, non potevano non riportare alla mente di Leonardo l'immagine di Archimede nell'assedio di Siracusa." Vecce, *Leonardo*, 323.
104 Qtd. in Simms, "Archimedes' Weapons of War," 195.
105 Ibid., 197.
106 See Pedretti's introduction to Vecce, *Leonardo*, 7; and Kemp, *Leonardo: Marvellous Works*, 165.
107 Rose, *Italian Renaissance of Mathematics*, 29.
108 Laird, "Archimedes among the Humanists," 631–4.
109 From Borgo San Sepolcro, Pacioli came to the Sforza court in 1496 to tutor mathematics; there, he became close friends with Leonardo, who provided drawings of geometric figures for the woodcut illustrations that accompanied Pacioli's *De Divina Proportione*, finished in 1498 and published in 1509. After the duke's overthrow in 1499, Pacioli followed Leonardo to Florence, where he obtained a

position as a teacher of mathematics in the Florentine Studio and continued to work closely with Leonardo on the artist's studies of mathematics and geometry. Pacioli, *De Divina Proportione*; Pedretti, *Literary Works*, 2:335; Kemp, *Leonardo: Marvellous Works*, 133–5; Vecce, *Leonardo*, 209. For Leonardo and Luca Pacioli, see Azzolini, "Anatomy of a Dispute," 115–35.

110 Clagett, *Archimedes in the Renaissance*, 416, 461.

111 Simms, "Archimedes' Weapons of War," 203. None of the standard references in antiquity that describe the siege of Syracuse mention burning mirrors. The earliest account of Archimedes using such a weapon occurs in Anthemius of Tralles, 6th century CE, in his *On Paradoxical Mechanism*. See also Simms, "Archimedes and Burning Mirrors," 1–24, esp. 6–7, 10; Knorr, "Geometry of Burning-Mirrors," 53–73.

112 Ms. Bologna, Bibl. Univ. MS. 250, 200v; Clagett, *Archimedes in the Renaissance*, 460.

113 "Borges ti farà avere l'Archimede del vescovo di Padova e Vitellozo quello da il Borgo a San Sepolcro." Qtd. in Vecce, *Leonardo*, 209.

114 "archimenjde e intero appresso al fratel dj monsignore dj sca gusta in roma djsse averlo dato al fratello chessta in sardjgna era prima nella libreria del duca durbino – fv tolto al tempo del duca valentine." *Codex Atlanticus*, fol. 349v, Pedretti, *Literary Works*, 2:333.

115 Ibid.

116 Apuleius, *Apologia*, 42; Simms, "Archimedes and Burning Mirrors," 10.

117 Vecce, *Leonardo*, 323.

118 Fatini, "Giuliano de' Medici," lx. In exchange Giuliano received an annual gift of perfumes especially created by Isabella herself.

119 Richter, *Literary Works of Leonardo*, 2:409.

120 Ibid., 2:410; Laurenza, *Leonardo nella Roma*, 1–20.

121 Richter, *Literary Works of Leonardo*, 2:409.

122 Schultz, *Art and Anatomy*, 108.

123 Richter, *Literary Works of Leonardo*, 2:407–8.

124 Pedretti, *Literary Works*, 2:19.

125 Vecce, *Leonardo*, 323.

126 Clagett, *Archimedes in the Renaissance*, 421. See also Ferrajoli, *Il Ruolo della Corte*, 377.

127 Minnich, "Fifth Lateran Council," 189, no. 243.

128 Minnich, "Concepts of Reform," 189.

129 Setton, "Leo X and the Turkish Peril," 376.

130 Ibid.

131 Sanudo, *Diarii*, 17:414–15.

132 Ibid., 17:530.

133 Pedretti, *Leonardo Architect*, 246.

134 Simms, "Archimedes and Burning Mirrors," 1–2.

135 Sanudo, *Diarii*, 17:536.

136 Vasari relates an anecdote about the artist who, commissioned to paint a picture for the pope, began distilling oils and plants in order to prepare the varnish, whereupon the Pope is reported to have exclaimed: "This man will never do anything, for he begins to think of the end before the beginning!" Vasari (Hinds, trans.), *Lives*, 2:166.

137 For Leo X's dismissive attitude toward Leonardo, and the artist's move to France, see Jungić, "Leonardo da Vinci in Rome," 181–214, esp. 207–14.

CHAPTER 8

1 During Machiavelli's lifetime *The Prince* circulated in manuscript with a dedication letter addressed to Lorenzo, Giuliano's nephew. It was first published on 3 January 1532, five years after the author's death on 21 June 1527, under a privilege granted by Pope Clement VII (Cardinal Giulio de' Medici). Later in the sixteenth century the Inquisition placed *The Prince* on the *Index of Forbidden Books* together with all other works by Machiavelli. See Connell, *Prince*, 22–3.

2 See Viroli's introduction to Machiavelli (Bondanella, ed.), *Prince*, xviii.

3 See introduction by Mansfield and Tarcov to Machiavelli, *Discourses on Livy*, xx. *The Prince* was written in the autumn of 1513 (although according to some scholars the final chapter dates from the time he wrote the dedication to Lorenzo de' Medici, between 1515 and 1516), and the *Discourses* from 1513 to 1517 (although some historians argue it was composed mostly from 1515 to 1517, or others that it was not completed until 1519).

4 Atkinson and Sices, *Machiavelli and His Friends*, 264, 514–15n.15.

5 The idea was first broached by Clough in "Yet Again Machiavelli's Prince," 201–26, esp. 212–17; idem, *Machiavelli Researches*, 40–67.

6 Bausi (*Machiavelli*, 200) believes that, if the Medici had not returned to Florence in 1512, and especially if Giovanni de' Medici had not been elected pope, Machiavelli in all probability would not have composed a work on principalities.

7 Atkinson and Sices, *Machiavelli and His Friends*, 264.

8 Richardson, "*The Prince* and Its Early Italian Readers," 20.

9 Ibid., 21–2.

10 Ibid., 20.

11 Atkinson and Sices, *Machiavelli and His Friends*, 313, 528n.7.

12 Clough, "Yet Again Machiavelli's Prince," 213–14; idem, *Machiavelli Researches*, 57.

13 In the summer of 1513, precipitated by Giuliano's move to Rome, there was much speculation, even among his own courtiers, that Leo X had plans to make him king of Naples and Lorenzo Duke of Milan. See Cerretani (Berti, ed.), *Dialogo della Mutatione*, 56; Nardi, *Istorie*, 2:32; Fatini, "Giuliano de' Medici," lv.

14 The earliest dated mention of *The Prince* occurs in a letter of 29 July 1517 that the young Niccolò wrote to his father, Luigi, showing that both were familiar with the text. See Connell, *Prince*, 143–5.

15 "Et veramente che a tutto el popolo forte fu in dispiacere la morte sua, perché in lui era una humanità singulare et gentileza, et verso tutti e ciptadini tanto facile et grata audientia et amore, che stimare non si potrebbe, et perché la humanità in simili Signori è la piú rara et piú amabile virtú che si possi considerare. Et era a tutti manifesto forte dispiacergli le cose che in Firenze si facevono, perché lui era piú prompto al farsi dagli huomini amare che temere, et desiderava piú presto con benificarli e sua nemici rendersegli propitii, che con vendetta opprimerli." N. Guicciardini, "Discorso," 368.

16 Clough, *Machiavelli Researches*, 53. See also A. Gilbert, *Machiavelli's Prince*.

17 Machiavelli (Bondanella, ed.), *Prince*, 53.

18 Ibid.

19 Machiavelli, *Discourses on Livy*, 15.

20 Machiavelli (Bondanella, ed.), *Prince*, 54–5.

21 "While wrong may be done, then, in either of two ways, that is, by force or by fraud, both are bestial: fraud seems to belong to the cunning fox, force to the lion; both are wholly unworthy of man, but fraud is the more contemptible." Cicero, *De officiis*, 1.13.41.

22 Viroli, *Machiavelli*, 52–3.

23 Machiavelli (Bondanella, ed.), *Prince*, 60.

24 Ibid., 61.

25 One commentator finds it difficult "not to read the account of Borgia's life [in *The Prince*] as a 'sick' joke," and wonders whether power "is really worth all the effort required to acquire and maintain it." See Mousley, "*The Prince* and Textual Politics," 167.

26 Machiavelli (Bondanella, ed.), *Prince*, 24, 25, 29.

27 Ibid., 57.

28 Ibid.

29 Guicciardini agrees with Machiavelli's assessment and blames the Florentine Signoria because they had allowed things to happen and had failed to take the necessary measures that would have quelled the disorders. See F. Guicciardini, *History of Florence*, 187.

30 Ibid., 186.

31 Pinto, *Storia di Pistoia III*, 3:62–72.

32 "Povera Italia, o pecore, che eleggono / Che i barbari emuli abitino Etruria! / Li animi soliti Itali retornino!" Giuliano de' Medici, *Poesie*, 76. See also Fatini, "Giuliano de' Medici," cxxix.

33 Machiavelli (Bondanella, ed.), *Prince*, 58.

34 Ibid., 27.

35 Connell, *Prince*, 5.

36 Woodward, *Cesare Borgia*, 255, 275–6.

37 The duke expressed his indignation to his subjects by revealing that Ramiro had received a yearly salary of 1,200 gold ducats, paid monthly in regular instalments,

and that he also received living and other expenses as well as gifts of fine clothes of great value. Alvisi, *Cesare Borgia*, 354, 554.

38 Ibid., 355.

39 Sacerdote, *Cesare Borgia*, 600.

40 Atkinson and Sices, *Machiavelli and His Friends*, 313, 529n12.

41 Najemy, *Between Friends*, 332; Simonetta, *Volpi e Leoni*, 109–10.

42 De Grazia, *Machiavelli*, 44.

43 Najemy, *Between Friends*, 332.

44 Ibid., 334.

45 Bullard, *Strozzi and the Medici*, 86–7.

46 Simonetta, *Volpi e Leoni*, 109–10.

47 Ardinghelli would later advise Giuliano, in a letter dated 14 February 1515, to avoid all contact with Machiavelli, showing his mistrust of the secretary, who was following Cardinal Giulio de' Medici, to be on target. Atkinson and Sices, *Machiavelli and His Friends*, 265, 515n.21.

48 Ibid., 264–5.

49 Ibid., 265.

50 Ibid., 269.

51 Ibid.

52 "Vettori's offhand reference to it must have disappointed Machiavelli, especially when Vettori, three paragraphs later, seems to get more pleasure from Machiavelli's letters than from his treatise." Ibid., 276, 518n.7.

53 Ibid., 261.

54 Sanudo, *Diarii*, 18:278, 292, 313–14.

55 For example, Clough (*Machiavelli Researches*, 66–7) suggested that Machiavelli, initially frustrated by Vettori in his attempt to present it to Giuliano, changed his mind about the dedicatee, because he "saw the weakness of Giuliano's character, and that he was not suitable," and presented his book to Lorenzo after Giuliano's death in March 1516.

56 Connell (*Prince*, 142) glosses and translates the account of Riccardo di Giovanni Riccardi (1558–1612), which relates how Machiavelli presented his book at the same time that hunting dogs were given to Lorenzo, who "gave greater thanks and responded in a friendlier way to the man who had given him the dogs than to [Machiavelli, who] went away offended."

57 Bausi, *Machiavelli*, 194–200.

58 Jaeckel, "'Tordi e il Principe Nuovo,'" 73–92.

59 Machiavelli, *Chief Works*, 2:1015. Subsequent quotations are from this translation by Gilbert. For the original Italian, see Machiavelli, "Io, Vi Mando, Giuliano, Alquanti Tordi," in *Scritti*, 282–3.

60 "e se d'intorno avete alcun che mordi / li possiate ne i denti dar con ello / acciò che mentre mangia questo Uccello / di lanïare altrui ei si discordi." Machiavelli, *Scritti*, 283.

61 Jaeckel, "'Tordi e il Principe Nuovo,'" 74–9.
62 Machiavelli, *Essential Writings*, 377.
63 "Lasci l'openïoni / vostra Magnificenzia, e palpi e tocchi, / e giudichi alle mani e non agli occhi." Machiavelli, *Scritti*, 283.
64 Fubini, "Postilla ai 'Tordi,'" 93–6.
65 "'State di buon animo, perchè ora lo vedo lacrimante, ed avrà compassione di noi.' E il più vecchio rispose: 'Figlio mio, non guardargli agli occhi, ma alle mani.' E mostrò come si non debba por mente alle parole, ma bensì alle opere." Bracciolini, *Facezie di Poggio Fiorentino*, 205–6.
66 Machiavelli (Bondandella, ed.), *Prince*, 62.
67 Jaeckel, "'Tordi e il Principe Nuovo,'" 81.
68 Machiavelli (Bondanella, ed.), *Prince*, 87.
69 Connell, *Prince*, 19; idem, "New Light on Machiavelli's Letter," 95, 121–3.
70 Baron, "Date of Chapter 26," 83–102, esp. 91–5.
71 Machiavelli (Bondanella, ed.), *Prince*, 90.
72 Bausi, *Machiavelli,* 214–16; Machiavelli*, Il Principe*, 38–9.
73 Whitfield, *Machiavelli*, 63–4.
74 Machiavelli (Bondanella, ed.), *Prince*, 87–8.
75 Ibid., 88.
76 Petrarch's poem "Italia mia" (My Italy) from the *Canzoniere* (128.93–6) appears to be appropriate in this context since it was written to denounce the depredations of a German mercenary soldier near Parma in 1344–45. Machiavelli (Bondanella, ed.), *Prince*, 90, 113 (note).
77 Gilbert and others maintain that this poem, written between 1513 and 1519, was meant to eulogize Lorenzo. Machiavelli, *Chief Works*, 1:99–100, lines 64–75, 97–8.
78 Weinberger, *Michelangelo*, 330.
79 "Partissi il magnifico Giuliano de' Medici a dì 9 di giennaio 1515 in sull'aurora da Roma per adare a sposare la moglie in Sovoia." Richter, *Literary Works*, 2:417.
80 Simonetta, *Volpi e Leoni*, 114.
81 Chambers, *Popes, Cardinals and War*, 134–6.
82 Fatini, "Giuliano de' Medici," lxviii.
83 "Io ho qualche altra pratica di parentado per me, che più mi satisfa che quelli che si è ragionato di costà … et benchè cotesta Maestà facessi tucto quello che vuole el Papa, io non voglio fare nessuno di cotesti parentadi … perchè in facto el parentado di Cardona si disegna per Lorenzo." Guasti, *I Manoscritti Torrigiani*, 42.
84 Fatini, "Giuliano de' Medici," lxix.
85 Tomas, *Medici Women*, 131.
86 Letter dated 9 February 1514 from Alfonsina Orsini to Lorenzo de'Medici. ASF, MAP, 114, fol. 51. "Hora tu ti vedi: ad Giuliano piacciono queste conditione, et ha decto ad questo homo del Duca, che, quanto per sè, dice di si absolutamente. Ad M. Luigi piacciono, etiam credo che ad Santa Maria in Portico piacciono. El Cardinale nostro sta così neutrale, et non dice si, nè no … El Papa ch' el debbi dir

prima, li pare un poco strano: pure e' non lo nega resoluto et non dice di no, ma si scontorce et fa di spalluccie." Zobi, *Delle Nozze del Magnifico*, 28; Tommasini, *La Vita e Gli Scritti*, 992. See also Simonetta, *Volpi e Leoni*, 110–14.

87 "tu facevi mille dispecti ad Jacopo [Salviati], et del parentado di Averardo [de' Medici], et della divisione della casa fra Giovanni et Pier Francesco [de' Medici], et di tutti s'è biasimata et ramaricata crudelmente ... Da una banda è il Magnifico [Giuliano], [Bernardo Dovizi da Bibbiena, Cardinale di] S.ta Maria in Portico, M. Luigi [de Rossi], la Contessina [Ridolfi], et Mona Lucretia [de' Medici]; da l'altro canto el Cardinale [Giulio] de' Medici, Lorenzo de' Medici, io, Mona Magdalena, et Cardinale Cibo, el Signore Francesco [Cibo], et ciascuno degli altri adherenti." Tommasini, *La Vita e Gli Scritti*, 992–3.

88 Letter dated 16 February 1514 from Alfonsina Orsini to Lorenzo de' Medici, ASF, MAP, 114, fol. 57: "Pure lui ci è tanto infiammato, che ha detto al Papa, che se non gli dà questa moglie, non faccia pensieri che ne tolgha più, et che pensi di fargli una cherica." Zobi, *Delle Nozze del Magnifico*, 32; Tommasini, *La Vita e Gli Scritti*, 1007.

89 Sacerdote, *Cesare Borgia*, 567.

90 Boone, *Claude de Seyssel*, 45–6.

91 Caviglia, *Claudio di Seyssel*, 273. Seyssel wrote a short treatise *Monarchie de France* for Francis I between February and March 1515, following his departure from Rome. Scholars have long seen the parallels between this text and Machiavelli's *Prince* because both works subvert the genre of advice books that teach princes how to be virtuous. Since there is no evidence of any direct contact between Machiavelli and Seyssel at this time, a likely explanation for the similarities between the two texts could be that Seyssel had access in Rome to Giuliano's copy of *The Prince*.

92 Fatini, "Giuliano de' Medici," lxx.

93 Zobi, *Delle Nozze del Magnifico*, 11n.2.

94 Moncallero, *Il Cardinale Bernardo Dovizi*, 396.

95 Gattoni, *Leone X e la Geo-Politica*, 108.

96 Moncallero, *Il Cardinale Bernardo Dovizi*, 395.

97 Pastor, *History of the Popes*, 7:106.

98 "Et quanto al concludere quì la lega con lo Imperatore, Spagna ec., V. Excellentia stia con lo animo quieto, che non sarà prima (quando si habbi ad fare) che dopo le noze, et forse V. Excellentia sarà tornata." Guasti, *I Manoscritti Torrigiani*, 61.

99 "perchè Sancta Maria in Portico [Cardinal Bibbiena] mi ha decto che expressamente li commisse, che per parte di N. S. referissi a V. Excellentia che non vi andassi in gnun modo, trovando scusa di havere ad tornare subito a Roma ad fare la compagnia de le genti d'arme, et chiamato et sollecitato da Sua Santità per altre occurrentie." Ibid.

100 "Ricordoli per parte di N. S., che non perda tempo, et consumi el matrimonio prima che si può, usando col Duca quelli termini amorevoli che per altre li ho scripto." Ibid., 63.

101 “et maxime havendo inteso da la Excellentia V., che N. S. non è inclinato ad far decta lega. Questa vostra participatione de la mente di Sua Santità è molto dispiaciuta a Sancta Maria in Portico, et se N. S. ne harà notitia, sarà più scarso in conferirmi un’altra volta e pensieri sui. Ricordo a la Excellentia V. andar cauto, et maxime con simili che hanno passione ne le cose di Francia.” Ibid.

102 Ibid., 64–5. See also Richard, “Une Correspondance Diplomatique,” 19.

103 “Io so bene che a N. S. è dispiaciuto quello che V. Excellentia comunicò al Doge di Genova o a lo Arcivescovo suo fratello, che Sua Beatitudine fussi inclinata a Francia; et dubita che loro non se ne sieno alterati, et fare lor forse scrivere in contrario. Se la Excellentia V. è di oppinione che Sua Santità debbi esser palese o secreto amico di Francia, o almeno starsi di mezzo, non sarà fuor di proposito li scriva una buona lettera, mostrando discorrere, et non scriver per lo adviso mio; et io poi l’accompagnerò con quelle parole che mi occorreranno.” Guasti, *I Manoscritti Torrigiani*, 65.

104 Pastor, *History of the Popes*, 7:107.

105 Zobi, *Delle Nozze del Magnifico*, 16.

106 Fatini, “Giuliano de’ Medici,” lxxii, n.1.

107 Roscoe, *Life and Pontificate of Leo the Tenth*, 2:8.

108 Gattoni, *Leone X e la Geo-Politica*, 96.

109 Guasti, *I Manoscritti Torrigiani*, 68.

110 Gattoni, *Leo X e la Geo-Politica*, 111.

111 “Il Magnifico è dil tutto diventà francese poi che andò in Savoia, e si parla per una altra forma di quello si parlava per avanti.” Sanudo, *Diarii*, 20:103.

112 Guasti, *I Manoscritti Torrigiani*, 68–71.

113 Zobi, *Delle Nozze del Magnifico*, 16–17.

114 Cerretani (Berti, ed.), *Dialogo della Mutatione*, 68; Simonetta, *Volpi e Leoni*, 333n.61.

115 It is not surprising to learn that, when Lorenzo returned to Florence in May 1515, he was successful in obtaining for himself captain-generalship of the Florentine forces despite massive opposition in the city. Within the Medici family, Alfonsina and Leo X were in favour while Giuliano was opposed because the law of the republic, with good reason, prohibited private Florentine citizens from occupying the post. Butters, *Governors and Government*, 260–5.

116 Sanuto, *Diarii*, 20:103.

117 “La felicità dei due sposi, cosí, era completa, e forse nell’onda di gioia che li travolgeva non videro le nubi minacciose che la politica di Leone X andava addensando anche sul loro cielo.” Fatini, “Giuliano de’ Medici,” lxxiv.

CHAPTER 9

1 De Vecchi, *Raphael*, 2–5.

2 Chapman, Henry, and Plazzotta, *Raphael from Urbino to Rome*, 45, Fig. 30.

3 Shearman, *Raphael*, 1:101–3.

4 Castiglione, *Courtier*, 60.

5 Pugliese, *Castiglione's* Courtier, 84.
6 Castiglione, *Courtier*, 173. See also Jungić, "Raphael at Bologna," 580–95.
7 Shearman (*Raphael*, 1:201–3) has doubts as to whether this notation refers in fact to Raphael because, he argues, a commission for a portrait alone should not necessarily lead to an appointment in a household, and furthermore, his name appears in strange company, between individuals holding such low-ranking positions as assistant purveyor and porter.
8 Henry and Joannides, *Late Raphael*, 264.
9 Jules Bache Collection, 1949 (inv. 49.7.12). The painting measures 83.2 × 66 cm. and was painted on canvas that was stretched over panel in the mid-nineteenth century. Henry and Joannides, *Late Raphael*, 262–6, 269, 287, 292, 294.
10 Shearman, *Raphael*, 2:1049. Henry and Joannides (*Late Raphael*, 262) note that, despite reports of the inscription by restorer Angiolo Tricca, and repetition of it throughout the literature on the painting as well as in the museum's own records, "no trace of it exists today and it cannot be seen in any of the old photographs."
11 Fatini, "Giuliano de' Medici," lxxviii.
12 Henry and Joannides, *Late Raphael*, 264.
13 Baker, *The Fruit of Liberty*, 80.
14 Zeri, *Italian Paintings*, 79; Henry and Joannides, *Late Raphael*, 264.
15 Miguel Falomir, "The Court Portrait," in Lorne Campbell and Philip Atwood, eds., *Renaissance Faces: Van Eyck to Titian* (London: National Gallery, Yale University Press, 2008), 68. See also n.9 above.
16 Shearman, *Raphael*, 1:240–1.
17 "parrebbono di mano d'uno de garzoni di Raphaello." Qtd. in Henry and Joannides, *Late Raphael*, 264.
18 Stephens, *Fall of the Florentine Republic*, 101; Knecht, *Renaissance Warrior and Patron*, 82.
19 Bembo (Travi, ed.), *Pietro Bembo Lettere*, 2:112.
20 Vasari, *Lives*, 2:327; Henry and Joannides, *Late Raphael*, 262.
21 Others who see the Met version as the original, either in part or entirely by Raphael, include: von Liphart, *Notice Historique*; Sedelmeyer, *Illustrated Catalogue of the Tenth Series of 100 Paintings by Old Masters*, 68–9; Fischel, "Porträts des Giuliano de' Medici, Herzogs von Nemours," 121, 126–30; Rosenberg and Gronau, *Raffael, des Meisters Gemälde*, 239, 255, 259, 267; von Bode, *Die Sammlung Oscar Huldschinsky*, 6–7, 39; Young, *The Medici*, 1:394–5; Mendelsohn, *Das Werk der Dossi*, 189; Venturi, *Storia dell'Arte Italiana*, 275–7, 279–80; Mayer, "Die Sammlung Jules Bache in New York," 541; van Marle, "An Early Portrait of Giuliano de' Medici," 17–18; Berenson, *Italian Pictures of the Renaissance*, 481; Venturi, *Italian Paintings in America*, vol. 3; Suida, *Raphael*, 25, 29; Jebb, "The Classical Renaissance," 76; Fischel, *Raphael*, 1:114, 365; Venturi, *Raffaello*, 181; Freedberg, *Painting of the High Renaissance in Rome and Florence*, 1:177–9; "Collectors' Questions," 770; Lecchini Giovannoni, "Alcune Proposte per l'Attività Ritrattistica di Alessandro Allori," 50; Henry and Joannides, *Late Raphael*, 262.

22 Zeri, *Italian Paintings*, 79; De Vecchi, *Raffaello, la Pittura*, 259; Oberhuber, *Raffaello*, 202 [copy, possibly by Francesco Penni]; Langedijk, *Portraits of the Medici*, 2:1048–9 [as workshop, attributed to Penni]; Jones and Penny, *Raphael*, 162; Oberhuber, *Raphael: The Paintings*, 199; Höper, *Raffael und die Folgen*, 240, no. B24; Volk-Knüttel, *Peter Candid (um 1548–1628)*, 135 [Luca Penni].
23 Meyer zur Capellen, *The Roman Portraits*, 7, 15.
24 Henry and Joannides, *Late Raphael*, 262–5.
25 Zeri, *Italian Paintings*, 79.
26 Meyer zur Capellen, *The Roman Portraits*, 183.
27 De' Maffei, "Il Ritratto di Giuliano, Fratello di Leone X, Dipinto da Raffaello."
28 Zeri, *Italian Paintings*, 79.
29 Langdon, *Medici Women*, 110.
30 Henry and Joannides, *Late Raphael*, 264.
31 Gamba, *Raphaël*, 103 [Castel conceived by someone other than Raphael]; Oskar Fischel, "Santi (Sanzio), Raffaello," in Thieme, Becker, and Vollmer, eds., *Allgemeines Lexikon der bildenden Künstler*, 29:439 [Castel obviously a later addition]; and idem, *Raphael*, 1:114, 365 [completely foreign to Raphael]; Ortolani, *Raffaello*, 59 [Castel added by copyist].
32 Meyer zur Capellen, *The Roman Portraits*, 9.
33 Henry and Joannides (*Late Raphael*, 292) have proposed that the Louvre picture represents the second of two portraits of Castiglione by Raphael, painted in 1519, and that the earlier version referenced by Bembo is now lost.
34 Meyer zur Capellen, *The Roman Portraits*, 15–16.
35 Ibid., 183.
36 Jenkins, *The State Portrait Its Origin and Evolution*, 11.
37 Cerretani (Berti, ed.), *Dialogo della Mutatione*, 77.
38 Henry and Joannides, *Late Raphael*, 264.
39 "calze fatte alla divisa del comune, bianca e rossa." Nardi, *Istorie*, 2:8.
40 Pucci reassured the cardinal: "Che non credeva vi fosse deformità e poco impedimento ... non appariva." Fatini, "Giuliano de' Medici," xi.
41 For a further discussion, see Weisz et al., "Who Was Pontormo's Halberdier?"
42 Falomir, "Court Portrait," 72.
43 Zeri, *Italian Paintings*, 79; Jones and Penny, *Raphael*, 162; Meyer zur Capellen, *The Roman Portraits*, 15.
44 Sanudo, *Diarii*, 20:363; Fatini, "Giuliano de' Medici," lxxxi.
45 Chambers, *Popes, Cardinals and War*, 28.
46 Langedijk, *Portraits of the Medici*, 1:57, 2:1049.
47 Fatini, "Giuliano de' Medici," lxxxii.
48 Sanudo, *Diarii*, 20:363.
49 D'Onofrio, *Castel S. Angelo*, 7–8.
50 Ibid., 30.
51 Sacerdote, *Cesare Borgia*, 686.
52 Howe, "Via Alessandrina," 62–72.

53 Petrucci, "L'Apertura della Via Alessandrina," 34–5.
54 Machiavelli (Bondanella, ed.), *Prince*, 41. See also Pellerin, "Machiavelli's Best Fiend," 423–53.
55 Machiavelli (Bondanella, ed.), *Prince*, 42.
56 Ibid.
57 Ibid., 42–3.
58 Ibid., 50.

CHAPTER 10

1 McManamon, "Marketing a Medici Regime," 1.
2 "si soppellì in S. Lorenzo, con una honoranza, che per insino a oggi non fu mai in Firenze fatta a uomo nessuno la simile." Cambi, *Istorie Fiorentine*, 3:93.
3 McManamon, "Marketing a Medici Regime," 1.
4 "scrive che il magnifico Juliano, come scrisse, partito di Roma, andò a Ugubio per esser a parlamento col ducha di Urbin, et cussì fue, persuadendolo a esser italian e non francese." Sanudo, *Diarii*, 20:383; Fatini, "Giuliano de' Medici," lxxxii.
5 Dialogo Giraldi, Vat. Ottob. MS 3153, trans. in Dennistoun, *Memoirs*, 2:361; Cartwright, *Baldassare Castiglione*, 1:400.
6 Dennistoun, *Memoirs*, 2:315.
7 Boulton, *Knights of the Crown*, 443–7.
8 Clough, "Clement VII," 78, 80, 82.
9 "el qual voleva menar il Magnifico a Urbin e preparava di honorarlo assai et veniva con 100 cavali solamente; ma sopravene do stafete del Papa, che fo causa il Magnifico mulasse il camin verso Roma, sichè non andò più di longo. Si dize, inteso la resolution dil prefato Ducha, non volesse altro; el qual Magnifico è a Viterbo." Sanudo, *Diarii*, 20:383; Fatini, "Giuliano de' Medici," lxxxii.
10 Butters, *Governors and Government*, 268.
11 Clough, "Clement VII," 82.
12 Pastor, *History of the Popes*, 7:111–12.
13 Bullard, *Filippo Strozzi*, 83; Devonshire Jones, *Francesco Vettori*, 112.
14 Giorgetti, "Lorenzo de' Medici," 194–215.
15 Devonshire Jones, *Francesco Vettori*, 112. Lorenzo was allotted 250 soldiers for his own personal guard and the further 250 soldiers of the Signoria also came under his command. See Cambi, *Istorie Fiorentine*, 3:67.
16 Trexler and Lewis, "New Light on the Medici Chapel," 102.
17 Giorgetti, "Lorenzo de' Medici," 209, 314–16.
18 Devonshire Jones, *Francesco Vettori*, 112.
19 Bullard, *Filippo Strozzi*, 85.
20 Frick, *Dressing Renaissance Florence*, 93, 113, 167.
21 Bullard, *Filippo Strozzi*, 88.
22 Butters, *Governors and Government*, 265–6.
23 Ibid.

24 Ibid.

25 "li amici dicevon che gli era ben fatto, e che meglio era dare i denari a noi medesimi che a Francia et altri conduttieri." Cerretani (Berti, ed.), *Dialogo della Mutatione*, 68.

26 Cambi, *Istorie Fiorentine*, 3:67.

27 Nerli, *Commentari*, 129.

28 "La qual cosa, come privò la ciptà di tutti la authorità et forze che appena gli erono restate, cosí ancora a lui tanta riputatione attribuí, che pareva che legitimamente non si potessi alle sua voluntà et imprese contradire." N. Guicciardini "Discorso," 369.

29 Stephens, *Fall of the Republic*, 99.

30 Nerli, *Commentari*, 130.

31 Fatini, "Giuliano de' Medici," lxxxii.

32 Tomas, "Alfonsina Orsini," 77. Landucci (*Diary*, 278) noted that Alfonsina arrived in Florence on 4 June 1515.

33 "et di poi, con ogni quiete et restauratione, ripigliare le forze del corpo." Guasti, *I Manoscritti Torrigiani*, 77. Sanudo reports receiving a notice of Giuliano's fever two days earlier, on 18 July. See Sanudo, *Diarii*, 22:406.

34 "che questo poco suo male, dal fastidio in fori, non interromperà alcuno disegno publico o privato di N. S. o vostro." Guasti, *I Manoscritti Torrigiani*, 78.

35 "Et quando pure la indispositione fussi più lunga (che Dio ne guardi) che non vuole la ragione, ad ogni modo sarebbe a tempo ad trovarvi in Lombardia, quando bene fussi necessità farvi portare in lettica, in convalescentia vostra: benchè le imprese si vanno tanto differendo, et N. S. non vuole fare cosa alcuna sanza la presentia vostra." Ibid.

36 "el Papa havea disegnato mandare in campo el Cardinale de' Medici Legato, et domattina era l'ordine di crearlo et publicarlo; stando fermo nel proposito che il Magnifico Lorenzo non partissi di Firenze, et parendoli che li condoctieri non habbino ad fare difficultà di obedire a uno Legato … come la Excellentia del Signore era forte migliorato, et speravono in brevi dì potessi cavalcare … et se per di quì a domatttina venissino lettere et confirmassino questo miglioramento, non si farebbe electione di Legato." Ibid., 79. Fatini, "Giuliano de' Medici," lxxxvi, records that Philiberte was finally given permission by the pope to visit her husband in Florence and she arrived with the legate on 14 August.

37 "Hiersera si spacciò in diligentia al Duca d'Urbino, che non tardassi più; et se la Excellentia Sua non servirà come è il debito suo et la speranza che havea N. S., dubito, ne la gratia di Sua Santità non vadi da extremo a extremo; perchè move troppe difficultà et tiene la cosa in lungo et dà parole. Et come, per le offerte et bona dispositione che a li giorni passati et prefato Duca havea facto et dimostro a Sua Santità et a la Excellentia V., havea guadagnato el Papa; se li effecti non corresponderanno, verrà in tanta indignatione, che Dio vogli non sia la ruina sua. Io non vi scrivo a caso; et però, se la Excellentia V. lo ama o desidera la

conservatione sua, li scriva subito che non tardi più ad servire Sancta Chiesa." Guasti, *I Manoscritti Torrigiani*, 80.

38 "che le cose non scorressino tanto avanti che la piaga diventasse incurabile." Da Camogli, *Leone X e la Geo-Politica dello Stato Pontificio*, 123.

39 "Et come noi crediamo che la maggior parte de la nostra infirmità sia proceduta da dispiacere preso per non vedere unito el papa con Sua Maestà per la servitù et affinità che habbiamo con quella, cosi confidiamo che se lo accordo seguisse, il contento che ne sentiremo saria la salutare medicina d'ogni nostra indispositione." Nitti, "Documenti ed osservasioni," 216.

40 Ibid., 217.

41 Butters, *Governors and Government*, 272.

42 Pastor, *History of the Popes*, 7:127.

43 Gattoni da Camogli, *Leone X e la Geo-Politica dello Stato Pontificio*, 127n.89.

44 "en considération de l'alliance nouvellement conclue entre François Ier et le pape Léon X." Académie des sciences morales et politiques, *Catalogue des actes de François Ier*, 64, no. 379. Following Giuliano's death, these rights were formally transferred to his widow on 12 November 1516; Stephens, *Fall of the Florentine Republic*, 101n.7.

45 Gattoni da Camogli, *Leone X e la Geo-Politica dello Stato Pontificio*, 132; Pastor, *History of the Popes*, 7:135–40.

46 For a summary of these sources, see Mitchell, *Italian Civic Pageantry*; Shearman, "Florentine *Entrata* of Leo X," 136n.2; Cox-Rearick, *Dynasty and Destiny*.

47 Shearman, "Florentine *Entrata* of Leo X," 144.

48 Ciseri, *L'Ingresso Trionfale*, 55–141.

49 Cox-Rearick, *Dynasty and Destiny*, 34–5, 98.

50 Ciseri, *L'Ingresso Trionfale*, 12–13.

51 "Voluimus nobilitatem tuam facere certiorem teque hortari et in domino require ut omne studium, atque omnem industriam, vimque animi et ingenii tui, que permagna est in eam curam conferre velis, ut nos et comitatus noster totus, qui et maximums et orbis terrarum clarissimus atque honoreficentissimus est omnibus, tam hospiciorum quam annone, et ceterarum rerum ad victum cultumque pertinentium non solum necessitatibus verum etiam commodiatibus ample, largitur, honesteque excipiatur." Ciseri, *L'Ingresso Trionfale*, 248. See also Tomas, *Medici Women*, 173.

52 Tomas, *Medici Women*, 173.

53 Ciseri, *L'Ingresso Trionfale*, 21, says that the Signoria waited for the pope's arrival at the Porta Romana, the normal route approaching Florence from Rome; however, the plan was changed to the gate of San Piero Gattolini because of last-minute difficulties with the Sienese. See Shearman, "The Florentine *Entrata* of Leo X," 149n.39.

54 Trexler, *Public Life in Renaissance Florence*, 500.

55 Ciseri, *L'Ingresso Trionfale*, 21.

56 Shearman, "The Florentine *Entrata* of Leo X," 152n.56.

57 Landucci, *Florentine Diary*, 279–80.
58 Ibid., 279.
59 Ibid., 285.
60 Ciseri, *L'Ingresso Trionfale*, 314.
61 Trexler, *Public Life in Renaissance Florence*, 500.
62 Ibid.
63 Pastor, *History of the Popes*, 7:133.
64 Ibid., 7:114-40; Simonetta, "Le Roi et l'Italie," 31–5.
65 Cambi, *Istorie Fiorentine*, 3:91.
66 Cerretani (Berti, ed.), *Dialogo della Metatione*, 76.
67 "Sextum lenones, Iul[i]um rexere cinedi; / imperium vani scurra Leonis habet. / Glandibus a pulcro consumptis robore quercus, / successere leves, quas creat ipsa, pilae. / Perdita libertas post hac, Florentia, nam te / femina ab Ursino sanguine sola regit. / Supplex ante aras petit, en, Florentia saepe / fiat uti mitra pontificum celebris. / Fit voti compos: crevit genus omne malorum; / grandia fert onera civis ubique suus. / [Iu]ra, magistratus patrii rapiuntur in horas; / ambitio, luxus, dira tyrannis adest." Translated by James Willis in Polizzotto, "The Making of a Saint," 363.
68 Clough, "Clement VII," 89 and n.62.
69 Gattoni da Camogli, *Leone X e la Geo-Politica dello Stato Pontificio*, 158.
70 Clough, "Clement VII," 85–6.
71 "Scrive, il Papa *omnino* ha terminato luor impresa contra il duca di Urbin, persuaso dal magnifico Lorenzin, *licet* il magnifico Juliano non voria per alcun modo, dicendo, quando i fono scaziati, da dito Ducha fo acetati et fatoli le spese. El qual Juliano, questi zorni de carlevar è sta malissimo; pur intrato in quaresema, sta meglio, e il Papa si doleva assai." Sanudo, *Diarii*, 21:510.
72 "Finito il parlamento in Bologna tra il Papa, e il Re, sene ritornò il Papa a Firenze quasi risoluto di contentare il nipote; pure procedeva nel muover tale impresa per conto di Giuliano con qualche rispetto; ma aggravando Giuliano nel male, si morì alla Badia di Fiesole, dove per migliorare aria s'era ritirato nel mese di Marzo del 1516." Nerli, *Commentari,* 130; Masi, *Ricordanze*, 196.
73 "che non credo che in Firenze restassi persona che non l'andassi a vedere; e non lo vedeva persona che non gli venissi voglia di piagniere." Masi, *Ricordanze*, 196.
74 Polizzotto, *Elect Nation*, 265.
75 Ibid.
76 Polizzotto, "The Making of a Saint," 362.
77 "Sollevarono queste così fatte predicazioni non solamente alcuni frati a predicare e pronunziare rinnovazioni e flagelli sopra la Chiesa, ma ogni dì surgevano monache, pinzochere, fanciulle, contadini, a fare lo simigliante, con attenzione di tutti quanti gl'animi torbidi." Pitti, *Istoria Fiorentina*, 119.
78 Polizzotto, "Prophecy, Politics and History," 107–31.
79 On Benivieni, see Re, *Girolamo Benivieni Fiorentino*; Polizzotto, *Elect Nation*, 141–6, 15–18, 248–50.

80 Polizzotto, *Elect Nation*, 143.

81 "Cum enim sol post MmDm XVm sex menses evolverit tunc erunt Italis peiora prioribus illata discrimina ... cum rex, ex meo genere per lineam directam progressus ... ut alter Hercules ad opus arduum cum multo militie progredientur ac tali vi actuque quod nullus ante eum rex unquam ausus fuerit non, ut multi putabunt, contra ius ecclesiae sed pro iure ecclesiastico ... Deinde fraudulentorum urbe capta. F. ingredietur, ibique magna civium perpetrata strage ipsam per 120 dies suae subiciet dictionj. Postmodum vero almum illum ducem quem quidam impij expulserunt proprio imperio restituetur. Interim totam Italiam devastabit, civitatisque civitatibus de bono regimine providebit. Ille autem qui Summus dicitur Sacerdos his auditis dolore vehementij animam exhalabit. Tanteque sanctitis creabitur Pastor qui cuncta per regem Francorum acta caelesti benedictione intuetur." University of Toronto Library, MS 5223, no. 7, fol. 2r, cited in Pugliese, "Franciscan Prophecy," 133. See also Jungić, "Savonarolan Prophecy in Leonardo's *Allegory*," 252–60.

82 Benivieni, *Opere*, 199–204.

83 Weinstein, *Savonarola and Florence*, 351.

84 Cerretani (Berti, ed.), *Dialogo della Mutatione*, 66.

85 Cambi, *Istorie Fiorentine*, 3:61–2.

86 Polizzotto, *Elect Nation*, 284.

87 Stephens, *Fall of the Florentine Republic*, 100.

88 Strocchia, *Death and Ritual*, 22.

89 Ibid.

90 Clough, "Clement VII," 89 and n.60.

91 Dennistoun, *Memoirs*, 2:361; Cartwright, *Baldassare Castiglione*, 1:400.

92 "E posti a sedere e prefati magistrati, uscì fuori Lorenzo col capperuccione inbastito, con tutta la famiglia del Duca e di madama vestita a nero con capperuccioni." Cerretani (Berti, ed.), *Dialogo della Mutatione*, 77.

93 "El mag.co Lorenzo a di 18 partì di qui con celerità grandissima, la causa etiam non si intese, ma fu ex abrupto." Quoted in Verdi, *Gli Ultimi Anni di Lorenzo*, 24–5n.7.

94 Verdi, *Gli Ultimi Anni di Lorenzo*, 24.

95 "Cum notitia in urbem pervenisset de obitu Juliani de Medicis fratris Papae, multi ex natione et ex familia Papae censebant tali in casu, cum ageretur de duce, de capitaneo generali Ecclesiae et de germano Papae, luctum generalem ostendi debere per vestes pullas longas assumendas cum caputiis, et per pubblicas et solemnes exequias. Verum aliter sentiebat Pontifex qui putavit neque ipsam suam familiam causam habere, ob quam ubique publica moestitiae indicia praeseferet, et solummodo annuit cardinales de Medicis aut Cibo, aut S. Mariae in porticu vel alium quamlibet consanguineum ex particulai affectu permotum, curare posse ut praesentibus suis, missa aliqua emortualis pro d. Juliano private tamen, et non publice celebraretur." Grassi, *Il Diario di Leone X*, 31–2.

96 McManamon, "Marketing a Medici Regime," 27–38.

97 Ibid., 4.

98 "licereque omnibus quod virtuti suae respondeat confidentius quarere – nuptias, magistratus, honores, clientelas, et imperia … dum licet in consortio et societate reipublicae esse et, quod aequae libertatis est, sortito et invicem annuis magistratibus parere atque imperitare, eo incrementi et gloriae res vestra erducta est ut rerum gestarum gloriae imperium accesserit." Ibid., 29–30.

99 "Cosmo, Medicae gentis ornamento omnium maxim …" Ibid., 30.

100 Ibid., 38.

101 Ibid., 13.

102 "Aderit nepoti suo quem non minore fortuna et gloria humana tractare voluit." Ibid., 37.

103 "Ite ergo et qua solitus in vita ille erat humanitate quae in eo civilis, prudentia quae paterna, consilio quod antiqu[u]um et domesticum, pietate vero quae propria in eo fuit, rempublicam vestram patriamque suam praecedere, humanitate pietateque … vos quod reliqu[u] ex eo nobis superest sequimini, optimum et maximum Deum precibus et lacrimis vestris exorantes, ut meliore loco constitutum adesse vobis ubique velit … Ite tandem qui ex tota republica cives huc venistis memineritisque semper civitatis et reipublicae vestrae fuisse hunc egregium ducem, cuius auspiciis foelicia semper et gloriosa omina fuerint." Ibid., 38.

104 "Nota la ruota di questo mondo, che tre mesi, e mezzo erano passati, che il Papa venne in Firenze con gran trionfo per portarossa, e per Merchato nuovo, e piazza de Signori, e da' fondamenti, e del chanto alla paglia, portato insur una barella con gran trionfo, e oggi el suo fratello charnale portato morto per la medesima via a riscontro di lui, ed era tutta la Ciptà a vederlo morto detto Giuliano, quanto a vedere il Papa vivo." Cambi, *Istorie Fiorentine*, 3:95.

BIBLIOGRAPHY

Académie des Sciences Morales et Politiques (France). *Catalogue des Actes de François I.* Vol. 1, *1515–1530*. Collection des Ordonnances des Rois de France. Paris: Imprimerie Nationale 1887.

Achillini, Giovanni Filoteo. *Collettanee Grece, Latine, e Vulgari per Diversi Auctori Moderni, nella Morte del l'Adente Seraphino Aquilano*. Bologna: Caligula Bazaliero 1504.

Ady, Cecilia M. *The Bentivoglio of Bologna: A Study in Despotism*. Oxford: Oxford University Press 1937. Repr. 1969.

Alberigo, Giuseppe. "The Reform of the Episcopate in the Libellus to Leo X by the Camaldolese Hermits Vincenzo Querini and Tommaso Giustiniani." In Christopher M. Bellitto and Louis I. Hamilton, eds., *Reforming the Church before Modernity: Patterns, Problems, and Approaches*. Aldershot, UK, and Burlington, VT: Ashgate 2005. 139–52.

– "Sul *Libellus ad Leonem X* degli Eremiti Camaldolesi: Vincenzo Querini e Tommaso Giustiniani." In Patrick Gilli, ed., *Humanisme et Église en Italie et en France Méridionale: XVe Siècle – Milieu du XVIe Siècle*. Rome: École Française de Rome 2004. 349–59.

Albertini, Rudolf von. *Firenze dalla Repubblica al Principato. Storia e Coscienza Politica*. Turin: Giulio Einaudi 1970.

Allen, Michael J.B., Valery Rees, and Martin Davis, eds. *Marsilio Ficino: His Theology, His Philosophy, His Legacy*. Leiden: Brill 2001.

Altieri, Marco Antonio. *Giuliano de' Medici, Eletto Cittadino Romano Ovvero il Natale di Roma nel 1513*. Edited by Loreto Pasqualucci. Rome: Artero 1881.

Alvisi, Edoardo. *Cesare Borgia: Duca di Romagna: Notizie e Documenti*. Imola: Tip. d'Ignazio Galeati e Figlio 1878.

Anderson, Jaynie. "Altobello Melone, *Portrait of a Gentleman (Cesare Borgia?)*." In Ron Radford, ed., *Renaissance: 15th and 16th Century Italian Paintings from the Accademia Carrara, Bergamo*. Canberra: National Gallery of Australia 2011. 186.

Angiolini, Enrico. "La Politica dei Borgia in Romagna." In Carla Frova and M. Grazia Nico Ottaviani, eds., *Alessandro VI e lo Stato della Chiesa*. Rome: Ministero per i Beni e le Attività Culturali, Direzione Generale per gli Archivi, 2003. 147–74.

Apuleius. *Apologia*. Translated by H.E. Butler. Oxford: Clarendon Press 1909.

Arrighi, Vanna. "Giacomini Tebalducci, Antonio." In *Dizionario Biografico degli Italiani*. Vol. 54. Rome: Istituto della Enciclopedia Italiana 2000.

– "Giovanni Folchi." In *Dizionario Biografico degli Italiani*. Vol. 48. Rome: Istituto della Enciclopedia Italiana 1997.

Atkinson, James B. "Niccolò Machiavelli: A Portrait." In John M. Najemy, ed., *The Cambridge Companion to Machiavelli*. Cambridge: Cambridge University Press 2010. 14–30.

Atkinson, James B., and David Sices, eds. *Machiavelli and His Friends: Their Personal Correspondence*. DeKalb: Northern Illinois University Press 1996.

Azzolini, Monica. "Anatomy of a Dispute: Leonardo, Pacioli and Scientific Courtly Entertainment in Renaissance Milan." *Early Science and Medicine* 9, no. 2 (2004): 115–35.

Baker, Nicholas Scott. *The Fruit of Liberty: Political Culture in the Florentine Renaissance, 1480–1550*. Cambridge, MA: Harvard University Press 2013.

– "For Reasons of State: Political Executions, Republicanism, and the Medici in Florence, 1480–1560." *Renaissance Quarterly* 62, no. 2 (2009): 444–78.

Bambach, Carmen C. "Leonardo and Raphael in Rome in 1513–16." In Miguel Falomir, ed., *Late Raphael: Proceedings of the International Symposium Actas del Congreso Internacional: Madrid. Museo Nacional del Prado. October 2012*. Turnhout, Belgium: Brepols 2013. 26–37.

– ed. *Leonardo da Vinci, Master Draftsman*. New Haven, CT, and London: Yale University Press 2003.

Baron, Hans. "The Principe and the Puzzle of the Date of Chapter 26." *Journal of Medieval and Renaissance Studies* 21, no. 1 (1991): 83–102.

Baumgartner, Frederic J. *Louis XII*. New York: St Martin's Press 1994.

Bausi, Francesco, "Jacopo Nardi, Lorenzo Duca d'Urbino e Machiavelli: L' 'Occasione' del 1518." *Interpres* 7 (1987): 191–204.

– *Machiavelli*. Rome: Salerno 2005.

Bayley, C.C. *War and Society in Renaissance Florence: The* De Militia *of Leonardo Bruni*. Toronto: University of Toronto Press 1961.

Beatis, Antonio de. *The Travel Journal: Germany, Switzerland, the Low Countries, France and Italy*. Translated by J.R. Hale and J.M.A. Lindon. Edited by J.R. Hale. London: Hakluyt Society 1979.

Bembo, Pietro. *Pietro Bembo Lettere*. Edited by Ernesto Travi. 4 vols. Bologna: Commissione per i Testi di Lingua 1987–93.

– *Prose e Rime di Pietro Bembo*. Edited by Carlo Dionisotti. Turin: Unione Tipografico-Editrice Torinese 1960.

Benivieni, Girolamo. *Opere Novissamente Rivedute et da Molti Errori Espurgate con una Canzone della Amore Celeste et Divino, col Commento dello III: Conte Giovanni Pio Mirandolano Distinto in libri III*. Venice, 1522.

Berenson, Bernard. *Italian Pictures of the Renaissance: A List of the Principal Artists and Their Works, with an Index of Places*. Oxford: Clarendon Press 1932.

Black, Robert. "Machiavelli, Servant of the Florentine Republic." In Gisela Bock, Quentin Skinner, and Maurizio Viroli, eds., *Machiavelli and Republicanism*. Cambridge: Cambridge University Press 1993. 71–99.

Bock, Gisela, Quentin Skinner, and Maurizio Viroli, eds. *Machiavelli and Republicanism*. Cambridge: Cambridge University Press 1993.

Bode, Wilhelm von. *Die Sammlung Oscar Huldschinsky*. Frankfurt: Joseph Baer 1909.

Bolzoni, Lina. *Il Cuore di Cristallo: Ragionamenti d'Amore, Poesia, e Ritratto nel Rinascimento*. Turin: G. Einaudi 2010.

Boone, Rebecca Ard. *War, Domination, and the Monarchy of France: Claude de Seyssel and the Language of Politics in the Renaissance*. Leiden and Boston: Brill 2007.

Boulton, D'Arcy Jonathan Dacré. *The Knights of the Crown: The Monarchical Orders of Knighthood in Later Medieval Europe, 1325–1520*. Woodbridge, UK: Boydell 1987.

Bowd, Stephen D. *Reform before the Reformation: Vincenzo Querini and the Religious Renaissance in Italy*. Leiden: Brill 2002.

– "Swarming with Hermits: Religious Friendship in Renaissance Italy, 1490–1540." In Abigail Brundin and Matthew Treherne, eds., *Forms of Faith in Sixteenth-Century Italy: Culture and Religion*. Aldershot, UK, and Burlington, VT: Ashgate 2009. 9–31.

Bracciolini, Poggio. *Facezie di Poggio Fiorentino*. 2nd ed. Rome: Sommaruga 1885.

– "In Praise of the Venetian Republic." Translated by Martin Davies. In Jill Kraye, ed., *Cambridge Translations of Philosophical Texts*. Vol. 2, *Political Philosophy*. Cambridge: Cambridge University Press 1997. 135–45.

Braden, Gordon. *Petrarchan Love and the Continental Renaissance*. New Haven, CT, and London: Yale University Press 1999.

Brown, Alison. "Lorenzo and Public Opinion in Florence: The Problem of Opposition." In Gian Carlo Garfagnini, ed., *Lorenzo il Magnifico e il Suo Mondo*. Florence: L.S. Olschki 1994. 61–85.

– "Public and Private Interest: Lorenzo, the Monte and the Seventeen Reformers." In Gian Carlo Garfagnini, ed., *Lorenzo de' Medici: Studi*. Florence: L.S. Olschk 1992. 103–42.

– "The Revolution of 1494 in Florence and Its Aftermath: A Reassessment." In J.E. Everson and Diego Zancani, eds., *Italy in Crisis: 1494*. Oxford: Legenda, 2000. 13–40.

Brown, David Allen. *Virtue and Beauty: Leonardo's Ginevra de' Benci and Renaissance Portraits of Women*. Washington, DC: National Gallery of Art 2001.

Brundin, Abigail, and Matthew Treherne, eds. *Forms of Faith in Sixteenth-Century Italy: Culture and Religion*. Aldershot, UK, and Burlington, VT: Ashgate 2009.

Bullard, Melissa Meriam. *Filippo Strozzi and the Medici: Favor and Finance in Sixteenth-Century Florence and Rome*. Cambridge: Cambridge University Press 1980.

– *Lorenzo il Magnifico: Image and Anxiety, Politics and Finance*. Florence: L.S. Olschki 1994.

Buonaccorsi, Biagio. *Diario dall'Anno 1498 all'Anno 1512 e Altri Scritti*. Edited by Enrico Niccolini. Rome: Istituto Palazzo Borromini 1999.

Buonarroti, Michelangelo. *Il Carteggio Indiretto di Michelangelo*. Edited by Paola Barocchi, Kathleen Loach Bramanti, and Renzo Ristori. Florence: SPES 1988.

– *Il Carteggio di Michelangelo*. Vol. 1. *Lettere di Michelangelo e Suoi Corrispondenti dal 2 Luglio 1496 al 27 Aprile 1518*. Edited by Paola Barrochi and Renzo Ristori. Florence: Sansoni 1965.
– *Complete Poems and Selected Letters of Michelangelo*. Translated by Creighton Gilbert. Edited by Robert N. Linscott. 3rd ed. Princeton, NJ: Princeton University Press 1980.
Burchard, Johann. *At the Court of the Borgia*. Translated by Geoffrey Parker. London: Folio Society 1963.
Butters, Humfrey C. *Governors and Government in Early Sixteenth-Century Florence, 1502–1519*. Oxford: Clarendon Press 1985.
– "Machiavelli and the Medici." In John M. Najemy, ed., *The Cambridge Companion to Machiavelli*. Cambridge: Cambridge University Press 2010. 64–79.
Caby, Cécile. *De l'Erémitisme Rural au Monachisme Urbain: Les Camaldules en Italie à la Fin du Moyen Âge*. Rome: Ecole Française de Rome 1999.
Calitti, Floriana. "Pier Francesco Giustolo." *Dizionario Biografico degli Italiani*. Vol. 57. Rome: Istituto della Enciclopedia Iitaliana 2001.
Calmeta, Vincenzo. *Prose e Lettere Edite e Inedite: Con due Appendici di Altri Inediti*. Edited by Cecil Grayson. Bologna: Commisione per i Testi di Lingua 1959.
Cambi, Giovanni. *Istorie di Giovanni Cambi Cittadino Fiorentino* Pubblicate*, e di Annotazioni, e di Antichi Munimenti Accresciute, ed Illustrate da Fr. Ildefonso di San Luigi*. 4 vols. Florence: G. Cambiagi 1785–86.
Campbell, Lorne. *Renaissance Portraits: European Portrait Painting*. New Haven, CT, and London: Yale University Press 1990.
Campbell, Lorne, and Philip Attwood, eds. *Renaissance Faces: Van Eyck to Titian*. London: National Gallery 2008.
Campioni, Rosaria, ed. *Leonardo Artista delle Macchine e Cartografo*. Florence: Giunti 1994.
Cartwright, Julia. *Isabella d'Este Marchioness of Mantua 1474–1539: A Study of the Renaissance*. 2 vols. London: John Murray 1915.
– *Perfect Courtier: Baldassare Castiglione, His Life and Letters, 1478–1529*. 2 vols. London: John Murray 1908.
Castiglione, Baldassare. *The Book of the Courtier*. Translated by Charles S. Singleton. New York: Anchor Books 1959.
– *Il Cortegiano con una Scelta della Opere Minori*. Edited by Bruno Maier. Turin: Unione Tipografico-Editrice Torinese 1955.
Cavicchi, Filippo. "Girolamo da Casio (1464–1533)." *Giornale Storico della Letteratura Italiana* 66 (1915).
Caviglia, Alberto. *Claudio di Seyssel (1450–1520): La Vita nella Storia de' Suoi Tempi*. Miscellanea di Storia Italiana, 3 ser. Vol. 23. Turin: Bocca 1928.
Cermenati, Mario. "Leonardo a Roma." *Nuova Antologia*, 6th ser., 202 (1919): 308–31.
Cerretani, Bartolomeo. *Dialogo della Mutatione di Firenze*. Edited by Giuliana Berti. Florence: L.S. Olschki 1993.
– *Dialogo della Mutatione di Firenze*. Edited by Raul Mordenti. Rome: Edizioni di Storia e Letteratura 1990.

– *Ricordi*. Edited by Giuliana Berti. Florence: L.S. Olschki 1993.

– *Storia Fiorentina*. Edited by Giuliana Berti. Florence: L.S. Olschki 1994.

Chambers, David Sanderson. *Patrons and Artists in the Italian Renaissance*. London and Basingstoke, UK: Macmillan 1970.

– *Popes, Cardinals and War: The Military Church in Renaissance and Early Modern Europe*. London and New York: I.B. Tauris 2006.

Chapman, Hugo, Tom Henry, and Carol Plazzotta. *Raphael from Urbino to Rome*. London: National Gallery Company and Yale University Press 2004.

Chiabò, Maria, ed. *Roma di Fronte all' Europa al Tempo di Alessandro VI: Atti del Convegno (Città del Vaticano – Roma, 1–4 dicembre 1999)*. 3 vols. Rome: Ministero per i Beni e le Attività Culturali, Direzione Generale per gli Archivi, 2001.

Christian, Kathleen Wren, and David J. Drogin, eds. *Patronage and Italian Renaissance Sculpture*. Surrey, UK, and Burlington, VT: Ashgate 2010.

Cian, Vittorio. "Per Bernardo Bembo: Le Sue Relazioni coi Medici." *Giornale Storico della Letteratura Italiana* 28 (1910): 348–64.

– *Un Illustre Nunzio Pontificio del Rinascimento: Baldassar Castiglione*. Città del Vaticano: Biblioteca Apostolica Vaticana 1951.

– *Musa Medicea: Di Giuliano di Lorenzo de' Medici e delle Sue Rime Inedite*. Turin: Baglione 1895.

Cicero. *De officiis*. Translated by Walter Miller. London: William Heinemann 1928.

Ciseri, Ilaria. *L'Ingresso Trionfale di Leone X nel 1515*. Florence: L.S. Olschki 1990.

Clagett, Marshall. *Archimedes in the Middle Ages*. Vol. 3.3. *The Medieval Archimedes in the Renaissance, 1450–1565*. Philadelphia: American Philosophical Society 1978.

Clark, Kenneth. *Leonardo da Vinci: An Account of His Development as an Artist*. Middlesex, UK: Penguin 1967.

Clayton, Martin. *Leonardo da Vinci: A Curious Vision*. London: Merell Holberton 1996.

– *Leonardo da Vinci: The Divine and the Grotesque*. London: Royal Collection 2003.

Clough, Cecil H. "Clement VII and Francesco Maria Della Rovere, Duke of Urbino." In Kenneth Gouwens and Sheryl E. Reiss, eds., *The Pontificate of Clement VII: History, Politics, Culture*. Aldershot, UK, and Burlington, VT: Ashgate 2005. 75–108.

– *Machiavelli Researches*. Naples: Istituto Universitario Orientale 1967.

– "Yet Again Machiavelli's Prince." *Annali dell'Istituto Universitario Orientale, sez. romanza* 5 (1963): 201–26.

Coffin, David R. *The Villa in the Life of Renaissance Rome*. Princeton, NJ: Princeton University Press 1979.

"Collectors' Questions: A Young Medici." *Country Life* (6 April 1967): 770.

Connell, William J. "New Light on Machiavelli's Letter to Vettori 10 December 1513." In Paola Guglielmotti, ed., *Europa e Italia: Studi in Onore di Giorgio Chittolini*. Florence: Florence University Press 2011. 93–127.

– ed. *The Prince by Niccolò Machiavelli with Related Documents*. Boston: Bedford/St Martin's 2005.

Cotton, Juliana Hill. "Il Lucco del Poliziano ed Altre Allusioni al Lucco Fiorentino." *Italica* 32, no. 1 (1966): 353–67.

Cox-Rearick, Janet. *Dynasty and Destiny in Medici Art: Pontormo, Leo X, and the Two Cosimos*. Princeton, NJ: Princeton University Press 1984.
Coyle, Martin, ed. *Niccolò Machiavelli's* The Prince*: New Interdisciplinary Essays*. Manchester, UK: Manchester University Press 1995.
Coyle, Martin, and Anthony M. Cummings. *The Politicized Muse: Music for Medici Festivals, 1512–1537*. Princeton, NJ: Princeton University Press 1992.
Danzi, Massimo. *La Biblioteca del Cardinal Pietro Bembo*. Geneva and Paris: Droz 2005.
Dean, Trevor, and Kate J.P. Lowe, eds. *Crime, Society and the Law in Renaissance Italy*. Cambridge: Cambridge University Press 1994.
De Grazia, Sebastian. *Machiavelli in Hell*. Princeton, NJ: Princeton University Press 1989.
De' Maffei, Fernanda. "Il Ritratto di Giuliano, Fratello di Leone X, Dipinto da Raffaello." *L'Arte*, new ser. 24, no. 4 (1959): 309–36.
De Matteis, Maria Consiglia. "Alessandro VI: Alle Origini di un Mito Negativo." In Maria Chiabò, ed., *Roma di Fronte all'Europa al Tempo di Alessandro VI*. Rome: Ministero per i Beni e le Attività Culturali, Direzione Generale per gli Archivi, 2001. 85–97.
Denley, Peter, and Caroline Elam, eds. *Florence and Italy: Renaissance Studies in Honour of Nicolai Rubinstein*. London: Committee for Medieval Studies, Westfield College, 1988.
Dennistoun, James. *Memoirs of the Dukes of Urbino: Illustrating the Arms, Arts and Literature of Italy, 1440–1630*. 3 vols. London: John Lane the Bodley Head 1909.
D'Onofrio, Cesare. *Castel S. Angelo: Images and History*. Rome: Romana Società Editrice 1984.
De Tolnay, Charles. *Michelangelo*. Vol. 3, *The Medici Chapel*. Princeton, NJ: Princeton University Press 1970.
De Tolnay, Charles, and Paola Squellati Brizio. *Michelangelo e i Medici*. Florence: Centro Di 1980.
De Vecchi, Pierluigi. *Raffaello, la Pittura*. Firenze: Giunti Martello 1981.
– *Raphael*. New York and London: Abbeville Press 2002.
Devonshire Jones, Rosemary. *Francesco Vettori: Florentine Citizen and Medici Servant*. London: University of London 1972.
Dionisotti, Carlo. *Machiavellerie: Storia e Fortuna di Machiavelli*. Turin: Einaudi 1980.
– "Pietro Bembo." *Dizionario Biografico degli Italiani*. Vol. 8 (1966).
Dizionario Biografico degli Italiani. 83 vols. Rome: Istituto della Enciclopedia Italiana 1960–2015.
Dorfman, John. "The 'Mona Lisa': Case Closed." *Art and Antiques* 32, no. 3 (2008): 39.
Dotti, Ugo. *Machiavelli Rivoluzionario: Vita e Opere*. Rome: Carocci 2003.
Dovizi, Bernardo. *Epistolario di Bernardo Dovizi da Bibbiena*. Edited by Giuseppe L. Moncallero. 2 vols. Florence: L.S. Olschki 1955–65.
Dupré, Sven. "Optics, Pictures and Evidence: Leonardo's Drawings of Mirrors and Machinery." *Early Science and Medicine* 10, no. 2 (2005): 211–36.
Elam, Caroline. "Lorenzo de' Medici's Sculpture Garden." *Mitteilungen des Kunthistorischen Institutes in Florenz* 36 (1992): 41–84.

Everson, Jane E., and Diego Zancani, eds. *Italy in Crisis, 1494*. Oxford: European Humanities Research Centre 2000.

Falomir, Miguel. "The Court Portrait." In Lorne Campbell and Philip Atwood, eds., *Renaissance Faces: Van Eyck to Titian*. London: National Gallery 2008. 66–82.

Fatini, Giuseppe. "Di Giuliano de'Medici Duca di Nemours e delle Sue Poesie (1479–1516): Cenni Biografici." In *Poesie* by Giuliano de' Medici. Florence: Le Monnier 1939. vii–xcvi.

Ferrajoli, Alessandro. *Il Ruolo della Corte di Leone X (1514–1516)*. Edited by Vincenzo De Caprio. Rome: Bulzoni 1984.

Ficino, Marsilio. *Le Lettere (1499–1513)*. Edited by Pierre Jodogne. 10 vols. Rome: Istituto Storico Italiano 1986.

– *The Letters of Marsilio Ficino*. Translated by members of the Language Department of the School of Economic Science. 7 vols. London: Shepherd-Walwyn 1978.

Finlay, Robert. "The Immortal Republic: The Myth of Venice during the Italian Wars (1494–1530)." *Sixteenth Century Journal* 30, no. 4 (1999): 931–44.

Firenze e la Toscana dei Medici nell'Europa del' 500. 3 vols. Florence: L.S. Olschki 1983.

Fischel, Oskar. "Porträts des Giuliano de' Medici, Herzogs von Nemours." *Jahrbuch der königlich preuszischen Kunstsammlungen* 28 (1907): 117–30.

– "Santi (Sanzio), Raffaello." In Ulrich Thieme and Felix Becker, eds., *Allgemeines Lexikon der Bildenden Künstler von der Antike bis zur Gegenwart*. Leipzig: Seemann 1935. 29:433–46.

– *Raphael*. London: K. Paul 1948.

Floriani, Piero. *I Gentiluomini Letterati: Studi sul Dibattio Culturale nel Primo Cinquecento*. Naples: Ligouri 1981.

Fosi, Irene, and Guido Rebecchini. "Ippolito de' Medici." *Dizionario Biografico degli Italiani*. Vol. 73, 2009.

Frazier, Alison Knowles. "Luca Della Robbia's Narrative on the Execution of Pietro Paolo Boscoli and Agostino Capponi." In Nicholas Terpstra, ed., *The Art of Executing Well: Rituals of Execution in Renaissance Italy*. Kirksville, MO: Truman State University Press 2008. 293–326.

Fredona, Robert. "Carnival of Law: Bartolomeo Scala's Dialogue *De Legibus et Iudiciis*." *Viator* 39, no. 2 (2008): 193–214.

Freedberg, Sydney J. *Painting of the High Renaissance in Rome and Florence*. Cambridge, MA: Harvard University Press 1961.

Frick, Carole Collier. *Dressing Renaissance Florence: Families, Fortunes, & Fine Clothing*. Baltimore, MD, and London: Johns Hopkins University Press 2002.

Frova, Carla, Maria Grazia, and Nico Ottaviani, eds. *Alessandro VI e lo Stato della Chiesa*. Rome: Ministero per I Beni e le Attività Culturali, Direzione per gli Archivi, 2003.

Fubini, Riccardo. "Postilla ai 'Tordi.'" *Archivio Storico Italiano* 156, no. 1 (1998): 93–6.

Fuller, Timothy, ed. *Machiavelli's Legacy:* The Prince *after Five Hundred Years*. Philadelphia: University of Pennsylvania Press 2016.

Galluzzi, Paolo. *Renaissance Engineers: From Brunelleschi to Leonardo da Vinci*. Florence: Istituto e Museo di Storia della Scienza 1996.

Gamba, Carlo. *Raphaël*. Paris: Crès 1932.

Gar, Tommaso. "Documenti Eiguardanti Giuliano de' Medici e il Pontefice Leone X." *Archivio Storico Italiano* 1, appendix (1842–44): 291–324.

– ed. "Instructione al Magnifico Lorenzo." In "Documenti Riguardanti Giuliano de' Medici e il Pontefice Leone X." *Archivio Storico Italiano* 1, appendix (1842–44): 291–324.

Garfagnini, Gian Carlo. *Lorenzo il Magnifico e il Suo Mondo: Convegno Internazionale di Studi (Firenze, 9–13 Giugno 1992)*. Florence: L.S. Olschki 1994.

– *Lorenzo de' Medici: Studi*. Florence: L.S. Olschki 1992.

Gattoni da Camogli, Maurizio. *Leone X e la Geo-Politica dello Stato Pontificio, 1513–1521*. Città del Vaticano: Archivio Segreto Vaticano 2000.

Giannetto, Nella. *Bernardo Bembo, Umanista e Politico Veneziano*. Florence: L.S. Olschki 1985.

Gilbert, Allan H. *Machiavelli's Prince and Its Forerunners: The Prince as a Typical Book de Regimine Principum*. New York: Barnes and Noble 1938. Repr. 1968.

Gilbert, Allan H., trans. *Machiavelli: The Chief Works and Others*. 3 vols. Durham, NC, and London: Duke University Press 1989.

Gilbert, Creighton. "Texts and Contexts of the Medici Chapel." *Art Quarterly* 34, no. 4 (1971): 391–410.

Gilbert, Felix. "Bernardo Rucellai and the Orti Oricellari: A Study on the Origin of Modern Political Thought." *Journal of the Warburg and Courtauld Institutes* 12 (1949): 101–31.

– "Cristianesimo, Umanesimo e la Bolla 'Apostolici Regiminis' del 1513." *Rivista Storica Italiania* 79, no. 4 (1967): 976–90.

– *Machiavelli and Guicciardini: Politics and History in Sixteenth Century Florence*. Princeton, NJ: Princeton University Press 1965.

– "The Venetian Constitution in Florentine Political Thought." In Nicolai Rubinstein, ed., *Florentine Studies: Politics and Society in Renaissance Florence*. Evanston, IL: Northwestern University Press 1968. 463–500.

Gilli, Patrick, ed. *Humanisme et Eglise en Italie et en France Méridionale: XVe Siècle – Milieu du XVIe Siècle*. Rome: Ecole Française 2004.

Giorgetti, Alceste. "Lorenzo de' Medici, Capitano Generale della Repubblica Fiorentina." *Archivio Storico Italiano*, 4th ser. 11 (1883): 194–215.

Giuliani, Luca. "Kästchen oder Quader? Zur Sizstatue des Lorenzo de'Medici in der Sagrestia Nuova und zum Problem der Materialität in den Skulpturen Michelangelos." *Mitteilungen des Kunsthistorischen Institutes in Florenz* 55, no. 3 (2013): 334–57.

Godman, Peter. *From Poliziano to Machiavelli: Florentine Humanism in the High Renaissance*. Princeton, NJ: Princeton University Press 1998.

Golzio, Vincenzo. *Raffaello nei Documenti nelle Testimonianze dei Contemporanei e Nella Letteratura del Suo Secolo*. Rome: Città del Vaticano 1936.

Gombrich, E.H. *Norm and Form: Studies in the Art of the Renaissance*. London: Phaidon 1966.

Gouwens, Kenneth, and Sheryl E. Reiss, eds. *The Pontificate of Clement VII: History, Politics, Culture*. Aldershot, UK, and Burlington, VT: Ashgate 2005.

Grassi, Paride de. *Il Diario di Leone X di Paride de Grass i … dai Volumi Manoscritti dagli Archivi Vaticani dell S. Sede, con Note di M. Armellini. Mons. Pio Delicati*. Rome: Tipografia F. Cuggiani 1884.

Grimm, Herman. *Life of Michael Angelo*. Translated by Fanny Elizabeth Bunnett. 2 vols. London: Smith, Elder 1865.

Guasti, Cesare. *I Manoscritti Torrigiani Donati al R. Archivio di Stato di Firenze: Descrizione e Saggio*. Florence: M. Cellini 1878.

– *Il Sacco di Prato e il Ritorno de' Medici in Firenze nel MDXII*. 2 vols. 1880.

– "Una Scrittura di Niccolò Machiavelli Sinora Inedita: Ricordo a' Palleschi 1512." *Archivio Storico Italiano*, 3rd ser. 7, no. 1 (1868): 182–5.

– ed. "I Manoscritti Torrigiani Donati al R. Archivio Centrale di Stato di Firenze." *Archivio Storico Italiano*, 3rd. ser. 19 (1874): 221–53.

Guicciardini, Francesco. *The History of Florence*. Translated by Mario Domandi. New York and London: Harper and Row 1970.

– *The History of Italy*. Edited by Sidney Alexander. New York: Macmillan 1969.

– *Le Lettere (1499–1513)*. Edited by Pierre Jodogne. 10 vols. Rome: Istituto Storico Italiano 1986.

– *Scritti Autobiografici e Rari*. Edited by Roberto Palmarocchi. Bari: G. Laterza 1936.

– *Storia d'Italia*. Edited by Silvana Seidel Menchi. Turin: Einaudi 1971.

Guicciardini, Niccolò. "Discorso di Messer Niccolò Guicciardni del Modo del Procedere della Famiglia de' Medici in Firenze et del Fine Che Poteva Havere lo Stato di Quelle Famiglia." In Rudolf von Albertini, ed., *Firenze dalla Repubblica al Principato: Storia e Coscienza Politica*. Turin: Giulio Einaudi 1970. Appendix 3, 365–75.

Guidoni, Enrico, and Giulia Petrucci, eds. *Urbanistica per i Giubilei: Roma, Via Alessandrina, una Strada "Tra due Fondali" nell'Italia Delle Corti, 1492–1499*. Rome: Edizioni Kappa 1997.

Gullino, Giuseppe. "Girolamo Lippomano." *Dizionario Biografico degli Italiani*. Vol. 65. Rome: Istituto della Enciclopedia Italiana 2005.

Hale, J.R. *Florence and the Medici: The Pattern of Control*. London: Thames and Hudson 1977.

– *Machiavelli and Renaissance Italy*. London: English Universities Press 1961.

Henry, Tom, and Paul Joannides, eds. *Late Raphael*. London: Thames and Hudson 2013.

Herlihy, David, et al., eds. *Florentine Renaissance Resources, Online Tratte of Office Holders, 1282–1532*. Machine readable data file. Florentine Renaissance Resources/STG: Providence, RI: Brown University 2002.

Heydenreich, Ludwig H., Bern Dibner, and Ladislau Reti, eds. *Leonardo the Inventor*. New York: McGraw-Hill 1980.

Hibbard, Howard. *Michelangelo*. 2nd ed. London: Folio Society 1974. Repr. 2007.

Hill, George F. *A Corpus of Italian Medals of the Renaissance before Cellini*. 2 vols. London: British Museum 1930.

Hill George F., and J. Graham Pollard. *Renaissance Medals from the Samuel H. Kress Collection at the National Gallery of Art*. Washington, DC, London, and New York, 1967.

Hollingsworth, Mary. *Patronage in Renaissance Italy from 1400 to the Early Sixteenth Century*. London: John Murray 1994.

Höper, Corinna, Wolfgang Brückle, and Udo Felbinger. *Raffael und die Folgen: Das Kunstwerk in Zeitaltern Seiner Graphischen Reproduzierbarkeit*. Ostfildern: Hatje Cantz 2001.

Hörnqvist, Mikael. "Approaching the Medici: Machiavelli as Co-Author of Paolo Vettori's *Ricordi* of 1512?" In David S. Peterson and Daniel E. Bornstein, eds., *Florence and Beyond: Culture, Society and Politics in Renaissance Italy*. Toronto: Centre for Reformation and Renaissance Studies 2008. 399–417.

Howe, Eunice D. "Alexander VI, Pinturicchio and the Fabrication of the Via Alessandrina in the Vatican Borgo." In Henry A. Millon, ed., *An Architectural Progress in the Renaissance and Baroque: Sojourns In and Out of Italy: Essays in Architectural History presented to Helmut Hager on His Sixty-Sixth Birthday*. University Park: Pennsylvania State University Press 1992. 62–72.

Hozier, Jean François Louis d', and Michel Popoff, eds. *Recueil Historique des Chevaliers de l'Ordre de Saint-Michel*. Vol. 1, *1469–1560*. Paris: Le Léopard d'Or 1998.

Hughes, R.J.F. "Francesco Vettori: His Place in Florentine Diplomacy and Politics." PhD thesis, University of London, 1958.

Hurtubise, Pierre. *Une Famille-Témoin: Les Salviati*. Città del Vaticano: Biblioteca Apostolica Vaticana 1985.

Iarocci, Irene. "Camillo Paleotti." *Dizionario Biografico degli Italiani*. Vol. 80. Rome: Istituto della Enciclopedia Italiana 2014.

Inglese, Giorgio. Review of *Opere, III: Lettere* by Niccolò Machiavelli, edited by Franco Gaeta. *La Bibliofilia* 86 (1984): 271–80.

Jaeckel, Hugo. "'Tordi e il Principe Nuovo': Note sulle Dediche del 'Principe' di Machiavelli a Giuliano e a Lorenzo de' Medici." *Archivio Storico* 156, no. 1 (1998): 73–92.

Jebb, Richard C. "The Classical Renaissance." *Metropolitan Museum of Art Bulletin*, new ser., 5, no. 3 (November 1946).

Jenkins, Marianna. *The State Portrait: Its Origin and Evolution*. New York: College Art Association of America 1947.

Johnson, Geraldine A. "The Lion on the Piazza: Patrician Politics and Public Statuary in Central Florence." In Phillip Lindley and Thomas Frangenberg, eds., *Secular Sculpture 1300–1550*. Stamford, UK: Shaun Tyas 2000. 54–73.

Jones, Lars, and Louisa Chevalier Matthew, eds. *Coming About – A Festschrift for John Shearman*. Cambridge, MA: Harvard University Art Museums 2000.

Jones, Roger, and Nicholas Penny. *Raphael*. New Haven, CT: Yale University Press 1983.

Jungić, Josephine. "Leonardo da Vinci in Rome: Meditations on the Sermons of Savonarola." *Raccolta Vinciana* 31 (2005): 184–214.

– "Prophecies of the Angelic Pastor in Sebastiano del Piombo's *Portrait of Cardinal Bandinello Sauli and Three Companions*." In Marjorie Reeves, ed., *Prophetic Rome in the High Renaissance Period*. Oxford: Clarendon Press 1992. 345–70.

– "Raphael at Bologna and Savonarola's Prophecies of a 'Renovatio Ecclesiae.'" *Art History* 16, no. 4 (1993): 580–99.

– "Savonarolan Prophecy in Leonardo's *Allegory with Wolf and Eagle.*" *Journal of the Warburg and Courtauld Institutes* 60 (1997): 253–60.

Jurdjevic, Mark. *Guardians of Republicanism: The Valori Family in the Florentine Renaissance*. Oxford: Oxford University Press 2008.

– Review of Dale Kent, *Friendship, Love, and Trust in Renaissance Florence*. In *Renaissance Quarterly* 62, no. 3 (2009): 960–2.

Kecks, Ronald G., ed. *Musagetes: Festschrift für Wolfram Prinz zu seinem 60. Geburtstag am 5. Februar 1989*. Berlin: Gebr. Mann 1991.

Kemp Martin. *Leonardo da Vinci*. London: South Bank Centre, Haywood Gallery, 1989.

– *Leonardo da Vinci: The Marvellous Works of Nature and Man*. Rev. ed. Oxford: Oxford University Press 2006.

Kent, Dale. *Cosimo de' Medici and the Florentine Renaissance: The Patron's Oeuvre*. New Haven, CT, and London: Yale University Press 2000.

– *Friendship, Love, and Trust in Renaissance Florence*. Cambridge, MA: Harvard University Press 2009.

Kent, F.W. "*Lorenzo … Amico degli Uomini da Bene*: Lorenzo de' Medici and Oligarchy." In Gian Carlo Garfagnini, ed., *Lorenzo Il Magnifico e il Suo Mondo*. Florence: L.S. Olschki 1994. 43–60.

Kidwell, Carol. *Pietro Bembo: Lover, Linguist, Cardinal*. Montreal and Kingston: McGill-Queen's University Press 2004.

King, Margaret L. *Venetian Humanism in an Age of Patrician Dominance*. Princeton, NJ: Princeton University Press 1986.

Knecht, R.J. *Renaissance Warrior and Patron: The Reign of Francis I*. Cambridge: Cambridge University Press 1994.

Knorr, Wilbur. "The Geometry of Burning-Mirrors in Antiquity." *Isis* 74, no. 1 (1983): 53–73.

Kolsky, Stephen D. "The Courtier as Critic: Vincenzo Calmeta's *Vita del Facondo Poeta Vulgare Serafino Aquilano*." In Stephen D. Kolsky, ed., *Courts and Courtiers in Renaissance Northern Italy*. Aldershot, UK, and Burlington, VT: Ashgate 2003. 161–72.

– ed. *Courts and Courtiers in Renaissance Northern Italy*. Aldershot, UK, and Burlington, VT: Ashgate 2003.

Kraye, Jill, ed. *Cambridge Companion to Renaissance Humanism*. Cambridge: Cambridge University Press 1996.

– ed. *Cambridge Translations of Renaissance Philosophical Texts*. 2 vols. Cambridge: Cambridge University Press 1997.

Lackner, Dennis F. "The Camaldolese Academy: Ambrogio Traversari, Marsilio Ficino and the Christian Platonic Tradition." In Michael J.B. Allen, Valery Rees, and Martin Davies, eds., *Marsilio Ficino: His Theology, His Philosophy, His Legacy*. Leiden: Brill 2002. 15–44.

Laird, W.R. "Archimedes among the Humanists." *Isis* 82, no. 4 (1991): 628–38.

Landucci, Luca. *A Florentine Diary from 1450 to 1516 by Luca Landucci, Continued by an Anonymous Writer till 1542*. Edited by Iodoco del Badia. Translated by Alice de Rosen Jervis. London: J.M. Dent 1927.

Langdon, Gabrielle. *Medici Women: Portraits of Power, Love and Betrayal from the Court of Duke Cosimo I*. Toronto: University of Toronto Press 2006.

Langedijk, Karla. *The Portraits of the Medici 15th–18th Centuries*. 3 vols. Florence: SPES 1981–87.

Laurenza, Domenico. *Leonardo nella Roma di Leone X (c. 1513–16): Gli Studi Anatomici, la Vita, l'Arte*. Florence: Giunti 2004.

Lecchini Giovannoni, Simona. "Alcune Proposte per l'Attività Ritrattistica di Alessandro Allori." *Antichità Viva* 7, no. 1 (1968): 48–57.

Lindley, Phillip and Thomas Frangenberg, eds. *Secular Sculpture 1300–1550*. Stamford, UK: Shaun Tyas 2000.

Liphart, Karl Eduard von. *Notice Historique sur un Tableau de Raphaël Représentant Julien de Médicis Duc de Nemours*. Paris: Claye 1867.

Londei, Enrico Ferdinando. "I Progetti Leonardiani di Macchine Scavatrici per il Canale di Cesena per Cesare Borgia." In Carlo Pedretti and Learco Andalò, eds., *Leonardo, Machiavelli, Cesare Borgia: Arte Storia e Scienza in Romagna 1500–1503*. Rome: De Luca 2003. 55–71.

Lowe, Kate J.P. "An Alternative Account of the Alleged Cardinals' Conspiracy of 1517 against Pope Leo X." *Roma Moderna e Contemporanea* 11, nos. 1–2 (2003): 53–78.

– "The Political Crime of Conspiracy in Fifteenth- and Sixteenth-Century Rome." In Trevor Dean and Kate J.P. Lowe, eds., *Crime, Society and the Law in Renaissance Italy*. Cambridge: Cambridge University Press 1994. 184–203.

Luzio, Alessandro. "Isabella d'Este ne'Primordi del Papato di Leone X e il Suo Viaggio a Roma nel 1514–1515." *Archivio Storico Italiano*, 4th ser., 6 (1906): 99–180.

Machiavelli, Niccolò. *Art of War*. Translated and edited by Christopher Lynch. Chicago and London: University of Chicago Press 2003.

– *L'Arte della Guerra: Scritti Politici Minori*. Edited by Jean-Jacques Marchand, Denis Fachard, and Giorgio Masi. Rome: Salerno 2001.

– *Discorsi Sopra la Prima Deca di Tito Livio*. Florence: G. Barbèra 1900.

– *Discourses on Livy*. Translated by Harvey C. Mansfield and Nathan Tarcov. Chicago and London: University of Chicago Press 1996.

– *The Essential Writings of Machiavelli*. Edited and translated by Peter Constantine. Introduced by Albert Russell Ascoli. New York: Modern Library 2007.

– *Florentine Histories*. Edited by Laura F. Banfield and Harvey C. Marsfield, Jr. Princeton, NJ: Princeton University Press 1988.

– *Legazioni, Commissarie, Scritti di Governo*. Edited by Jean-Jacques Marchand et al. 7 vols. Rome: Salerno 2002–11.

– *Lust for Liberty: The Poems of Machiavelli*. Translated by Joseph Tusiani. New York: Ivan Obolensky 1963.

– *Machiavelli: The Chief Works and Others*. Translated by Allan Gilbert. 3 vols. Durham, NC: Duke University Press 1989.

– *Niccolò Machiavelli, Il Principe*. Edited by Mario Martelli. Rome: Salerno 2–-2005.

– *Opere di Niccolò Machiavelli*. Edited by Ezio Raimondi. 4th ed. Milan: Mursia 1969.

– *Opere di Niccolò Machiavelli*, 3: *Lettere*. Edited by Franco Gaeta. Turin: Unione Tipografico-Editrice Torinese 1984.

– *Opere di Niccolò Machiavelli*, 4: *Scritti letterari*. Edited by Luigi Blasucci and Alberto Casadei. Turin: Unione Tipografico-Editrice Torinese 1989.

– *Opere Poetiche di Niccolò Machiavelli*. Edited by Giuseppe Gigli. Florence: Le Monnier 1908.

– *The Prince*. Translated and edited by Peter Bondanella. Introduced by Maurizio Viroli. Oxford: Oxford University Press 2005.

– *The Prince by Niccolò Machiavelli with Related Documents*. Translated and edited by William J. Connell. Boston: Bedford/St Martin's 2005.

– *Il Principe*. Edited by Mario Martelli. Rome: Salerno Editrice 2006.

– "Ricordo a' Palleschi 1512." *Archivio Storico Italiano*, 3rd ser., 7, no. 1 (1868): 183–5.

– *Scritti in Poesia e in Prosa*. Edited by Antonio Corsaro et al. Rome: Salerno 2012.

Malanima, Paolo. "Bartolomeo Cerretani." *Dizionario Biografico degli Italiani*. Vol. 23. Rome: Istituto della Enciclopedia Italiana 1979.

Malato, Enrico, ed. *Storia della Letteratura Italiana*. 4: *Il Primo Cinquecento*. Rome: Salerno 1996.

Mallett, Michael. *The Borgias: The Rise and Fall of a Renaissance Dynasty*. London: Paladin 1972.

Mallett, Michael, and Nicholas Mann. *Lorenzo the Magnificent: Culture and Politics*. London: Warburg Institute 1996.

Marani, Pietro C. *L'Architettura Fortificata Negli Studi di Leonardo da Vinci con il Catalogo Completo dei Designi*. Florence: L.S. Olschki 1984.

– "Leonardo, Fortified Architecture and Its Structural Problems." In Paolo Galluzzi and Jean Guillaume, eds., *Leonardo da Vinci, Engineer and Architect*. Montreal: Montreal Museum of Fine Arts 1987. 303–14.

Marchand, Jean-Jacques. *Niccolò Machiavelli: I Primi Scritti Politici (1499–1512)*. Padua: Antenore 1975.

Marchi, Gian Paolo, ed. *Testi Cinquecenteschi sulla Ribellione Politica*. Verona: Fiorini 2005.

Mariani, Pietro C., ed. *Francesco di Giorgio II Codice Ashburnham 361 della Biblioteca Medicea Laurenziana di Firenze Trattato di Architettura di Francesco di Giorgio Martini*. 2 vols. Florence: Giunti 1979.

Marinoni, Augusto, ed. *Il Manoscritto dell'Institut de France*. Florence: Giunti-Barbèra 1987.

– "La Pianta di Imola." In Rosaria Campioni, ed., *Leonardo Artista delle Macchine e Cartografo*. Florence: Giunti 1994. 77–82.

Marle, Raimond van. "An Early Portrait of Giuliano de' Medici." *International Studio* 99 (May 1931): 17–19.

Martelli, Mario. "Firenze." In Alberto Asor Rosa, ed., *Letteratura Italiana: Storia e Geografia*. Vol. 2, book 1, *L'Età Moderna*. Turin: Einaudi 1988. 25–201.

– "Preistoria (Medicea) di Machiavelli." *Studi di Filologia Italiana* 29 (1971): 377–405.

Martelli, Mario, and Francesco Bausi. "Politica, Storia e Letteratura: Machiavelli e Guicciardini." In Enrico Malato, ed., *Storia della Letteratura Italiana*, vol. 4. *Il Primo Cinquecento*. Rome: Salerno 1996. 251–351.

Masi, Bartolomeo. *Ricordanze di Bartolomeo Masi: Calderaio Fiorentino dal 1478 al 1526*. Edited by Gius. Odoardo Corazzini. Florence: G.C. Sansoni 1906.

Massa, Eugenio. *L'Eremo, la Bibbia e il Medioevo in Umanisti Veneti del Primo Cinquecento*. Naples: Liguori 1992.

– *I Manoscritti Originali del Beato Paolo Giustiniani, Custoditi nell'Eremo di Frascati*. Rome: Edizioni Storia e Letteratura 1967.

Mayer, August L. "Die Sammlung Jules Bache in New York." *Pantheon* 6 (December 1930): 537–42.

McManamon, SJ, John M. "Marketing a Medici Regime: The Funeral Oration of Marcello Virgilio Adriani for Giuliano de' Medici (1516)." *Renaissance Quarterly* 44, no. 1 (1991): 1–41.

Medici, Giuliano de'. *Poesie*. Edited and introduced by Giuseppe Fatini. Florence: Le Monnier 1939.

Medici, Lorenzo de'. *Lettere*. Vol. 8, *1484–1485*. Edited by Humfrey Butters. Florence: Giunti Barbèra 2001.

– *Lettere di Lorenzo de' Medici*. Edited by Riccardo Fubini et al. 16 vols. Florence: Giunti Barbèra 1977–2011.

Mendelsohn, Henriette. *Das Werk der Dossi*. Munich: G. Müller and E. Rentsch 1914.

Meyer zur Capellen, Jürg. *The Roman Portraits, ca. 1508-1420*. Vol. 3 of *Raphael: A Critical Catalogue of His Paintings*. Translated and edited by Stefan B. Polter. Landshut: Arcos 2008.

Millon, Henry A., Susan C. Scott, and Helmut Hager, eds. *An Architectural Progress in the Renaissance and Baroque: Sojourns In and Out of Italy: Essays in Architectural History Presented to Helmut Hager on His Sixty-Sixth Birthday*. University Park: Pennsylvania State University Press 1992.

Minnich, Nelson H. "Concepts of Reform Proposed at the Fifth Lateran Council (with New Appendices)." *Archivum Historiae Pontificiae* 7 (1969): 163–253.

– *Councils of the Catholic Reformation: Pisa I (1409) to Trent (1545–63)*. Aldershot, UK: Ashgate Variorum 2008.

– *The Fifth Lateran Council (1512–17): Studies on Its Membership, Diplomacy and Proposals for Reform*. Aldershot, UK: Ashgate Variorum 1993.

– "The Images of Julius II in the *Acta* of the Councils of Pisa-Milan-Asti-Lyon (1511–12) and Lateran V (1512–17)." In Giovanna Rotondi Terminiello and Giulio Nepi, eds., *Giulio II: Papa, Politico, Mecenate: Atti del Convegno, Savona, Fortezza del Priamar, Salla della Sibilla, 25–26–27 Marzo 2004*. Genoa: De Ferrari 2005. 79–90.

– "The Official Edition (1521) of the Fifth Lateran Council (1512–1517)." In *Councils of the Catholic Reformation. Pisa I (1409) to Trent (1545–63)*. Aldershot, UK: Ashgate Variorum 2008). Pt. 3: 1–14.

– "The Participants at the Fifth Lateran Council." *Archivum Historiae Pontificiae* 12 (1974): 157–206.

– "The Role of Schools of Theology in the Councils of the Late Medieval and Renaissance Periods." In Johannes Grohe, Jerónimo Leal, and Vito Reale, eds., *I Padri e le Scuole Teologiche nei Concili: Atti del VII Simposio Internazionale della Facoltà di Teologia, Roma, 6–7 Marzo 2003*. Città del Vaticano: Libreria Editrice Vaticana 2006. 59–95.

Mitchell, Bonner. *Italian Civic Pageantry in the High Renaissance*. Florence: L.S. Olschki 1979.

Modesti, Jacopo. "Il Miserando Sacco Dato alla Terra di Prato dagli Spagnoli l'Anno 1512 Scritto per M. Jacopo Modesti." In Cesare Guasti, ed., *Il Sacco di Prato e il Ritorno de' Medici in Firenze nel MDXII*. Bologna: Gaetano Romagnoli 1880. 94–110.

Moncallero, Giuseppe Lorenzo. *Il Cardinale Bernardo Dovizi da Bibbiena: Umanista e Diplomatico (1470–1520)*. Florence: L.S. Olschki 1953.

Mousley, Andrew. "*The Prince* and Textual Politics." In Martin Coyle, ed., *Niccolò Machiavelli's The Prince: New Interdisciplinary Essays*. Manchester, UK: Manchester University Press 1995. 151–73.

Najemy, John M. *Between Friends: Discourses of Power and Desire in the Machiavelli–Vettori Letters of 1513–1515*. Princeton, NJ: Princeton University Press 1993.

– "The Controversy Surrounding Machiavelli's Service to the Republic." In Gisela Bock, Quentin Skinner, and Maurizio Viroli, eds., *Machiavelli and Republicanism*. Cambridge: Cambridge University Press 1993. 101–18.

– *A History of Florence 1200–1575*. Malden, MA: Blackwell Publishing 2006.

– "Machiavelli and Cesare Borgia: A Reconsideration of Chapter 7 of *The Prince*." *Review of Politics* 75 (2013): 539–56.

– ed. *Cambridge Companion to Machiavelli*. Cambridge: Cambridge University Press 2010.

Nardi, Jacopo. *Istorie della Città di Firenze*. Edited by Agenore Gelli, 2 vols. Florence: Felice Le Monnier 1858.

– *Vita di Antonio Giacomini*. Florence: Semartelli 1597.

Nathan, Johannes. "Engineering and Machinery Studies." In Frank Zöllner, ed., *Leonardo da Vinci, 1452–1519: Paintings, Sketches, and Drawings*. New York: Taschen 2006. 372–93.

Nerli, Filippo de'. *Commentari de' Fatti Civili Occorsi Dentro la Città di Firenze dall'Anno MCCXV al MDXXXVII*. Augusta: D.R. Mertz and G.J. Majer 1728.

Newbigin, Nerida. "Piety and Politics in the *Feste* of Lorenzo's Florence." In Gian Carlo Garfagnini, ed., *Lorenzo Magnifico e il Suo Mondo: Convegno Internazionale di Studi (Firenze, 9–13 Giugno 1992)*. Florence: L.S. Olschki 1994. 17–41.

Niccolini, Enrico, ed. *Vita di Lorenzo de' Medici Scritta in Lingua Latina da Niccolò Valori: Resa in Volgare dal Figlio Filippo Valori*. Vicenza: Accademia Olimpica 1991.

Niccolini, G.B. *Filippo Strozzi, Tragedia*. Florence: Le Monnier 1847.

Nitti, Francesco. "Documenti ed Osservazioni Riguardanti la Politica di Leone X." *Archivio della Società Romana* 16 (1893): 181–232.

– *Leone X e la Sua Politica Secondo Documenti e Carteggi Inediti*. Florence: Barbèra 1892.

Oberhuber, Konrad. *Raffaello*. Milano: A. Mondadori 1982.

– *Raphael: The Paintings*. Munich and New York: Prestel 1999.

Ortolani, Sergio. *Raffaello*. Bergamo: Istituto Italiano d'Arti Grafiche 1945.

Orwin, Clifford. "The Riddle of Cesare Borgia and the Legacy of Machiavelli's *Prince*." In Timothy Fuller, ed., *Machiavelli's Legacy:* The Prince *after Five Hundred Years*. Philadelphia: University of Pennsylvania Press 2016. 156–70.

Pacioli, Luca. *De Divina Proportione*. Introduction by Augusto Marioni. 2 vols. Milan: Silvana 1982.

Parenti, Piero di Marco. *Storia Fiorentina*. 2 vols. Edited by Andrea Matucci. Florence: L.S. Olschki 1994 and 2005.

Pastor, Ludwig. *The History of the Popes, from the Close of the Middle Ages. Drawn from the Secret Archives of the Vatican and Other Original Sources*. Vols. 7 and 8. *A.D. 1513–1521*. Edited by Ralph Francis Kerr. 3rd ed. London: Routledge and Kegan Paul 1950.

Pedretti, Carlo. *A Chronology of Leonardo da Vinci's Architectural Studies after 1500*. Geneva: E. Droz 1962.

– *Disegni di Leonardo da Vinci e della Sua Scuola alla Biblioteca Reale di Torino*. Florence: Giunti Barbèra 1975.

– *Leonardo: Le Macchine*. Florence: Giunt 2000.

– *Leonardo & Io*. Milan: Mondadori 2008.

– ed. *Documenti e Memorie Riguardanti Leonardo da Vinci a Bologna e in Emilia*. Bologna: Editoriale Fiammenghi 1953.

– ed. *Leonardo da Vinci, Engineer and Architect*. Montreal: Montreal Museum of Fine Arts 1987.

– *The Literary Works of Leonardo da Vinci Compiled and Edited from the Original Manuscripts by Jean Paul Richter*. Berkeley and Los Angeles: University of California Press 1977.

Pedretti, Carlo, and Learco Andalò, eds. *Leonardo, Machiavelli, Cesare Borgia: Arte Storia e Scienza in Romagna, 1500–1503*. Rome: De Luca 2003.

Pellegrini, Marco. "Leone X." In *Dizionario Biografico degli Italiani*. Vol. 64. Rome: Istituto della Enciclopedia Italiana 2005.

Pellerin, Daniel. "Machiavelli's Best Friend." *History of Political Thought* 27, no. 3 (2006): 423–53.

Pesman Cooper, Roslyn. "La Caduta di Pier Soderini e il 'Governo Popolare': Pressioni Esterne e Dissenso Interno." *Archivio Storico Italiano* 193, no. 525 (1985): 225–60.

– "L'Elezione di Pier Soderini a Gonfaloniere a Vita: Note Storiche." *Archivio Storico Italiano* 125, no. 454 (1967): 145.

– "The Florentine Ruling Group under the 'Governo Popolare,' 1494–1512." *Studies in Medieval and Renaissance History* 7 (1985): 71–181.

– "Machiavelli, Piero Soderini, and the Republic of 1494–1512." In John M. Najemy, ed., *The Cambridge Companion to Machiavelli*. Cambridge: Cambridge University Press 2010. 48–63.

Peterson, David S., and Daniel E. Bornstein, eds. *Florence and Beyond: Culture, Society and Politics in Renaissance Italy*. Toronto: Centre for Reformation and Renaissance Studies 2008.

Petrucci, Giulia. "L'Apertura della Via Alessandrina: Idée e Progetti, Realizzazione, 'Derivazioni' Cinquecentesche." In Enrico Guidoni and Giulia Petrucci, eds., *Urbanistica per i Giubilei: Roma, Via Alessandrina, una Strada "Tra due Fondali" nell'Italia delle Corti, 1492–1499*. Rome: Edizioni Kappa 1997. 27–58.

Picotti, G.B. "La Congiura dei Cardinali contro Leone X." *Rivista Storica*, 40–1 (1923–24).

Pieraccini, Gaetano. *La Stirpe de' Medici di Cafaggiolo: Saggio di Ricerche sulla Trasmissione Ereditaria dei Caratteri Biologici*. 2nd ed. 3 vols. Florence: Vallecchi 1947.

Pincus, Debra. "The Humanist and the Poet: Bernardo Bembo's Portrait of Dante." In Kathleen Wren Christian and David J. Drogin, eds., *Patronage and Italian Renaissance Sculpture*. Surrey, UK, and Burlington, VT: Ashgate 2010. 61–94.

Pinto, Giuliano, ed. *Storia di Pistoia III: Dentro Lo Stato Fiorentino dalla Metà del XIV alla Fine del XVIII Secolo*. 4 vols. Florence: Felice Le Monnier 1999.

Pitti, Jacopo. *Istoria Fiorentina*. Edited by Adriana Mauriello. Naples: Liguori 2007.

– "Sulla Vita di Antonio Giacomini e l'Apologia de' Cappucci." *Archivio Storico Italiano* 4, no. 2 (1853): 75–384.

Pocock, J.G.A. *The Machiavellian Moment: Florentine Political Thought and the Atlantic Republican Tradition*. Princeton, NJ: Princeton University Press 2003.

Poliziano, Angelo. *The Stanze of Angelo Poliziano*. Translated by David Quint. Amherst: University of Massachusetts Press 1979.

Polizzotto, Lorenzo. *The Elect Nation: The Savonarolan Movement in Florence 1495–1545*. Oxford: Clarendon Press 1994.

– "The Making of a Saint: The Canonization of St. Antonio, 1516–1523." *Journal of Medieval and Renaissance Studies* 22, no. 3 (1992): 353–81.

– "Prophecy, Politics and History in Early Sixteenth-Century Florence: The Admonitory Letters of Francesco d' Antonio de' Ricci." In Peter Denley and Caroline Elam, eds., *Florence and Italy: Renaissance Studies in Honour of Nicolai Rubinstein*. London: Committee for Medieval Studies, Westfield College, 1988. 107–31.

Pollard, Graham. "Niccolò di Forzore Spinelli, called Niccolò Fiorentino (1430–1514)." In Stephen K. Scher, ed., *The Currency of Fame: Portrait Medals of the Renaissance*. New York: Harry N. Abrams 1994. 132–6.

– *Renaissance Medals*, vol. 1, *Italy*. Oxford: Oxford University Press 2007.

Prodi, Paolo. "Relazione Diplomatiche fra il Ducato di Milano e Roma Sotto il Duca Massimiliano Sforza (151–1515)." *Aevum* 30, nos. 5/6 (1956): 437–94.

Pugliese, Olga Zorzi. "Apocalyptic and Dantesque Elements in a Franciscan Prophecy of the Renaissance." *Proceedings of the PMR Conference: Annual Publication of the Patristic, Medieval and Renaissance Conference* 10 (1985).

– *Castiglione's* The Book of the Courtier (Il Libro del Cortegiano)*: A Classic in the Making*. Naples: Edizioni Scientifiche Italiane 2008.

Radford, Ron, ed. *Renaissance: 15th and 16th Century Italian Paintings from the Accademia Carrara, Bergamo*. Canberra: National Gallery of Australia 2011.

Raffini, Christine. *Marsilio Ficino, Pietro Bembo, Baldassare Castiglione: Philosophical, Aesthetic, and Political Approaches in Renaissance Platonism*. Renaissance and Baroque Studies and Texts 21. New York: Peter Lang 1998.

Randolph, Adrian W.B. "Il Marzocco: Lionizing the Florentine State." In Lars R. Jones and Louisa Chevalier Matthew, eds., *Coming About – A Festschrift for John Shearman*. Cambridge, MA: Harvard University Art Museums 2000. 11–18.

Re, Caterina. *Girolamo Benivieni Fiorentino: Cenni sulla Vita e sulle Opere*. Città di Castello: S. Lapi 1906.

Rebecchini, Guido. *"Un Altro Lorenzo" Ippolito de' Medici tra Firenze e Roma (1511–1535)*. Venice: Marsilio Editori 2010.

Reeves, Marjorie, ed. *Prophetic Rome in the High Renaissance Period*. Oxford: Clarendon Press 1992.

Rendina, Claudio. *I Capitani di Ventura: Storia e Segreti*. Rome: Newton Compton 1985.

Reti, Ladislao. "The Engineer." In Ludwig H. Heydenreich, Bern Dibner, and Ladislao Reti, eds., *Leonardo the Inventor*. New York: McGraw-Hill 1980. 124–84.

Richard, P. "Une Correspondance Diplomatique de la Curie Romaine à la Veille de Marignan, 1515." *Revue d'Histoire et de Littérature Religieuses* 9, nos. 1, 2, and 4 (1904).

Richardson, Brian. "La Lettera a una Gentildonna del Machiavelli." *La Bibliofilia* 84, no. 3 (1982): 271–6.

– "*The Prince* and Its Early Italian Readers." In Martin Coyle, ed., *Niccolò Machiavelli's The Prince: New Interdisciplinary Essays*. Manchester, UK: Manchester University Press 1995. 18–39.

Richter, Jean Paul, ed. *The Literary Works of Leonardo da Vinci Compiled and Edited from the Original Manuscripts*. 2 vols. London: Sampson Low, Marston, Searle and Rivington 1883.

Ridolfi, Roberto. *The Life of Girolamo Savonarola*. Translated by Cecil Grayson. London: Routledge and Kegan Paul 1959.

– *The Life of Niccolò Machiavelli*. Translated by Cecil Grayson. London: Routledge and Kegan Paul 1963.

– *Vita di Machiavelli*. Florence: Sansoni 1978.

Robbia, Luca della. "Recitazione del Caso di Pietro Paolo Boscoli e di Agostino Capponi, Scritta da Luca Della Robbia l'Anno MDXIII." *Archivio Storico Italiano* 1 (1842): 283–312.

Roscoe, William. *Life and Pontificate of Leo the Tenth*. 2 vols. London: Bohn 1846.

Rose, Paul Lawrence. *The Italian Renaissance of Mathematics: Studies on Humanists and Mathematicians from Petrarch to Galileo*. Geneva: Droz 1975.

Rosenberg, Adolf, and Georg Gronau. *Raffael, des Meisters Gemälde*. Stuttgart: Deutsche Verlags Anstalt 1908.

Ross, James Bruce. "Gasparo Contarini and His Friends." *Studies in the Renaissance* 17 (1970): 192–232.

Rotondi Terminiello, Giovanna, and Giulio Nepi, eds. *Giulio II: Papa, Politico, Mecenate: Atti del Convegno, Savona, Fortezza del Priamar, Salla della Sibilla, 25–26–27 Marzo 2004*. Genoa: De Ferrari 2005.

Rowland, Ingrid D. *The Culture of the High Renaissance: Ancients and Moderns in Sixteenth-Century Rome*. Cambridge: Cambridge University Press 1998.

Rubinstein, Nicolai. *The Government of Florence under the Medici (1434 to 1494)*. Oxford: Clarendon Press 1997.

– "Machiavelli and the Mural Decoration of the Hall of the Great Council of Florence." In Ronald G. Kecks, ed., *Musagetes: Festschrift für Wolfram Prinz zu seinem 60. Geburtstag am 5. Februar 1989*. Berlin: Gebr. Mann 1991. 275–85.

– *The Palazzo Vecchio 1298–1532: Government, Architecture and Imagery in the Civic Palace of the Florentine Republic*. Oxford: Clarendon Press 1995.

– "Dalla Repubblica al Principato." In Gian Carlo Garfagnini, ed., *Firenze e la Toscana dei Medici nell'Europa del '500*. Vol. 1, *Strumenti e Veicoli della Cultura: Relazioni Politiche ed Economiche*. Florence: L.S. Olschki 1983. 160–76.

– ed. *Florentine Studies: Politics and Society in Renaissance Florence*. Evanston, IL: Northwestern University Press 1968.

Sacerdote, Gustavo. *Cesare Borgia: La Sua Vita, la Sua Famiglia, i Suoi Tempi*. Milan: Rizzoli 1950.

Sallares, Robert. *Malaria and Rome: A History of Malaria in Ancient Italy*. Oxford: Oxford University Press 2002.

Sanudo, Marino. *Cità Excelentissima*. Edited by Patricia H. Labalme and Laura Sangineti White. Translated by Linda L. Carroll. Baltimore: Johns Hopkins University Press 2008.

– *I Diarii di Marino Sanuto*. Edited by Nicolò Barozzi et al. 58 vols. Venice: F. Visentini 1879–1903. Repr. Bologna: Forni 1969–70.

Savonarola, Girolamo. *Selected Writings of Girolamo Savonarola: Religion and Politics, 1490–1498*. Translated and edited by Anne Borelli and Maria Pastore Passaro. New Haven, CT, and London: Yale University Press 2006.

Scala, Bartolomeo. "Dialogue on Laws and Legal Judgments." Translated by David Marsh. In Jill Kraye, ed., *Cambridge Translations of Renaissance Philosophical Texts*. Vol. 2, *Political Philosophy*. Cambridge: Cambridge University Press 1997. 173–99.

Scarpa, Emanuela. "Un 'Poeta' in 'Geti': I Sonnetti dal Carcere di Machiavelli a Giuliano de' Medici." In Gian Paolo Marchi, ed., *Testi Cinquecenteschi sulla Ribellione Politica*. Verona: Fiorini 2005. 139–60.

Scher, Stephen K. "An Introduction to the Renaissance Portrait Medal." In Stephen K. Scher, ed., *Perspectives on the Renaissance Medal*. New York: Garland 2000. 1–25.

– ed. *The Currency of Fame: Portrait Medals of the Renaissance*. New York: Harry N. Abrams 1994.

– ed. *Perspectives on the Renaissance Medal*. New York: Garland 2000.

Schultz, Bernard. *Art and Anatomy in Renaissance Italy*. Ann Arbor, MI: UMI Research Press 1985.

Sedelmeyer, Charles. *Illustrated Catalogue of the Tenth Series of 100 Paintings by Old Masters*. Paris: Sedelmeyer 1906.

Setton, Kenneth M. "Pope Leo X and the Turkish Peril." *Proceedings of the American Philosophical Society* 113 (1969): 367–424.

Shaw, Christine. *Julius II: The Warrior Pope*. Oxford: Blackwell 1993.

– "The Papacy and the European Powers." In Christine Shaw, ed., *Italy and the European Powers: The Impact of War 1500–1530*. Leiden, Boston: Brill 2006. 107–27.

Shearman, John. "The Florentine Entrata of Leo X, 1515." *Journal of the Warburg and Courtauld Institutes* 38 (1975): 136–54.

– *Raphael in Early Modern Sources (1483–1602)*. 2 vols. New Haven, CT, and London: Yale University Press 2003.

– "Pontormo and Andrea del Sarto, 1513." *Burlington Magazine* 104 (1962).

Silvano, Giovanni. *"Vivere Civile" e "Governo Misto" a Firenze nel Primo Cinquecento*. Bologna: Pàtron 1985.

Simms, Dennis L. "Archimedes and the Burning Mirrors of Syracuse." *Technology and Culture* 18 (1977): 1–24.

– "Archimedes' Weapons of War and Leonardo." *British Journal for the History of Science* 21, no. 2 (June 1988): 195–210.

Simonetta, Marcello. "Le Roi et l'Italie: L'Attraction Fatale." In Olivier Bosc and Maxence Hermant, ed., *Le Siècle de François Ier: Du Roi Guerrier au Roi Mécène*. Chantilly: Éditions Cercle d'Art 2015. 31–5.

– *Volpi e Leoni: I Medici, Machiavelli e la Rovina d'Italia*. Milan: Bompiani 2014.

Solmi, Edmondo. *Scritti Vinciani*. Edited by Arrigo Solmi. Florence: Soc. Anon. Editrice "La Voce" 1924.

Steinmann, Ernst. *Das Geheimnis der Medicigräber Michelangelos*. Leipzig: Hiersemann 1907.

Stephens, J.N. *The Fall of the Florentine Republic 1512–1530*. Oxford: Oxford University Press 1983.

Stephens, J.N., and Humfrey C. Butters. "Notes and Documents: New Light on Machiavelli." *English Historical Review* 97 (1982): 54–69.

Strathern, Paul. *The Artist, the Philosopher, and the Warrior: The Intersecting Lives of Da Vinci, Machiavelli, and Borgia and the World They Shaped*. New York: Bantam Books 2009.

Strocchia, Sharon T. *Death and Ritual in Renaissance Florence*. Baltimore and London: Johns Hopkins University Press 1992.

Suida, Wilhelm. *Raphael*. New York: Phaidon 1941.

Syson, Luke. *Leonardo da Vinci: Painter at the Court of Milan*. London: National Gallery 2011.

Syson, Luke, and Dora Thornton. *Objects of Virtue: Art in Renaissance Italy*. Los Angeles: J. Paul Getty Museum 2001.

Tabacchi, Stefano. "Giuliano de' Medici." In *Dizionario Biografico degli Italiani*. Vol. 73. Rome: Istituto della Enciclopedia Italiana 2009.

Terpstra, Nicholas, ed. *The Art of Executing Well: Rituals of Execution in Renaissance Italy*. Kirksville, MS: Truman State University Press 2008.

Thieme, Ulrich, Felix Becker, and Hans Vollmer, eds. *Allgemeines Lexikon der Bildenden Künstler von der Antike bis zur Gegenwart*. Vol. 29. Leipzig: Seemann 1935.

Tomas, Natalie R. "Alfonsina Orsini de' Medici and the 'Problem' of a Female Ruler in Early Sixteenth-Century Florence." *Renaissance Studies* 14, no. 1 (2000), 70–90.

– *The Medici Women: Gender and Power in Renaissance Florence.* Aldershot, UK, and Burlington, VT: Ashgate 2003.

Tommasini, Oreste. *La Vita e gli Scritti di Niccolò Machiavelli nella Loro Relazione col Machiavellismo.* 2 vols. Rome: E. Loescher 1883–1911.

Trexler, Richard C. *Public Life in Renaissance Florence.* New York: Academic Press 1980.

– "True Light Shining vs. Obscurantism in the Study of Michelangelo's New Sacristy." *Artibus et Historae* 21, no. 42 (2000): 101–17.

Trexler, Richard C., and Mary Elizabeth Lewis. "Two Captains and Three Kings: New Light on the Medici Chapel." *Studies in Medieval and Renaissance History* 4 (1981): 93–177.

Valentiner, Wilhelm R. "Leonardo as Verrocchio's Coworker." *Art Bulletin* 12, no. 1 (1930): 43–89.

Valori, Niccolò. *Ricordanze.* In *Memorie di Casa Valori*, Ms. Biblioteca Nazionale di Firenze, Fondo Panciatichiano, 134, fols.17r–18v.

Vasari, Giorgio. *The Lives of the Painters, Sculptors and Architects.* 4 vols. Translated by A.B. Hinds and edited by William Gaunt. London: Dent 1963.

– *Lives of the Painters, Sculptors, and Architects.* 2 vols. Translated by Gaston du C. de Vere. Edited by David Ekserdjian. New York: Alfred A. Knopf 1996.

Vecce, Carlo. *Leonardo.* 2nd ed. Rome: Salerno 2006.

Ventrone, Paola. "Lorenzo's *Politica Festiva.*" In Michael Mallett and Nicholas Mann, ed., *Lorenzo the Magnificent: Culture and Politics.* London: Warburg Institute 1996. 105–16.

Venturi, Adolfo. *Raffaello.* Milan: A. Mondadori 1952.

– *Storia dell'Arte Italiana: La Pittura del Cinquecento.* Milan: Hoepli 1926.

Venturi, Lionello. *Italian Paintings in America.* Vol. 3, *Sixteenth to Eighteenth Century.* New York: E. Wyhe 1933.

Verdi, Adolfo. *Gli Ultimi Anni di Lorenzo de' Medici, Duca d'Urbino, 1515–1519.* Este: G. Pietrogrande 1888.

Vettori, Francesco. *Scritti Storici e Politici.* Edited by Enrico Niccolini. Bari: Laterza 1972.

– "Sommario della Storia d'Italia dal 1511 al 1527." In Enrico Niccolini, ed., *Scritti Storici e Politici.* Bari: Laterza 1972. 133–246.

Vettori, Paolo. "Memorandum to Cardinal de' Medici about the Affairs of Florence." Translated by Russell Price. In Jill Kraye, ed., *Cambridge Translations of Renaissance Philosophical Texts.* Vol. 2, *Political Philosophy.* Cambridge: Cambridge University Press 1997. 238–44.

– "Ricordi di Paolo Vettori al Cardinale de' Medici Sopra le Cose di Firenze." In Rudolf von Albertini, ed., *Firenze dalla Repubblica al Principato: Storia e Coscienza Politica.* Turin: Giulio Einaudi 1970. 359–9.

Villari, Pasquale. *The Life and Times of Niccolò Machiavelli.* Translated by Linda Villari. London: Fisher Unwin 1898.

– *Niccolò Machiavelli e i Suoi Tempi.* 4th ed. 2 vols. Milan: Hoepli 1927.

– *La Storia di Girolamo Savonarola e de' Suoi Tempi*. 2 vols. Florence: Felice Le Monnier 1926.

Villata, Edoardo, ed. *Leonardo da Vinci: I Documenti e le Testimonianze Contemporanee*. Milan: Castello Sforzesco: Ente Raccolta Vinciana 1999.

Viroli, Maurizio. *Machiavelli*. Oxford: Oxford University Press 1998.

Vitruvius. *The Architecture of Marcus Vitruvius Pollio, in Ten Books*. Translated by Joseph Gwilt. London: John Weale 1860.

Volk-Knüttel, Brigitte. *Peter Candid (um 1548–1628): Gemälde, Zeichnungen, Druckgraphik*. Berlin: Dt. Verl. für Kunstwissenschaft 2010.

Weinberger, Martin. *Michelangelo the Sculptor*. 2 vols. London: Routledge and Kegan Paul 1967.

Weinstein, Donald. "The Myth of Florence." In Nicolai Rubinstein, ed., *Florentine Studies: Politics and Society in Renaissance Florence*. Evanston, IL: Northwestern University Press 1968. 15–44.

– *Savonarola and Florence: Prophecy and Patriotism in the Renaissance*. Princeton, NJ: Princeton University Press 1970.

Weisz, George M., et al. "Who Was Pontormo's Halberdier? The Evidence from Pathology." *Rheumatology International* 32, no. 7 (2012): 1915–20.

Whitfield, J.H. *Machiavelli*. New York: Russell and Russell 1965.

Wilson, Charles Heath. *Life and Works of Michelangelo Buonarroti*. London: J. Murray 1876.

Woodhouse, John Robert. *Baldesar Castiglione: A Reassessment of* The Courtier. Edinburgh: Edinburgh University Press 1978.

Woodward, William Harrison. *Cesare Borgia: A Biography*. New York: E.P. Dutton 1914.

Young, G.F. *The Medici*. London: J. Murray 1913.

Zeri, Federico. *Italian Paintings: A Catalogue of the Collection of the Metropolitan Museum of Art, Sienese and Central Italian Schools*. New York: Metropolitan Museum of Art 1980.

Zobi, Antonio. *Della Nozze del Magnifico Giuliano de' Medici con la Principessa Filiberta di Savoia*. Florence: Eredi Botta 1868.

Zöllner, Frank. *Leonardo da Vinci, 1452–1519*. New York: Taschen 2000.

INDEX